PUBLISHING

Collection Directors and authors : Dominique AUZIAS et Jean-Paul LABOURDETTE
Publishing manager : Isabelle DREZEN
In collaboration with : Jean Marc BELLONE
Authors : Eileen GIACOLETTO, Elodie CABRERA, Gérard BERNAR, Claire CAMARASA, Mélodie MARCQ, Isabelle DREZEN, Laure Lambert, Noëlle MOUSKA, Noël FANTONI, Valérie PELLEGRINI, Marjorie MODI, Karine CANTET, Marleyne MATI, Aurélie CARUCHET, Caroline DHERBEY, Jean-Paul LABOURDETTE, Dominique AUZIAS et alter
Publishing director : Stéphan SZEREMETA
Publishing team (France) : Elisabeth COL, Maurane CHEVALIER, Silvia FOLIGNO, Tony DE SOUSA
Publishing team (World) : Patrick MARINGE, Caroline MICHELOT, Morgane VESLIN, Pierre-Yves SOUCHET, Talatah FAVREAU

STUDIO

Studio Manager : Sophie LECHERTIER assisted by Romain AUDREN
Layout : Julie BORDES, Sandrine MECKING, Delphine PAGANO, Laurie PILLOIS
Pictures management : Anne DIOT
Mapping management : Jordan EL OUARDI

WEB

Web Director : Louis GENEAU de LAMARLIERE
Web management and Development : Cédric MAILLOUX, Nicolas GUENIN, Florian FAZER, Caroline LAFFAITEUR, Andrei UNGUREANU, Nicolas VAPPEREAU
Community Manager : Cyprien de CANSON

NATIONAL PUBLICITY

Publicity director : Caroline CHOLLET
Local publicity management : Michel GRANSEIGNE
Customer relations management : Vimla MEETTOO and Sandra RUFFIEUX
Heads of National Publicity : Caroline AUBRY, François BRIANCON-MARJOLLET, Perrine DE CARNE MARCEIN, Caroline GENTELET, Caroline PREAU

INTERNATIONAL PUBLICITY

Heads of Publicity : Jean-Marc FARAGUET, Guillaume LABOUREUR assisted by Michelle MAYER

CIRCULATION AND PROMOTION

Sales promotion Director : Bénédicte MOULET assisted by Aissatou DIOP, Vianney LAVERNE
Sales Manager : Jean-Pierre GHEZ assisted by Nathalie GONCALVES
Press and sponsor partnership management : Jean-Mary MARCHAL

ADMINISTRATION

Chairman : Jean-Paul LABOURDETTE
Administrative and financial Director : Valérie DECOTTIGNIES
Human Resources Director : Dina BOURDEAU assisted by Sandra MORAIS
Information and Technology Manager : Pascal LE GOFF
Accounting : Jeannine DEMIRDJIAN, Christelle MANEBARD and Adrien PRIGENT
Collection : Fabien BONNAN assisted by Sandra BRIJLALL and Belinda MILLE
Siwtchboard : Jehanne AOUMEUR

PETIT FUTE BEST OF COTE D'AZUR 2017-2018

Petit Futé was founded by Dominique AUZIAS.
It is published by Les Nouvelles Editions de l'Université
18, rue des Volontaires - 75015 Paris.
✆ 01 53 69 70 00 - Fax 01 42 73 15 24
Internet : www.petitfute.com
SAS au capital de 1 000 000 € -
RC PARIS B 309 769 966
Couverture : Sanary harbor on the Cote d'Azur
© ivan bastien
Impression : IMPRIMERIE CHIRAT - 42540 Saint-Just-la-Pendue
Dépôt légal : 09/08/2017
ISBN : 9791033162148

To email us, type the surname (lowercase) followed by @petitfute.com
Write to the editor : info@petitfute.com

"(... *would never turn it back on it. It discovered the French Riviera, settled there and was quite content to stay there. It has remained ever since.*" Louis Nucéra, 1928-2000 .

Cosmopolitan Mediterranean destination located in the heart of Europe, from the glowing Esterel mountains on the west to the Italian border on the east, from the Mercantour National Park on the north to the shores of the Mediterranean on the South, the Riviera Coast offers a privileged climate blessed by the gods with over 300 shiny days per year in a unique natural setting. Accessible, thanks to the international Nice Côte d'Azur airport, the second airport of the country, by its road network but also well served by the TGV several times a day from many French cities, this land of geographical contrasts offers an unimaginable amount of different landscapes and attractions.

An exceptional and emotional land, the «French Riviera» owes much of its success to its unique diversity and richness. It has first of all a unique identity showing contrast between sea and mountains with a preserved landscape ranging from the Mediterranean coastline to the Southern Alps allowing those who like heliotropism and animations to clump to the seaside to enjoy the beaches, festive and night activities, and investigators of authenticity to escape to the back country and its preserved areas and to set off-road to discover peacefully the numerous perched villages. Then there is its extraordinary cultural heritage that embraces much of the history of humanity: great creative workshop for artists around the world, art lovers follow the footsteps of Matisse, Chagall, Picasso, Dufy, Renoir and Bonnard, famous painters fascinated by the blue colour of the sky and the brightness of the region while culture-lovers are interested in the rich architectural heritage of the Alpes-Maritimes. There is also a sunny gastronomy that has been revisited by top chefs: gourmets will enjoy all the good restaurants swarming in the department where almost forty establishments hold a Michelin star, gourmets go to markets to buy local produce of the sunny cuisine while others visit vineyards to taste the wines of the region. There is also the abundance of festivals and major international events that punctuate the calendar of the Riviera every season, the wide range of leisure activities, from the coastal snowy backcountry trails, which have seduced visitors from around the world for more than a century and a half. What else?

PEFC™
10-31-1895
Certifié PEFC
Ce produit est issu de forêts gérées durablement et de sources contrôlées.
pefc-france.org

PRINTED IN FRANCE

See page 131

CONTENTS

CONTENTS

FENCH RIVIERA: THE MOUTAINSIDE

The Rock of Monaco.

MONACO

MONACO

MONACO GOVERNMENT TURIST AND CONVENTION BUREAU

2, boulevard des Moulins
✆ +37 (0)7 92 16 61 16
www.visitmonaco.com – dtc@gouv.mc

Open from 9am to 7pm every day. Sunday and public holidays, from 11am to 1pm.

You will find there all the information needed to have a pleasant stay in the Principality. Very charming hostesses who speak several languages are at your disposal: they will advise you both on the availability of your stay and on business and leisure turism. The website www.visitmonaco.com/fr also provides a valuable source of information: available in different languages, it is updated regularly and includes all activities and events organized in Monaco.

MONACO TOURS – MINI TRAIN

Departure from the towers in front of the oceanographic Museum of Monaco
✆ +37 (0)7 92 05 64 38
www.monacotours.mc

Closed from mid-November to February. The mini trains works every day depending on climatic conditions and events in the Principality. Duration: approximately 30 minutes. Capacity 60 places maximum. Adult: €9. Child (from 2 to 8 years old): €5. Guided tour in 12 languages, by audio helmets, simultaneous translation. "Tout comfort" Visit. Ticket office located in front of the oceanographic Museum. Regulation: species and credit card. Possible privatization for your events (wedding, birthday, baptism, transfers of guests…). This train is the best way to visit the principality and its major tourist attractions. Departure and arrival in front of the Oceanographic Museum on the Rock. Smart advice: leave your car in the parking des Pecheurs located avenue de la Quarantaine and then join the museum using the free lift. The circuit follows the most beautiful sites in Monaco: Place d'Armes, Port Hercule, the Grand Prix Formula 1, Monte Carlo with the Casino Square and luxury hotels, city centre, and finally the old town with the Department of State, the Princes palace and the Cathedral.

Smart advice: park your car at the parking des Pecheurs located at the end of the boulevard de la Quarantaine. Then take the free lift that brings you in front of the Oceanographic museum. The mini train is the best way to visit the Prinicipality in a ludic way.

Good tips in Monaco

The website of the tourist office is wonderful. Go on www.visitmonaco.com and you'll find all the latest news of the Principality and all the good attractions! Once on the site, go on "Enchante-moi Monaco." Open an account "My Monaco" magic pass to access many discounts as football tickets as from € 5, stays in hotels at low prices or entrys to some exhibitions at discounted prices.

GETTING THERE

To get to the Principality of Monaco, you can choose arriving by the sea, by plane or by car.

CARBACK & DRIVE PREMIUM SERVICES

9, rue des Oliviers
✆ +33 (0)6 80 86 40 11 / +33 (0)6 80 86 41 64
www.car-back.mc
info@car-back.mc

Service of custom-tailored driver: €35 per hour including all taxes. Other day rates, half-day, day and night on request. Service of convoying: price on request. Concierge service of vehicles: monthly regular maintenance of your car 70 €/car, washing €50 + price of washing + other services on request (maintenance, glossing…), passage of your vehicle to technical control: €50. Service airport, station or boat for Nice €60 the trip or €100 for a return ticket from Monaco and the cities bordering (Cap d'Ail, Beausoleil, La Turbie, Roquebrune- Cap-Martin). Other departures, price on request. Service back from night.

The team of CarBack & Drive offers a range of services designed both to facilitate your travels as well as for your vehicle. Airport station or boat transfer via the tailored-service driver, the return at night, transfer of your hosts during a festive evening, convoying or the conciergerie of your vehicles… The service is good and very professional. Rates are displayed on the website for all these services. Possibility of online reservation or by e-mail.

By Plane

If you want to spend a few days in Monaco, when arriving by plane you will land at Nice airport. With 10 million passengers, Nice-Côte d'Azur is the first international airport in France after Paris.

Located a few minutes' drive from the city centre of Nice, about thirty minutes from Monaco and a few hours from winter sports stations, various means of locomotion more or less rapid, will be available when you arrive: taxis, cars, motorcycles, bicycles ...

INTERNATIONAL AIRPORT NICE-CÔTE D'AZUR
Rue Costes et Bellonte
NICE (FRANCE)
✆ +33 (0)8 20 42 33 33
www.nice.aeroport.fr
nice.aeroport@cote-azur.aeroport.fr
♿

Nice-Cote d'Azur Airport is the third among the French airports after those of Paris (Charles de Gaulle and Orly) and the second business French airport after the Bourget. Built on an area partially taken over the sea, it connects the French Riviera to many worldwide destinations. It is divided into two poles: Terminal 1 for international flights and Terminal 2 for domestic flights. Many companies have a desk there.

Helicopter

You can reach Monaco by helicopter from Nice airport. A conveyance which admittedly is a bit expensive but indeed so convenient! Only 7 minutes flight with a budget of approximately € 200 return ticket (adult). Frequencies are numerous, almost every half hour. Once in Monaco, a free shuttle service will drop you off at your hotel or at your appointment.

MONACAIR
✆ +37 (0)7 97 97 39 00
www.monacair.mc
info@monacair.mc
Possibility of having a private flight. 7 minutes Monaco to Nice Côte d' Azur airport. Service of free shuttle-minibus.
Created in 1988 by Stefano Casiraghi, the company Monacair obtained in 1999 the prestigious title of Official Supplier of HSH the Sovereign Prince of Monaco. From this date, Monacair has been providing helicopter transportation to the Princely Family, the Government of Monaco and the many Heads of State who go to the Principality. With departures every 15 minutes from Nice and Monaco, enjoy the opportunity to take a flight. Possibility to reach Saint-Tropez, Corsica, Sicily, Sardinia but also Courchevel, Val d'isere, Méribel, St. moritz, or Gstaad, Auron, Isola 2000 without forgetting Venice, Milan, Rome, Florence, Toulouse, Paris, Lyon or Barcelona. Just ask!
Innovation 2016/2017: Monacair associated with Easyjet. Passengers from Monaco, with their boarding pass and one cabine baggage will be, from now on, directly transferred to the boarding area to their Easyjet flight in Nice Airport

HELI AIR MONACO
From Monaco heliport
Avenue des Ligures
✆ +37 (0)7 92 05 00 50 / +37 (0)7 92 05 00 10
www.heliairmonaco.com
reservations@heliairmonaco.com
Private flights. Transfers. Panoramic flights.
Perfect for avoiding traffic jams, Heli Air Monaco is the ideal solution if you are in a hurry or if you wish to have an original experience. The company organises regular transfers between the Nice Côte d'azur airport to Monaco (and vice versa) every 30 minutes all year round. You can also fly to other destinations: Saint-Tropez (25 minutes), Cannes (15 minutes) or Isola 2000 (20 minutes) but also to other ski resorts such as Courchevel, Megève, Albertville or Avoriaz. Heli Air Monaco also offers private flights to all destinations, panoramic flights and first flights on the French Riviera and the back country. To be noted a free shuttle service offered by the company in the Principality and package formulas for weekend in Monaco and a limousine service in the region.

By Train

All trains of the SNCF network stop at the station in Monaco Monte-Carlo. The TGV to and from Paris (5h30 drive) insure a day and night trip. Day trains to Milan, Genes or Bale pass 4 times per day. Night trains also serve the cities of Strasbourg, Paris, Toulouse, Irun, Port-Bou, Milan, Venice, Pisa and Rome. The TER (Regional Express Trains) provide long distance service to the Riviera cities from Ventimiglia (Italy) and from Menton for the eastern side, and from Grasse, Cannes or Les Arcs Draguignan for the western side. Since 2009, the Principality has contributed to increase the frequency of the number of TER and therefore also the number of passengers transported (450 seats) on the regional network between Menton and Nice by purchasing 5 reams decorated with the colours of the country. The TER run every day (about one every 15 minutes at peak times, every half hour during the day, if not every hour).

STATION SNCF OF MONACO MONTE CARLO
Place Sainte-Dévote ✆ +33 (0)800 11 40 23
♿
Open every day from 5am to 2am.
Inaugurated in December 1999, the Monaco Monte-Carlo station is operated by the National Society of French Railways (SNCF). The particularity of this station is its underground location: it is also characterized by the number of pedestrian accesses which serve the four corners of the Principality, from the Sainte-Devote bridge via a serie of elevators and escalators, from the Sainte Devote square at the corner of rue Grimaldi and Port Hercule, from the elevators of Boulevard de Belgique leading to Sainte Devote gallery, from the former SNCF station via the new gallery Prince Pierre near the Place d'Armes whose access is recommended for disabled people. Within the station, you will find the offices of the SNCF , some souvenir shops and a tourist office desk.

By Bus

The Urban Community of Nice Côte d' Azur has established a network of buses and coaches providing many connections between Nice and Menton, going through Monaco. All tickets can be purchased directly on board of each line by the driver which allows you to have a free correspondence within 2h30 (only for connections on French territory).

- **Line No. 100** runs daily from 6am to 8.30pm from Ségurane stop in Nice or from the bus station of Menton. Monday to Saturday, a departure every quarter of an hour is ensured while the frequency is slower on Sundays and French bank holidays: on these days, every 25 minutes there is a bus. Please note, buses of line 100 are often very crowded, probably victims of their success the ticket being at 1.50 € ... A good advice: arm yourself with patience, especially during major events or during summer! Enjoy the view along the seafront and if you find a seat, this will probably be your lucky day! In the Principality of Monaco, line 100 serves seven stops: Les Carabiniers, Place des Moulins, Casino, Stade nautique / Sainte Devote, Place d'Armes and cemetary.
- **Another much faster** and less crowded line connects Nice to Monaco but from the motorway: the **Xpress bus 100**. You will pay 4 € for a ticket. Beware: This line runs only every 50 minutes during peak periods.
- **For those who want to enjoy Monaco by night,** the **Noctambus 100** connecting Nice to Menton via The Principality runs every Thursday, Friday, Saturday and on the eve of public holidays from 10pm to 4am. Expect, however, that one passes every hour and a half in the Principality.

By Boat

The Principality of Monaco covers 2 km^2 but has 2 deep water marinas, arranged on both sides of the Rock. The welcome, the assistance and monitoring are carried out all year round 24h/24 year.

HERCULE PORT
Quai Albert-Ier
✆ +37 (0)7 97 77 30 00
www.ports-monaco.com
Guarded harbour 7/7 and 24/24. Freshwater, electricity on the dock and pontoons(220V/380V), 20 showers, 20 toilets, public phone and phone on board on request. TV on dock, laundromat downtown, containers for wasted oils and batteries, rubbish collect. Fuel. VHF channel 12 (24/24). From May 1st to September 30th from 8am to 11pm. From October 1st to April 30th from 8am to 8pm.
Located in the heart of the Condamine area, the port Hercule welcomes cruise ships and offers all the facilities to sailors and tourists who will find the commercial and leisure activities in the immediate vicinity. With a capacity of 700 places, it is one of the rare ports on the French Riviera with deep water, it therfore can welcome very big and luxurious boats. Note that postal delivery is free of charge for the sailors in the harbour office and a free pumping of wasted water can be made upon request at the petrol station.

PORT OF FONTVIEILLE
Quai Jean-Charles-Rey ✆ +37 (0)7 97 77 30 30
www.ports-monaco.com
VHF channel 9. From May 1st to September 30th from 8am to 10pm. From October 1st to April 30th from 8am to 8pm. Freshwater, electricity on dock and pontoons (220V/380V), 4 showers, 4 toilets, Public phone and phone on board on request. Guarded harbour 7 days a week and 24/24. TV on dock, laundromat downtown, containers for wasted oils and batteries.
Real marina, Fontvieille cannot welcome ships in stopover. Located in the heart of the residential area of the same name, this marina has all the necessary comfort for a very nice arrival in the principality.

GETTING AROUND

Public Transport

COMPANY OF BUSES OF MONACO – CAM
3, avenue Président- J.-F.-Kennedy
✆ +37 (0)7 97 70 22 22 – www.cam.mc
info@cam.mc
♿
Desks open from 8.30am to 4.30pm Monday to Friday. Ticket 1 trip: €2 (sold on the bus). Free -5 years. Pass 1 day (24 hours) unlimited: €5.50 and Pass 2 days (48h): €8.50. Free - 7 years. Cards 6 trips: €11. Boat-bus every day every 20 minutes from 8am to 7.40pm.
It is an eco green transport company (the public buses run on diester and are standard EEV), the CAM offers to the public transport users several lines of buses and a solar sea shuttle with a frequency of 10 minutes (20 minutes for the water bus) until midnight and a night service until 4am on weekends. The tickets are bought directly from the drivers when getting on the bus, in ticket machines, on Internet or in the company offices. To be noted that you can combine your tickets with the TER train service of the SNCF at reasonable prices for subscriptions rates.

Green Transport

MOBEE
c/o MC2D
41, avenue Hector-Otto – Patio Palace
✆ +37 (0)7 97 70 22 22
www.mobee.mc
Mobee, carsharing of electric vehicles. Licence B required. 25 accessible vehicles 24/24.
Mobee is a 100% project of electric mobility, an eco-responsible solution to move around in Monaco. Whether you are a resident, a company or a tourist, this innovating auto-sharing service is based

Port Hercule.

Traffic access control for campers or caravans

Beware, if you want to go to Monaco-Ville (The Rock) by car, the access is controlled: only vehicles registered in Monaco and the Alpes-Maritimes are authorized. For new French license plates, only those bearing the territorial identification of the Alpes-Maritimes and whose owner justifies his actual residence in this department will be allowed to enter the Rocher (Rock). The police officer on duty on the Place d'Armes will ask for some documents (registration certificate, vehicle registration and identity papers). Others will have to go to the Parking des Pecheurs at the end of the Avenue de la Quarantaine, where an elevator provides direct access within minutes to the old town.
Although motorhomes are welcome in the Principality, it is not the most appropriate way to get around in the streets of Monaco. Their parking is prohibited on public roads: only the parking des Ecoles can accommodate this type of vehicle but in limited quantities and the welcome is only possible when there are no major events. Information can be obtained from the Department of Public Parkings – 24, rue du Gabian 98000 Monaco ✆ +37 (0)7 98 98 81 83

on the principle of *free floating* («I take and I return my vehicle where I want»). Whether you are a resident, a company or a tourist, this service constitutes a sure and practical way to move around on the Monagasque territory. Via a smartphone app, a cartography of the points indicates to you in real time when to take your car: after use, you will be able to restore the vehicle anywhere freely in Monaco. The parking is free on the roadways (2 or 4 wheels) and in 14 parkings partners of the service. A smart solution to discover the Principality in a playful manner, in total autonomy. Download the list of partner parkings from their website.

Taxi

MONACO TAXI PRESTIGE
✆ +37 (0)7 93 15 01 01
www.taximonacoprestige.com
♿

Service available 24/24 and 7 days a week.

For an urgent personal or professional appointment, a departure towards an airport (Nice, Mandelieu, Marseille, Albenga or Genes), for a long distance journey or simply to discover the French and Italian Riviera with a high quality service, the taxis in Monaco are at your service. Drivers will pick you up directly at your home or at your hotel according to your expectations. Beware: in peak season or during major events, the drivers are often overflowed and the waiting can sometimes be very long! A booking service is possible via the website where you simply fill in the form with the date, destination and schedule to the central reservation which will forward your request to a driver. The site also allows you to have an idea about the prices of each service performed during the day and at night.

YOUR PRIVATE DRIVER
✆ +33 (0)6 78 82 00 72
www.yourprivatedriver.fr

Rates studied according to the destination and the number of passengers. Possibility of renting a chauffeur-driven car for transfers, possibility of renting top-of-the-range cars, helicopter, private jet, yatch rentals.

Your Private Driver, company of limousine drivers (V.I.P.), puts at your disposal several types of services, small or long distance all destinations tansfers, car rental with driver, sports car, yacht, helicopter or of private jet. You will have understood, whatever your waitings and your budget, they do their best to satisfy you!

Car Rental

LIVEN UP
2, rue Princesse-Florestine
✆ +37 (0)7 97 97 17 16
www.livenup.fr/livenup

Ferrari or Lamborghini tour from €119 the 15 minutes. Possible departure from Monaco, Eze village or Nice. Ferrari Baptism (15 minutes, 30 minutes or 1 hour). Possibility of gift coupon. Tourist excursion in minivan with a driver-guide. Boat rental.

Liven Up Nice and Liven Up Monaco are specialized in sports and leisure events organisation. The agency offers a wide choice of activities: Ferrari or Lamborghini baptisms, guided excursions, boat rentals, tours on sailing ships, rentals of terraces for F1 Grand Prix... to live an unforgettable experience. For a stroll in Ferrari or in Lamborghini, the departure is from the parking of Fragonard perfumery in Eze village: discover the pleasures of driving on board a genuine racing car, along the corniches. To do as a copilot or a pilot if you like sport cars. An original idea of gift!

SIGHTSEEING

Although the Principality of Monaco is a small country (2 km2), it is important to structure your visit to avoid wasting time. A tip how to save time and to have a wise visit: use car parks and urban elevators, fast and secure operating 24h/24.

Fontvieille and the exotic Garden. Located down against the Rock, the Fontvieille district was built on the sea. It consists of homes, offices, a heliport, factories, the Louis II stadium and a small port. If you arrive in Monaco by the medium corniche, you will arrive by the Exotique garden.

The Rocher (the Rock). It is the old town with narrow alleys of the Middle Ages. It is better to leave the car in the parking des Pecheurs located down against the Rock: a lift then enables you to reach the main sites (Prince's Palace, Cathedral, Oceanographic Museum, etc.)

The Condamine. Important shopping area, this sector of La Condamine includes Grimaldi Street, the Place d'Armes and the little church of Sainte-Devote, the Boulevard Albert I and the Port Hercule.

Monte-Carlo and the Larvotto. Worldwide famous, it is in the district of Monte-Carlo (some pronounce it Monte-Carl ') that are the Casino, the Opera and the Carré d'Or. Not far away, the Larvotto includes private and public beaches, the Grimaldi Forum and Villa Sauber.

Monuments

CHURCH SAINTE-DÉVOTE

Port
Condamine
✆ + 37 (0)7 93 50 52 60
www.sainte-devote.com
mouvementstedevote@hotmail.com

Sunday Mass every Sunday at 6pm except during school holidays.

Sainte Dévote is the holy patroness and guardian of the Principality. The roman Emperor Diocletian Roman led the last bloody wave of persecution against the followers of the new religion that was Christianity. The corsican Dévote was one of his victims towards the end of his reign in 304. A legend perpetuates her memory: by fear her body would be desecrated, her circle of friends manadged to get her remains and put her in a boat which came ashore in the small valley of Gaumates in Monaco. The martyr, became Saint, and was buried there. The edification of a church dedicated to her was given to the monks of the abbey of Saint-Pons. The actual church dates back to 1870, under the reign of Prince Charles III. Every January 27th, the miraculous return of the holy patroness is commemorated by igniting a boat on the church square.

MONACO CATHEDRAL

4, rue Colonel-Bellando-de-Castro
✆ +37 (0)7 93 30 87 70
www.cathedrale.mc
cathedrale@cathedrale.mc

Open all year. Masses Monday to Friday at 6pm in the chapel Notre-Dame de la Miséricorde and Tuesday at 9am at the cathedral in the chapel of Saint-Sacrement. Sunday masses Saturday at 6pm at the cathedral. Sunday at 8.30am at the chapel Notre-Dame de la Miséricorde then at 10.30am at the cathedral. Free. Cathedral open from October 1st to April 30th from 8.30am to 6pm. From May 1st to September 30th, the cathedral is open from 8am to 7pm.

This cathedral of Romanesque revival style was built in 1875 with the white stones of La Turbie on the exact location where the old saint-Nicolas church once was. Inside, a magnificent altarpiece painted by Louis Bréa at the beginning of the 16th century represents saint-Nicolas on his green episcopal throne surrounded by saints with a prédelle of 17 small different paintings. The majestic white marble altar encrusted with mosaics gives a glimpse of *the* white Penitents *Pietà* behind it. In the crypt, the tombs of the Princes of Monaco: that of the Princess Grace and Prince Rainier III are on the left side of the transept. During summer, you can hear every Sunday at 10am the mass sung by the Petits Chanteurs de Monaco.

Tour of The Prince's palace of Monaco.

Museums

COLLECTION OF VINTAGE CARS OF THE PRINCE OF MONACO – MONACO TOP CARS COLLECTION

Les Terrasses de Fontvieille
✆ + 37 (0)7 92 05 28 56
www.palais.mc
mtcc@mtcc.mc
Direct access to the Terraces of Fontvieille by elevators and escalators; parking of Fontvieille.

♿

Closed on December 25th. The schedule and opening dates can be changed. Ticket twinned with the Palace: €11.50 adult, from 6 to 14 years old child and students: €5. Open every day from 10am to 5.30pm. Ticket twinned with the Oceanographic Museum: €18 adult, child +12 years: €11, from 8 to 12 years old child: €8, from 4 to 7 years old child: €7 and students: €11. Free for under 5-year-olds. Adult: €6.50. Child (from 6 to 14 years old): €3. Students and disabled guests: €3.

Prince Rainier III, car passionate, built up for more than thirty years, when he got the opportunity or when he came across a favourite, an important personal collection of cars of all ages and from all countries, popular or unique. His son Prince Albert II took over the collection. A hundred vehicles built by the most famous European and American companies and, which have played a major role during their era, were collected and restored. This unique collection is displayed on 5000 m^2 as wished by Prince Rainier in a specially designed hall overlooking the Terrasses de Fontvieille at the foot of the Rock. If you are lover of great cars, you can't miss that visit.

NEW NATIONAL MUSEUM OF MONACO (NMNM) – PALOMA VILLA

56, boulevard du Jardin-Exotique
✆ +37 (0)7 98 98 48 60
www.nmnm.mc

Open every day for exhibitions from 10am to 6pm from October 1st to May 31st and from 11am to 7pm from June 1st to September 30th. Closed on January 1st, May 1st, 4 days of Grand Prix, November 19th and December 25th. Entrance Villa Paloma + Villa Sauber: €6. Group rate €4 minimum 15 people. Twinned ticket NMNM + Exotic Garden + Musée d'Anthropologie Préhistorique: €10. Free admission every Sunday. Free -26 years, pupils and children, Monegasques, members of the Association of the Friends of the NMNM, members ICOM and CIMAM, unemployed people on written proof, disabled people. Free guided tours on reservation by e-mail: public@nmnm.mc

The New National museum of Monaco (NMNM) consists of two villas: villa Paloma located on the heights of the boulevard du jardin exotique and villa Sauber on the beachfront in Larvotto area. Built in 1910, Villa Paloma is one of the most beautiful residences of the Principality for its architecture and urbanism. Since 2010 it welcomes temporary exhibitions. Do not hesitate to visit its garden designed by Octave Godard, pupil of the famous landscape architect Edouard André (1840-1911) from which the view of Monaco is unique.

NEW NATIONAL MUSEUM OF MONACO (NMNM) – SAUBER VILLA

17, avenue Princesse-Grace
✆ +37 (0)7 98 98 91 26
www.nmnm.mc
contact@nmnm.mc

Open every day during exhibitions from 10am to 6pm from October 1st to May 31st and from 11am to 7pm from June 1st to September 30th. Closed on January 1st, May 1st, 4 days of Grand Prix, November 19th and December 25th. Tarifs Villa Paloma + Villa Sauber €6. Group rate €4 minimum 15 people. Twinned ticket NMNM + Exotic garden + museum of Prehistoric anthropology: €10. Free admission every Sunday. Free -26 years, pupils and children, Monegasques, members of the Association of the friends of the NMNM, members ICOM and CIMAM, unemployed people on written proof, disabled people. Free guided tours on reservation by e-mail: public@nmnm.mc

The New National museum of Monaco (NMNM) is composed by two villas: villa Paloma located on the heights of the boulevard du jardin exotique and villa Sauber on the beachfront in the Larvotto area. Belonging to the last Belle Epoque residences in the Principality, and often wrongly attributed to Charles Garnier because of its similarities with the Opera built at the same period, it was bought by the painter Robert Sauber who gave it its name before it became the Monegasque state property in 1969. La Villa Sauber exposed from 1972 to 2009 the Galéa collection (dolls, robots, miniatures...). Today, it hosts various exhibitions. During your visit, do not miss its garden where many cítricos bloom, and a rose garden dedicated to Francis Meilland as well as exotic plants. A pleasant walk, far from the hustle and bustle of the city.

GRAND APARTMENTS OF THE PRINCES PALACE

Place du Palais
✆ +37 (0)7 93 25 18 31
www.palais.mc
visites@palais.mc

Access: local bus of Monaco lines 1 and 2, stop Visitation then 5 minutes on foot through the narrow streets of the Rock. Access by the Place d'Armes by the ramp Major: 10 minutes on foot. The schedule and opening dates are likely to change. Annual closing from mid-October to end of March. From July 1st to August 31st, open from 10am to 7pm; last entrance 6.30pm. From April 2nd to June 30th and from September 1st to October 15th, open every day from 10am to 6pm; last entrance 5.30pm. Free for under 5-year-olds. Adult: €8. Child (from 8 to 14 years old): €4 (same rate for the students). Ticket twinned with the Oceanographic Museum: adults €19, from 4 to 7 years old €7, from 8 to 12 years old €9, + 12 years and students €11; tickets only valid from April to end of October. The palace has a sophisticated system of audio-guided visits in 11 languages. Site non accessible to people in wheel chair (staircases). Ticket twinned with the Car collection museum: €11.50 adult, from 8 to 14 years old child and students: €5. Guided tour (possible on request). Shop.

Count about 40 minutes to visit the large flats of this private residence. The building was built in the late 13th century in the early days of the Grimaldi dynasty on the remains of a castle built in 1215. It was then developed and embellished during the Renaissance. Each year, an impressive procession of tourists comes to visit and discover some of the Princes of Monaco intimacy through their large flats. It's an opportunity to see the beautiful Italian arcaded gallery with large wall paintings, the Prince lounges or the throne room which has hosted major events since the 16th century. You will see how each element has been decorated pompously and luxuriously like the courtyard with its staircase made with Carrara marble or the palatine chapel. One of the Rocher classic postcards shows the standard bearing the princely arms when the Prince was in the Palace on the Sainte-Marie tower, white in La Turbie stones and built at the beginning of the century by Prince Albert I. On the Palace Square, you can enjoy a beautiful view of the city and the harbour. The changing of the Carabiniers' guard in their famous local suit which is white in summer and black in winter, takes place every day at 11.55am. If you arrive late, you can catch up by listening to their band which appears on stage during major ceremonies or during public concerts. The Palace also includes the parish of Saint-Jean-Baptiste which is not open to the public: built between 1654 and 1656 by the Genoese

The oceanographic Museum of Monaco

architect Jacques Cantone on the request of Prince Honoré II, it was fully restored during the reign of Prince Charles III (1818-1889).

OCEANOGRAPHIC MUSEUM OF MONACO

Avenue Saint-Martin ✆ +37 (0)7 93 15 36 00
www.oceano.mc
musee@oceano.mc

♿

Open every day except on December 25th and the F1 Grand Prix weekend at the end of May. January, February, March, October, November, December: from 10am to 6pm. April, May, June, September: from 10am to 7pm. July and August from 9.30am to 8pm. Rates of the museum (individual rates, reduced, twinned, family offer, freedom pass) on the website: www.oceano.org. Armchair loan. No pets allowed except blind dogs. Guided tour. Catering facilities (Terrace of the Oceanographic Museum). Shop. Activities.

Built on the side of the Rock, the oceanographic Museum of Monaco contemplates the Mediterranean from its 85 meters since more than one century. In this establishment dedicated to the marine world, history and scientific news are supplemented with wonder. On several floors, the visitor discovers the path of Prince Albert 1st Monaco (1848-1922), founder of this museum and pionnier of modern oceanography. Between exploration, arts and sciences, the visit is marked by impressive collection items highlighted by the spaces of these majestic rooms where models and large skeletons of marine mammals take all their dimensions. Temporary interesting exhibitions supplement the discovery of this attractive place: from May 5th to September 30th, 2017, discover the Borderline event by Philippe Pasqua. The painter and sculptor with an incisive and powerful art, will invest the place in its totality, from the entrance square to the panoramic terrace with his monumental works – 12 on the whole, and new achievements. Through them, Philippe Pasqua questions and challenges the public whose aim is to cause an awakening in favour of marine and terrestrial life. In the basement, the aquarium constitutes one of the key moments of the visit: the lagoon with sharks, in a 6 meters depth and 400 000 liters aquarium and the extraordinary diversity of the coral reef. The alive ecosystems are presented in a realistic way sensitizing the visitors to durable management of the ocean. The visitor strolls in a bluish, soft and mysterious atmosphere. Several spaces also mark the course: a patrimonial stone staircase, a space acidification of the oceans which illustrates the effect of massive absorption by the seas of carbonic gas produced by human activity, a news area equipped with screens which enables the visitors to share the daily life of the boarders and news concerning Méditerranée, a games space for children to learn while having fun. This year, discover a new space around fluo corals for a night dive in the tropical seas. An commitment area concludes this splendid submarine visit and makes it possible to visitors to mention their desire to protect the Mediterranean. To finish this enthralling outing, the roof terrace accommodates on 600 m^2 tortoises of Mali offered to Prince Albert II. If you are hungry, the La Terrasse du Musée restaurant offers a cuisine with Mediterranean flavours and a stunning view on the Sea and the Principality.

Walks & Strolls

ANIMALIST GARDEN

Les Terrasses de Fontvieille
✆ + 37 (0)7 93 50 40 30
jardinanimalierdemonaco@monaco.mc

The schedule and opening dates can be changed. Open every day from 9am to 12pm and from 2pm to 7pm from June to September. Open from 10am to 12pm and from 2pm to 6pm from March 1st to May 31st. Open from 10am to 12pm and from 2pm to 5pm from October 1st to February 28th. Free - 6 years. Adult: €5. From 6 to 14 years old child: €3. Children welcome. Access strollers, disabled guests and wheel chairs.

Overlooking the port of Fontvieille on the southern slope of the Rock, this garden sheltered from violent easterly winds was founded in 1954 by Prince Rainier III. It shelters nearly 250 animals of fifty different species: exotic birds, turtles, alligators, hippos, reptiles, primates, farm animals, which live in exemplary comfortable conditions. The particularity of this park is to collect animals after donations from individuals or after seizures by different authorities. During your visit, immerse yourself in this almost wild world in the middle of this modern world of the Principality of Monaco: change of scenery guaranteed!

EXOTIC GARDEN AND CAVE OF THE OBSERVATORY ★★
62 boulevard du Jardin-Exotique
✆ + 37 (0)7 93 15 29 80
www.jardin-exotique.mc
jardin-exotique@mairie.mc

Open all year. Closed on November 19th (national day) and on December 25th. Open from May 1st to September 30th from 9am to 7pm. In February, March, April and October from 9am to 6pm. In January, November and December from 9am to 5pm. From 4 to 18 years old: €3.80. Adult: €7.20. Students (with card): €3.80. More than 65 years: €5.50. For groups, possible reservation Monday to Friday from 9am to 5pm at ✆+37 (0)7 93 15 29 80. Free for under 4-year-olds. Possibility of twinned ticket with Nouveau Musée National de Monaco (Villa Paloma) and Oceanographic museum. Partnership with Parc Alpha (on presentation of ticket): entrance with the exotic garden with €5.50/adult (instead of €7.20) and €2.70/child (instead of €3.80). Access limited to the garden for the people in wheel chair (free admission for accompanying) and the strollers. No pets allowed. Free kennels. The admission ticket includes the visit to the exotic garden, the cave of the Observatory and the museum of anthropology.

The rocky walls of the Exotic garden benefit all year round of an exceptional microclimate. Work of Jean Gastaud, this garden offers a magnificent collection of cacti and agave plants since 1933. The site offers a unique and exceptional panoramic view of the Principality of Monaco and the Italian Riviera. Bridges and arches allow to move freely among the huge and amazing plants. The 2,400 hours of sunshine per year favours the development of coloured flowers with varied sizes throughout the year. At the bottom of the garden there is the Observatory Cave (compulsory guided tour, about 30 minutes) where stalactites and stalagmites, draperies and concretions accentuate the scenery. Note that it is possible to rent the exotic garden outside opening hours for private events and that the site offers a special package for wedding photos. Before leaving, you can go to the shop facing the entrance: 55 m^2 with more than 400 products, (T-shirts, teddy bears, pens, key rings, magnets, post cards... without forgetting an exclusive collection of leather goods) most of them bearing the colours of the Exotic garden..

KNIFE & FORK

AMICI MIEI
16, quai Jean-Charles-Rey
✆ +37 (0)7 92 05 92 14
www.amici-miei.com
amici-miei@monte-carlo.mc

Open all year. 7 days a week for lunch and dinner. From 12pm to 3pm and from 7pm to 11pm. In July, August and September, open all day nonstop. Booking advised. Menu business lunch at €26 (excluding drinks). À la carte: Around €35. Lunch menu: €16 (daily special + dessert + coffee). Main course + coffee + glass of wine €18. American Express. Groups welcome. Terrace. Take-away. Parking. Pets allowed.

When you arrive, you will like the friendly setting of the place: a beautiful terrace on Fontvieille harbour, a splendid view of the lower part of the Rock and the most beautiful yachts of the Mediterranean. Inside, photos of celebrities who regularly come to eat there adorn the walls of this restaurant with a friendly atmosphere. Here Giorgio Colombesi and his partner Lucia perpetuate a tradition that exists for more than twenty years: that is an excellent italian cuisine. Very good quality meals with flavours and scents that the gourmet chef, Donatella Colombesi, prepares with care and rigour, homemade pasta is then cooked al dente upon the customer's order (bigoli lobster, fusilli cherry tomatoes lobster and artichoke...) and fish is wild (red tuna tagliata with mint sauce, busara scampi and its polenta or salt crust wolf). All ingredients used are purchased in the morning! Also taste the Venetian veal liver with polenta, it is really good. The restaurant also offers a range of exceptional Italian and French wines. Business lunch menu served daily for lunch is admirable and allows you to enjoy a range of house specialties. A gourmet address where Italian flavors are being honored in a pure spirit of gastronomy.

BEEFBAR
42, quai Jean-Charles-Rey
✆ +37 (0)7 97 77 09 29
monaco@beefbar.com

Open all year. Monday to Thursday from 8am to 11pm. Friday to Saturday from 8am to midnight. Sunday from 8am to 11pm. Booking advised. À la carte: Around €28 (dish). Wine by the glass. Business lunch €20. Plate from €18. Menu Is in hiding €26. Tagliata menu €27. American Express. Groups welcome. Terrace. Valet. Take-away.

This address combines elegance and charms. Benefit as of your arrival from the magnificent panorama on the port from Fontvieille. Inside, the déco is purified, mixing wood and metal harmoniously. Behind the wide fully glazed facade nest a table of quality: with an impeccable service, original dishes and of a great diversity will be brought to you. The à la carte proposes salads and also leaves place to the charcuterie with the pata will negra imported live at Spain and the meat with beef fine pieces like the incredible beef Chateaubriant Angus, the beef of Kobe style Gold Selection, Beefbar black burgers of Black Angus, inter alia. Side fish, you will be allured by the ceviche of octopus, lemon grass and coriander, or the Tartar of crab, avocado and pink lady. An excellent address. Also discover The Beefbar Butcher Shop, the top-of-the-range butcher which sells the meats and the emblematic charcuteries of the à la carte of Beefbar: a place nested in an ecrin where luxury and modernity

are interfered in wood and brass, black marble, white marble a decor made, revealing exclusive meat cuttings. Possible home delivery.

THE MICHELANGELO

8, quai Jean-Charles-Rey
✆ + 37 (0)7 92 05 77 33
www.michelangelo-arturo.com
lemichelangelo.monaco@hotmail.fr

Open all year. Monday to Friday from 12pm to 2pm and from 7.30pm to 10.30pm. Saturdays from 7.30pm to 10.30pm. Closed on Sunday. À la carte: Around €55. Fixed rate formula Business lunch from €48 (starter + main course + dessert). American Express. Label Artisan du Gout. Covered terrace.

Unmissable establishment on the Fontvieille harbour for over twenty years, it has welcomed many personalities such as Prince Albert II, Luciano Pavarotti, Roger Moore or Whitney Houston, and also the greatest professionals of Formula 1. This beautiful restaurant is perfectly run by its illustrious owner Arturo, which continues over the years. People come here to enjoy a variety of Italian and Mediterranean inspirations, good for their body and taste buds. Taste the «basket of Arturo» with its extraordinary tomatoes coming from Sicily, the artichoke salad, the mozzarella *di buffala* and the wonderful Alba truffle, but also the seafood specialties such as the carpaccio of smoked cod on a bed of warm potatoes. All the fish are wild and the meats are certified Angus or Limousin. Pizza lovers will not be left behind. Note that there are also Monegasque specialties like the barbajuan.

Exotic garden

BELLA VITA

21, rue Princesse-Caroline
✆ +37 (0)7 93 50 42 02 – www.bellavita.mc
info@bellavita.mc

Open all year. Open 7 days a week from 7am to 11pm. Non-stop service. Service delivery (ask for information). À la carte: Around €25. Daily special: €15 (Monday to Friday from 12pm to 3pm). Breakfasts from €5. Afternoon snack €8. Snack carte: Around €13. Pizza from €14. Happy hours from 6pm to 8pm. Formula adapted for private groups or events. Terrace. Label Artisan du Gout.

La vita è bella ma la bella vita è meglio: here is the motto of this establishment that welcomes you in the morning with its tasty breakfasts. Start out on the right foot with an Italian coffee or a freshly squeezed orange juice, with delicious pastries. Belle Vita also offers for lunch homemade menus prepared upon request (paninis served with foccacia bread, sandwiches, salads or burgers), daily specials and the chef's specialities displayed on the menu: mussels in Calabrian way, spaghetti reda, artichokes salad and Parmesan, Bolognese tagliatelle, ravioli with pumpkin in mantovene way, baked salmon, fried artichokes, pine nuts and seasonal vegetables, slices of grilled beef, chianti sauce, homemade mashed potatoes or fried squid and prawns. Bella Vita is also the perfect place to have a drink while nibbling some tapas after work, back from the beach or after *shopping* seated on the sunny terrace or in the large indoor room with a modern and warm decor: a beautiful life, after all!

BRASSERIE OF MONACO

Port of Monaco – 36, route de la Piscine
✆ +37 (0)7 97 98 51 20
www.brasseriedemonaco.com
contact@brasseriedemonaco.fr

Open all year. Every day from 12pm to 2am of the morning. DJ 7 days a week. Happy Hour every day 6pm at 8pm. Pressure from €4. Soft €5. Cocktails from €10. Booking advised. À la carte: Around €17 (dish). Lunch menu: €16 (dish + drink). Wine by the glass. Pizza from €10. Salad from €14. Dish from €12. American Express. Groups welcome. Terrace. Take-away. Shop. Activities.

The Brasserie is known for its famous beer of Monaco, its *afterworks* or its evening entertainments but it is also a nice canteen with the relaxed atmosphere. One lunches there readily on the outdoor terrace with the sun, even in winter. The à la carte displays suggestions of type brasserie: pizza, salad Caesar, salad of hot goat cheese, shrimps & chips, fish & chips, onion, chiffonade of Italian charcuterie... The products come or are primarily elaborate in Monaco or in the French regions and Italian located not far from there. To come to the Brasserie ensures you one friendly moment to divide with your friends.

CASA TUA

4 ,rue Reymond-Suffren
✆ +37 (0)7 97 98 68 28
http://casatuamonaco.com

Open all year. For lunch and dinner. À la carte: Around €20 (dish). Lunch menu: €15 or €17 (Monday to Saturday).

Casa Tua is a restaurant with simple cuisine where italian local products are enhanced, meat polpette della mamma with tomato sauce, fried squid and crunchy courgettes with balsamic vinegar, fusilloni del gargano with swordfish and eggplant, risotto, turbot with clams and cherry tomatoes, royal sautéed (clams, mussels, fasolari and knives of sea), Black Angus steak... The decoration is refined, the atmosphere is cosy, the staff friendly. You will feel at home in Casa Tua...

GRAN CAFFE

57, rue Grimaldi ✆ +37 (0)7 97 97 78 88
www.grancaffe.net
info@grancaffe.net

Open all year. Open Monday to Friday 7am until midnight. Lunch menu: €19. Terrace. Air conditioning. Free wi-fi.

In a friendly atmosphere with a bright and trendy decor, discover the gourmet and contemporary italian cuisine sublimating regional products of the Italian lands. The creative cuisine inspired by fresh seasonal ingredients is declined regularly according to the lucky finds of the market and the chef's inspirations. It is a subtle cuisine with accents of the South: roasted Scallops on an artichoke salad with chickpea cream and rosemary, roasted squids on a candied bed of mixed green salad with dried tomatos, spelt flour spaghettis with clams and broccolis, cod fish à la vicentine... The dishes are colourfull and nicely presented. The desserts are remarkable, the ice cream cups are exquisite. Excellent French and Italian wine list. The Dolce Vita in Monaco!

LE HUIT ET DEMI

4, rue Langlé ✆ +37 (0)7 93 50 97 02
www.huitetdemi.mc
info@huitetdemi.mc

Open all year. Monday to Saturday from 12pm to 2.30pm and from 7pm to 11pm. Closed on Sunday. Booking advised. À la carte: Around €45 (starter, main course, dessert). Daily special: €14. Wine by the glass. Daily special + dessert of the day: €20. Groups welcome. Terrace. Label Craftsman of Taste.

Special mention for this friendly address with a decor fully dedicated to cinema. You arrive in the indoor room with some portraits of cinema stars by a long red carpet which echoes with the one that the celebrities in Cannes climb during the film festival. On the beautiful outdoor terrace, large white parasols shelter tables and chairs which remind us of the famous directors armchairs while the facade presents illustrations framed with original cinema reels. The carte offers a Mediterranean cuisine: duck breast with bilberries and maple syrup, Anna apples and flat beans; coalfish fillet braised with mustard, tulip of candied vegetables; sautée piglet grandma's style, crushed potatoes; haddock sauce bonne femme, vegetable bayaldi and steamed potatoes; cod loin with candied jasmine and Thai rice; crusty whiting champagne sauce and 3 colours rice... Yes, a pleasure for everybody!

JACK MONACO

32, route de la Piscine
✆ +37 (0)7 97 98 34 56
www.jack.mc
info@jack.mc

Open all year. Monday to Sunday from 12pm to 3 in the morning. Lunch menu €17. Daily special €14. Happy hours. Terrace. Animations. Concerts.

Comfortably seated on the sunny terrace (covered and heated in winter) or in the large interior room with exposed stone walls, let yourself be tempted by a simple and gourmet carte: Greek salad (salad, feta, sweet peppers, cucumbers, olives, tomatos cherries, coriander, onions); fresh fusilli, fresh tomatos and basil; risotto with wild mushrooms and Parmesan tiles; wok of shrimps, crunchy vegetables and noodles; fillet of cod with coconut and rice pistachio; sliced chicken à la thaïe and its crunchy vegetables without forgetting the variation of classical pizzas. In the evening, the atmosphere gets warmer: concerts and DJ animate the place. Enjoy the XL cocktails and other drinks accompanied by tapas.

MARCELLO RESTAURANT, WINERY & STORE

22 bis, rue Grimaldi ✆ +37 (0)7 97 98 37 81
www.marcellofoodvalley.com
info@marcellofoodvalley.com

Open all year. Every day from 12pm to 11pm. Shop open from 8am. À la carte: Around €25. Children's menu: €12. Lunch menu: €16 (daily special + dessert + coffee Monday to Friday). Antipasto + daily special + dessert + coffee: €19 Monday to Friday for lunch only. Groups welcome (on reservation). Terrace.

Delicate mixture between modernity and tradition, Marcello honours Italian excellence around a subtle concept that combines traditional catering, catering, wine bar and deli. The decor in a *trattoria* way is neat and bright, and you'll find generosity as well in the hearty dishes as with the friendly and attentive team, always smiling and always of good advice. Salads, pasta, cheese, cold meats, risottos. . . find all the italian flavours at Marcello's!

O LIBAN

La Condamine
3, place d'Armes ✆ +37 (0)7 93 50 00 00
www.oliban.mc

Open all year. À la carte: Around €30 (dish). Tasting menu (min 2 people) €55 (possibility of vegetarian menu). Menu OLiban (4 people) €90. Daily special: €15 Monday to Friday, only for lunch (except bank holidays). Terrace. Take-away. Organization of all types of events. Theme parties. Catering with sandwiches containing Lebanese bread from €8 and other menu at €10, €14 and €18.

A change of scenery that you can reach from Place d'armes, by the staircase on the right. Succumb to Lebanese specialties which you'll enjoy on a musical and relaxing background: homous, kibbé (minced meat with wheat, onions, cream and parsley), manahich, pancake with ewe's milk cheese... Gourmands will also appreciate the tasty desserts. Very nice selection of Lebanese wines. The setting is warm and cosy, the atmosphere pleasant and the service elegant. O Liban also regularly organises evenings with oriental dancers, *belly dancing*, percussion, DJs... Do not hesitate to visit their Facebook page to know the program! A culinary stopover not to be missed in the Principality.

RESTAURANT DE LA SOCIÉTÉ NAUTIQUE DE MONACO

1, quai Louis-II ✆ 37 (0)7 93 50 51 30
www.avironmonaco.com
restaurantsnm@gmail.com

Open all year. From 8am to 4pm Monday to Saturday. For dinner from 7pm to midnight Thursday to Saturday. Closed on Sunday. Tea room from 3pm; aperitif from 5pm. À la carte: Around €30. Children's menu: €10. Daily special: €14.

In a bright and modern decor, discover the restaurant of the Nautical Company of Monaco. Equipped with a splendid and pleasant sunny terrace opened on the Mediterranean and the moored yachts, and a superb room where white and beige dominate, the cuisine is turned towards regional flavours: homemade raviolis tomato sauce, homemade tagliatelle bolognaise sauce, beef tartare with French fries, salmon filet and ratatouille, risotto of the sea... A delicious stopover with an attentive and friendly welcome and service!

ROYAL THAÏ

18, rue Millo ✆ +37 (0)7 93 30 16 14
www.royalthaimonaco.com

Open 7 days a week from 12pm to 3pm and from 7pm to 10.30pm. Average price à la carte €20. Daily special €13. Menu €16.50.

Desire for tasting some Thai dishes? In neat surroundings, this establishment has a beautiful terrace whose clientele can largely profit as of the first sunbeams. Side cuisine, place with the tradition with often raised preparations and delicately prepared: chicken with cashews, noodles of rice poêlées with vegetables or the tofu, vegetable donuts, beef or chicken jumped to the ginger, marinated pork chops sauce with honey or shrimp soup. Entrance with the dessert, expatriation is guaranteed!

BLUE BAY

40, evenue Princesse-Grace
✆ +37 (0)7 98 06 03 60
www.montecarlobay.com
reservation-mcbay@montecarlobay.mc

Open Tuesday to Saturday from 7.30pm to 10.30pm. Annual closing from February to March. 1 Michelin star. Booking advised. Menu Escapade 4 dishes €88 and 5 dishes €108. Wine by the glass. Menu étoilé €108 (excluding drinks). Special meeting, privatization or semi-privatization for lunch: from €51 with the menu business 3 dishes, excluding drinks. Sunday brunch from 12.30pm to 3pm: consult the website. American Express, Diners Club. Groups welcome. Terrace. Car valet.

From one rock to another... Marcel Ravin left his native Martinique to settle in Monaco at the Blue Bay. A hint of the Caribbean on the French Riviera. His cuisine is made of an alchemy of spices and herbs precisely proportioned to intensifie the taste of the selected local products. He offers a subtle combination of flavours and textures as in the garden of Antipodes, the macaroni of conger with crab and pink bays, the Bresse poulard with crayfish and foie gras, the back of venison with maniguette pepper. For dessert, choose the apple/pear caramel with maple syrup, or the chocolate partition maracudja, a classic! As Marcel Ravin says: «When one comes to eat at the Monte-Carlo Bay, I wish that one finds something good and beautiful. Whether to test a main course by curiosity or to return by pleasure.» Besides, his passion has been rewarded, Michelin Guide awarded him his first star.

MAYA BAY

Roccabella
24, avenue Princesse-Grace
Monte Carlo
✆ +37 (0)7 97 70 74 67
www.mayabay.mc
mayabay@mayabay.mc

Closed in November. Closed on Sunday and Monday. Open from 12pm to 2pm and from 7.30pm to 11pm. The outdoor terraces are open from April 15th to end of October. Booking advised. À la carte: Around €70. Lunch menu: €18 (starter + main course + dessert). Wine by the glass. American Express. Groups welcome (except the weekend). Garden. Terrace. Car valet. Take-away. Shop. Animations. Parking. Garage.

The Maya Bay has a chic and Zen atmosphere which combines two restaurants: Christophe Dupuy controls the Thai restaurant assisted exclusively by Thai chefs insuring their culinary culture while the Chef Ryuji Kakizaki manages the Japanese restaurant with revisited traditional dishes offering an explosion of new flavours in the mouth. The menu is magnificent and invites you to travel: dim sum lobster or shrimp, sushi, uramaki, grilled salmon, grilled lobster, tempura moriawase, scallop ravioli and kimchi, fresh crab accompanied by Chinese chives and sweeten-spiced sauce... Delicious Asian flavours, friendly service, a wine list worthy of a large hotel combining affordable rates and grand crus. A real favourite! On site, be sure to visit Maya Shop, an unusual space where you'll find vintage pieces, jewellery, seasonal collections, upscale brand or original accessories coming direcltly from Japan.

STARS'N' BARS

6, quai Antoine-Ier ✆ +37 (0)7 97 97 95 95
www.starsnbars.com
info@starsnbars.com

Open all year 7 days a week. Non-stop service from 11am to midnight. Terrace. À la carte around €23 (dish). Brunchs from 11am to 3pm Saturday, Sunday and public holidays only. Daily special: €11. Lunch menu €17. Possible privatization.

The Stars'n'Bars is a must for all those who love the «made in USA» atmosphere. With a beautiful view on the moored yachts of Port Hercule and a large terrace, the menu offers simple and generous dishes: salads (with or without meat), BBQ pork ribs, grilled fillet with egg, steak tartare, grilled chicken fillets topped with melted gorgonzola and all kinds of burgers, as well as more exotic flavours such as tortillas, sliced beef fillet marinated in ginger and soy slightly spicy served with vegetables. A non-stop casual service. In the evening, after dinner, go to the Star Deck upstairs for a drink and dance on DJ rhythms! A very good address.

SONG QI

7, avenue Princess-Grace
✆ + 37 (0)7 99 99 33 33 – www.song-qi.mc

Open all year. Service from 12pm to 2.30pm and from 7.30pm to 11pm. À la carte: Around €100. Lunch menus between €26 and €29. Terrace. Valet.

Alan Yau and Riccardo Giraudi are perfectionists: they have imagined and created a new and sublime concept. The Song Qi is the first Chinese gourmet restaurant of the Cote d'Azur. A luxurious decor erected in a lacquerware setting spread on 100m^2. An outdoor terrace completes the room for you to have lunch in the sun. It is a blend of traditional and gourmet Chinese cuisine prepared with French local products. The lunch menu offers 3 formulas, glass of wine included: The Dim Sum Lunch (assortment of homemade Dim sun), the All in One Lunch (salad of the day, daily special...) and the Personal Noodle Menu (noodles with choice of sauces). The menu changes every 15 days. In the evening, the menu is wonderful: you really have to try specialities like the whole roasted duck of Song Qi (to be ordered when booking, because it takes 60 minutes to prepare), the range of homemade Dim Sun, the crispy squid served with green mango salad or even the wok of entire sole... Also discover in the evening the concept "personal wok" where you can choose yourself your meat, fish with the sauce of your choice (sweet & sour, Indonesian curry, secret Song Qi sauce...). A true gourmet journey in China, totally off beaten tracks where each detail aims to reach perfection.

LE PINOCCHIO

30, rue Comte-Felix-Gastaldi
✆ +37 (0)7 93 30 96 20
office@lepinocchiomonaco.com

Open all year. Open 7 days a week days; for lunch from 12pm to 2.30pm and for dinner from 7pm to 11pm. From April to October the service is continuous during the afternoon with a simplified à la carte. Booking advised. À la carte: Around €50. Starter and main course + a drink. Wifi. Air conditioning. Terrace.

Settled in the heart of the narrow streets of the historic Monegasque city, Pinocchio is a restaurant of Italian specialties, an institution on the Rock! It has just been repurchased last year and has been beautifully redecorated: the outdoor terrace is flowered, the completely renovated indoor room preserves her chic bistro appearance with her wood panelling on the walls and her nice tablecloths... You will even find there the portholes of boat that recalls the Pinocchio's story to visitors, absorbed by the whale! The cuisine is resolutely Italian. The specialties are declined on the themes of the sea and the ground while thoroughly following the stages of the Italian cuisine, very generous in culinary stages. Start with the antipasti then the secondi while stopping on the pasta or risotto... You settle down on the little square facing the street, or in the elegant dining room with a more intimate atmosphere and enjoy yourself with a warm octopus and potatoes' salad, a salad of rocket, artichokes, tomatoes cherries, or the restaurants speciality, the famous «blue fairy pappardelle». The pastas are flamed in a grinding stone with parmesan, marcapone and a Cointreau liqueur of 1849...To conclude? A tiramisu, obviously! Fresh ingredients, elaborate homemade hearty dishes, a friendly and attentive service... In short, a nice address.

L'EXPRESS

22, rue Comte-Félix-Gastaldi
✆ +37 (0)7 97 77 59 09
www.lexpressmonaco.com
restaurantexpress@hotmail.fr

Open all year. From April 1st to September 30th from 12pm to 10pm nonstop 7 days a week and from October 1st to March 31st from 12pm to 4pm (closed on Wednesday). Menu Gourmand €26. À la carte: Around €25. Children's menu: €10.90. Lunch menu: €18 (daily specials + dessert of the day). Pizza from €10.50. Starter from €13.50. Pasta from €12.50. Fish from €14.50. Risotto from €14. Terrace.

Situated in an alley of the old town, this small restaurant offers a wide range of typical local dishes and a very warm welcome. The carte is varied: it offers stuffed veal cutlets, or beef tournedos; fish side, try the casserole of fresh salmon with crunchy vegetables, roasted prawns with garlic, or the roasted sea bass with fennel. in the evening only, the Chef offers a nice selection of risottos: cep and foie gras, Scallops and their juice, or vegan, a la milanaise... As for pasta, spaghettis, raviolis, tagliatelles are served with a variety of sauces. You'll finish your meal with a selection of homemade desserts such as mousse au chocolat, lemon pie, or fondant au chocolat. The terrace has lounge-style sofas and is ideal for a delicious and refreshing break. The service is all day long in summer.

LA MONTGOLFIERE

16, rue Basse
✆ +37 (0)7 97 98 61 59 / +33 (0)6 80 86 86 25
www.lamontgolfiere.mc
hgeraci@libello.com
Bus Monaco-Ville

Closed Wednesday and Sunday for lunch and evening. Annual leave from end of January to beginning of March. To lunch until 1.45pm. To dine from 7.45pm to 9.30pm. Booking advised. Menu from €47 to €54. À la carte: Around €35 (main course). Wine by the glass. Menu any truffle (starter, main course and dessert): €70. Menu any truffle (starter, main course, cheese and dessert): €78. Terrace. Public parkings of the Abbey, the Bishopric and the Fishermen.

What if a greedy pleasure was just to enjoy good and simple well-prepared dishes? Henri Géraci combines a cuisine with Mediterranean, Asian and local flavours: maki of foie gras Japanese Style, carpaccio of scallops, carnaroli risotto, black cod gindara no saikyo yaki, or the sea bass from cap Corse with seaweed butter, potato parmentier, and wakame, artichoke.... The restaurant with a friendly atmosphere . Henri Géraci found the right formula. What are you waiting for to discover this amazing place?

THE TERRASSE OF THE OCEANOGRAPHIC MUSEUM

Avenue Saint-Martin
✆ +37 (0)7 93 15 36 16
www.restaurore.com
restaurant@oceano.mc

Open at the same times as those of the Oceanographic Museum, every day except on December 25th and weekend of F1 Grand Prix at the end of May. From January to March: open from 10am to 6pm. From April to June from 10am to 7pm. July and August from 9.30am to 8pm. September from 10am at 7pm. From October to December from 10am to 6pm. Lunch until 3pm. Fixed rate formula from €23 (starter + meat or fish + dessert). Terrace with sea view.

This panoramic restaurant perched 85 m above the Mediterranean sea offers an impressive 360° view over the Principality of Monaco and the sea. Located on the terrace of the eponymous museum, the atmosphere is friendly in an Italian style: the owner and all the waiters have this beautiful melodious accent. As for the cuisine, the pasta is showcased in all its forms, seasoned with all sauces. A brasserie-style menu with classics is also available. Note that you can also have a drink and relax at any time of day in the *lounge* on the island with the turtles... Guaranteed change of scenery.

ALAIN DUCASSE AT THE HOTEL DE PARIS

Hôtel de Paris Monte-Carlo
Place du Casino
✆ +37 (0)7 98 06 88 64
www.alain-ducasse.com
adhp@sbm.mc
♿

The restaurant is open Wednesday to Monday for dinner only. The restaurant is open from 8pm to 9.45pm. Booking is essential. Menu from €230 to €310. À la carte: Around €120 (main course). American Express, Diners Club. Groups welcome. Terrace. Car valet. Parking of the Casino. Jacket is requiered during winter and will be appreciated in summer.

Alain Ducasse cooks with emotion, passion, rigour, simplicity and perfection and his cuisine is still present today thanks to Dominique Lory who perfectly reproduces this culinary style that magnifies the best products for the pleasure of the senses. In a sublime room signed by the designers Patrick Jouin and Sanjit Manku, you can enjoy masterpieces such as refreshed langoustines and chickpeas, pourpier crushed in a mortar; the blue lobster with bays of myrtle and ginger; the suab, duck foie gras nad roasted potatoes or even the u'stocafi à la monégasque. As for the wines, the sommelier offers one of his many references among 400,000 bottles in the cellar. One is conquered by watching the ballet of the service carried out since the opened central office.

BUDDHA BAR

Place du Casino
✆ +37 (0)7 98 06 19 19
buddhabarmontecarlo@sbm.mc
♿

Open all year. Open Tuesday to Saturday from 6pm to 2am. Booking advised. À la carte: around €80 (starter, main course and dessert). Wine by the glass. American Express, Diners Club. Groups welcome. Terrace. Car valet. Shop. Parking. Entertainment (DJ).

Those who expect to enjoy traditional chinese cuisine get prepared to a complete surprise: the Chef creates innovative combinations with perfect mix of Asia and French excellence. Let yourself be tempted by the mild satay of salmon with black rice of mountains, the grilled fillet of sea bass and its steamed vegetables with a scent of ginger, by beef fillet teppanyaki way, Tom yum soup and his squid noodles or by red curry shrimp in Thai way. For sashimi and others rolls fans, you will be surprised by unique creations. Change of scenery guaranteed!

LE CAFÉ DE PARIS

Place du Casino
✆ +37 (0)7 98 06 76 23
✆ +37 (0)7 98 06 76 24
www.montecarloresort.com
brasseriecp@sbm.mc
♿

Open all year. Every day. Non-stop service from 8am to 1am (2am in summer). Booking advised. À la carte: Around €60. Wine by the glass. Menus for groups from €40. A daily suggestion from €19. American Express, Diners Club. Groups welcome (organization of events and receptions in the Bellevue room and its terraces on the 1st floor). Terrace. Take-away. Shop. Musical entertainment on summer evenings from June to September.

The Café de Paris is the place by excellence to see and to be seen on the famous Casino square. Its Belle Epoque decor is worthy of a top-of-the-range brasserie cuisine. The carte offers classics but also more current dishes: vegetable cream with croutons, rock fish soup with home-made rust, salmon tartar with chives, salad Caesar with grilled chicken, ravioli à ricotta and spinach tomato sauce with basil, bouquetière of vegetables English manner, andouillette of Troyes and French fries, sauté of beef fillet and its green pepper sauce, veal paillard, sea-bream fillet and rice Greek way and cocktail of shrimps, avocado virgin and beef mimosa heart, between others. If the indoor room offers a felted and refined decoration, the large sunny terrace remains a distinguished position all year round.

L'HIRONDELLE

Place du Casino
2 avenue de Monte-Carlo
✆ +37 (0)7 98 06 69 30
www.fr.montecarlosbm.com

Open with the lunch from 12pm to 5.45pm. Suggestions à la carte from 12pm to 4pm. Closed with the dinner. Booking advised. Menu health or menu of the excluding drinks market: €58. À la carte: Around €35 (main course). Wine by the glass. Starter €15, main course €30 and dessert €10 for lunch. American Express, Diners Club. Groups welcome. Terrace. Valet. Shop. Parking.

The restaurant has a room with floor-to-ceiling windows and a pretty terrace overlooking Port Hercule. The Chef offers cuisine that is mediterranean in lightness with tasty menus, balanced and made with seasonal produce in the spirit of the services provided in the Thermes Marins adjoining: me shrimpś diterrané e tempura on its mango carpaccio, avocado Tartar à fresh tomato, ponzu sauce; multicoloured tomato, AOC Parma ham pé tales and mozzarella di Buffala; rigatoni à the cré toise, eggplant, tomatoes confit fraî ches and sheep's milk cheese; duo of organic quinoa, lé gumes melting; cod fillet roasted on the skin and à ricotta gnocchi and chard in the country... All breads are made with organic flours 100%. A place to combine taste buds and well-being of the spirit.

JOËL ROBUCHON MONTE-CARLO

4, avenue de la Madone
Monte Carlo
✆ +37 (0)7 93 15 15 10
www.joel-robuchon.com
restaurant@metropole.com

Open every day for breakfast, lunch from 12.15pm to 2pm and dinner from 7.30pm to 10.30pm. Booking advised. À la carte: Around €75 (dish). Wine by the glass. Menu Food & Life €98. Lunches of Joel from €56. American Express, Diners Club. Groups welcome. Garden. Terrace. Valet. Parking.

This address is perfectly adapted to the Mediterranean and timeless universe of Hôtel Métropole, and was fully thought by the famous *designer* Jacques Garcia. Authenticity and modernity are combined with simplicity and conviviality. A simple cuisine which sublimates the exceptional quality of the products and the dishes signed Joël Robuchon and Christophe Cussac. On the carte, you will be happy to discover: scottish smoked salmon with home made toasted bread, scallops with crunchy chicories in virgin olive oil with lemon, soft boiled egg with impérial caviar and smoked salmon, cod dish with gratiné polenta with white truffles of Alba, whole turbot roast and relevé of condiments with pistachio oil, sucking lamb in roasted chops with thyme and aubergine... The most delicate tastebuds will let themselves be charmed by the degustation carte in small portions to satisfy their culinary curiosity.

LE LOGA

25, boulevard des Moulins
✆ +37 (0)7 93 30 87 72
www.loga.mc

Open all year. Closed weekly Wednesday for dinner and Sunday. From 8am to 11pm. À la carte: Around €35 (dish). Wine by the glass. Lunch menu from €15. Salad of the day €16. Full menu in the evening: €38. Terrace. Label Craftsman of the Taste.

Ketty Gastraldi and her Chef have created this address halfway between a brasserie, a tea room and a traditional restaurant, is a major gourmet establishment in the Principality. It has a beautiful cosy interior room, very popular both for its food and for its warm welcome. The carte offers tasty and creative dishes: mid-cooked duck foie gras and jams, smoked salmon, the famous *barbajuans*, linguine mantecate with clams, pistachio risotto with gorgonzola, sea bass back and vegetables.... The greediest will be tempted by a medley of flavours with homemade pastrys, or crème caramel. The restaurant has been awarded the 2015 Price of Restauration in Monaco and the label Craftsmen of Taste thanks to products of quality and a healthy cuisine. An address to discover without hesitation!

NOBU

Fairmont Monte Carlo
12, avenue des Spélugues
✆ +37 (0)7 97 70 70 97
www.noburestaurants.com
nobu@fairmont.com

Open all year. Every day from 7pm to 9pm for a musical aperitif, the seven2nine. Every evening diner from 7pm. About €120 on average per person. Monday to Sunday from 7pm to 11.30pm. Valet. Open to the guests of Fairmont Monte Carlo and external guests. Pets allowed. Possibility of privatization.

Nobuyuki «Nobu» Matsuhisa began his career in the country of the Rising sun in his brothers restaurant. His japanese cuisine was influenced during his many travels, in particular in Alaska and in Peru. Located in the preserved universe of the Fairmont Monte Carlo in the heart of the historical district and nested in a delicate and elegant atmosphere, this establishment offers an exceptional view on the Principality, France and Italy. The bright dining room with trendy decoration mixes carefully and nicely contemporaneity and Japanese atmosphere opening on a huge *sushi bar* behind which they are prepared with fresh ingredients sashimis, makis, bento, tempuras or sushi. The culinary travel continues with the carte: roasted langoustine and shiso salsa, pasta inaniwa and lobster, beef fillet, tacos of lobster with wasabi or mushroom shiitake salad, and king crab of Alaska with spicy and creamy sauce. From the welcome to the service via the atmosphere: all is perfect. Booking highly recommended!

NOVOTEL CAFE BY FRED RAMOS

Novotel Monte Carlo
16, boulevard Princesse-Charlotte
✆ +37 (0)7 99 99 83 00
www.novotel.com
h5275@accor.com

♿

Open all year. Every day from 12pm to 2.30pm and from 7pm to 10.30pm. À la carte: Around €28 (dish). Menu for lunch €25.50. City Dinner starter + main course or main course + dessert €28. Starter + main course + dessert in the evening €35. Label Craftsman of Taste.

Novotel Café by Fred Ramos is a contemporary address turned towards flavours of the South: organic soup with five vegetables, home made mid-cooked duck foie gras with fig jelly, melting Marcellin with honey and pine nuts accompanied by small potatoes and bresaola chips, fresh tagliatelle of two salmons and Parmesan cream, roasted beef fillet with truffle sauce or turbot fillet poached with red butter, between others. A real gourmet address.

POLPETTA

2, rue Paradis
✆ + 37 (0)7 93 50 67 84
www.restaurantpolpetta.com

♿

Open all year. 7 days a week. For lunch from 12 pm to 2 pm and for dinner from 7: 30 pm to 11 pm. Closed Saturday for lunch. À la carte: around €40 (for lunch about €25). Daily specials: €12 (to €15 on weekdays only). Wine by the glass. American Express. Groups welcome. Car valet. Terrace in summer and closed veranda in winter.

High place of Monegasque's restaurant for over thirty-five years, good Italian cuisine finds its full meaning here. Polpetta is a famous restaurant nestled in the tangled little streets of the Principality not far from the historic Monte Carlo Casino. Let yourself be tempted by tortellini with truffle cream, tagliatelle with black or white truffles, homemade ravioli, wolffish in salt crust or fillet with pepper. We also like the Italian charcuterie and the seasonal products such as the white truffle from Alba, asparagus, artichokes and porcini mushrooms. Happiness and good humour reign in this restaurant conveyed by all the team. You do not need to go to Italy to enjoy and appreciate their culinary specialties: you're already there! A car valet is very useful at night.

RAMPOLDI

3, avenue des Spélugues
Monte Carlo
✆ +37 (0)7 93 30 70 65

Open every day. From 12pm to 2pm and from 7.30pm to 11pm (midnight in season). At lunchtime, daily special from €22 to €24, à la carte around €35. For dinner, à la carte between €70 to €90.

This smart address has just celebrated its 70 years! Inaugurated in 1946 within walking distance of the famous historic Casino, Rampoldi displays a new style as well in the cuisine where an young and already experienced chef has just taken control as for the decor which has been fully reconsidered with noble materials. A cosy atmosphere which recalls the Belle Epoque, this restaurant promises a single culinary experience, delicious and surprising. The dishes are composed of fresh ingredients rigorously selected, like the truffles, mushrooms, asparagus, red shrimps of Sanremo, oysters, caviar and meats of top quality. The reception is absolutely perfect and the subtle ballet of the caring waiters adds to the quality of the place. As of June, you can enjoy the terrace. Two new spaces are now opened to public: the smoking-room with the cigar club exclusively accessible to the members and the music lounge for live music evenings!

VALENTIN

Park Palace Gallery – 27, avenue de la Costa
✆ +37 (0)7 93 50 60 00
www.valentin.mc
info@valentin.mc

Open all year. Monday to Friday from 7am to 6pm non stop. Friday night aperitif a l'italienne from 6pm to 11pm. Booking advised. À la carte: Around €20 (for a dish). Lunch menu: €20 (dish + soft drink + coffee). Wine by the glass. Covered terrace within the boundary of the gallery of Park Palace.

We loved the conviviality which emanates as soon you pass the door! A fancy decoration, warm welcome and a cuisine centered on the local products. The carte changes every day. You can start with breakfast with fixed formulas on the blackboard or complete. For lunch, suggestions are declined. The trend is resolutely Italian with recipes «like at home» revisited by the Chef: homemade pie with artichokes, pumpkin soup and small chips of roasted bacon, salad of salmon stove vegetables, rollers of beef stuffed with ceps and smoked ham... The house also does delicatessen and wine cellar to bring back some souvenirs of this tasty Italian culinary stop! It is advisable to book... success! it is often full midday.

THE VISTAMAR

Hotel Hermitage Monte-carlo
Square Beaumarchais
✆ +37 (0)7 98 06 98 98
http://fr.hotelhermitagemontecarlo.com

♿

Open all year. Lunch from 12pm to 2pm. Dinner from 7.30pm to 10pm. Booking advised. Wine by the glass. Menus from €49 (business menu for lunch), €68 (menu season) and €135 (gourmet menu). American Express, Diners Club. Groups welcome (up to 16 people). Terrace. Valet. Label Craftsman of the Taste. Parking. Garage. 1 Michelin star. Chef Joel Garault named to the rank of Knight of the National order of Merit for his 42 years of services. Elegance recommended, necessary jacket. No pets allowed.

The room bathed in natural light opens onto a beautiful terrace with a wonderful view of port Hercule and the Rock. The Vistamar was designed to enter in perfect harmony with the cuisine of the south proposed by the new Chef Benoit Witz: centred around essential and authentic culinary values, the new carte celebrates seasonal products, the accuracy of cookings, and the simplicity of the dishes like the spring salad with lobster and fresh herbs, or the fresh hake, gambero rosso with fennel.

YOSHI

Metropole Hotel
4, avenue de la Madone
✆ +37 (0)7 93 15 13 13
www.metropole.com
yoshi@metropole.com

Open Wednesday to Sunday from 12.15pm to 2pm for lunch and from 7.30pm to 10.30pm for dinner. Booking advised. À la carte: Around €65 (fish or meat). Lunch menu: €35 (Bento). Wine by the glass. Yoshi menu €199 served for dinner only. Aki menu €142. American Express, Diners Club. Garden. Valet. Parking.

Yoshi is located within the boundary of Hôtel Métropole Monte-Carlo. In a decor created by the French *designer* Didier Gomez, the guests are transported through the Japanese culture that Joël Robuchon expresses through a refined table and an elegant setting, a contemporary and poetic vision of this country which he is particulary fond of. In the room, the guests installed at the Sushi Bar can attend the show of the Chef and his team thanks to an open cuisine allowing to watch the realization of their dishes. The carte: selection of sushi and sashimis, snow crab with algue salad, octopus salad hot sauce, chicken skewers and cébette, sirloin roulé with vegetables and enoki mushrooms, crayfish or steamed veal raviolis, inter alia. The menu Bento offers each midday in an elegant black box enamelled an entrance, a main course and a choice of desserts on the concept of traditional Japanese *lunch box* for the guests in search of a gourmet meal the time of a business lunch.

SLEEPING

HÔTEL COLUMBUS MONTE-CARLO

23, avenue des Papalins
✆ +37 (0)7 92 05 90 00
www.columbushotels.com
sales@columbus.mc

Open all year. 53 Classical rooms including 6 twins. 100 Deluxe rooms including 42 twins. 14 Junior Suites with terrace and sea view. 13 Suites and Top Floor suites with terrace and sea view. Apartment with 2 double rooms. Room from €210. Rates change depending on the duration of the stay and the season. Buffet breakfast: €25. Extra bed: €50 (free -12 years). Free wi-fi in all the rooms and public parts. Air conditioning. Excursions. Beaches in the vicinity, access to an open heated outdoor swimming pool in season, fitness room. Free shuttle depending on availability. Catering facilities, possible delivery in room. Wine tasting. Organization of private events.

Ideally located between the sea and the Princesse Grace rose garden, the Columbus Monte Carlo Hotel welcomes you in a soft and contemporary décor with natural colours. An alternative to the luxurious hotels of the principality, you will discover a place with a real identity that offers you its expertise. The rooms and suites have a chic and relaxing atmosphere where confort and refinement perfectly mix. Most of them have a balcony or a terrace. In this relaxing and chic setting, everything is done to satisfy you: personalized welcome, common areas, free wi-fi access in all rooms, gym and an outdoor pool. A charming address where refined elegance and relaxed lifestyle are combined.

Monte Carlo Bay Hotel & Resort

LE MERIDIEN BEACH PLAZA

22, avenue Princesse-Grace
✆ +37 (0)7 93 30 98 80
www.lemeridienmontecarlo.com
reservations.montecarlo@lemeridien.com

Open all year. Reception 24/24 (spoken languages: French, English, Italian, Spanish, German, Arabic and Chinese). 403 rooms (including 12 suites; half non-smoking). Breakfast: €36 (buffet). Parking covered with valet. Room from €212 per night. Parking with valet: 46€. American Express, Diners Club. Babysitting. Pets allowed. Seminars. Receptions and weddings. Internet corner. Internet access available for a fee. Wifi fee. Cleaning service. Restaurant (with ocean view and kitchen facing the guests). Private beach with direct access. Satellite TV, Canal+. Sauna. Activities. Excursions (reservations possible at the concierge service).

Staying in Méridien Beach Plaza is like having a disorientating sensory journey in an oasis of relaxation and pleasure. As soon as you arrive, the ambient scents and natural sounds give a huge feeling of wellness. Ideally located near the beach, this establishment has bright rooms with modern decor, private balcony and a view over the Sea. It is the only hotel of Monaco to have a private beach supplemented by three swimming pools and a fitness center. On the spot, there are several catering facilities. L'Intempo is contemporary, trendy and relaxing: with a menu rich in suggestions, it is open all the year from 7am to 11pm. It is the perfect place for a gourmet break with sea view and four distinct atmospheres, the *Lounge*, the *Live Cooking*, the *Brasserie* and the *Salon*. In summer, discover every day, from midday to dawn, another trendy catering area, Muse, with its tasty and creative cuisine. As for the bar, the Longitude 7° 26' open 24 hours a day invites you to discover with its menu of creative coffees Illy and its éclairs with exquisite flavours, unless you prefer the Alang Bar, open only in summer with its parasidiac atmosphere.

MONTE CARLO BAY HOTEL & RESORT

40, avenue Princesse-Grace
✆ +37 (0)7 98 06 02 00
www.montecarlobay.com
resort@sbm.mc

Open all year. Reception 24/24 (spoken languages: French, English, Italian, Russian and Japanese). 334 rooms (including 22 suites). American breakfast: €34, Continental: €29. Room from €191 per day. Parking: €30 per day. American Express, Diners Club. Seminars. Receptions and weddings. Internet access available for a fee. Wifi fee. Cleaning service. Catering facilities. Sale. Satellite TV. Whirlpool, sauna. Excursions.

On a peninsula of 4 acres with 334 rooms and suites, most with a sea view, , the Monte Carlo Bay Hotel & Resort also has a hotel residence, a freshwater lagoon with fine sand, an indoor pool, the «Cinq Mondes» spa, three restaurants (the Blue Bay – 1 Michelin star, the Orange Verte, Las Brisas), a bar, the Blue Gin with a terrace overlooking the sea, 15 flexible meeting & banquet rooms, without forgetting a casino. A chic resort, active and casual, whose decor immerses you in a tropical atmosphere. A haven of peace by the sea far from the hustle and bustle of the city centre. Exceptional!

FAIRMONT MONTE CARLO

12 avenue des Spélugues
✆ +37 (0)7 93 50 65 00
www.fairmont.fr/monte-carlo/
montecarlo@fairmont.com

Open all year. Reception 24/24 (room from €276 in low season, €690 in high season). 602 rooms (140 smoking rooms, 26 suites). Possibility of having breakfast at the buffet or in the room. Extra bed: €68. Parking: €45. Spoken languages: French, English, Italian, Spanish, German, Japanese and Russian (in summer season). American Express, Diners Club. Pets allowed (on request). Seminars. Receptions and weddings. Wifi fee. Cleaning service. Catering facilities. Sale. Satellite TV, Canal+. Hammam, whirlpool, sauna. Activities. Excursions (bicycles available free).

A temple of luxury regularly awarded for the excellence of its services and the offered products, Fairmont Monte-Carlo is equipped with a range of facilities designed for wellness: Spa Willow Stream of 900 m², fitness center, solarium, heated swimming pool between sky and sea without forgetting the lush shopping arcade. The decoration, inspired by a luxurious cruise ship is appealing and cordial. The restaurant L'Horizon Deck & Champagne Bar (open from April to October) located on the seventh floor on the roof, offers a tasty mediterranean cuisine, while the Nobu – opened all the year round – offers an unforgettable gourmet adventure. As for the bar Saphir 24, it is open day and night: it is the ideal place to have a coffee, have lunch or enjoy a tea or drink the aperitif with the sea as only horizon. It should be noted that Fairmont Monte Carlo has just been voted Monaco's Leading Spa Resort 2016 by the World Travel Awards.

HÔTEL DE PARIS MONTE CARLO

Place du Casino
✆ +37 (0)7 98 06 30 00
www.hoteldeparismontecarlo.com
resort@sbm.mc

Open all year. Reception 24/24 (spoken languages: French, English, Italian, Spanish, Russian). 47 rooms (reduced capacity, certain smoker). Breakfast: €39 continental and €44 American. Extra bed: €122. Closed parking: €39 (per day). Room from €294 per night depending on the season. American Express, Diners Club. Pets allowed (in the hotel, small, prohibited in the restaurants and the bar). Seminars. Receptions and weddings. Internet access available for a fee. Cleaning service. Catering facilities: 3 restaurants Le Louis XV-Alain Ducasse, the Grill and Côté Jardin. 1 Bar Américain. Product sales. An access to Thermes Marins Monte Carlo (swimming pool, fitness room, hammam, sauna, solarium… Access to the Monte Carlo Beach from April to October, free shuttle. Satellite TV, Canal+. Hammam, whirlpool, sauna. Activities. Excursions, visits via the concierge. Cryotherapy.

This is simply a legend of luxury and high-class at the top of the hotel hierarchy. Built in 1864, it is in itself a historical monument into which famous personalities came to associate their name like Alain Ducasse who transmits his expertise in the sumptuous decor of the eponymous restaurant since 1987. Without forgetting the famous Bar Américain that has welcomed the most famous stars of the last century. The Hôtel de Paris has also access to the Thermes Marins, a complex of more than 7000m² combining high technology and well-being. An institution that remains the flagship of the Société des Bains de Mer, which in addition celebrated its one hundred and fifty years in 2013. Since 2014, Hôtel de Paris is in renovation phase: up to standard, creation of a patio and a dozen luxury boutiques, transformation of the Churchill suite into a villa, creation of a spa on the last floor and increasing the size of the rooms and suites. During the renovation, which should last until 2018, the Hôtel de Paris remains partially open.

HÔTEL HERMITAGE MONTE CARLO

Square Beaumarchais
✆ +37 (0)7 98 06 40 00 / +37 (0)7 98 06 41 51 / +37 (0)7 98 06 17 17
www.hotelhermitagemontecarlo.com
hh@sbm.mc

Open all year. Reception 24/24. 278 rooms (100% non smoker). Breakfast: €38. Extra bed: €120. Garage: €39. Double room from €257. Variable rates depending on duration of the stay and season. Valet service. Currency exchange. Room service 24/24. American Express, Diners Club. Pets allowed (dogs of -20 kg). Seminars. Receptions and weddings. Internet corner. Internet access available for a fee. Wifi fee. Cleaning service. Catering facilities. Sale. Satellite TV, Canal+. Hammam, whirlpool, sauna. Activities. Excursions, visits on request with the concierge. Cryotherapy. Service helicopter Nice/Monaco.

This monegasque hotel is a real jewel. It has received awards many times, and offers an absolute comfort and a majestic scenery. Its «winter garden» designed by Gustave Eiffel is classified as a historical monument. On the golden square, it adjoins the Casino of Monte-Carlo and overlooks Port Hercule. Its magnificent façade has Italian loggias and frescoes inspired by the galleries of the Prince's palace. The rooms have a Belle Epoque decor in tones of beige and red or beige and blue. The hotel also has a restaurant The Vistamar with the Chef Benoit Witz and for lighter menus, The Hirondelle, facing the sea. For a drink, head for the Crystal Bar with a beautiful view where to smoke a cigar with a grand cru. As for the Limùn Bar which is ideal for a cup of tea and delicious homemade pastries. The hotel is directly linked to the thermal baths of Monte-Carlo and a private beach at the Monte Carlo Beach Club. An exceptional address.

HÔTEL MÉTROPOLE MONTE CARLO

4, avenue de la Madone
✆ +37 (0)7 93 15 15 20
www.metropole.com
metropole@metropole.com

*Open all year. Reception 24/24 (spoken languages: English, Russian, Italian, German, French). 133 rooms (and suites). Double room from €450. Breakfast €38. Parking €39. Seminars. Receptions and weddings. Three restaurants: Joël Robuchon Monte Carlo **, Yoshi* and Odyssey. Metropolis ESPA (swimming pool, fitness, heat experience, treatments and massages). American Express, Diners Club. Pets allowed. Internet corner. Free Internet access. Free Wifi. Cleaning service. Satellite TV, Canal+. Hammam, whirlpool, sauna. Excursions (via the concierge).*

Hôtel Métropole, luxurious Belle Epoque style palace, is located in the heart of Monte-Carlo. The entrance is magnified by a superb boxwood arch which marks the beginning of the trip inviting you to go along a cypress path to reach the square of the hotel. Once in the lobby, with subtle scents of musc, you will discover the *atrium* and its impressive glass dome which will bring you in a real Italian palace. Here, the designer Jacques Garcia was inspired by the spirit of the early 19th century added a touch of modernity that makes the Métropole Monte-Carlo a hotel full of charm and character. Charming welcome, professionalism and the smile of the teams are the philosophy of the place. The Mediterranean style present in all rooms and suites, will carry you in the heart of a palace of the last century. On the last floor, in a sumptuous setting, the suite offers from its terrace an incomparable view of the Casino and the Mediterranean. In the early evening, the lobby bar is an ideal place to enjoy delicious cocktails accompanied with some appetizers. Continue the adventure to the restaurant Joël Robuchon (2 Michelin stars) where a refined cuisine with Mediterranean accents will delight you. It is by the swimming pool designed by Karl Lagerfeld that you can also enjoy your breakfast... A haven of peace and relaxation which incites you to discover the Métropole ESPA: you just have to choose from a wide range of holistic and therapeutic cares according to your desires. At lunchtime, immerse yourself into the heart of Japan in the refined and warm universe designed by Didier Gomez: Yoshi, the first Japanese restaurant of Joël Robuchon (1 Michelin star) offers a selection of sushi, sashimi, maki and à la carte dishes. Glamorous, elegance and refinement are the key words which perfectly summarizes the Hôtel Métropole Monte-Carlo... An exceptional journey in the heart of Monaco.

Givenchy should open at the end of February 2017 within the boundary of the Hotel Metropole, a relaxation area with a range of treatments adapted to each type of skin. A pure pleasure!

■ **HÔTEL FORUM**
16, avenue d'Alsace – BEAUSOLEIL (FRANCE)
✆ +33 (0)4 93 78 96 36 – www.forumhotel.net

Open all year. Reception 24/24 (spoken languages: Italian, English, Russian, Portuguese). 39 rooms (soundproofed with bathroom). Single room from €120 to €160; double room from €140 to €190; triple room from €160 to €210. Buffet breakfast included (continental buffet). Public parking at 150 meters: €20/day. Child free up to 12 years. Rates rooms non applicable during the GP F1 of Monaco, Christmas, New year, Easter and periods of congress. American Express, Diners Club. Lift. Pets allowed. Seminars. Receptions and weddings. Internet corner. Free Internet access. Free Wifi. Cleaning service. Catering facilities (open from 12pm to 2pm and from 7.30pm to 9.30pm. Daily special from €8.50. Menu from €9. Full menu €25). Satellite TV. Bar open until 11.30pm. Panoramic terrace. Solarium.

Modern and bright, the rooms of the Hotel Forum (certain have a beautiful view on the harbour) mix comfort and functionality: soundproofing, air conditioning, bright bathrooms, minibar and Satellite TV with foreign channels. The restaurant offers a cuisine with Mediterranean accents: famous *bruschetta*, pasta prepared with all sauces but also salads, beef carpaccios and pizzas. The products are fresh and home made. *The must* of this establishment is its incredible panoramic terrace on the roof of the building which offers a stunning view of Monaco! A convenient place for a quiet stay and ideal for your business or leisure without forgetting the very charming reception of the team.

LEISURE

■ **THE THERMES MARINS MONTE-CARLO**
2, avenue de Monte-Carlo
✆ +37 (0)7 98 06 69 00
www.fr.thermesmarinsmontecarlo.com

Sea water indoor pool heated at 30 degrees. Fitness. Hammam. Sauna. Cryotherapy. New: a Ferrari Training Lab which enables you to practise like the pilots of the Ferrari team. American Express, Diners Club. Open every day from 8am to 8pm. Beauty salon from 9am to 7pm (beginning of the treatments at 9.30am). Hair salon from 10am to 7pm.

This ultramodern center is a temple of the relaxation with 7,000 m² on four floors offering an effective answer to the stress of the daily life with thalassotherapy and high technology, the best for well being, fitness and relaxation. This largest spa of Europe offers a whole range of services thus: cryotherapy, cures, massages, revitalizations, health programs, beauty, advices...

GOING OUT

Tea Rooms

■ **LE LIMÙN**
Square Beaumarchais – Hotel Hermitage
Monte Carlo ✆ +37 (0)7 98 06 98 48

Open every day from 8am to 8pm. Smart relaxed outfit.

For an afternoon with friends, enjoy a pastry with a delicious tea from a wide choice. Le Limùn is also the perfect place where you can enjoy a hearty breakfast to start the day. You can also discover at lunch time the gourmet dishes prepared by the Chef Joël Garault.

■ **PATISSERIE RIVIERA**
27, boulevard des Moulins
✆ +37 (0)7 93 50 63 23

Open Tuesday to Saturday from 8am to 7pm. Sunday from 8am to 1pm. This address will transport you to a gourmet and delicate universe where cakes, brownies, macaroons, biscuits, logs, cookies and pastries are endlessly present. They especially create beautiful custom-made cakes that will delight your guests, traditional with fruits or chocolate, to the most amazing in the shape of Chanel bag, football, iPhone, a piano, a computer or even film rolls… Birthday, birth, wedding, Valentine's Day and celebrations of all kinds, the team of the pastry shop Riviera will charm you both by their talent where imagination has no limit and by their sense of hospitality!

Bars & Pubs

GERHARD' S CAFE MONACO

42, quai Jean-Charles-Rey
✆ +37 (0)7 92 05 25 79
www.gerhardscafe-monaco.com

Open all year. Every day from 8am to 3 in the morning. Sunday from 11am to 3 in the morning. Multilingual staff. Free Wifi. Terrace. Catering facilities.

Gerhard' s is a meeting point, very popular for the accustomed yachtmen and regulars, in particular during Oktoberfest, the Bavarian beer festival famous for the love of life and good atmosphere. A wooden interior makes it cosy. The service is rapid, and the place promises beautiful evenings in a friendly atmosphere. A very pleasant terrace in summer.

SHIP & CASTLE

42, quai Jean-Charles-Rey
✆ +37 (0)7 92 05 76 72

Open 7 days a week, from Monday to Friday from 11am to 1am, Saturday from 6pm to 1am, and Sunday from 11am to 1am. The restaurant is open from noon to 2.30pm and from 7pm to 10.30pm. Wifi. Terrace. Catering facilities. Activities. Quiz evenings regularly organized.

Ship & Castle is located at the end of the quay of Fontvieille port: it has been one of the oldest places in the area run with great care by Annie for more than 26 years! It is the typical English pub as we like them: indoor wooden room with a large central bar, plasma screens on the walls that broadcast the major sporting events. People get together for a drink after work around a fine selection of beers and whiskys. The outdoor terrace is attractive and very pleasant on sunny days. Events are often organised. Check the Facebook page for their news.

BRASSERIE OF MONACO

Port of Monaco – 36, route de la Piscine
✆ +37 (0)7 97 98 51 20
www.brasseriedemonaco.com

Open all year every day from 12pm to 2am in the morning. DJ 7 days a week. Happy Hour every day from 6pm to 8pm. Draught beer from €4. Soft €5. Cocktails from €10. Salad from €14. Dish from €12. Pizza from €10. Lunch menu €16. Wine by the glass. American Express. Groups welcome. Terrace. Take-away. Shop. Activities.

The Brasserie is well known for its famous Monegasque beer unfiltered and unpasteurized made on the spot with organic malts revealing an authentic taste: the white 4,5° slightly spicy, the lager 5° finely hoppy, the amber the 5,5° rousse and tougher without forgetting the exceptional beer batches to be discovered every month around a unique vintage. The place gets lively in the evening with a DJ or a for a sports or musical event. A friendly moment to share with friends.

JACK MONACO

32, route de la Piscine
✆ +37 (0)7 97 98 34 56
www.jack.mc
info@jack.mc

Open all year. Monday to Sunday from 12pm to 3 in the morning. Lunch menu €17. Daily special €14. Happy hours. Terrace. Animations. Concerts.

With its slogan *anything is possible*, the Jack is one of the unmissable establishments in the Principality. After a good dinner on the pleasant terrace (covered and heated in winter) or in the large interior room with exposed stone walls, let yourself be transported by a heated atmosphere with concerts and DJ's that animate the place. Discover XL cocktails and others drinks with tapas.

LA RASCASSE

Quai Antoine-Ier
✆ +37 (0)7 98 06 16 16
www.larascassemontecarlo.com
♿

Open every day from 4pm to 4.45am. Afterwork from 4pm to 11pm with DJ and live music, finger food (50% discount on all drinks except the bottles and cocktails from 6.30pm to 8.30pm except during great events). Clubbing atmosphere from 11pm to 4.45am. Possible privatization. Wifi. Terrace. Catering facilities. Animations. Concerts.

Want to have fun and dance? On two floors *duplex*, the atmosphere is rather relaxed from 4 to 11pm, ideal for an *afterwork* between friends with music in the background. From 11pm until early in the morning, the atmosphere warms up when the DJ rises the sound, a promise of beautiful wild nights. Cosy seats to take a breath and have a little champagne or any other alcoholic drink or not. You will also appreciate the large terrace (heated in winter) which regularly hosts events. Many themed evenings: English speaking, Stand-up comedy, sports events broadcasting on a giant screen, Dolce Vita aperitif… Find the entire program on the website or Facebook page. A *designer* décor address with, as a bonus, a magnificent view on Port Hercule.

BLUE GIN

40, avenue Princesse-Grace
Monte Carlo Bay Hotel & Resort
✆ +37 (0)7 98 06 06 77
www.montecarlobay.com

Open all year from 5.30pm to 1am and from 6.30pm to 2am from June to August. Food Gin until 11pm. Retransmission of your preferred sporting events. Every Tuesday: Pink Tuesday! the first drink is offered to the women until 10pm. Happy hours. Privatizable or semi-privatizable place on request. Terrace. Catering facilities. Activities.

Le Blue Gin is splendid a *lounge bar* located within the boundary of Hôtel Monte Carlo Bay: refined designer, terrace in seaside, billiards, set of DJ all vendredis and saturday nights... A magical place and single to take the aperitif in Principality of Monaco. The barman proposes up to six different gins as well as a à la carte of cocktails out of commun run made up of daring and astonishing creations. The place proposes evenings also regularly.

TWIGA MONTE CARLO SHISHA LOUNGE

35, boulevard Louis-II ✆ +37 (0)7 97 98 47 81
www.twigamontecarlo.com
info@twigamontecarlo.com

Open all year. Open Tuesday to Sunday from 7pm. Snacks pizzas and focaccia until 4 in the morning.

Twiga Monte Carlo has several spaces and different atmospheres, from the contemporary Japanese restaurant to *the* very trendy *night club*. There is also a shisha bar and louge shisha on the elegant terrace overlooking the Mediterranean where you can enjoy a cocktail or a glass of wine by smoking traditional shisha or with fruity flavours of tobacco. Don't miss the chic and festive atmosphere of Twiga nightclub version, nor the Sumosan restaurant and its traditional japanese cuisine.

ZELO' S

Grimaldi Forum
10, avenue Princesse-Grace
✆ +37 (0)7 99 99 25 50
www.zelosworld.com
sales@zelosworld.com
Facebook: Zelo's Monaco

Open all year. Lounge: every evening of the week from 7pm to 2 in the morning. American Express. Free Wifi. Terrace. Car valet. Catering facilities.

The name Zelos comes from Greek mythology and means «ardour». Located on the top floor of the Grimaldi Forum facing the Mediterranean Sea with a contemporary and zen decor, this restaurant-bar-lounge offers after-work aperitifs with live music some evenings. As for the restaurant, two cartes: one with Mediterranean accents and the other Japanese. The atmosphere becomes more festive with a DJ mixing as of 11.30pm every week end.

Casinos

In the hope of making fortunes or simply for trying your luck, do you want to get in one of the temples of game in Monaco? It is possible only if being of age and correctly attired. Jacket and tie are required in the private rooms as from 22h. Do not forget to bring an ID with photo. You can get more information at: www.montecarlocasinos.com

Casino of Monte Carlo

MONTE-CARLO BAY CASINO

40, avenue Princesse-Grace
✆ +37 (0)7 98 06 07 81
www.montecarlocasinos.com

Open every day from 2pm to 2am.

Within Goes up Carlo Bay Hôtel & Resort, this casino raises a designer ultra-contemporary. Nearly 145 slot machines the arms in a space equipped with technology tighten you «ticket out in/ticket» single in Europe of the South. It is the perfect place for one evening combining wellness and distraction.

CASINO CAFÉ DE PARIS

Place du Casino
✆ +37 (0)7 98 06 21 21 / +37 (0)7 98 06 76 23
vip@montecarlocasinos.com

Open 24/24 and 7 days a week. Free admission accessible to any +18 year old person nonprohibited from game. No particular dress code. Catering facilities.

Inaugurated in July 1988, Casino de Paris is a mythical place with a very futuristic decoration where arches diffuse a light which varies along the day. Side games, you will have the embarrassment of the choice among more than 550 machines: electronic casters, machines with theme (Alien versus Predator, King Kong, Wizard of OZ, Jurassic Park, Playboy, Harley Davidson, Betty Boop, Rolling Stones, Le Retour de la Momie, Sherlock Holmes, Twilight Zone, Lord of the Boxing ring, Phantom of the Opera...), screen machines and machines with classical rollers allowing to gain a car... Note that a furnished terrace makes it possible to smoke while playing and that a catering service is also possible.

CASINO OF MONTE CARLO

Place du Casino
✆ +37 (0)7 98 06 21 21
www.casinomontecarlo.com
vip@montecarlocasinos.com

Open all year. Formal dress required (neither shorts, nor beach or sport shoes). Jacket recommended after 8pm. Admission individual visitors: €12 (low season) and €17 (high season) with audioguide accessible to any person +18 years nonprohibited from game between 9am and 1pm. No pets allowed. €12 extra of admission fee to reach the private rooms in low season and €17 in high season (from 2pm). Strictly prohibited photographs and videos. Bags, except ladies hand bags must be left at the free cloakroom at the entrance of the Casino.

Place of legend, the building was designed by Charles Garnier. The mythical steps lead to a sumptuous marble atrium before entering 4 successive rooms and the common area on the right. The Opéra house – The Garnier room – is just opposite. Once you enter the gambling rooms, you'll be dazzled by the choice between slot machines, green carpets or the roulettes... A planetary reference to the most prestigious choice of gambling tables in Europe. In summer, you can also play on the tables of the Terrasse Salle Blanche with a panoramic view. Enough to gamble under your lucky star! The restaurants Le Train Bleu, Le Salon Rose, and the Restaurant des Privés complete the offer.

Monaco and casinos

As for the games, the Sovereign Charles III wanted to perpetuate the economic and tourist development of the Principality by combinating them with thermal activities ... Mission accomplished for the Société des Bains de Mer (SBM), which now has a monopoly on gambling in Monaco. The most famous is the Casino de Monte-Carlo, beautiful building built in the last century. Two steps further, the Casino of Café de Paris renovated in the late nineties on the theme of the Grand Prix and also the Casino of Sporting Monte-Carlo, open only in summer, the Sun Casino located in the Fairmont and the Bay Casino in the eponymous hotel located in Larvotto.

Place your bets! Casinos have contributed to the touristic reputation of Côte d' Azur. Among them, the famous and essential Casino de Monte-Carlo! Established in 1865 on the deserted hill of Spéluges by François Blanc, a very popular casino operator at the Second Empire period, the establishment attracts people in the Principality and in only a few years the whole European elite. A wealthy area rapidly emerges around it: Monte -Carlo, the «Mount Charles» named in tribute to the Sovereign Prince Charles III. Money flows there and the Prince decides to remove all taxes in his country. In 1879, the builiding is completely redesigned by Mary Blanc (wife of Francois) who adds an opera there and whose construction was entrusted to the architect Charles Garnier, the author of the Paris Opera. 130 years later, the gaming Casino de Monte- Carlo is still shining both for the quality of its games and for the beauty of its scenery. Now the tradition is that the superstitious players enter the lobby of the Hotel de Paris, close neighbour of the Casino and they do this, before going to play: touch the knee of the horse of the equestrian statue of Louis XIV to bring luck. ..

The Salon de l'Europe was the first game-room to open officially in the Principality. Restored at the end of the nineteenth by the architect Henry Schmitt, frescoes depicting the four seasons have been painted in beautiful landscapes. The room is lit since the beginning of the twentieth century by a monumental chandelier over 150 pounds made of Bohemian crystal. The Salon hosts games like the European roulette and the English roulette or the thirties and forties.

The White Dove or the Atrium, originally designed and used as a chat room, was built in 1903, at that time, the Casino, which received more and more players, needed to expand its playgrounds. The most surprising decorative element is the famous painting of Gervais representing the Graces Florestines: a work depicting three characters whose resemblance with the much courted and very accustomed at that time (Cleo de Merode, Liane de Pougy and Otero) provoked many questions... This room which has been renovated in 1991 now hosts slot machines.

The Touzet lounge is divided into two small rooms whose fine harmonious decor highlights the precious woods and the bucolic paintings. Opened in 1890, the year when all the game rooms were lit for the first time with electricity, this lounge was created by the architect Jules Touzet: note that when its doors were opened to players for the first time, the decorative elements were not all yet installed. Some additional adjustments were made in 1891 and in 1988 though the atmosphere and general ambience of the place was kept intact.

The Medical Room located in the west wing of the Casino bears the name of the architect François Doctor. Also known as the Empire room, it was inaugurated in 1910, when Massenet created Don Quixote in the Principality. Today the room has a luxurious private lounge for the «big players» and hosts entertainment like the European roulette, English roulette, thirties and forties, the railroad, the two tables-bank or the Punto Banco ...

SUN CASINO
12, avenue des Spélugues
Fairmont Monte-Carlo ✆ +37 (0)7 98 06 20 00
vip@montecarlocasino.com
Open every day, from 2pm until 2am of the morning. Free admission, accessible to any person of more than 18 years, nonprohibited of game. Presentation of an ID with photograph required. No particular dress code. Entièrement rénové, le Sun Casino offre désormais de nombreux jeux de table ainsi que des machines à sous en exclusivité. Musique *live* et animations complètent l'offre de ce lieu chic et atemporel. Sur place, vous pourrez également profiter du restaurant et du bar situés au cœur des jeux. Une adresse qui conjugue parfaitement divertissement et plaisirs.

Nightclubs

JIMMY' Z MONTE CARLO

Sporting Monte-Carlo – 26, avenue Princesse-Grace ✆ + 37 (0)7 98 06 70 68
jimmyz@sbm.mc

Open every day from 11.30pm to dawn. Closed for works starting from October 22nd. Valet.

The spirit of the Jimmy'z located in the heart of the Monte Carlo Sporting is distinguished by its international atmosphere, its customers selected for their *clubbing attitude*, its comfort, its *light-effects*, its exceptional *sound system*, its ideal architecture and its breath-taking décor with a lake surrounded by a Japanese garden. It offers high-quality services such as a driver at disposal to bring back guests within the Principality and a security service worthy of Monaco, cornerstone of an evening spent in an absolute carelessness. The know-how of a real night professionals team, competent and generous: car valet, hostess, staff room, bartenders... Trades in the service of party signed by Monte-Carlo SBM!

SHOPPING

SHOP OF THE EXOTIC GARDEN OF MONACO

62, boulevard du Jardin-Exotique
✆ +37 (0)7 93 15 29 80
www.jardin-exotique.mc

Open all year except on November 19th and on December 25th. From November to January from 9am to 5pm. From February to April, and in October from 9am to 6pm. From May to September from 9am to 7pm. Shop accessible to the visitors leaving the Exotic Garden Monaco and to all people who wish entering freely without visiting the Garden.

Located in front of the entrance, the shop provides four free parking spaces in the parking of the buses and sells on 55 m^2 over 400 items (t-shirts, pens, key, magnets, post cards... and an exclusive collection of leather goods) most of them being engraved with the colours of the Exotic Garden of Monaco. The theme of cactus and succulent plants is naturally honoured with a series of various products: candles, pieces of work, teddy bears, educational games, specialized books, toys, living cacti, seeds and flower baskets ready to plant or gardening articles.

THE MANUFACTURE OF MONACO

36, boulevard des Moulins
✆ +37 (0)7 92 05 77 55
www.mdpm.com
boutique@mdpm.com

Shops open Monday to Saturday from 10am to 7.30pm.

Supplier of His Serene Highness the Prince of Monaco, the Manufacture of Monaco was founded in 1972 by Erich Różewicz with the support of Prince Rainier III and Princess Grace. Here is created luxury porcelain with multiple qualities (white, hard and translucent) obtained thanks to the expertise of specialized craftsmen. For a chic and refined souvenir, as a practical or decorative element, each piece presented in the shop was rigorously selected. The collections made in Limoges or in German workshops have decorative motifs inspired by the rosettes and mosaics of the princely palace but also works of art from the Mediterranean civilisations. Others more contemporary, are decorated with geometric patterns or are equipped with metal supports silver and gold, sometimes even with Swarovski crystals. Today, it is Joram Ró żewicz who perpetuates the tradition of this unsurpassed know-how. Note that the shop located inside the Metropole shopping center manages wedding lists.

OPERA GALLERY MONACO

Scala palace – 1 avenue Henri Dunant
✆ +37 (0)7 97 97 54 24
www.operagallery.com

Open every day from 10am to 7pm except on Sunday. Free admission except exceptional exhibition.

Located opposite Hôtel Hermitage within the Scala palace in the heart of Monte-Carlo, the Opéra Gallery of Monaco offers a unique collection of modern and contemporary art which traces the main artistic movements of the end of the 19th century to today. Over 400 m^2 of exhibition, many levels gather more than 110 works: paintings and sculptures artistically mixed with photos and art furniture. A must for lovers of art and good taste.

Gourmet Basket

CENERI & FILS

Market Condamine ✆ +37 (0)7 97 98 13 02
www.fromagerie-ceneri.com

Open Tuesday to Sunday from 8am to 3pm and from 6pm to 9pm. Orders and deliveries. In the Cénéri family,they are cheesemonger- refiner from generation to generation since 1968, when the grandfather founded the shop. The brand has become over time the unmissable reference in the region for cheese with more than 250 varieties which are popular but also the passing tourists. The specialty is the Brie with truffles made on site in the purest craft traditions. You compose the plateau of your dreams according to the number of people, your tastes and your budget. It is however recommended to order upstream .

COSTA

Condamine Market ✆ +37 (0)7 93 30 94 72
samcosta@monaco.mc

The shop is open during the market. 8 other addresses in Monaco.

Costa is the reference in Monaco regarding bakery. This is a real family saga which dates back to 1979. Their strong points? Their professional and smiling welcome and the quality of products entirely made traditionally in their own laboratory. The activities are divided into several professions: bakery, pastry and caterer. No less than 8 shops spread over the Principality. Difficult to mention all their specialties and the famous monegasque barbagiuan is their trademark.

L'ABUS D'ALCOOL EST DANGEREUX POUR LA SANTÉ, À CONSOMMER AVEC MODÉRATION

THE GELATERIA
57, rue Grimaldi ✆ +37 (0)7 97 77 36 34
www.lagelateriamonaco.com
info@lagelateriamonaco.com

Monday to Sunday from 10am to midnight in summer season. Closed on Mondays off-season. Cakes, verrines and ice creams on order.
Note for gourmets! Ice creams, milk shakes, sorbets and cakes are made here in the purest Italian gastronomic tradition by revealing the tastes and authentic flavours: mint, flower milk chocolate sorbet, mango, stracciatella, licorice, vanilla, strawberry, lemon, banana, Malaga rum-grapes, cherries, coconut, hazelnut, crème caramel, bacio, tiramisu, natural yoghurt, pistachio, coffee, chocolate fondant, raspberry, Nutella, black chocolate... La Gelateria also offers tasty appetisers with the enchanting perfumes, an original idea to fill a gourmet or want to surprise your guests during a meal. Note that the cakes are made using scoops of ice-cream or sponge cake. Everything with helpfulness and kindness.

MARCELLO RESTAURANT, WINERY & STORE
22 bis, rue Grimaldi ✆ +37 (0)7 97 98 37 81
www.marcellofoodvalley.com
info@marcellofoodvalley.com
Open all year. Monday to Friday from 8am to 3pm and from 5.30pm to midnight. Saturdays from 10am to 3pm and from 6pm to midnight. Closed on Sunday. Catering facilities on the premises or take-away. Delicatessen.
This place combines with delicacy traditional catering, restaurant and wine bar and also offers a grocery shopping service. As always at Marcello, Italian products are enhanced and selected with the utmost care among the best producers and artisans of the boot: exceptional wines, charcuterie (coppa, pancetta, speck ham, salami, ham...), pasta, cheese and coffee. An address that perpetuates the love of the Italian tradition.

CHOCOLATE SHOP OF MONACO
Place de la Visitation ✆ +37 (0)7 97 97 88 88
www.chocolateriedemonaco.com
info@chocolateriedemonaco.com
WiFi on the premises. Online sales on the website. News on the https://www.facebook.com/chocolateriedemonaco page. American Express. Open from 9.30am to 6.30pm nonstop Monday to Saturday. Tea room from 9.30am to 5.30pm. Open a few Sundays depending on events.
The legendary chocolate of Monaco was designed, at the time, for the commemoration of the wedding of Prince Rainier III with Grace Kelly. Created in 1920, it became the qualified supplier of Prince of Monaco, this place will delight you with pleasure... Real palace of chocolate which is declined in all other types (pistachio, mocha, extra black, hazelnuts, caramel, puffed rice, nougatine, tiramisu, caramel, gianduja or tangerine), it is the perfect place to have a gourmet break. A shop part and a tea room, do not hesitate: go for a tasty walk just a few steps away from the Prince's Palace! Before leaving, some extra purchases will allow you, when you get home, to continue the pleasure and to let your friends taste this unmissable weakness of the Monegasques.

GELATORINO
4, boulevard de France ✆ +37 (0)7 97 98 28 91
www.gelatorino.com
monaco@gelatorino.com
Open all year. Eco label Friendly.
Here is an exceptional ice-cream shop which prepares in front of you its delicacies coloured with fresh ingredients, without artificial ingredients, in the pure Italian tradition. Know-how is there, traditional machines to the precision of the gestures which fit in perfect rhythmic, without forgetting the quality of the ingredients selected in Turin and in the Piedmont region, warm welcome and singing with the Italian accents, the whole accompanied by an unequalled passion. Yield to the temptation of these tasty ice creams with multiple flavours which one tastes in cup, horn, biscuit gelato or in affogato cup. You can even order and bring back home your frozen dessert in a box. To (Re) discover without waiting no more!

Wines & Spirits

CAVES ET GOURMANDISES
25, boulevard Albert-1st
✆ +37 (0)7 97 70 54 94
www.cavesetgourmandises.com
cavesetgourmandises@monaco.mc
Open all year from 10am to 7.30pm Monday to Saturday.
This is an address for epicureans! «Cellar» side, you will find a selection of French wines (Bordeaux, Bourgogne, Vallée du Rhône, Loire, Sud-Ouest or Provence) as well as a large champagne diversity, Italian wines, Whisky, Cognac, Armagnac, Grappa, Vodka and Téquila. As for «delicacies», the house invites you to discover several kinds of caviar but also Italian products like dried tomatoes, aubergines or the roasted artichokes which will bring a touch of originality to your aperitifs. This is without forgetting the olive oil and balsamic vinegars which will sublimate your salads and other dishes! Elegant information: possibility of making custom-made baskets to offer on site.

Markets

THE CONDAMINE MARKET AND GOURMET FOOD MARKET
Place d'Armes
Covered market open all year from 7am to 3.30pm Monday to Sunday included, and in the evening from 6pm to 9.30pm Tuesday to Saturday. Condamine Market open every day from 7am to 3pm.
Located at the foot of the Rock on the place d'armes, the Condamine market opens your appetite and transcends your needs of South. The place offers pleasant terraces, a newsstand, a kiosk with souvenirs and a playground. Ideal place to rub with the authentic monegasque life and sample the local specialties, the place is a daily pretty market where the stalls honour the colourful flowers with the fruit and vegetables of the country, fragrant and tasty. The halles located under the arches and in the neighbouring buildings hold fishmongers, manufacturers of fresh pasta, butchers, bakers, butchers and caterers. You'll also enjoy on site the areas for consumption.

General view of Eze.

FRENCH RIVIERA:
THE COASTLINE

FRENCH RIVIERA: THE BEACHES

Some people, while opening this guide, will ask about the utility of a thematic document on beaches ... Friends-visitors, you must first understand what the word «beach» in the Riviera vocabulary means! It is not only a stretch of sand (or pebbles) along the coast, where it is usual to sunbathe, to swim ... Here, when « we go to the beach « is often a private beach where you must pay for your deckchair or your parasol, where you can have a drink, have lunch and sometimes dinner and do water activities... on the Côte d' Azur, the private beaches are subject to restrictions set by local councils. No building can be built in concrete to enforce the 1986 law on the management, the protection and the enhancement of the coastline. But who says «legality» does not necessarily mean quality. If, in general , sunbathers compete in originality in their concept and increase annually the level of services, some go too far during the summer season: prohibitive tariffs, questionable cleanliness, non-existent welcome ... If you do not wish to see these annoyances then follow the guide and you can rely on our small selection of private beaches. Some of our favourite are quite expensive but for the criteria of quality, you will always be satisfied. And as our selections are never exhaustive, do not hesitate to share your discoveries of the year!

The eastern part of the Riviera coast is full of different beaches. On the East coast of the Riviera, pebbles replace the fine sand on the west coast. However, the landscape is no less grandiose in some places. The large equipped and supervised beaches are very populated during peak season. Nevertheless they are next to shaded coves that are more difficult to access and therefore are wilder. Public or private, quiet or busy, whether you are sportsmen or leisure-lovers, you're sure to find your little piece of paradise on each beach – or nearly – offers a lot of games, water or sensational activities. Those who love wildlife will prefer snorkelling in small intimate rocky coves where the water is clearer, fresher and have more fish!

EAST COAST TO ITALY

Nice ★★★★

The 8 km beaches of Nice, covered with white pebbles, are mainly public and free. Water is regularly checked there and bathing is supervised. Two spaces handiplages are located on both sides of the city (Carras and the Centenaire). 15 private beaches with rental mattresses and catering mark the bay from one end of the Promenade des Anglais to another.

Handiplage and Handisport labels

In partnership with the municipalities, the department of Alpes-Maritimes is involved in the accessibility of structures and sites of the Riviera that benefit from the label of quality «Tourism and Handicap» which meets the specifications developed by associations of people with disabilities. Municipalities offering a total of 14 sites Handibeach: Antibes, Cagnes-sur-Mer, Cannes, Cap d'Ail, Mandelieu, Nice, Roquebrune, Saint-Laurent-du-Var, Theoule-sur-Mer, Villeneuve-Loubet and the Principality of Monaco.

During handisport, the access for handicapped person to sports and water activities is also favoured. Structures Labelled Handisport: the Moana Diving Club in Cagnes-sur-Mer and the nautical base of Moure Rouge in Cannes.

■ **BLUE BEACH**
31, promenade des Anglais
Opposite Negresco
✆ +33 (0)4 93 87 10 36
www.bluebeach.fr
contact@bluebeach.fr

Qualité Tourisme label. Open all year. 7 days a week from 9am to 7pm. For lunch and dinner until 11pm from end of May to end of September. Organization of events: family meal, birthday, business, weddings or banquets. À la carte: Around €40. Children's menu: €11. Wine by the glass. À la carte and suggestions on the board. Snacking service on the beach for lunch. Checks are not accepted. American Express. Groups welcome (up to 300 people and 700 people standing). Beach 4 buoys. Deckchair from €16/ day. Umbrella: €6.

On the Promenade Des Anglais, between the legendary luxury hotel Le Negresco and the imposing Palais de la Méditerranée, all the Blue Beach team welcomes you in a good mood. This elegant beach where you can sunbathe all year round and enjoy water sports in season is also known to be a nice restaurant: light and refreshing, the inventive cuisine of the chef falls under the concept of «gastro-beach» where the Mediterranean specialties are honoured. Sole, sea bream, sea bass or red mullet are cooked in the oven or are served grilled, sometimes flavoured with saffron or thyme and also lobster direct from the tank. The wine list offers local vintages like those of Domaine de Bellet. And if you do not want to leave your deckchair, a snack at low prices is available at lunchtime: an initiative that rejoices children and all *finger food lovers*. The good atmosphere participates in the relaxation.

NEPTUNE BEACH

Promenade des Anglais
✆ +33 (0)4 93 87 16 60
www.neptuneplage.com
contact@neptuneplage.com

Closed from December 21st to January 31st. Open every day from 9am to 8pm. À la carte: Around €36 (starter + main course + dessert). Children's menu: €14. Breakfast from €9. Snack from €6. Salad from €14. Holiday voucher. Beach rates: around €20 the day (deckchair, cloakroom, shower, umbrella). 1/2 day from 2pm from €14. Bath sheets €6. Cabin €6.

Located opposite Negresco, this beach invites you to a change of scenery and peacefulness with its blue azure decor and flowering plants along the path leading to the deckchairs. Elegant, Neptune Plage offers services that make it a little paradise: playgrounds for children, supervised swimming, rental of pedal-boat and individual or two-seats kayaks. We like the ancient pontoon and its ladder to go into the water. The subscription options are interesting for a local clientele (card on a yearly basis with unlimited entry, the restaurant is open eleven months out of twelve) and for passing customers (cards from 10 to 80 entrances valid 2 years with declining prices). A dismountable roof installed from mid-May to the end of September creates a shaded area offering a fresh and cool lunch in summer. A large variety of *snacks* is available for those who do not want to leave their place on the pebbles. You will also find on the menu traditional dishes of fish and meat, excellent homemade omelettes, pasta and an original soup bar to stay in shape. Fresh fruit, ice-creams and homemade pancakes complete the offer for gourmands without forgetting the breakfasts to get all the vitamins you need. The very friendly reception and the attentive and smiling service finish to build customer loyalty.

© JEAN CHARLES DUSANTER

Place Garibaldi.

REGENCY BEACH BY RADISSON BLU
223, promenade des Anglais
✆ +33 (0)4 97 07 03 09
www.radissonblu.fr/hotel-nice
info.regence@radissonblu.com

Beach open from end of March to mid-October. Restaurant open daily for lunch and evenings in high season. Cabins available for people having a physical disability. Cloakrooms and hot showers. Lounge space. Snacks between 4pm and 7pm. Beach rates: Deckchair with umbrella from €14 and €18 in July/August. Bath sheet: €4. Possibility of Menu groups with or without privatization.

Facing the contemporary universe of the Radisson Blu, this private beach is not exclusively reserved to the clientele of the eponymous hotel: discover the performance of the 4* and its attentive service mixing simplicity and elegance. The prices are very reasonable and you will be welcomed as a privileged guest. Lying on one of the 200 white deckchairs along the pebbles under a parasol, it is the guaranteed relaxation free of noise, other than the sea! You can choose to lunch there because the service is ensured on the beach unless you choose a table on the vast sheltered wooden bridge to enjoy the daily specials, salads or grilled fish. All the dishes are prepared on the spot with fresh products. During the season a mini carte is available between 4 and 7pm. For a drink with friends, the lounge area is ideal, and you can enjoy between 6 and 7pm the «Aperitieu», with a plate of Nice specialties offered for each cocktail bought. A nice address with a fancy decoration and a maximum comfort, a true invitation to relaxation in front of the panoramic view of Baie des Anges.

RUHL BEACH
1, promenade des Anglais
✆ +33 (0)4 93 87 09 70
www.ruhl-plage.com
info@ruhl-plage.com

Open from beginning of March to end of October. Restaurant open for lunch and dinner, closed Sunday for dinner. Booking advised. À la carte: Around €55 (starter + main course + dessert). Fixed rate formula: daily special + dessert + drink: €28. Mattress €21. Mattress + umbrella €27. Mattress + umbrella + bath sheet €33. Possibility of subscriptions. Swimming pool with sea water changed every day. Lifeguard for children. Checks are not accepted. American Express. Groups welcome. Terrace. Spoken languages: French, English, Spanish, Italian, German, Russian, Arab and Chinese.

Created in 1920, it is one of the oldest beaches of Nice: the establishment is a family-run business where the generations follow one another. Today, it is Marie-José Malacarne who gives to the place a serene and warm spirit where regular customers get together. Warm welcome and impeccable service await you in this prestigious setting with terrace-solarium, private cabins equipped with hot showers and seawater pool for children supervised by a lifeguard. The restaurant, opening onto the sea offers a refined cuisine of Provençal specialties, including dishes made with fresh fish. When you sit in this elegant and stylish setting, your senses are teased by the marine air and you enjoy these relaxing moments. The service is discreet and attentive. The future is assured in the family whose destiny is linked to this beautiful restaurant of the Nice coastline.

Saint-Jean-Cap-Ferrat ★★★★

There is a reason if the greatest fortunes in the world in search of tranquility and beauty are settled on this peninsula connected to the mainland by an isthmus: thus, the place is dotted with luxury villas hidden in sumptuous and highly secure parks. You must visit the site to understand why Somerset Maugham, F. Scott Fitzgerald, King Leopold II of Belgium or Gregory Peck (among many others) have found refuge in this land of choice. You can go around the Cap Ferrat by sea, by road or by the 10 km tourist trail in 3 hours without hurrying with a few stops to admire the landscape: you will discover the Ganivette peak, Coisse peak, the Crau de Nao to Malalongue peak that bears a lighthouse of 33 m with a 50 km range. The tourist trail then goes through the most jagged part of the peninsula bypassing Fosses bay and the Saint-Hospice peak, port of the Maurice Rouvier promenade up to the Baratier peak at the entrance of Beaulieu-sur-Mer. Of all the sea-side promenades, it is the most spectacular for the scenic beauty and the diversity of the landscape. Warning: the days of high winds, waves can be violent and access to the promenade is highly inadvisable.

© THOMAS DUPAIGNE

Villa Ephrusi Rothschild.

Beach in Nice.

© VIRGIL PRUDHOMME

Eze.

© OFFICE DU TOURISME D'EZE

PALOMA BEACH
1, route de Sainte-Hospice
✆ +33 (0)4 93 01 64 71 / +33 (0)6 04 59 66 82
www.paloma-beach.com

Beach open from beginning of April to end of September from 9am to 7pm. Restaurant open 7 days a week at lunchtime from Easter to the end of September and for dinner from end of May to beginning of September. Snack service all day. À la carte: around €20 (for lunch; €50 in the evening). Deckchair: €26 per day. Towel: €7. Checks are not accepted. American Express. Groups welcome (organization of all types of events up to 250 people (cocktails, seminars, weddings, birthdays, presentation of products). Terrace. Car valet. Animations. Boat shuttle (tender). Supervised swimming with lifeguard. Free WiFi.

A unique place nestled in an idyllic cove, the place has a private pontoon with water sports, skiing, parasailing, towed buoys or jet-skiing. During the day, you can have lunch on your deckchair or the terrace overlooking the bay. On the menu, a fine selection of salads, grilled meats and fish nicely prepared. In the evening, the atmosphere becomes more stylish and romantic: you can have candlelight dinner, with your feet in the water. The reception is professional and delicate.

Eze ★★★★

Difficult to access and relatively calm, the Eze beach remains one of the quietest of the region, even in high season. Nestled at the foot of the cliffs, you will enjoy a breathtaking view! And above all silence... heavenly.

ANJUNA BEACH
Eze Seafront
Avenue de la Liberté Basse Corniche RD 698
✆ +33 (0)4 93 01 58 21
✆ +33 (0)6 98 46 48 36
www.anjunabay.com
contact@anjunabay.com

Closed from October to March. It is recommended to park on the level of the real estate agency and to take the underground passage under the railway. Private beach and restaurant. Open from April to September 7 days a week for lunch and dinner. Open for dinner as from May only. Restaurant open from 12pm to 11pm. The beach opens at 10am. Booking advised. À la carte. Average bill between €50 and €75 (including wine). Boat service, WiFi free on the premises. Reservation only by telephone. Activities.

Anjuna Beach is a small paradise reinvented each year, we return there for a chic «robinsonnade» on the beach in the middle of a protected bay to spend a magical day in a festive and exotic atmosphere or even a magical romantic evening the head in the stars in a cosy setting with candlelights. It is a getaway on unbeaten tracks. The menu offers a gourmet and Mediterranean cuisine which does not lack originality: sea bass in sea salt crust prepared in front of you or the smoked saddle of lamb with rosemary... This is a generous and warm restaurant which honours taste in a balinese decor: colourful fishing boats transformed into tables and chairs; superb gazebo for the bar, a shady and ventilated terrace adorned with exotic plants, varnished wooden surfing boards hung to the walls. The service is neat with a warm welcome. Little extra: possibility of menus for professional or private events. Anjuna Beach is an unique place with various facets.

Friedrich Nietzsche trail

From Eze village (427 m height), it is possible to walk down to the waterfront by a delightful walk. In approximately 1 hour, you walk under the pines and olive trees in the footsteps of the famous philosopher who gave his name to the path as it would have been here that Friedrich Wilhelm Nietzsche would have composed his last work, entitled Thus Spoke Zarathustra.

Cap D'ail ★★★

Coming from Nice by the basse cornice, it is the last small resort before arriving in Monaco. You can also get there by train from Nice or Monaco or by the bus line Monaco- Nice every 15 minutes, Sunday every 20 min. Nestled between the massif of Tête de Chien and the sea, it has as big advantage, its beautiful sheltered beaches. You can admire: the outdoor amphitheater Jean Cocteau, where many shows are held during the season.

© OFFICE DU TOURISME D'EZE – P. MASSON

The Fortified Postern of Eze.

The most beautiful places for swimming

- **Marquet beach**. Accessible to all, it is next to the port of Cap d'Ail and offers all sorts of entertainment.
- **Pointe des douaniers**. Wild volcanic site with small coves.
- **Mala Beach**. Reserved for sportsmen (15 min walk to reach the beach from the parking of Beaverbrook), this little piece of paradise offers a majestic setting.
- **Les Pissarelles**. This wild (and naturist) corner is worthy! It is accessible only by a small road from the Basse Corniche: facing the service station, turn left towards the subdivision «the Pissarelles» then down for about 1 km. You will then arrive in a beautiful cove surrounded by rocks.

EDEN BEACH MALA

Allée Mala
✆ +33 (0)4 93 78 17 06
www.edenplagelamala.com
plagemala@gmail.com

Beach open every day from 9am from Easter to October and for dinner (until midnight) from end of May to beginning of September. Restaurant and bar open every day. Breakfast from 9am to 11am. Continuous service for lunch and dinner from 12pm to 10pm. Booking advised. À la carte: Around €35 (dish + glass of wine + coffee). Mattress whole day €30 in peak season and €25 half-day (from 2pm). In September and October, mattress rental €10 (on weekdays) and €20 (weekend and public holidays). Umbrella all year €6 and towels €5. Groups welcome (up to 150 people and 200 in buffet). Shop. Shuttle boat. Massages. Lifeguard rescuer.

Eden Plage Mala is one of the most beautiful places in Cap-d'Ail and of the French Riviera. Its access is a reward as you have to walk a little and go down a lot of steep steps from the town centre or follow the Chemin des Douaniers from the port. But the effort is worthwhile: a splendid beach nestled in the middle of the rocks. The Eden Plage welcomes you for a sweet relaxing moment. Everything is within reach from breakfast to dinner for a pleasant moment of well-being and taste: mid-cooked tuna, spaghetti vongole, crunchy pizzas, hearty fritto misto, beef tartar, risotto...Escape guaranteed!

Monaco ★★★★

The public and private beaches of Monaco are in Larvotto area, west of the Principality: bathing is supervised, and the beaches arranged. Easy to park your car in nearby parkings, another swimming spot also exists on the side of Port Hercule: take avenue de la Quarantaine. At the end, stairs descend on the new pier in the back of which you will find a solarium and ladders allowing easy access to swimming. Finally, do not forget the Marquet beach of Cap D'ail which offers, like the private beaches of Monaco, a whole range of water activities during the season.

LA ROSE DES VENTS

Larvotto beach ✆ +37 (0)7 97 70 46 96
www.larosedesventsmonaco.com

Open 7 days a week in season. Annual closing from November to February. Service from 12.30pm to 3.30pm and from 7pm to 10.30pm. Average price à la carte: from €30 to €35. Menu groups on reservation.

As soon as the warm weather returns La Rose des Vents beach restaurant invites you to relax, lying comfortably on deckchairs in the shade of parasols facing the Mediterranean Sea. You will also have the opportunity to dine on the terrace or in the large modern room. As for the food, the Chef works with fresh products and prepares tasty dishes with a Monegasque and Italian influence. The service is friendly and kind. More than enough to spend a wonderful day on the shore!

Beach of Monte Carlo.

Coastal path.

© VILLE DE CAP D'AIL

Beach in Mandelieu La Napoule.

WEST COAST TO CANNES

On the west coast of the Riviera, the sandy beach with golden reflections replaces the small pebbles and gravel of the east coast ... Here, the beaches are narrower but longer, and there are many small coves with turquoise waters. As for the east coast, large beaches are equipped, supervised during peak season and are densely populated in summer. You have the choice between public and private beaches, family beaches or furiously trendy ones. Each offers a lot of water, playful or sensational activities.

Saint-Laurent-du-Var ★★★

Set in the middle of the Alpes Maritimes coast line, halfway between Cannes and Monaco, Saint-Laurent-du-Var has all the advantages of a modern city and an old village with the bonus of a whole range of nautical pleasures. Ancient natural border of Nice county until 1860, the city was the border between France and the Sardinian kingdom. The crossing of Var river was often made when water was low. The wooden bridge that made it possible to cross the river has often been worn by water or was demolished during the wars. It is only after 1860 that a stone bridge was built for the road and the railway side-by-side. The city, very much affected by the bombings of 1943 and 1944, was mainly rebuilt but many monuments of the old Saint-Laurent remain as the church place Castillon rebuilt in the 12th century and remodelled in the 16th century with a Provençal romanesque style that houses a reliquary containing a tibia of saint Benoit, founder of the Benedictines. Around the church remains a part of the old village with its old characteristic streets. The port of Saint-Laurent with its 18 acres of mooring, shops, restaurants and bars is the stronghold of daytime and night time entertainment of the town relayed by the large mall of Cap 3000.

BEACH CLUB

Beach, Restaurant, Lounge Bar
2, promenade des Flots-Bleus
✆ +33 (0)4 69 00 13 48
www.beachclub-saintlaurentduvar.fr

♿

Open all year. Monday to Saturday from 9am to 11.45pm; Sunday from 9am to 6pm. Booking advised. À la carte: Around €32 (starter + main course + dessert). Checks are not accepted. American Express, Holiday voucher, Chèque Restaurant. Groups welcome. Terrace. Lounge bar. Themed nights. Organization of private events. Playground with several structures at disposal for young children.

The only fine sandy beach of Saint-Laurent-du-Var is the setting of this restaurant at the beginning of the Promenade des Flots Bleus. With white and wine-coloured parasols it is an ideal scenery for meals on the beach. The patio chairs and teak tables occupies one of the largest sandy terraces of the French Riviera. We have lunch and dinner in the open air with view on the sea. The rich menu favours fresh products and delights everyone with meats, fish, pastas, pizzas, bruschettas, tartars and carpaccios (meat and fish). Children and gourmets are not forgotten with a nice range of desserts and a delicious gourmet coffee. As for the beach, the deck chairs on the sand await those who like to relax in the sun.

Cagnes-sur-Mer

In the medieval village of Cagnes-sur-Mer, the ancient fortress became museum and on the coastal side, you can enjoy visiting the port where the you can still find «pointus» boats. In Cagnes, where the painter Auguste Renoir ended his days, life evolves around art.

STONE BEACH

15 B, promenade de la Plage
✆ +33 (0)4 93 89 96 28
www.plagestonebeach.com

Restaurant-snack-salad bar every day for lunch. In winter, only the snack is open. Beach open from June 15th to September 15th. Supervised swimming. Deckchair €11, €13 for the first rank. Daily special: €13. Large salad to compose yourself €10. Hamburger homemade €10. Holiday voucher, Chèque Restaurant.

This fine restaurant is the ideal holiday destination if you want to taste the pleasures of a relaxing day on the seaside without spending too much money. The colours are bright and flashy on the large terrace overlooking the pebble beach; the deck chairs are comfortable with their matching cushions and parasols; music is trendy; the warm and friendly team offers a fast-food service at the counter in a cool and family atmosphere. Nothing but happiness! The food is prepared on the spot every day. At the salad bar, you make your own dish from the buffet of various fresh products. You can also find classic snacks: hamburger, bruschetta, pan bagnat, and the traditional minced steak and French fries. At the sweet section, lots of sweets, pancakes, fresh fruits, wafers and 24 perfumes of handmade ice-creams. You can eat on the beach while admiring the horizon. Children have games available. A reasonable corner of paradise to enjoy alone, between friends or in family.

World championship square balls.

Antibes and Cap d'Antibes/ Juan-les-Pins ★★★★

The history of Antibes-Juan-les-Pins is that of an exceptional site that has been inhabited for 2000 years. Founded in the 5th century BC under the name of Antipolis – which probably means the city opposite... from Nice - the city was often attacked and ravaged by the Ligurians. The Roman occupation brought safety and a relative prosperity. In the 2nd century AD, the city became a bishopric and took the name Antiboul. Its proximity to Italy makes it a stronghold. In the middle Ages, it went through incessant attacks of the Barbarians. In the 12th century, Antibes became a Major component of the fortifications of the Provence County. It is the only town on the coast to have been surrounded by ramparts. But in 1244, the episcopal seat was transferred to Grasse, again for safety reasons, given that the fortified town of Grasse was less exposed as compared to the coast which experienced barbaric attacks on its shores. In the 14th century, Queen Marie of Anjou confiscates the Antibes fiefdom from the Grasse Bishop and entrusted it to the Pope of Avignon. In 1482, finally united to Provence, Antibes will experience a new period of prosperity. The Fort Carré was built a hundred years later in 1588. It was so well designed and so well armed that it was never fully conquered. In 1746, the city was besieged by the Austrian army. Louis XIV entrusted the development of the city to Vauban who completed the fortifications of the city. They will be demolished at the end of the 19th century under the pressure of the growth of the city beyond its walls. Remains of these remarkable fortifications are the Fort Carré, Antibes pride. Napoleon 1 had a stay there. Indeed, after the fall of Robespierre, he will be held some time in Fort Carré. Finally, in March 1815, after his landing at Golfe-Juan -les cent jours- the city of Antibes as well as that of Cannes, refused to receive him and he directly went to Grasse, starting point of the famous route Napoléon. The seaside resort of Juan-les-Pins was created in 1882. Antibes continued to thrive after the First World War. Many artists have succumbed to its charm: Prévert, Audiberti, Greene, Picasso or Monet. Between heritage (archaeological museum), cultural events (jazz) and luxury tourism (palaces, Cap d'Antibes) the city preserves its environment and thus its identity. Antibes was one of the first towns in the county to sign the States environment charter.

PLAGE KELLER – RESTAURANT LE CÉSAR

Cap d'Antibes

✆ +33 (0)4 93 61 33 74

www.restaurant-plage-cesar-antibes.fr

Private beach open from March to beginning of October from 9am to 11.30pm. Le César restaurant open for lunch as from March and for dinner as from April. Swimming lessons. Net anti-jellyfish. Supervised swimming. Labeled beach 4 Buoys. À la carte: Around €50 (starters from €15, main courses around €26, desserts €9). Deckchair: €23 per day and €26 for the pontoon or on the first rank. Valet service or Free parking. Shuttle boat. Free Wifi access.

The turquoise blue of Cap d'Antibes is the dominant colour when you arrive on this beach. A small paradise offering a striking view over the *Baie des Anges* (Bay of Angels) and the Southern Alps overlooking it. Here, you take your time lazing in the sun when you are not cooling off in the crystal-clear water... And when it's time to eat, you joyfully go to the Le César restaurant to enjoy a Mediterranean cuisine made with fresh and seasonal ingredients: sea bass in salt crust with artichoke ravioli, royal bouillabaisse, breeded meats... Happiness, relaxation and conviviality are guaranteed in an elegant setting by the sea. This place even takes care of organising your custom receptions, banquets and weddings.

La vieille ville.

Plage de Garoupe.

BIJOU PLAGE

Boulevard du Littoral
✆ +33 (0)4 93 61 39 07 / +33 (0)4 93 67 69 72
www.bijouplage.com
bijou.plage@free.fr

Restaurant open 7 days a week from 12pm to 3pm and from 7pm to 10.30pm in summer and from 2.30pm to 10pm in winter Tuesday to Sunday for lunch. Beach open from Easter to mid-October from 9am to 6pm. Booking advised. Menu from €25 to €35. À la carte: Around €30 (fishing of the day from €8 to €12 the 100 grs. Bouillabaisse from €48 to €92). Children's menu: €14.50. Daily special: €16.50. Seafood platters from €43 to €135. Charter quality Mer de Lérins 2015. Groups welcome (up to 350 seats). Terrace. Free Wifi.

One of the most elegant beaches of the riviera coast where you spread your towel on one of the transats facing the Mediterranean blue horizon while slipping your feet into hot sand. Located between Cap d'antibes and the hills of Golfe-juan, this beach has a privileged location. It also offers restaurant with an impeccable service that offers a menu based on seafood: carpaccio of marinated salmon, fritto mixto, fish soup, mussels mariniere, fresh grilled fish of the day, seafood, bouillabaisse and shellfish. The beach offers an elaborate and varied menu, a buffet and deckchairs for an excellent time with family or friends. We liked the pleasures of relaxation, the sea water and sunbathing in this idyllic setting where swimming is supervised.

BRETAGNE BEACH

Boulevard du Littoral ✆ +33 (0)4 93 61 46 55
www.bretagne-beach.perso.neuf.fr
contact@bretagne-beach.fr

Label Quality Tourism. Off-season, the restaurant is open for lunch (weekends and holidays). The beach is open every day from April to end of October from 9am to 6pm (from 9am to 7pm from mid-June to end of September). À la carte: Around €20. Fixed rate formula: €25 (1 deckchair + marine salad or mussels + 1 glass of wine or 1/2 free bottle of mineral water + dessert of the day or ice-cream 2 balls Monday to Friday). Checks are not accepted. Free wi-fi. Label Pavillon Bleu (eco-environmental).

An underground pedestrian passage leads you directly from Dulys 2 parking to this pretty beach. The blue signpost and the blue and white of the deck chairs and parasols evoke the colours of summer. The restaurant obtained the «Qualité Tourisme» label in 2011 and the Pavillon Bleu ecolabel for the quality of its services and also for the good environmental quality. On week days, a «Deck chair + Lunch» formula is offered giving access to the whole set of services: changing cabins, hot shower or furnished pontoon. At the restaurant, on the menu you will enjoy a sunny cuisine with fish from the south (sea bass, sea bream, St Pierre, scampis provençal style) or traditional food with saucy or roast meats. The daily suggestions offers only fresh fish from the market. You are served on the shady covered terrace opposite the Lérins islands. Complete relaxation is guaranteed on this convivial beach open only during the day.

ESTÉREL BEACH

28, boulevard Charles-Guillaumont
✆ +33 (0)4 93 61 04 18
www.esterel-plage-juan-les-pins.fr

Closed from November to end of January. Restaurant open every day from 9am to 6pm. From May to September open for lunch and dinner, from 9am to 0h30. Booking advised. À la carte: Around €20 (starter and main course around €20, dessert around €10). Checks are not accepted. Groups welcome (up to 180 people). Terrace. Organization of any type of events.

A change of scene on this beach is guaranteed with an exotic hut decoration: bamboo furniture, wooden terrace, tables on the soft sand, till the front of the deck chairs near the water. The brown and white cushions and

Antibes.

parasols give a fresh look and a tanned complexion... You can find on the menu specialties as well as the classic Mediterranean ones as mussels in marine way, beef tartar, cod fillet, chorizo crumble and Parmesan, puree with basil, salmon with tandoori, rice sautéed with vegetables and minth sauce, etc. Everything is well presented and well served. The café is hearty, the desserts generous and the cocktails inventive (mango/red fruits mojito). Didier and Eric are supported by an efficient and dynamic team and guest benefit from the festive and warm atmosphere which prevails on this beautiful beach. You will definitely relax in front of this dreamlike panorama. Booking is recommended especially if you want a place on the pontoon.

PLAGE DES ILES
Boulevard Guillaumont
✆ +33 (0)4 93 61 09 46 / +33 (0)6 83 22 13 14
Open every day from April to end of October. Open for lunch and dinner in July and August. À la carte: Around €25. Children's menu: €10. Menu and fixed rate formula served for lunch weekdays, except public holidays. Deckchair rental for a day.
Held by beach owners from father to son for three generations, Plage des Iles has evolved according to its faithful clientele. Created in 1946, it is now managed by Gérard and his team. The address is inhabited by a true marine spirit, friendship and good mood reign there. Everything gets animated very early, the relaxation day starts on a deckchair in a perfect setting combining comfort and conviviality. Many games are available for children and in the middle of the season, bathing is supervised by a lifeguard. You have lunch with feet in the sand or on the shaded and open terrace. The cuisine with Provencal and Mediterranean flavours offers great gourmet moments since it is prepared with vegetables and fresh ingredients: mixed salads, roasted fish or griddled meats, homemade desserts (tiramisu dessert, caramel custard, etc.). On summer evenings, you have a candle lighted diner and some entertainments and themed evenings make very festive some end of the day. Not to be missed, for the warm and family atmosphere.

PLAGE DU GARDEN BEACH
15-17, boulevard Édouard-Baudoin
✆ +33 (0)4 92 93 57 57
www.hotel-gardenbeach.com
contact@hotel-gardenbeach.com
Beach open from April to October. Restaurant open 7 days a week for lunch from May to end of September and for lunch and for dinner from mid-June to mid-September. Open every day from 12pm to 3pm and from 7pm to 10pm. Booking advised. Children's menu: €12. Fixed rate formula: €29 (main course + dessert+ ½ water or drink of vin+ coffee). Suggestion or daily special from €19. Lunch menu and Deckchair: €35. Deckchair from €15 per day. Checks are not accepted. American Express. Valet. Free Wifi.
It is the beach restaurant of the hotel Garden Beach. A pleasant setting with its private pontoon. A beautiful break for a casual lunch or a romantic dinner on the waterfront. You will like the pontoon to improve your sun tan. A fresh cuisine created by the chef Cédric Milliot and his team. Also book a massage session inside the hotel, which also a spa as well, for an exceptional relaxing day.

Golfe-juan ★★★★

Golfe-juan is a small seaside resort surrounded by hills and attached to the town of Vallauris. It takes its name from the protected bay where it is located, lined with kilometers of fine sandy beaches on both sides of the center. It has an atmosphere of family village, despite the presence of two ports: the Old Port with fishing boats and «pointus», a bench sales of fresh fish opened in the morning, the shuttle to the Sainte Marguerite island, the old captaincy, etc. The port Camille Rayon is more recent, where yachts and pleasure boats are anchored. You will find the shipyard Rodriguez, shipchandlers, and many restaurants. The vehicles circulating behind the buildings, the terraces are set on the unique pedestrian promenade of the Riviera. The Jean Marais theater, in the shape of an ancient outdoor circus is a place for concerts and shows in summer. The red and black Fourmigue lighthouse emerges in the middle of the bay to signal a dangerous reef to navigation. This site offers many opportunities for divers who can admire at the foot of the lighthouse the remains of a miniature village that was designed for the creation of a film (the child and the siren). Napoleon takes part in its fame by landing here on March 1st, 1815 in charge of a small fleet after his escape from Elba island. Later, the novelist Juliette Adam settled there and invited the intelligentsia of the time. Picasso had his habits on the beach, as Jean Marais in some restaurants... Movie and show stars never fail to stop at Golfe-juan to enjoy there the sweetness of life.

PASSOÂ BEACH
Plages du Midi – Avenue des Frères-Roustan
✆ +33 (0)4 93 63 10 59
Open from beginning of April to mid-October. Beach open every day from 9am to 6pm. Restaurant open daily for lunch; for dinner for the fireworks and on request for any type of private events. Booking advised. À la carte from €20 to €30. Children's menu: €10. Daily special: €15. Wine by the glass. Deckchair: €16 per day depending on location, €12 1/2 day depending on location. Holiday voucher, Chèque Restaurant. Groups welcome. Terrace. Free Wifi for the guests. The road from Théâtre de la Mer of Golfe-Juan to Juan-les-Pins goes along the beaches of the Midi. Among them, Passoa Beach is facing the Cap d'Antibes. As you enter, you are seduced by the green color which illuminates the lines of deckchairs on the white sand. It is a green world, soothing and invigorating at the same time, guaranteeing relaxation, tanning and bathing. Here, the atmosphere is family-like and relaxed. The traditional and Provencal cuisine is based on fresh fish, tasty mixed salads, and homemade gourmet desserts. For sea or land, the menu suits all tastes, the suggestions are displayed on the slate each day. The meals are served on the beach or on the large covered terrace. For the little hungers apart from lunch, take-away snacks (panini, sandwiches, pan bagnat...) are offered nonstop. The restaurant is opened the evenings of fireworks or on request. A guarranteed good moment to share...

Cannes ★★★★

The English nobility discovered it when it was only a village. Movie stars made it a myth, brands installed their windows, and visitors perceive it as a privileged stopover. Cannes, dream destination, continues today to deliver its secrets. Here mingle in an incomparable atmosphere, the luxury hotels of the Croisette, the ancient stones of the historic district of Suquet, the authenticity of the old fishing port, the bright beauty of the islands, the beaches bathed in sunshine and the liveliness of the events organised at the famous Palais des festivals et des congres. Leader of the French Riviera, city of congresses, of international events, of movie stars and glamour, beyond its famous croisette, Cannes, reveals a precious heritage, natural and artistic. The heart of its history vibrates in the pedestrian streets and steep streets of Suquet district, area above the old port which reveals a provencal soul. The Meynadier shopping street and the Forville market preserve a village atmosphere, as for the Iles De Lerins, green lung overflowing with history, they face the flashy croisette where the great brands of luxury and the famous palaces mingle. All facets are offered to the curious visitors who want to see beyond *the sunlights*.

LA PLAGE 45

Opposite the Grand Hotel
45, la Croisette
✆ +33 (0)4 93 38 15 45
www.grand-hotel-cannes.com
info@grand-hotel-cannes.com

Open from mid-April to end of September 7 days a week. À la carte: Around €30.

It is the beach of the Grand Hôtel located a few steps away, on the other side of the Croisette: an exotic and contemporary decor with bamboo vegetation and colorful fabrics. We appreciate the magnificent pontoon and its large VIP relaxation beds, «gazebos» (Balinese beds), not to mention a superb bar on the sand. A chic and trendy place for a drink, lunch or simple "relaxation" at the end of the day.

PLAGE DU FESTIVAL

52, boulevard de la Croisette
✆ +33 (0)4 93 39 37 37
www.plage-festival-cannes.com
contact@plage-festival-cannes.com

Open all year from 10am until 6pm into off-season. In season, open from 9am to midnight. Booking advised. À la carte: Around €60. Rates beach: deckchair, umbrella, sheet bath €30 in July and August, €20 the rest of the year. wi-fi. Organization of all private or professional events.

It is one of the oldest beaches of the Croisette, rested by the girl of Jean Mineur, the pionnier of publicity in France. Thus, it was always closely related to the cinema world, the more so as it is close to the Palace and its famous steps. New departure since 2011 thanks to the rerun of the beach by a local family. The famous architect Jean-Michel Wilmotte revisited space, and it is successful. A resolutely elegant, simple and contemporary decoration. This spirit is liked: wood, white, greenery, fine touches coloured thanks to the sparse flowers on the tables. The cuisine signed by the chef François Vadala is of mediterranean influence. One finds in the dishes this breath smart and purified simply worked quality ingredients. You will undoubtedly pass wonderful moments.

VEGALUNA BEACH

61, boulevard de la Croisette
✆ +33 (0)4 93 43 67 05
www.vegaluna.com

Open all year. Every day from 12pm to 4pm and every evening in July, August (last orders 10.30pm). À la carte: Around €60 (starter, main course, dessert). Children's menu: €13 (for lunch and €28 for dinner). Beach rates (deckchair + umbrella + shelf): in season from €26 to €35 depending on the row. Off-season from €15 to €20. Free Wifi on all the beach.

La Plage Vegaluna opposite the InterContinental Carlton hotel owes its charm to its relaxing atmosphere and its captivating setting combining talent, sobriety, trend and elegance. A refined decor, teak furniture with a sleek design, a large bar with a mosaic of coloured glasses

The port of Suquet.

The gulf of Napoule and peaks of Theoule-sur-Mer.

from Murano... everything has been conceived to blend harmoniously the natural elements of the beach and the sea. Chef Antoine Regnault offers authentic flavours of the Mediterranean sea and beautiful dishes. Add to this a nice welcome of the young owner Cécile and the friendly team.

RADO BEACH

La Croisette
✆ +33 (0)4 93 94 20 68
www.rado-plage.fr
events@rado-plage.fr

Open all year. Beach open every day from 9am to 7pm. Restaurant open 7 days a week for lunch all year and Fridays and Saturday for dinner in July and August. Dancing parties every Saturday in July and August. À la carte: Around €55. Fixed rate formula: €18 (dish + drink + coffee except weekends and public holidays). American Express, Chèque Restaurant. Terrace.

Between the Carlton and Martinez hotels facing the Miramar, the Rado beach has occupied the seafront since 1958. It is one of the oldest in Cannes, run from father to son by the Rotondaro family. Each table of this air conditioned restaurant offers a sea view, summer and winter. The large terrace is fully heated and sheltered in winter. On the menu, you will find daily specials and a menu which changes regularly. While enjoying the sunshine on your deckchair, you can nibble light snacks chosen from the «spécial plage» menu. Its long experience in the organisation of events enables the beach to offer its know-how and its spaces for professional or private events. Listening, sharing and warm welcoming motivate the team in the festive spirit inspired by the famous Croisette.

Théoule-sur-Mer ★★★

In Antiquity, Théoule was one of the biggest ports of mooring between Antibes and Toulon. From the Var coast, it is the first town at the entrance of Esterel which reveals the Provencal French Riviera with a rock red-garnet colour, very typical. Formerly, the city was mainly devoted to fishing, had only thirty dwellings and access was done by a small path not suitable for motor vehicles commonly called «chemin du Trayas». Recognized as one of the most beautiful routes in Europe along the Mediterranean offering superb views, the main road of «Corniche d'Or» opened in 1902, truly marks the extension of the town. Protected in the hollow of a small cove, Théoule is a seaside resort today with a pretty marina with its red stone mini lighthouse. The site fills both lovers of seaside activities and lovers of nature that can walk along the paths in the direction of the surrounding mountains such as the «Grosses Grues» whose highest point reaches 440 meters.

LES FRÈRES DE LA BAIE

Parking du Chateau
Promenade de la Darse
✆ +33 (0)4 92 97 80 20
www.lesfreresdelabaie.fr
contact@lesfreresdelabaie.com

Restaurant open in winter Friday to Monday from 12pm to 3pm. Open in summer 7 days a week from 12pm to 3pm and from 7pm to 10pm. Beach open from 9am to 7pm. Non-stop service all day. Booking advised. Menu from €30 to €36. À la carte: Around €45. Children's menu: €12. On the waterfront. Deckchairs on the beach.

In one of the most beautiful parts of the coast with the Esterel on one side, the mountains of the Mercantour on the other and the ocean just in front, the beach restaurant Les frères de la Baie has been welcoming guests for nearly 20 years now. Whether in the water-front restaurant, on the terrace or in the hut, you will find a Provencal cuisine made with fresh ingredients, beautiful and generous salads and also meat or fish tartars, risotto, grilled fish, beef rib, a fisherman's pot (the evening suggestions)... Without forgetting the bouchot mussels with cream in season. The wine list is reasonable for the prices and lovers of rosé wine will find the biggest classics. An address operating summer after summer for the greatest satisfaction of the regulars.

NICE

★★★★

Nice is a city on the move and where it is nice to be all year round. Historical, due to its architectural heritage of incredible richness; cultural, due to several museums; dynamic, due to its major urban projects... There are so many ways to approach the capital of Riviera! The city is divided into two parts delimited by a very capricious river, the Paillon, now largely channelled under the Massena Square which is the urban heart of the city. On the east is the old town (Vieux Nice), the hill of the Castle, the Port and Mont Boron. To the west lie the new districts of the Arenas, the business center of the city but also the hills of Bellet and the residential neighbourhoods of Fabron and Sainte-Marguerite. To the north, the hill of Cimiez where once there was the Roman fortress (oppidum) and where today the old buildings of the Belle Epoque are alongside more modern ones...

To discover Nice, you must have at least a full day. But the city has such a concentration of museums and monuments that a complete and detailed inspection will take several days! Therefore, depending on the length of your stay, you can choose in advance and establish a clever route that will allow you to move from one site to another without having to go back your way: Take the time to enjoy the mild climate and beautiful scenery. Enjoy the numerous events, strolled through the old streets of the town and along beaches of the Promenade des Anglais, enjoy trendy evenings or opera and you will realize that there is always something to do in Nice. Gastronomy, culture, heritage, recreation? So much pleasures to discover and to share!

Nice – Nikaïa

The city would have taken the name of Nikaia, name of the goddess Athena Nikkel which means "the goddess who gives victory" after the victory of the Greeks over the Ligurians in 540 BC. Another hypothesis, Nice would be derived from "Nis" Ligurian radical which means "source" in reference to the source of drinking water that flowed at the foot of hill of the Castle.

REGIONAL COMMITTEE OF TOURISM - CRT
455, promenade des Anglais
✆ +33 (0)4 93 37 78 78
www.cotedazur-tourisme.com

Tourism label & Disability. Find on the site more than 50 labeled sites.

For touristic information on your stay, the website of the Comité Régional de Tourisme Riviera Côte d'Azur (CRT) is there for you! Essential for organising your holidays, find your accommodation in the Alpes-Maritimes a holiday rental on the French Riviera as well as your sports activities, tours and excursions.

Pass Côte d'Azur Card, a distillation of ideas and good deals! Developed by the Comité Régional du Tourisme Côte d'Azur and the Departmental Council of Alpes-Maritimes, created and supported by all the stakeholders in Azure tourism, Côte d'Azur Card is a genuine sesame with good plans. Sold as a prepaid electronic passport card, it gives its holder access to numerous activities to do on the whole Azure coastline as well as in the mountain resorts. Museums, strolls in the open air, visits of unmissable sites, family stay, theme parks, boat trips... here is a beautiful opportunity to compose you a customised stay at the best price for active and enriching holidays. A catalogue indexing all the activities is given at each card purchase gathering all of the proposed offer. More information on the website www.cotedazur-card.com

TOURIST AND CONVENTION OFFICE OF NICE
5, promenade des Anglais ✆ 0 892 707 407
www.nicetourisme.com

Desk of the railway station: from mid-September to mid-June, open from 8am to 7pm Monday to Saturday and from 10am to 5pm Sunday. From mid-June to mid-September, open from 8am to 8pm Monday to Saturday and from 9am to 7pm Sunday. Desk of the Promenade des Anglais: from mid-September to mid-June, open from 9am to 6pm Monday to Saturday. From mid-June to mid-September, from 8am to 8pm Monday to Saturday and from 9am to 7pm Sunday. Desk of airport T1 and T2: from October to March open from 9am to 6pm Monday to Sunday. From April to September from 9am to 8pm Monday to Sunday.

You are visiting Nice and do not know what to do during the day or at night or where to go? Just go to the Tourist and Congress Office of Nice where advisors will welcome you, inform you and direct you. They will give you all the necessary information to make your stay a perfect and successful one. You will find there the activities and events organised in Nice and in the neighbouring communes. Free brochures in different languages are available there.

FRIEND IN FRANCE ★★
City Center – 9, rue Gubernatis
✆ +33 (0)6 99 16 22 33 / +33 (0)4 93 80 27 07
www.friend-in-france.com
info@friend-in-france.com

Open every except Sunday from 9.30am to 7pm. Possibility of booking on the website. Airports transfers to Nice, Cannes, Monaco, Saint-Tropez. Guided tours Best of the Riviera Tour, Provence Tour or A Day in Italy.

Friend in France invites you to discover the region around several themes accompanied by passionate and professional bilingual English guides. Regardless the option you choose – in a group or a private tour – it will be an opportunity to learn about historical and cultural anecdotes and the not to be missed visits. The company also organises transfers to the Nice Côte d'azur airport from Monaco and Italy to Saint-Tropez.

NICE AZUR VISIT ★★

✆ +33 (0)6 23 42 40 73
www.nice-azur-visit.com
sam@nice-azur-visite.com

Guided tour on foot from €14. Stroll discovery by bike from €37. Electric bicycle tour from €47. Excursion with mini van from €47. Activity at sea from €39. Conference national guide Lecturer Approved by the Ministry of Tourism and Culture.

Feel like discovering the French Riviera differently? Nice Azur Visit proposes guided and commented tours with a National Guide Lecturer Approved by the Ministry of Tourism and Culture on foot, by electric bicycle, bicycle, mini-van or with a solex! An original opportunity, sportive, educational and ludic in a friendly atmosphere for all you have to know on the unmissable sites of Nice and surrounding areas.

VU PAS VU ★★★

City Center
18, rue Pastorelli
✆ +33 (0)6 12 26 41 69
www.vupasvu.com
joel@vupasvu.fr

Art lovers? Vu pas Vu offers seminars, conferences, debates, guided tours of exhibitions, meetings or workshops allowing you to widen your knowledge and to share moments with intense cultural professionals and lovers of culture coming from diverse backgrounds: artists, art historians, museum curators, art critics, experts, gallery owners, antique dealers, auctioneers and guide-lecturers. Find the news on the website or their Facebook page.

© VALÉRY TRILLAUD

Rauba Capeu.

GETTING THERE

Station SCNF Monaco Monte Carlo: 1st station of France

The SNCF train station in Monaco Monte Carlo, excavated in the valley of Sainte Devote, is surprising: underground, it is through a starry sky of bright lights, over twelve meters high, that the travellers arrive. The station hosts a volume of about 4 to 5 million passengers per year since its creation in 2000 and has won the title of «first station in France» in terms of quality and welcoming conditions. Third Station of the region of PACA after Nice and Marseille, the station has the label «Access +» as it is adapted for people with reduced mobility. With a simple booking, support is organised when needed.

By Plane

INTERNATIONAL AIRPORT NICE-CÔTE D'AZUR
Rue Costes and Bellonte ✆ 08 20 42 33 33
See page 9.

AIR FRANCE
Nice Côte d'azur airport – Terminal 2
✆ +33 36 54 / +33 (0)8 92 70 22 22
www.airfrance.fr

Service for disabled people or with reduced mobility Service Saphir ✆ +33 (0)9 69 36 72 77 and mail.saphir@airfrance.fr.
The company offers with KLM and Delta Air Lines partners a large number of flights every week from Nice-Côte d'Azur: 4 destinations operated by Air France (Lille, Lyon, Nantes and Paris), 2 European destinations (Amsterdam operated by KLM, Rome operated by Alitalia and 1 international with direct flight to New York (4 frequencies every week operated throughout the year by Delta Air Lines). HOP! Air France now also sells 3 destinations: Biarritz, Caen and Clermont Ferrand. All year round. HOP! Air France now also serves from Nice Airport: Lyon, Toulouse, Bordeaux, Lille, Nantes, Strasbourg, Metz-Nancy-Lorraine and Rennes.

By Train

CHEMINS DE FER DE PROVENCE
Liberation
4, bis rue Alfred-Binet
Nice train station
✆ +33 (0)4 97 03 80 80 / +33 (0)4 93 29 82 82
www.trainprovence.com
One-way rates: Nice Digne les Bains: €23.30. Nice Entrevaux: €11.80. Allianz Riviera station €5 return ticket.
A trip between sea and mountains: discover the Mediterranean back country with the Train des Pignes! Between Nice and Digne Les Bains, on a very picturesque line, discover hilltop villages and impressive gorges. From the palm trees of the French Riviera go to the thyme scents of the highland, the crops of olives and the snowy mountains. Terroir and discovery are there for a unique trip in the heart of Provence. The Chemins de Fer de Provence climbs up to 1000 m altitude and serves 50 stops and stations, including the towns of Villars sur Var, Touët-sur-Var, Puget-Théniers in the Alpes Maritimes, Entrevaux, Annot, Thorame, Saint André-les-Alpes and Digne-les-Bains in the Alpes de Haute Provence. Fast and reliable way to travel on a daily basis, the company also provides 22 shuttle services per day in average between Nice and Plan du Var but also 4 round trips per day between Nice and Digne-les-Bains. Leave your car at the station in Nice (paid parking) or that of Lingostière (free parking) and discover Nices backcountry with a picturesque means of transport that operates 365 days a year! Stop at the Allianz Riviera Stadium on match days with the possibility of booking tickets in advance. A unique and incomparable tourist offer: sales of excursions in the villages (train+lunch) and voucher gifts for your relatives for an original ride aboard Train des Pignes. In summer, a steam train runs on Sundays from May to October and in winter, the winter-sports train brings you to the station of Foux D'allos. Information and reservations ✆ +33 (0)4 97 03 80 80 or on www.trainprovence.com

Bypass

Nice is served by the A8 highway, the «Provençale», from Aix-en-Provence to the Italian border. There are different exits, which enable you to quickly reach all sections of the city: exit 50 serving the Promenade des Anglais, the 51 district of St. Augustin, the 52 the district of Saint-Isidore (which allows you to join the main road 202 or 202bis to the ski resorts), the 54 will take you to Nice-north and exit 55 takes you to the districts of Nice-east and to the harbour. Except exit 50, you will have to add a few extra euros when paying to reach the other exits linking Nice to A8 motorway «bypass»: you will save valuable time and avoid the downtown and congestion, especially during peak hours or during the summer season.

Nice – Colours of the French Riviera.

■ **SNCF TRAIN STATION OF NICE-VILLE**
City Center – 11, avenue Thiers
✆ 08 00 11 40 23 – www.sncf.com
Open from 5am to 00.30am.
Served by nearly 130 TER, 30 high-speed trains and 15 InterCités every day, the Nice main train station is located in the heart of the city, a few steps away from the tram. The retail space welcomes you on weekdays from 06: 10am to 9pm and on weekends and holidays from 7am to 8pm. More information on the TER by calling Contact'Ter on the +33 (0)8 00 11 40 23 (everyday from 7am to 9.30pm, free call from a landline telephone), on the TER Paca website or on the TER Mobile application. More information on the high-speed trains and InterCités on the 3635 or on the sncf.com website.

GETTING AROUND

Public Transport

■ **LIGNES D'AZUR**
City Center
1, rue d'Italie ✆ +33 (0)8 10 06 10 06
Telephone call (€ 0.06/min)
♿
Ticket solo 1 travel: €1.50. Multi 10: €10. Pass 1 day: €5. Open Monday to Friday from 7.30am to 7pm and Saturday from 9.30am to 6pm. Information bus and tram (schedule, itineraries, disturbances, ideas of stroll on www.lignesdazur.com and application Lignes d'Azur Mobile for smartphone). Retail outlets tickets bus and tram in the commercial agencies Lignes d'Azur, the points relay, the buses, Parcazurs (P+R) and on the docks of the tram stations. L'Infobus furrows Metropolis NCA: planning available on www.lignesdazur.com. Center of customer relation open Monday to Saturday from 7am to 8pm. Sunday from 8am to 6pm.

▸ **Move smart with Lignes d'azur.** The Lignes d'azur network provides connections throughout the country by bus and tram. Do not forget to validate your ticket while getting into the bus or tram. If you have a card Lignes d'azur, you can recharge it in the Lignes d'azur agencies or by Internet on www.lignesdazur.com: it is then necessary to create an account before selecting free pack of your choice. After 48hours, your card is reloaded automatically during your next validation on the network.

▸ **The tram. It** is strongly advised for your travels north-south in Nice: you will not only avoid the congestions but also trying to find a parking space. The line of the tram connects north of Nice via the downtown. It functions every day except on May 1st and makes it possible to move according to the following itinerary: Henri Sappia, Comte of Falicon, Le Ray, Gorbella, Valrose Université, Borriglione, Libération, Gare Thiers, Jean-Médecin, Masséna, Opéra Vieille Ville, Cathédrale Vieille Ville, Garibaldi, Acropolis, Palais des Expositions, Vauban, Saint-Jean-d'Angély Université, Saint-Roch, Virgile-Barel, Saint-Charles, Pont Michel et Hôpital Pasteur. For the schedule, the first departures are early the morning until late the evening from each terminus. Count approximately 4 minutes between two trams during the day and 15 minutes on average during the off-peak hours.

▸ **The Parcazur parks.** Since the commissioning of the tram, the motorists also take advantage of parkings: the Parcazur parks. You enter freely with your car , park there the time there that you wish without exceeding the day in progress. With your subscription or a ticket Lignes d'Azur, easily go downtown by bus or tram at an attractive price. The access to the parks is for clients of Lignes d'Azur, or to those having a multimode subscription card Carte d'Azur. To leave the parks, you must be in possession of a title validated the very same day on an urban line of Nice Côte d' Azur which must correspond at least to a round-trip. The title solo 1 travels and the ticket Azure do not allow the outing of the vehicle. The parking is limited for a day in progress. Vauban: opened from 5am to 1.50am; Henri Sappia: connected to the highway A8 outing n° 54. Opened from 4am to 2.30am; Pont-Michel: connected to the highway A8 outing n° 55. Opened from 4.55am to 1.45am; Palais des Expositions: level 3 of the public car park Acropolis Jean Bouin. Opened from 4.15am to 2.15am.

▸ **Purchase of tickets. For the** buses, you can buy your tickets directly near the drivers. It is recommended to give the exact money. Caution: the drivers of the tram do not sell tickets and there is no sale of tickets on board: it is thus necessary to buy your tickets at the cash machines installed on the docks of each tram station, with the distributors of the ParcAzur parks or at the agents of the network and the commercial agencies of Lines of Azure. New application NFC Nice Ticket enables you to buy and validate directly your tickets since your mobile with function NFC (more information on www.lignesdazur.com).

▸ **Pricing**. The network Lines of Azure proposes a single pricing on the whole of the Metropolis Nice Côte d' Azur which gathers 49 towns: Aspremont – Bairols – Beaulieu-sur-Mer - Belvédère – Bonson – Cagnes-sur-Mer – Cap d'Ail – Carros – Castagniers – Clans – Colomars – Duranus – Eze – Falicon – Gattières – Gillette – Ilonse – Isola - La Bollène-Vésubie – La Gaude – La Roquette-sur-Var – La Tour-sur-Tinée – La Trinité – Lantosque – Le Broc – Levens – Marie – Nice – Rimplas – Roquebillière – Roubion – Roure – Saint-André-de-la-Roche – Saint-Blaise – Saint-Dalmas-le-Selvage – Saint-Etienne-de-Tinée – Saint-Jean-Cap-Ferrat – Saint-Jeannet – Saint-Laurent-du-Var – Saint-Martin-du-Var – Saint-Martin-Vésubie – Saint-Sauveur-sur-Tinée – Tournefort – Tourrette-Levens – Utelle – Valdeblore – Venanson – Vence – Villefranche-sur-Mer. Also on the trunk lines of the departmental network: 100 - 200 - 400 - 500 - 112 - 116 - 217 - 510 - 701A – 701B – 730 for the trips inside NCA.

Get carried away in the city

LIGNES D'AZUR
Nice Côte d'Azur en toute liberté

Parcazur park & rides are free for holders of a monthly or annual Lignes d'Azur or Carte Azur travel card

6 16 89 →	Connecting bus services near the station
LD06 →	Lignes d'Azur departmental lines
(train icon) →	Connection to the train station
LIGNES D'AZUR →	Lignes d'Azur travel agents
P tram bus Parcazur →	Park and Ride: Access information on +33 (0)8 1006 1006 or at www.lignesdazur.com

Informations: **www.lignesdazur.com**

From 7 a.m. to 8 p.m. Monday to Saturday. From 8 a.m. to 6 p.m. on Sunday

08 1006 1006 Service € 0,06 / min + call rates

MÉTROPOLE NICE CÔTE D'AZUR

NFC nice Ticket

With the new 'Lignes d'Azur' application, already used by many passengers and **available on Google Play, you can use your Android NFC smartphone to buy your tickets, validate them on our buses and/or trams.**

Fast, easy and secure

1. I download the application via Google Play
2. I buy my tickets on the bus or on the tram where I want, when I want
3. I pay securely with my credit card or with PayByPhone
4. I validate my journey by placing my activated smartphone on the validation terminal

During inspections, you may present your mobile as if it were a 'Lignes d'Azur' card. To travel correctly, you should always travel with a valid travel pass (ticket, 'Lignes d'Azur' card, Azur card or NFC Nice ticket).

Further information available at lignesdazur.com

ZENCOM zencommunication.fr

- **Solo:** € 1.50 for one trip on the urban lines Nice Côte d'azur with correspondence for 74 minutes (no ticket) except lines with special pricing for airport 98 and 99 (€ 6). Only one ticket is valid on all network (bus and tram) on the côte d'azur.
- **Parcazur** round-trip €3.
- **Multi 10 travels** sold €10 enables you to buy in only once 10 trips (with correspondences during 74 minutes which should not constitute a round-trip) which can be used simultaneously by several travellers. Ideal for small groups or families.
- **Pass 1 day** €5 ensures you unlimited travels during 24 hours on the urban lines (except lines specific pricing: Bus 100% snow and lines airport 98 and 99).
- **Pass 7 days** €15 enables you to travel freely and in an unlimited way during 7 days consecutive on the urban lines (except lines with specific pricing: Bus 100% snow and lines airport 98 and 99). possibility of using lines 98 and 99 for the airport.
- **In winter, enjoy the Bus 100% snow**. Direction Auron, La Colmiane, Saint-Martin-Vésubie, Isola 2000 or Valberg. Non accessible to classical pricing: ask for information. Many places available limited. Information from Monday to Saturday from 7am to 8pm number Azure +33 (0)8 1006 1006 (price of a local call) or on www.lignesdazur.com

Green Transport

VÉLO BLEU

✆ +33 (0)4 93 72 06 06

www.velobleu.org

The price of the service understands a right of access + a rate for the rental. Four offers for the right of access: 1 year (€25), 1 month (€10), 1 week (€5) or 1 day (€1.5). Annual rate reduced (€15) for the subscribers Lignes d'Azur and carte Auto Bleue. 1/2 hour free with each rental, €1 for following half an hour then €2 per hour extra. Accessible service 7 days a week and 24/24.

Self-service bicycle rental since 2009 is a set of 175 stations which allows you to take a bicycle in a place after registration and to leave it in another, in the towns of Cagnes sur Mer, Saint-Laurent-du-Var and Nice. The 1750 bicycles are available 365 days a year and 7/7 and 24/24. There are three ways of paying: with the contactless card (Carte Vélo Bleu or Ligne d'Azur) or your mobile phone or via NFC (BPASS) identification. The future subscribers have four defined time of commitment for the subscription: 1 year, 1 month, 1 week or 1 day. A telephone information service is permanently available through a vocal interactive server and a representative who will answer your questions from Monday to Saturday from 7.00 a.m. to 8.00 p.m. except on public holidays. It is possible to register online.

SIGHTSEEING

Nice is a city on the move where it is pleasant to be all year round. Historical, due to its architectural heritage of an incredible variety; cultural, due to numerous museums; dynamic, due to its major urban projects... There are so many ways to approach the capital of Riviera! The city is divided into two parts delimited by a very capricious river, the Paillon, now largely channelled under the Massena Square which is the urban heart of the city. On the east is the old town (Vieux Nice), the hill of the Castle, the Port and Mont Boron. To the west stands the new districts of the Arenas, the business center of the city but also the hills of Bellet and the residential neighbourhoods of Fabron and Sainte-Marguerite. To the north, the hill of Cimiez where once there was a Roman fortress (oppidum) and where today the old buildings of the Belle Epoque mix with more modern ones ...

To discover Nice, you must have at least a full day. But the city has such a concentration of museums and monuments that a complete and detailed inspection will take several days! Therefore, depending on the length of your stay, you can choose in advance and establish a clever route that will allow you to move from one site to another without having to go back your way: Take the time to enjoy the mild climate and beautiful scenery. Enjoy the numerous events, strolled through the old streets of the town and along the beaches of the Promenade des Anglais, enjoy trendy evenings or opera and you will realize that there is always something to do in Nice. Gastronomy, culture, heritage, animations? So many pleasures to be discovered and to share!

PROMENADE DES ANGLAIS ★★★★

It is hard to believe that this impressive promenade was just a modest earthy trail in the early 19th century! With the arrival of the first British for their winter holidays in 1760, the beach became a pleasant place to walk: in 1844, a first section of 12 m was built southeast of the Paillon. Ten years later, the path was extended to Magnan. In 1930, the site showed its real appearance: the villas and their gardens were destroyed and replaced by palaces, hotels, casinos and apartment buildings. You will notice that the Negresco or Opera palaces have their facades to the north, backing the promenade: remember that Nice was a winter resort popular for its mild climate, but not for the sea! During winter, only the English, who were numerous on the Riviera at this time of the year, enjoyed walks on the waterfront thus the name «Promenade des Anglais» ... Becoming legendary, it was extended on almost eight kilometers from the beachfront, following the almost perfect curve of the Baie des Anges. The 'Prom' «(as the nicois says), although sometimes overloaded with vehicles, became a place of rendezvous for lovers of rollers, running, bike rides (a cycle path has been arranged on the south sidewalk) or walking alone, with friends or in family. In addition to the many events (Carnival, flower parades, marathon...), the promenade is known for its «blue chairs» and pergolas, suitable to relaxation and contemplation. Curiously, its unique lampposts illuminate both the ground and the sky and serve as beacons to airline pilots landing at the Nice airport at night.

ON
HOLIDAY
ORIGINAL
PASSPORT
Adopt the style
Vélobleu
From 1€*
vélobleu
vélobleu
Vélobleu, self-service bike rental system
www.velobleu.org
(*) conditions available on www.velobleu.org
Allo vélobleu 04 93 72 06 06
LOCAL CALL
MÉTROPOLE
NICE CÔTE D'AZUR

French Riviera Pass

It allows you to access a number of sites and activities at discounted prices. Offered for 24, 48 or 72 hours, the pass "French Riviera" is a passport for discovery: embark as often as you wish aboard the double-decker bus "The Grand Tour" which will allow you to discover the city on a guided and commented tour. Discover the National Museum of Marc Chagall Biblical Message which has the largest collection in the world of public works by the artist. Then go towards the majestic Russian church. The pass also invites you to Phoenix Park with its 7 ha accommodating nearly 2,500 species of plants and animals. The small tourist train will finally allow you to sneak into the alleys of old Nice to the hill of the Castle during a guided tour of 50 min.
Info and prices on www.frenchrivierapass.com and pass@nicetourisme.com

OLD CITY ★★★★

The old town, tells us about the medieval times of Nice with its monuments, its baroque palaces and its nightlife. Particularly picturesque, it is characterised by its narrow streets, its tall buidings, belfry-topped arches on several floors crossing the streets, its steps linking the different levels, its winding and tortuous paths, its small squares and restaurant terraces. Built in the 16th and 17th centuries, and renovated in the 1950s is today well developed, it is a moving testimony of the past. Dotted with little boutiques of local specialities like spices, flavoured candles and scents of the South, the old Nice is also the place to find restaurants with secret rooms and pizzerias whose terrace extends into the street... Its streets offer to tourists its Franco-Italian Renaissance ambiance, ochre lights façades, half-closed shutters ensuring the privacy of the occupants, the liveliness of its merchants who speak to one another in authentic *nissart*, the local dialect. Here, you will find memories of Garibaldi, originally from Nice and the young artillery general Bonaparte who lived at number 6 of the street that now bears his name. Lets not forget the young Masséna, son of a wine merchant who left as a soldier and in a few years became Marshal Of France, duke of Rivoli and prince of Essling: Napoleon had named him "*l'enfant chéri de la victoire*" [The beloved child of victory]. Do not miss the visit the Cours Saleya which in the mornings holds under its colourful tents, its famous flower, fruit and vegetables market that fill the air with pleasant scents. This street is the place to go during your visit to Nice, in the heart of the old town. Surrounded by bars and restaurants, the Cour Saleya is constantly lively from 6 am until late at night, regardless the season. Note that this charming décor notably served for a speed chase in the movie Ronin with Robert De Niro and Jean Reno in 1998.

Old city of Nice.

Monuments

CATHÉDRALE SAINT-NICOLAS DITE ÉGLISE RUSSE ★★★

Quartier de la Gare
Avenue Nicolas-II
✆ +33 (0)6 63 28 98 99
www.cathedrale-russe-nice.fr

The cathedral is open Tuesday to Sunday from 9am to 12pm and from 2pm to 6pm. Closed with the visits at the time of the outfit of the private religious offices (baptisms, weddings, burials).

In order to meet at the request of an important Russian population in Nice, the construction of the orthodox cathedral Saint-Nicolas began in 1903 according to the plans of the architect Preobrajensky. Remarkable with its 52 metres high, this cathedral is considered the most beautiful building of this type built of Russia. It owes its name to the emperor Nicholas II who with his mother empress Maria Feodorovna ordered the construction of the building completely. They chose a ground in Piol, where they liked to live. Inspired by the style of the Saint-Basile de Moscou basilica, the cathedral was built with materials from the region and Italy: terracotta of Florence, marble and pink granite from Italy, white stone La Turbie. The tower is composed of six domes: highest symbolising Christ, the other four depicting the four evangelists and the smallest of blue dedicated to the Virgin Mary. The building is classified as a Historical Monument since 1987. Since 1923, it is a religious association which managed the orthodox parish Saint-Nicolas de Nice and therefore the cathedral. But in 2006, the Federation of Russia proclaimed the property of the cathedral and based on the fact that the land on which it was built belonged to the family of imperial Russia before the Russian revolution of 1917. The business was made in front of the justice who agreed with the Federation of Russia. The site is not visited freely any more.

CHÂTEAU DE L'ANGLAIS ★★

Mont Boron

Architectural curiosity. Does not visit itself.

Located on the Mont Boron hill, the building was constructed around 1856 by the Scottish colonel of the English engineering unit in the Indies called Robert Smith. The building is surprising, between a curious architecture of medieval British and Hindu style that earned it the nickname « la Folie de l'Anglais » or « la Folie Smith ». On the death of Smith in 1875, his son sold the building to Count Melchior Gurowsky of Wezel. Unfortunately, after the Second World War, the count sold the property to a real estate investor who divided it into several apartments, thereby destroying pavilions, houses and terraces. Today, the Botanical Garden is classified as a Historic monument since the year 2000, as well as its colourful and always amazing architecture.

Slavic rides in Nice

If the Riviera was attended sporadically by a few Russian intellectuals in the first half of the nineteenth century (Lermontov, Gogol and Tolstoy), it is from the time when members of the Russian imperial family stayed on the Riviera that the Slavic presence increased quickly on the azurian territory. You'll begin your journey by visiting the Château de Valrose, Sciences University of Nice, built by Baron Von Berwies, magnate of railways, who arrived in Nice in 1867.Go along the beautiful park in which the Baron constructed statues, caves and waterfalls. He even built an izba, coming from one of his properties in Kiev. While going back down, stop for a moment at the Church of St. Joan of Arc to admire the beautiful frescoes of Eugène Klemmentieff. Then head towards the Boulevard de Cimiez where the famous Chagall Museum whose collection, consisting of 17 paintings of the Biblical Message, is exceptional! Back downtown for lunch in the Old-Nice at «The Russian House»: blinis with salmon; bitkis and zakouska constitute a delicious gourmet stop. Continue your visit with the Russian Orthodox Church which was created due to funds from the Empress Alexandra Feodorovna, Empress Dowager, widow of Tsar Nicolas I. Then you will go to the Saint-Nicolas cathedral, picturesque witness of the Slavic past. This building of Byzantine style is wondrous, especially with the five cupolas, finely gilded with fine gold which draw colourful balloons in the sky. Not far away, the Hotel of Parc Imperial was built in 1900 for Russian winter holidays on another part of the Bermond estate. It is on its tennis courts that the champion Suzanne Lenglen was glorified and it was then transformed into a high school in 1924. End your walk in Bottéro Street to buy a lot of Russian products and crafts at the Isba grocery store before eating at the restaurant, The Transsiberian. You will drink happily your vodka. But be careful: here we do not follow the customs of throwing the empty-glass... Take care to book a room at the Chateau des Ollières, former residence of the Russian Prince Alexei Lobanov-Rostowsky. The next day, begin by having lunch at the Matrochka before walking along the paths of the Russian cemetery. Established in 1867, it was dedicated to the Grand Duke Nicolas Alexandrovitch. You will see, among the 3,000 graves , those of the Grand Duke Rostislav Romanoff, Count Stroganoff, Colonel Alexander Rajevsky, Princess Yourevski or that of Nicolas Fricero. To conclude your journey, go through the Museum of Fine Arts Jules-Cheret which was the residence of Princess Kotschoubey and which retains in its collections the works of Marie Bashkirtseff, which includes her famous self-portrait.

Museums

The museums and local art galleries owned by the City of Nice are free. A great initiative that the municipal team took during the summer 2008, to increase visits of its institutions and to facilitate access to culture for all. Be careful there is an entrance fee for the Museum of Biblical Message Marc Chagall: the site is managed by the state that offers to its visitors free entrance every first Sunday of the month!

MUSÉE D'ART MODERNE ET D'ART CONTEMPORAIN – MAMAC ★★★★

Centre Ville
Promenade des Arts ✆ +33 (0)4 97 13 42 01
www.nice.fr
mamac@ville-nice.fr

Open all year. Closed on Monday and on January 1st, Easter Sunday, on May 1st, on December 25th. Tuesday to Sunday from 10am to 6pm. Inhabitant of the metropolis Nice Côte d' Azur: free on presentation of a written proof of home and an identity card. Tourist individual ticket 48h €10 and Pass 7 days €20. Free for under 18-year-olds (and unemployed people, beneficiaries of the social minimums, students, journalists, teachers). Guided tour. Shop. Activities.

Opened in 1990, this museum of modern art and Contemporary Art (MMCA) is the result of several projects done in the course of the second half of 20th century. They are the architects Yves Bayard and Henri Vidal who by offering an architecture linking the course of and Straw the axis of the old RN7 won the votes of the elected representatives. The MAMAC is a large château-fort consisting of four towers with grey marble and connected by bridges to the large bay windows. The permanent artistic program of the museum stands are identity between the Pop Art and the Art of American assembly and the new school of European realism. Local movement of the Nice School is well highlighted with artists such as César and Arman whose famous works as adorn the museum entrance those with Yves Klein, by Niki de Saint-Phalle and Ben. The second floor, reserved for temporary exhibitions, hosts artists of the 1950s to the present day. From the roof (closed in case of bad weather), you can benefit from a circular walk from the view of the city. Some summer evenings, the wall of the fire made by Yves Klein and still in perfect condition of operation, is embraced for a show of burning beauty.

MUSÉE DES ARTS ASIATIQUES ★★★★

Arenas – 405, promenade des Anglais
✆ +33 (0)4 92 29 37 00
www.arts-asiatiques.com
arts-asiatiques@departement06.fr

Open all year. From May 2nd to October 15th, from 10am to 6pm. From October 16th to April 30th, from 10am to 5pm. Closed on January 1st, on May 1st and on December 25th. Inhabitant of the metropolis Nice Côte d' Azur: free on presentation of a written proof of home and an identity

The Ecole de Nice, the new postwar artistic trend

As from the fifties, a center of artistic creation is created in Nice around different means of expression and various currents but with a common position: the rejection of academicism. The founder of what is called «The School of Nice» is Yves Klein , a native of the region and pioneer of experimental art, known for the invention of his famous « IKB « (International Klein Blue), a deep over-sea blue which initiated many of his works. The group is composed by many artists, from Nice mostly; all are friends and pursuing the same goal of creating: Arman,Martial Raysse, César, Spoerri, Tinguely and Niki de Saint-Phalle are the main personalities. The origin of their creation is more rooted in a philosophical then artistic inbred: they denounce in an ironic way the contemporaries, react to answers provided by the abstraction made so far and refuse an hermetic art, which prevents them to denounce through their works, this alienating status that carries the object of current consumption in post-war France facing the evils of a booming consuming-society. For this, they have to invent a new way of creation, unconventional, with real objects as materials, in order to enhance the expression of their works: Arman accumulates and breaks objects while Caesar compresses them; Niki de Saint Phalle became well-known for her « girls « opulent and variegated kinds of creatures that illustrate some after-war economic prosperity and Jean Tinguely, her husband, built monstrous infernal machine, a kind of caricatures of war machines. Three movements thus characterize the School of Nice: the new realism, a kind of French pop art that appears in the fifties. Then the Fluxus movement in the sixties exposing dramatically the problem of the limits of art and genres: the support for creation becomes the artist himself and the artwork becomes ephemeral, characterized by performance and «happenings» of any kind in unusual places. In this movement, the leader, Benjamin Vautier, best known as «Ben», who also invented a writing that became famous and especially used on various objects of mass consumption, finally, the last movement specially in the School of Nice: « Support Area « in the 1970s who advocated that tools should be back and procedures of painting with Viallat, Dollan Charvolen, Chacallis , Isnard, Maccaferri, Miguel and Saytour. Other artists beyond all rankings: Bernar Venet, Albert Chubac, Malaval, Verdet and, more recently, Sosno or Mas.

card. Tourist individual ticket 48h €10 and Pass 7 days €20. Lift, approach ramp serving the various levels of the rooms of the museum, provision of a wheel chair to the reception of the museum, toilets for disabled people. Guided tour. Shop. Activities.

Meeting place and exchanges between Asian arts and the western culture, placed on a covered with artificial lake of water birds in the heart of a floral park of 7 acres, the museum of Asian Arts is the work of architect Tange Kenzo. Its glass building and marble (contrast between the empty and full) evokes one according to the principles Asian the ground (the square) and the sky (the circle): while on the first floor, the sacred rotunda of a glass pyramid is reserved for spiritual world of Buddhism, the basement is dedicated to the habitat, the furniture, objects and multimedia area. A space is reserved for temporary exhibitions. Four symmetrical areas have works of Chinese, Japanese, cambodian civilisations and indian where antiques, modern, traditional or precious illustrate the traditional cultures of Asia. The sunday two ceremonies of tea are offered alternating with visitors: ceremony of Japanese tea (*chanoyu*) and the Chinese tea (*gong fu cha*). The museum also offers conferences, shows on reservation and has a beautiful shop.

MUSÉE INTERNATIONAL D'ART NAÏF ANATOLE-JAKOVSKI ★★★

Nice Ouest
Avenue de Fabron
Château Sainte-Hélène
✆ +33 (0)4 93 71 78 33

Open all year. Open all the week except Tuesday from 10am to 6pm. Inhabitant of the metropolis Nice Côte d' Azur: free on presentation of a written proof of home and an identity card. Tourist individual ticket 48h €10 and Pass 7 days €20. Shop. Activities. Parking free visitor.

It is in Château Sainte-Hélène de Fabron, remains of the François Coty perfumer, that settled in 1982, the international museum of Naive Art of Nice. This site owes its existence to the donation of art critics Anatole and Renée Jakovsky that gave it its name. It has a collection of works unique in the world where you can retrace the History Of naive Art of 17th century to today: Haiti, South America, Croatia, Central Europe, Europe... Three themes articulate the permanent collections: the city in the countryside; popular fables and tales and the history of naïve Art. You will find paintings, sculptures, posters and pictures of more or less famous artists such as Rabuzin, Bauchant, Bombois, Ivan and Josip Généralic, Grandma Moses, O' Brady, Haddelsey, Rimbert, Vivin, Séraphine, Lefranc, Vivancos...

MUSÉE MASSÉNA ★★★

Centre Ville
65, rue de France
✆ +33 (0)4 93 91 19 10
musee.massena@ville-nice.fr

Open Wednesday to Monday from 10am to 6pm. Closed certain public holidays (Christmas, January 1st, Easter Sunday and May 1st). Free for under 18-year-olds (and unemployed, beneficiaries of the income of solidarity, disabled people, journalists, teachers, guide lecturer on presentation of a written proof). Inhabitant of the metropolis Nice Côte d' Azur: free on presentation of a written proof of home and an identity card. Tourist individual ticket 48h €10 and Pass 7 days €20. Guided tour. Activities.

Housed in a beautiful villa built at the end of the 19th century by the Danish architect Hans-Georg Tersling according to the model of the Italian and neo-classical villas of the First Empire, the site was Prince Victor of Essling's winter residence, grandson of the Nice native, André Masséna before he donated it to the City of Nice stipulating that the garden will be open to the public and the villa must become a museum. By 1921, the hotel therefore provides collections (paintings, graphic arts, sculptures, furniture and works of art) showcasing – marks of the influence of Nice from Bonaparte and napoleon's Empire up to 1939. From the Promenade Des Anglais, the view of the museum is beautiful: it is like an architectural jewel set in the middle of a very beautiful tree-filled park designed by Edouard André, one of the Masters of the 19th century gardens.

MUSÉE MATISSE ★★★★

Cimiez
164, avenue des Arènes-de-Cimiez
✆ +33 (0)4 93 81 08 08
www.musee-matisse-nice.org
musee.matisse@ville-nice.fr
♿

Open all year. Wednesday to Monday from 10am to 6pm. Closed for Christmas, on January 1st, Easter Sunday and on May 1st. Inhabitant of the metropolis Nice Côte d' Azur: free on presentation of a written proof of home and an identity card. Tourist individual ticket 48h €10 and Pass 7 days €20. Guided tour. Shop. Activities.

Created in 1963, the collection of the museum, presented around a pictorial journey of initiation, covers the period from 1869 to 1954. The museum presents an architectural feature that is reflected in the presentation of its collections. On the one hand, Villa des Arenes, a 17th century Genoese house, transformed into Matisse museum since 1963 focuses on the artistic development of the artist with his projections and his research for colour and graphics. On the other hand, the new wing, which opened in 1993, welcomes part of the permanent collection consisting of various donations (including the painter himself who lived in Nice from 1917 to 1954), a collection of drawings but also temporary exhibitions that give rise to a series of lectures and screenings of art films. The visit of the museum begins with rather dark works (they were open to Mediterranean light only under the influence of Cézanne) and other, more violent and colorful, when Matisse became a master of Fauvism. Further on, we find paintings of great expressiveness corresponding to the period when the artist lived in Nice: the artist's sensitivity is growing, inspired by the sea, women, heat, light and nature. The public then discovers almost all of sculpted work but also a hundred of photographic clichés, fifteen illustrated books, more than two hundred engravings, numerous drawings and very numerous objects which belonged to the artist. Note that some of the rooms are devoted to the tapestries, stained-glass windows and documents.

MUSÉE NATIONAL DU SPORT ★★★

Plaine du Var – Boulevard des Jardiniers
Stade Allianz Riviera
✆ +33 (0)4 89 22 44 00
www.museedusport.fr

Tuesday to Sunday from 10am to 6pm. Night Thursday until 9pm. Closed on Monday. From October to April: Tuesday at Sunday from 11am to 5pm. Full price: €6. Temporary exhibition + permanent exhibition: €8. Free -18 years, disabled people, titular Card Culture and Pass Education, administrative staff of the sports. Possibility of guided tour. Groups 10 people €3.

Labeled Musée de France since 2004, Musée National du Sport was created in 1963 at the request of Maurice Herzog. The establishment knew several successive phases: opening of the first galleries in 1988 to Parc des Princes (closing in 1997), opening of a provisional exhibition space in XIIIᵉ district of Paris in 2008, move in 2013 and establishment in Nice in June 2014 in Stade Allianz Riviera. The site understands permanent, temporary galleries and of news, an auditorium, a café of the sports, a shop and a immersif and interactive space. Its collections cover six hundred years of sporting history and are articulated around 45,000 objects, 400,000 documents (material, clothing, accessories, trophies, mascots, posters, paintings, films, photographs, archives...). For a visit full with feelings, he proposes to the visitors four big challenges: the challenge on oneself which conceives the sport like a going beyond oneself practitioner generally alone (athletics, swimming, cycling, gymnatisque, ski...), the challenge of man with man (the duel) or how the sport confronts two adversaries in a combat at the conclusion which only one will be victorious (boxes, judo, works hard, tennis...), the challenge of a collective vis-a-vis another which gathers all the team sports (football, Rugby, basketball, handball, volleyball...), and the challenge of the sport beyond the limits which evokes the natural barriers, physiological, psychological, social or technological.

Walks & Strolls

COLLINE DU CHÂTEAU

Vieux-Nice – Parc du Château

♿

Open all year. From September 1st to September 30th and from April 1st to May 31st from 8am to 7pm. From October 1st to March 31st of 8am at 18: 00 From June 1st to August 31st from 8am to 8pm. Children welcome (park with games). Catering facilities (in summer season).

The hill of the castle is a large limestone rock rising to 93 feet. A its summit, 2 plates: the first south housed for seven centuries the castle of Nice while the other, in the north, housed the first suburb of the citadel. Once you have climbed the stairs to the Park or favourite lift (paying), you can enjoy a superb view of the city as well as Baie des Anges. The hill of the castle is a huge green lung of nice: relaxation area and promenade, the 2 acre offer vegetation mainly composed of broad-leaved trees and some conifers. On the other succulent plants and hill, cacti were colonised the rock. An amazing waterfall (built on the site of the old keep of the castle) fed with water of Vésubie comes to cool the ambient air from the hot summer days: do not hesitate to make a wish by throwing a coin into the pool below! As you walk in a green setting in the heart of the paths built and decorated with pebbles (for some), you will notice the ruins of the old castle destroyed around 1706 on the orders of Louis XIV and those of the medieval cathedral dedicated to sainte Marie. In 18ᵗʰ century, with the arrival of many tourists on the azure coastline, the town commissioned the naturalist Antoine Risso with retimbering site in there important of many exotic species. Accompanied by others (Bottieri, Milonis and Touet), they offer Nice to a beautiful park. La Tour Bellanda (formerly Tour Saint Elme) comes to embellish the site with its architecture in the style of romantic landscaped decorations. A little further, do not miss one of the most beautiful cemeteries in France with a multitude of magnificent tombs of all styles: Roman, neo-gothic, Ligurian... Many local people are buried here. But it is certainly the evening, when the lights up and the farm park, and that the visitor contemplate the hill of the castle from the old town, that the place is most magical. Anyway, the site will offer beautiful souvenirs to you.

PHOENIX PARK

Western Nice – 405, promenade des Anglais
✆ +33 (0)4 92 29 77 00
www.parc-phoenix.org

♿ 🦻

Open all year every day from 9.30am to 6pm in winter and from 9.30am to 7.30pm in summer. Cash desks closing 1 hour before. Free for under 12-year-olds (within the limit of 3 children per paying adult. Admission prohibited to any 16 year old minor not accompanied). Adult: €4 (for the residents Metropolis Nice Côte d' Azur; €5 for the residents out of Metropolis Nice Côte d' Azur). The entry ticket also gives a free access to Musée d'Arts Asiatiques. Pets are strictly prohibited within the boundary of Park except guide dogs. Possibility of loan of 2 strollers and 2 wheel chairs on request. Buckle magnetic for the deaf people. Children welcome. Catering facilities (and drinking water fountain in the park). Activities. 2hours offered to the parking of Arenas, weekends and public holidays, during school holidays of the area B, and from June 15th to September 15th, after validation of the ticket at the counters of Parc Phoenix.

Park Phoenix has filled with wonder its visitors. If it owes its reputation to the diversity of its flora, children also adore it for its feathery and hairy inhabitants! On 7 ha, about 20 different gardens with sound themes, the park accommodates one of the largest greenhouses of Europe of 7 000 m² and 25 m high in which you'll discover six tropical climates... Birds, tortoises, iguanas and small crocodiles of the Nile are there and illustrate the biodiversity of nature. Discover their environment: old plants sometimes more than 8 million years, Rugs of odorous flowers, tree ferns, rare orchises... and many other extraordinary plants! In the gardens, hens, ducks, peacocks and swans in freedom will come to meet you. From the entrance, the visitor will also be able to discover a large otter pool. Birdcages gather also exotic birds (cranes, rheas, parrots, macaws...) while enclosures shelter wallabies, porks épics and lemurs "varis" classified in critical danger of extinction. On the lake evolve hundreds of birds, while in the aquarium, fish and alive insects offer an attractive show. The park accommodates throughout the year exhibitions, conferences, workshops and various entertainments for small ones and adults.

KNIFE & FORK

Since 2000, the label «Cuisine Nissarde» defends the values and the authenticity of the real specialties of Nice: the Nicoise salad, onion tart, pan bagnat, stuffed vegetables, ratatouille, tian of zucchini or squash, pocket of stuffed veal, meat stew, ravioli, gnocchi, stockfish, stuffed sardines, chard pie, loops and the apples-dried grapes donuts. A simple and tasty food that praises vegetables, fish , olive oil and the herb-garden of the South composed by basil , marjoram, thyme, savory and rosemary.

AGUA

Port – 41, boulevard Stalingrad
✆ +33 (0)4 97 19 08 15

Open Tuesday to Saturday for lunch and dinner. À la carte: Around €40 (starter + main course + dessert). Lunch menu: €19. Wine by the glass. Terrace.

The chef offers a fine selection of fishing of the day: Saint-Pierre, bream, skipjack, palamide, cuttlefish, clam, red mullet... In this trendy address, the dishes evolve according to the catch of the day: sea bass with fennel and chorizo, fried squid with Espelette pepper on fresh tomato puree and candied sweet peppers, lobster, stuffed capon with tomatos olives and basil, sea-bream tajine, risotto of Breton lobster with peas and chanterelle. A delicious address to be discovered!

LES AMOUREUX

Port – 46, boulevard Stalingrad
✆ +33 (0)4 93 07 59 73

Open all year. Tuesday to Saturday only for dinner. Booking advised. À la carte: Around €16 (dish). Tasting dishes from €9.60. Pastries from €6.70. Chianti €25.50 the bottle. Pizzas from €8. Take-away.

Discover the authentic Neapolitan pizza. Here, Ivan and Monica cultivate a real know-how with 100% Italian ingredients, AOP or Organic. From traditional recipes to more original pizzas with crispy pasta, all your senses will be awakened especially since the welcome is very pleasant, just like the decor. Victim of their success, remember to book if you don't want to wait until a table is available. A very nice address that cultivates with art the Neapolitan cuisine and the generosity.

ARDESIA

3, rue François-Guisol – Port
✆ +33 (0)9 81 34 03 02

♿

Open all year. Monday to Saturday from 12pm to 3pm; Monday and Wednesday to Saturday from 7pm to 11pm. Booking advised. À la carte: Around €35 (starter + main course + dessert). Lunch menu: €12. Chèque Restaurant. Groups welcome (up to 40 people. On reservation). Terrace.

In a pretty modern decor, enjoy a regional cuisine prepared with fresh ingredients selected according to the arrival of the market. According to the season, you will be able to taste artichoke salad and squids, Tartar of fresh tuna with citrus fruits, veal quasi with green pepper, risotto linguini with ceps of the country and for deserts, the delicious tarte tatin. The service is perfect. A nice address to be discovered as quick as possible!

ARTE E CUCINA

7, avenue Baquis ✆ +33 (0)6 66 56 69 64

Open Monday to Friday from 12pm to 1.45pm and from 7pm to 9pm. Daily special with 9€50. Possibility of takeouts. Possibility of privatization.

In a preserved setting in the heart of the City Center, Arte E Cucina expects you for a friendly moment. This restaurant of charm nicely combines culinary art with fine arts in a bright and contemporary decor with coloured paintings hung on the walls, on the floor or exposed on beautiful wooden trestles. In this beautiful environment sybarite let yourself be surprised by a beautiful carte with Mediterranean accents. An address as exquisite as artistic!

LA BAIE D'AMALFI

City Center – 9, rue Gustave-Deloye
✆ +33 (0)4 93 80 01 21
www.baie-amalfi.com
info@baie-amalfi.com

Open all year. Closed 1 week in January and 2 weeks mid-July, at the end of July. Closed on Sunday and Monday all day in low season, Monday all day in high season. Schedule of service from 12pm to 2.15pm and from 6.45pm to 10.30pm. Open until 10.45pm the weekend. Booking advised. Menu from €17.50 to €36.50. À la carte: Around €35 (starter + main course + dessert). Wine by the glass. Originality of the day from €11.50. Chèque Restaurant. Groups welcome (by reservation). Terrace. Take-away.

This Italian restaurant in the Neopolitan corner is, since a long time, very popular for the people living in Nice. The meats, fish, starters on the menu are prepared with transalpine accents: Trancio of swordfish a la plancha, Tagliata of mid-cooked red tuna on seasonal greenery and lime emulsion, Scialatielli with eggplants, provalo & pecorino, Spaghettata of the fishermen, Veal Saltimbocca alla Romana, crunchy Sfogliatella in profiteroles... Fresh fish arrives every day. The setting is elegant as the paintings and decorative objects awaken the spirit of Italian restaurants with the welcoming bar, the arches of the dining room and the frescoes paying tribute to Amalfitan sceneries. The wine list makes you discover the Italian PDOs: Vermentino di Sardegna La Cala, red Montepulciano d'Abruzzo, Costa d'Amalfi "Selva Delle monache", Cantine Sammaro. Meals for groups can be organised on request in this atmosphere dedicated to southern Italy and a few tables in the sun extend the charm of the place outside during summer.

BANTHAÏ SEA FOOD
Old Nice
9, rue Pairolière ✆ +33 (0)9 72 81 81 23

Open all year. Closed on Monday. Booking advised. À la carte: Around €30. All starters at €12. All fish at €18.

A new gourmet address has opened in the middle of Old Nice: Banthaï Sea Food. It is the younger sister of Banthaï, a thai restaurant nestled a few steps away. Welcome in the temple of the culinary delights of the Land of Smile. The decoration is resolutely zen with a kitchen open on the main room and a vaulted room in the basement. Some Buddhas quietly watch over the spot... The name of the establishment is evocative because here, fish and seafood are the kings of the dish. They are declined depending on the arrivals: everything is fresh except the shrimps from Asia. Squids, shrimps, crabs and fish are thus cooked by real Thai chefs, originating from Bangkok. The result? A true explosion of flavours in your dish! The spices arrive directly from Thailand, the sauces are made with sesame and tamarin, the steaming is done in a true steam oven... The lovers of thai cuisine will be satisfied with the excellent Tom Yum Kong soup with spices and shrimps. And in order to not forget our vegan friends, the menu offers a panoply of suggestions of vegetarian dishes. We like this high-quality restaurant which will certainly make some people happy among them the thai cuisine lovers. An exceptional value for money and an affordable prices. Warm and professional welcome from Stéphane and Sophie, and their small team. To discover without delay!

LE BARBECUE
Old Nice
3, rue du Four
✆ +33 (0)4 93 53 02 59

Open all year. Closed 2 weeks in February (ask for information). Closed on Tuesday. From 11.45am to 2.15pm and from 6.45pm to 10.15pm. Booking advised. À la carte: Around €24 (starter + main course + dessert). Wine by the glass. Lunch menus and evening: €13.50 (starter, main course, coffee); €17.50 (starter, main course, dessert); €19.50 (starter, main course, dessert, glass of wine). Daily special from €8.50. Checks are not accepted. Chèque Restaurant. Groups welcome (up to 50 people). Terrace.

Fany and Manu who exude conviviality and generosity welcome you in their charming hotel located in a colourful narrow street in the old city of Nice. The menu showcases Portuguese cuisine whose flavours mix sometimes, with delicacy, with the local cuisine. The dishes are copious like traditional homemade cod accras, grilled meats, flambéed prawns, sardine with coarse salt, pork spare ribs, clams in Provençal way, beef skewers, smoked sausages or cod steak grilled in aioli way. As for the desserts, let yourself be tempted by the pasteis de nata, delicious small Portuguese cakes, by the tart minute cooked with honey and cinnamon or by serradoura, a small tiramisu with Portuguese biscuit. A charming and pleasant meal break that can be enjoyed on the terrace as well as in the small room with traditional decoration.

LE BAR DES OISEAUX
Old Nice
6, rue de l'Abbaye
✆ +33 (0)4 93 80 21 93

♿

Open all year. Open from 11.30am to 2.30pm and from 6.30pm to 10.30pm. Booking advised. À la carte: Around €22. Menu €20 for lunch.

Le Bar des Oiseaux is the must of the historic city where we like to come (back). The menu offers daily revisited seasonal dishes, written on a large blackboard on the entrance. Seated in the dining room, you can look at the team in the kitchen preparing with passion and dexterity the dishes with delicate flavours: pollack marinated with lime, mashed sweet potatoes and avocadoes, red onions or mackerel bourride, pollacks, squids, shells and ink juice. As for dessert, try the must-eat rum baba, a wonder! We also love the smiling, very friendly and professional team in room and in cuisine as well.

LA BARQUE BLEUE
Port
7, quai des Deux-Emmanuels
✆ +33 (0)4 93 55 39 74
Tram: Garibaldi stop

Open all year. From 12pm to 2.30pm and from 7pm to 11.30pm on weekdays. From 12pm to midnight Friday and from 7pm to midnight Saturday. À la carte: Around €25 (main course and dessert). Menu at €26 (starter + main course + dessert). Chèque Restaurant. Terrace. Air conditioning.

Since 1982, this restaurant firmly moored at Nice harbour celebrates fresh fish cooked in all its forms: roasted, in curlpapers, with sauces... You can also enjoy dishes with an Italian consonance like in particular the famous minute cooked pasta with the sauce you choose. A real delight, at table on the terrace with a stunning view on the port, the pointus and coloured facades or in the charming blue room with wooden shelves furnished with grocery products.

LE BISTROT D'ANTOINE
Old Nice
27, rue de la Préfecture
✆ +33 (0)4 93 85 29 57

♿

Open Tuesday to Saturday from 12pm to 2pm and from 7pm to 10pm. Booking advised. À la carte: Around €26 (starter + main course + dessert). Wine by the glass. Checks are not accepted. Terrace.

The unmissable nicoise address by excellence, where we love to (Re) come. The team of Armand Crespo welcomes you with a smile and an exemplary professionalism. The Chef offers a traditional cuisine with dishes like sautéed squid, chicory spaghetti, chorizo, citrus sauce, roasted nuts of St Jacques with seasonal vegetables or rum baba delicately and meticulously prepared by Armand himself. We strongly advise you to book, regulars and tourists rush there!

LE BISTROT DU GILLOU
City Center – 30, rue Alberti
✆ +33 (0)4 93 76 84 97

Open all year. Fixed rate formula: €18 (starter and main course or main course and dessert). Starter from €6. Main course from €13. Desserts from €5.

The chef's cuisine is friendly and seasonal: toasted slices of black pudding on onion jam; creme brulee with ceps and soy; toasted slices of bread with goat cheese and honey on a spinach and endives bed; bœuf bourguignon; sausages of Morteau Label Rouge and lentils; sea-bream fillet poelee sweet mashed potatoes and carrot juice... The room is small but cordial just like the nice dishes. The service is friendly and in good mood.

LE BISTROT DE JENNIFER
Old Nice
36, cours Saleya
✆ +33 (0)4 93 80 52 50

Open all year. From 9am to 1am. À la carte: Around €20 (dish). Daily special from €9 to €11.50. Lunch menu from €10.90. Dinner daily menu from €14.90 to €22.90. Happy Hours from 5pm to 8pm. Terrace. Take-away.

In a nice setting with a friendly atmosphere, Le Bistrot de Jennifer is a pleasant place in the heart of the Old Nice. In the cosy dining room or on the beautiful outdoor terrace, you will discover a homemade cuisine prepared by the Chef with Mediterranean and italian influences. Discover the medley of pizzas but also delicious traditional dishes like rigatonis with salmon, courgettes from the market and fresh tomatoes, the revisited goat's cheese dish, ravioli nicoise, scallops tartar, mussels mariniere, chicken tartar or duck breast. Cocktails are as beautiful as good. A nice family address.

LE BISTROT DES VIVIERS
Downtown – 22, rue Alphonse-Karr
✆ +33 (0)4 93 16 00 48
www.les-viviers-nice.fr
viviers.bretons@wanadoo.fr

«Maîtres Cuisiniers» label. Open all year. Closed on Sunday. Open from 12pm to 2pm (last sitting at 2pm) and from 7.30pm to 10pm. Booking advised. Menu from €35 to €70. À la carte: Around €65. (Starter/main course or main course/dessert at €19.50 or starter/main course/dessert at €23.50 excluding drinks (except eve of public holidays and public holidays). Checks are not accepted. American Express, Chèque Restaurant. Groups welcome. Baby chairs. Terrace. Take-away. Le Louvre parking opposite the restaurant.

Here we are at Rolancy's brasserie as the two adjacent restaurants of the Meilleur Ouvrier de France 1996 are divided into the bistro for people in a hurry and the gastronomic restaurant. The lunch formula is unbeatable and this is what makes the success of this extraordinary bistro – it is always full at lunchtime. Jacques Rolancy prepares us an inventive traditional cuisine, with dishes such as chicken, steamed white cabbage and duck foie gras, mixed vegetable or the turbot with Collioure's anchovy grilled with parsley, rosettes of potatoes, onions, tomatoes and basil cooked in the oven in a dish. Note a beautiful wine list that you can taste by the glass. It is an excellent and impeccable address where the welcome is a real pleasure; cordiality, advice and smiles prevail.

LE BISTROT DU PORT
Port – 28, quai Lunel
✆ +33 (0)4 93 55 21 70
www.lebistrotduportdenice.fr
stephanie.leona@wanadoo.fr

Closed Tuesday and Wednesday all day. Open from 12.15pm to 1.45pm and from 7.30pm to 10pm. Booking advised. À la carte: Around €35 (starter + main course + dessert). Lunch menu: €14.50. Terrace.

The cuisine is resolutely dedicated to flavours niçoises and Mediterranean. The chef works with treatment and creativity of the fresh ingredients daily declined with blackboard: pumpkin tatin to the foie gras, carpaccio of Saint-Jacob endives to the tangerine, blinks of fresh cod to the mussels, soup of chestnuts truffles red mullet... As regards desserts, you let allure by a Tartar of pineapple to the caramel Palmito house, a pie black chocolate and raspberries or by a milfoil of pear roasted to the wine of Bellet. Liqueur of tangerine and cream of limoncello house accompany the end by the meals been useful in terrace overlooking with the port or in the clear room whose bays largely open.

LE BISTROT GOURMAND
Old Nice
3, rue Desboutin ✆ +33 (0)4 92 14 55 55
www.lebistrogourmand.fr
bistrotgourmand@live.fr

♿

«Maîtres Cuisiniers de France» label. Closed on Wednesday and Sunday. Open on Monday, Tuesday and Thursday to Saturday from 12pm to 1.45pm and from 7.30pm to 9.45pm. Booking advised. Menu from €23 to €145. À la carte: Around €68 (starter + main course + dessert). Wine by the glass. Menu for lunch €23 (starter and main course or main course and dessert) or €27 (starter + main course + dessert). American Express. Groups welcome (by reservation. €55 per person). Terrace.

The chef David Vaqué and his wife Laurence ensure the service and offer a beautiful facet of gastronomy. The tableware is in tune with the contemporary decor with colourful furniture in a bright dining room. David is constantly looking for new products. We love his well-presented and Mediterranean cuisine especially the rock octopus salad, spring's vegetables and fruits, creamy potato, dried tomatoes vinaigrette, fresh herbs, citrus fruit and white balsamic; the "royal" pigeon or even the «lou capoun» puree and garlic chips, pigeon juice, dried tomatoes and walnut oil. The staff performs high-standard service. Everything is perfect.

LE BISTROY

City Center
37, rue Maréchal Joffre
✆ +33 (0)9 82 47 33 44 / +33 (0)6 62 15 06 87
www.le-bistroy.fr
Le.Bistroy@bbox.fr

Open all year. Monday to Friday from 8am to 3pm. Open for dinner only each Thursday and Friday from 7pm to 10pm. Saturdays from 9am to 2pm exclusively for a brunch buffet. Booking advised. À la carte: Around €20 (main course and dessert). Lunch menu: €15.50 (daily special + choice of desserts + coffee). Set menu except weekend and public holidays: breakfast + breakfast formula. Take-away jars. Checks are not accepted. Chèque Restaurant. Groups welcome (possibility of privatization. Ask for information). Baby chairs. Take-away. Shop. Activities. Take-away wines and sterilized jars.

Two pretty colourful and flowered window boxes set the tone! The Bistroy is nicely and harmoniously decorated with recycled materials in a bright dining room. Bright, just like the chef's cuisine offering a selection of dishes prepared with products from the market. The menu is original and twists the classics like the «outdoor» double egg cocotte, fennel and smoked bacon compote, fromage frais and basil bread fingers. We chose the daily specials: two fillets of sea bass, green olive tapenade and basil on stir fried zucchini, the whole perfectly cooked and at very reasonable prices. You can even concoct a Bistroy meal thanks to a pretty choice of main courses, desserts and drinks to take-away back home.

CAFÉ BRETON

Pedestrian area
1, rue Dalpozzo
✆ +33 (0)9 54 39 83 73
cafebreton06@gmail.com

Open all year. All the week for lunch and dinner. Closed on Tuesday and Sunday for lunch. Breton products. 100% pure salted butter. Organic flours and ciders. Manufacturing 100% artisanal. Crepes from €3 to €11.90. Salads from €10.50 to €11.50.

Who has never dreamt of a delicious Breton crepe? Savoury or sweet, they have a childhood flavour and keep on enchanting us as adults. At Café Breton, a resolutely modern and elegant address, you will appreciate them in all their forms: classical, complete, flambeed, iced or with wheat flour. The scallop galette, with smoked andouille of Guémené, Gattières potatoes, garlic and herbs Bordier butter and Sichuan pepper is very appreciated. As a dessert, choose the homemade baked apples crepe, with Corsican chestnut cream and toasted almonds. The menu also has a part dedicated to the legendary salted butter caramel developed in various ways. Ingredients are of quality, with organic beer and cider. Get ready for an intense gourmet moment!

CAFÉ DES CHINEURS

Port
1, rue Cassini
✆ +33 (0)4 93 89 09 62
cafedeschineurs@gmail.com

Open all year. Every day from 11am to 00.30am. Closed on Sunday. À la carte: Around €20. Tapas from €6. Terrace.

The Café des Chineurs is before all the story of three enthusiasts from Nice who after having travelled throughout the world settled in their birthplace to create this café not like any other... An unusual and new style decoration created by a brilliant architect made of recycled and second-hand furniture. We love the bar, the club chairs or the Formica tables. The large outdoor terrace is a nice spot to enjoy your morning coffee. It must be said that the establishment offers several facets: people come here for a drink, to nibble some tapas, to have lunch on the run or dinner while taking your time. The chef is also a bargain hunter in his way: he leaves every morning to buy the best market ingredients for a simple and fresh cuisine. Tartar, sea plancha, burgers, big salads, pasta... It is good, it is beautifully presented and the bill is reasonable. Add to that a top welcome. Guaranteed result: it is always a pleasure to make a stop there.

LA CAMBUSE

Old Nice
5, cours Saleya
✆ +33 (0)4 93 80 82 40

Open all year. 7 days a week 11am to 11pm. À la carte: Around €34 (starter + main course + dessert). Wine by the glass. Single main course from €13. Groups welcome (by reservation). Terrace.

Here, there are neither large tables nor outdoor plastic furniture but nice small tables with tablecloths, elegantly set in a warm and refined atmosphere. On summer days, the beautiful sunny terrace is full. The menu highlights Nice specialities prepared on the spot with fresh local quality products. Enjoy among others the Nice stuffed vegetables without forgetting the Nice stew, the rack of lamb with rosemary, the prawns and the different dishes of wild fish depending on the catch at the port of Nice, the whole served with homemade side dishes. The life of the market a few meters away will accompany your meal... A real show! The complete wine list offers Provence, Chardonnay and Bordeaux wines to the glass.

CAMPO DI FIORI

Old Nice
18/20, Cours Saleya
✆ +33 (0)4 93 62 16 32
www.campo-di-fiori.com
chezfreddynice@neuf.fr

♿

Open all year. Non stop from 11.30am to midnight. Take-away. Set menu at €17.90 (1 starter + 1 main course or 1 main course + 1 dessert). À la carte: Around €20 (the main course). Wine by the glass. Pizza from €11.90. Full menu: €22.90. American Express, Holiday voucher, Chèque Restaurant. Groups welcome (by reservation. Possible group menus and banquets). Baby chairs. Terrace (heated in winter). WiFi free.

The priviledged location in the centre of Cours Saleya within a short distance from the Mediterranean sea gives to this restaurant a menu with mixed flavours inspired from all corners of the world: sushis, risottos, raviolis, gnocchis, pastas, pizzas, grilled meat and fish, wok dishes, various salads, fajitas or typical dishes from Nice as the pissaladière and the gourmet desserts like the homemade tiramisu. Amateurs of culinary specialities from here and elsewhere can get seated on the terrace (heated in winter) in the heart of animated Old Nice or inside the chic and contemporary restaurant. The meals for groups are served in the private lounges upstairs or on the terrace with a choice of adapted menus.

THE CHANTECLER
37, promenade des Anglais
Le Negresco ✆ +33 (0)4 93 16 64 00
chantecler@lenegresco.com
♿
Open all year. Tuesday to Saturday from 7pm to 10pm. Booking is essential. Menu from €110 to €230. À la carte: Around €150. Wine by the glass. Checks are not accepted. American Express, Diners Club. Groups welcome (up to 20 people in a private room). Terrace. Car valet. Shop.
A very subtle cuisine. Original, true and generous dishes, like red and yellow heirloom tomatoes, burrata with virgin oil, condiments of sucrine, tomato-basil sorbet with roast langoustines with Espelette peppers, crosmesquis of calf's head with arugula leaves or vapor of turbot with seaweed butter, artichokes and new carrots, solférino of seasonal vegetables with chervil or the supreme of Mieral pigeon cooked with green chard and coppa, crusty leg confit in creamy gorgonzola. You prolong the pleasure with a pretty dessert menu. The service, in the great tradition of French gastronomy, is exceptional. The cellar, famous for sheltering 15,000 bottles, will perfectly complete this unforgettable moment without forgetting the decor with the sumptuous wood panelling made in 1751.

LA CLEF D'OR
City Center
2, rue Chauvain
✆ +33 (0)4 93 54 83 18
Open all year for lunch and dinner. Closed on Saturday and Sunday for lunch. Open Monday to Friday from 12pm to 2.30pm and every day from 6.30pm to 0h30. À la carte: Around €28. Wine by the glass. Possible service delivery. Terrace. Activities. Activities for dinner, DJ Saturday.
This address consists of a restaurant and wine bar. The place has a cosy and contemporary decor designed by Steve Baldini: walls made of red bricks, suspended chandeliers, coffer... Some tables on terrace and a little of good trendy music animated by DJ above a wardrobe complete the picture. If the wine list is consistent with more than 80 references that you discover around tapas dishes and boards of Corsican charcuterie, La Clef d'or is also a nice restaurant where you can choose at lunchtime your formula among the daily specials depending on the mood of the chef and product of the market. At dinner time, the dishes listed on the slate are much more prepared as the camembert on oven and its truffle oil, pan-fried scallops, burger with foie gras, prawns with pastis or tuna steak with fresh basil. The dishes are copious and nicely presented. An original address.

CI GUSTA
Republique – 13, avenue de la République
✆ +33 (0)4 92 12 18 10
www.cigusta.com
Open all year. €5.50: 1 hot drink + 1 pastry.
Ci Gusta Nice is a franchized address full of charm which offers Italian artisanal products sweetened and salted selected for their gustatory qualities elaborated with originality. Home-made with a great know-how, discover the pancrocchino – the new version of the traditional pizza – but also the lasagnas cooked in the oven or the focaccino (a roasted Italian sandwich with ciabatta bread furnished with ham, salami, meat, cheese, tomato, a fillet of olive oil of Provence, herbs), a treat! As for the desserts, you'll taste the home made cake with cream, red fruits and banana, the chocolate fondant or the frozen cake... To be noted: Ci Gusta starts serving for breakfast cappucino, café latte, espresso and flavoured Italian café with chocolate, hazelnut, caramel, pistachio or vanilla, the whole accompanied by pastries. We also appreciated the efficient service and the friendly ambiance. An address which will charm the gourmets.

LE COMPTOIR DE MANON
Cessole – 110, boulevard de Cessole
✆ +33 (0)6 66 63 37 85
Open all year. From 8.30am to 7.30pm. Booking advised. Daily special: €8. Breakfast €3.50. Fresh pasta sale from €0.69 the 100 grams. Take-away. Shop.
Comptoir de Manon is a nice address with a warm atmosphere which brings together the lovers of delicacies and flavours all day long with hearty breakfasts, but also with seasonal daily specials: tartiflette, lasagnas, stew polenta or thinly sliced chicken forest sauce with tagliatelle which one can enjoy on the spot or take-away. The most hurried ones will choose a classical panini or a cold sandwich generously furnished. Softnesses go between caramel panna cotta, café or gourmet chocolate with coconut rocks, muffins or cookies, without forgetting the tiramisu. You can also make the pleasure last, by buying raw fresh pasta that you'll prepare at home: tagliatelle, panisses, gnocchis, green pasta, Nice raviolis, raviolis with ceps...

LE CONGRÈS
Downtown
14, boulevard Risso
✆ +33 (0)4 93 56 13 97
stemi6@orange.fr
Open all year. Thursday to Monday included. Services lunchtime and diner. À la carte: Around €25 (starter and main course or main course and dessert, excluding drinks). Groups welcome (on reservation). Terrace. Take-away.
An authenticate and unpretentious address which will make you (Re) discover flavours of the past! The carte honours some specialties of the county of Nice but also of Mediterranean dishes like delicious vegetable donuts, homemade gnocchis, tripe a la niçoise, the astonishing prawns with anise, lasagnas, the classical stew of Provence, raviolis or the beef steak perfectly cooked. The service is pleasant and friendly. As for the atmosphere? It is definitively cordial!

CRÊPERIE BRETONNE CORENTIN
Downtown
3, rue de Russie
✆ +33 (0)4 93 16 02 98
Open all year. For lunch Tuesday to Friday. Open for dinner Wednesday to Saturday from 7pm. Booking advised. À la carte: Around €20 (1 salty crepe + 1 sweet crepe + 1 drink). Jug of Cider.
Once you pass the door of this creperie, you are taken away to Brittany for a very pleasant gourmet escape! It starts with the déco, you, indeed, will be surrounded by traditional objects of yesteryear, old photographs, as well as famous black and white emblematic Breton flag. The travel continues with the carte which presents original or more traditional recipes of salty pancakes with buckwheat flour from the most classical (egg-cheese, egg-ham-cheese, butter) to the most inventive (bacon-mushroom-cream-egg, duck breast and goat cheese blazed with Cognac, three cheeses). You will also find a farandole of delicious sweet crepes: caramel with salted butter, jams, chocolate-banana and specialties mixing flavours and flavors. The service is pleasant and the welcome warm with a good value for money. Smart information: think of booking because, victim of its success, waiting to have a table is sometimes long.

THE DANDY
Petit Marais Niçois
21, rue Bonaparte
✆ +33 (0)4 93 07 07 73
www.ledandy-nice.fr
info@ledandy-nice.fr
Open all year. À la carte: Around €30 (main course and dessert). Daily specials: €14. Terrace. Activities. DJ.
With its elegant and trendy decor with acidulated touches, Le Dandy is *the place to be*! Sitting on the large terrace or in the indoor room, this restaurant declines the atmospheres throughout the day: restaurant, tea room and... "after tea" with wild evenings animated by a DJ. As for the cuisine, the dishes are very fresh and the plates are well presented: raviolis niçois with ricotta and truffles chips, slightly salted aïoli cod and garden vegetables, tapas shrimps hot sauce with Espelette pepper, jar of fresh vegetables and white cheese with chive, pata negra burger and vegetables brick with sesame, lamb wok, eggplant caviar, artichokes, cébettes and socca dentelles... Le Dandy? A deliciously chic address!

CHEZ DAVIA
Golden square
11bis, rue Grimaldi
✆ +33 (0)4 93 87 91 39
Open all year. Tuesday from 7pm to 10pm and Wednesday to Sunday from 12pm to 2pm and from 7pm to 10pm. À la carte: Around €30 (starter + main course + dessert). Children's menu: €10. Fixed rate formula: €22. Chèque Restaurant. Groups welcome (by reservation). Terrace. Spoken English and Italian. Air conditioning.
Since 1953, this family-run establishment treats lovers of Provençal cuisine. Served by a friendly and dynamic team, the homemade dishes are prepared with fresh products from local producers. The dishes are delicious with the restaurant's specialities: fresh cod, coq au vin, bouillabaisse, sirloin with pepper... A delight! A great address.

LES DEUX CANAILLES
Downtown – 6, rue Chauvain
✆ +33 (0)9 53 83 91 99
www.lesdeuxcanailles.com
restaurant@lesdeuxcanailles.com
Open all year. Open Monday to Saturday, closed Sunday and Saturday for lunch. Booking advised. Menu from €23 to €68. À la carte: Around €60. Wine by the glass. American Express, Chèque Restaurant. Groups welcome.
Creations that delight the tastebuds and the eyes: pan-fried foie gras from the Gers, risotto with gorgonzola gravy in Madeira way, venison pie cocoa sauce and vegetables poached in a minute, fine turnips salad with candied ginger, bluefin tuna carpaccio, fennel salad with lemon, eggplants marinated with dashi, Japanese wagyu beef steak walnut... In total, harmony with the chef's cuisine, also we should mention the excellent service of the sommelier who brings us to the discovery of new wines that she chooses with passion and the head waiter who ensures a pleasant and attentive service.

AUX DEUX CHEFS
Liberation
56, rue Dabray
✆ +33 (0)4 93 52 56 50
www.auxdeuxchefs.e-monsite.com
aux2chefs@hotmail.fr
♿
Open all year. Monday to Wednesday from 11am to 3.30pm. Thursday to Saturday from 11am to 3.30pm and from 7pm to 10.30pm. Closed Sunday and public holidays. Booking advised. À la carte: Around €35 (starter + main course + dessert). Daily special: €9.90. Wine by the glass. Checks are not accepted. Chèque Restaurant. Groups welcome (realization of personalized menus). Baby chairs. Take-away.
Wooden chairs, red and white checkered tablecloths, of old cookbooks and copper pans hanging on the walls bring you in the bistro of yesteryear. In this beautiful traditional niçoise restaurant, the cuisine is lived: you can talk about it, you can see it, you can breathe it and you can taste it, of course! Discover the menu: the roustida nissart, a toasted slice of bread in the niçoise way, large the merenda which will delight the big appetites or which could be shared, the roasted tuna steak and its caponata, the mignon filet of pork roasted with herbs from the garden. As for the sweet, enjoy the homemade soup of strawberries and sorbet basil or the unmissable triple chocolate mousse. An address with the family atmosphere which is full of generosity, a friendly, courteous and efficient service, original dishes that respect the seasonal products and homemade from the starter to the dessert. Go quickly at this address for a meal with friends, a business dinner, a birthday or a wedding.

L'EMPIRE
City Center – 54, boulevard Jean Jaurès
✆ +33 (0)4 93 01 30 40
www.empire-nice.com
contact@empire-nice.com

«Maître Restaurateur» label. Open all year. Tuesday to Sunday from 12pm to 2.30pm and from 7.30pm to 10.30pm; Sunday from 10.30am to 3pm. Menu from €18.50 to €68. À la carte: Around €48 (starter + main course + dessert). The Big Brunch at €23 only Sunday from 10am to 3pm.

This establishment has a modern decor and a refined cuisine. You can enjoy various types of fish from the catch of the day deliciously prepared by the chef: fried fillets of red mullets and sautéed chanterelles, roasted cod loin with hazelnut butter, lobster celery and currants. Try the excellent fillet of simmental beef roasted with bacon, mashed potatoes, frozen beets and Roman cauliflowers. Every Sunday lunch, the restaurant also prepares hearty *brunchs* with delicious homemade pastries to enjoy facing the Coulée Verte.

FARINELLI
39, rue Beaumont ✆ +33 (0)9 81 04 86 47
contact@lefarinelli.com

Open all year from 9am to 11pm. À la carte: Around €20 dish. Terrace. Possible privatization of the restaurant on request for your private events (birthday, wedding…). Children's menu €12.

Discover an authentic italian cuisine! The dishes are generous and reflect the good mood atmosphere of this establishment. The dishes all are prepared with fresh ingredients rigorously selected by the Chef. The carte changes according to the seasons. Taste as starter the gran beef smoked and marinated carpaccio, the mozzarella di bufala and riviera tomatoes or the warm octopus and potatoes pie on a bed of tapenade. A large choice of pasta and risottos: penne arrabbiate with three tomatos, Milanese risotto according to the original recipe of Giuseppe, risotto with squid ink juice, mussels and clams without forgetting the spaghettoni with poutargue (mule eggs) served on a bed of cream, between others. Meats and fish supplement this, already so appetizing carte: fish soup cacciucco of Tuscany, roasted tuna slice with white and black sesame crust with sauce salmoriglio, beef steak Café de Paris way and loin of lamb with tuna rillettes. Vegan lovers will also find happiness with seasonal vegetable dishes, tofu and fruits. We also liked the reception and the very cordial service.

LA FEMME DU BOULANGER
3, rue du Commandant-Raffali
✆ +33 (0)4 89 03 43 03
♿

Open all year. Every day from 11.30am to 2.30pm and from 6.30pm to 11pm. Wine by the glass. Poilâne toasted slices of bread. Dishes from €13. Groups welcome (by reservation). Terrace. WiFi.

Attentive welcome and fancy decoration in the vast and elegant indoor dining room or on the pleasant terrace… The decor of this charming address pays tribute to the cinema and Pagnol! The dishes are generous and the homemade dishes follow the seasons. Do not forget to taste the slices of bread Poilânes cooked with wood fire that come in all their flavours: with goat's cheese, with flower honey with pear comfit with spices and salad of mesclun; with Morteau sausage of Franche-Comté on a bed of potato gratin with morbier and his salad of mesclun; with chopped fresh steamed vegetables, gratin with feta… Without forgetting the delicious dishes such as veal stew in the old way accompanied by its rice and curry, beef lasagnes from the Chef, to the moussaka accompanied by salad or steamed potatoes, duck and foie gras. You can have breakfast or brunch. A gourmet address to discover urgently!

FINE GUEULE
Vieux-Nice – 2, rue de l'hôtel de Ville
✆ +33 (0)4 93 80 21 64
contact@finegueule.fr

Open all year. Monday to Saturday from 7pm to 10pm; Tuesday to Saturday from 12pm to 2pm. Booking advised. À la carte: Around €35. Daily special around €13 - €14. Checks are not accepted. Chèque Restaurant. Groups welcome. Terrace.

"Because who is a gourmet has nozzle, muzzle, nose… As a fine gourmet, he knows what is good and can not do without. It is a small amount of Audiard, powdered with rabble and slang of which we wanted to make a name. Moreover, if you are a gourmet, play fine: eat here…". You are welcomed with a smile while the service is very attentive. The Chef offers traditional and sought-after cuisine prepared with fresh ingredients. The menu consists of a dozen starters and many dishes and desserts. You can enjoy the cold ox tongue with gribiche sauce, burnt fresh tuna, eggplant caviar, stew beef cheek with its creamy polenta or salmon tartare, organic apple green and bulgur with herbs. As for the desserts, it will be a Valhrona 70% chocolate mousse or the Breton puck, exotic cream lime and fruit, among others. An address to (re) discover in the warm and bright dining room or on the terrace facing the Town hall.

LE FONÉTIC
Cessole – 107, boulevard de Cessole
✆ +33 (0)4 92 07 04 71 / +33 (0)6 22 74 23 18 / +33 (0)6 14 21 19 06
www.lefonetic.com

Open all year. Closed on Sunday. Open for lunch and dinner. À la carte: Around €25 (starter + main course + dessert). Daily special: €14. Terrace.

Fonétic has a warm and friendly atmosphere where humour is king. In this charming neighbourhood restaurant, the carte offers simple and tasty dishes: supion on a nest of Taglioni with ink juice, a beautiful variation of salads (niçoise, hot goat cheese, Italian, Caesar, etc), Simmental beef steak, plate of cheeses, pork spareribs and tomato sauce with sautéed potatoes, fresh salmon and homemade risotto. An delicious address for your tastebuds. The dinner ends with a selfie (the owner lends you his tablet) which will join the gallery of the restaurant on its website. The Fonétic? A restaurant not like the others and worth the detour!

CHEZ FREDDY
Old Nice
22, cours Saleya
✆ +33 (0)4 93 85 49 99
www.chezfreddy.fr
chezfreddynice@neuf.fr
♿

Open all year. Every day from 11.45am to 11.30pm. Service uninterrupted. Booking advised. Menu around €26.90. Children's menu: €12.90. Daily special: €15.90. Giant salads from €16.90. Pizza from €11.90. Seafood platter from €23.90. American Express, Holiday voucher, Chèque Restaurant. Groups welcome (up to 330 people and 300 extra at the Campo di Fiori restaurant. Possible group menus or banquet). Terrace. Take-away. Free Wifi.

Passionate about cooking, Freddy opened his first restaurant in 1987 after numerous apprenticeships with the «great chefs». This inhabitants of Nice specialised in aïoli and paella that he inherits from his family. Since then, his eponymous restaurant has become an instituton on the Cours Saleya in the middle of the old Nice. We find on the menu many kinds of aïoli, many types of paella directly served at table in typical plates, the unmissable bouillabaisse, the seafood spaghettis as well the daily catch of seafood from Oleron Island, meats, salads and pastas. The originality of the copious dishes, the quality of the taste and the presentation make the difference. We love the service, polite and efficient, and the ambiance with musical background.

LE FROG
Old Nice
3, rue Milton-Robbins
✆ +33 (0)4 93 85 85 65 / +33 (0)6 20 44 26 40
www.restaurantgroupesnice.fr
restaurantlefrog@orange.fr
♿

Closed from November 16th to December 10th. Open every day from 12pm to 2.30pm and from 7pm to 11pm. Booking advised. À la carte: Around €46 (starter + main course + dessert). Children's menu: €8. Wine by the glass. For lunch express formula €13: daily special + glass of wine + coffee. Lunch menu €15: starter and main course or main course and dessert chosen in the menu of the market. Lunch and dinner, menu of the market €27: starter + main course + dessert. Menu niçois €20. American Express, Chèque Restaurant. Groups welcome. Baby chairs. Terrace. Take-away. Activities.

In a very quiet small alley within walking distance of the Nice Opera House, the team of the Frog warmly awaits you. The service is attentive while the colourful decoration corroborates the atmosphere. The cuisine and the dishes have beautiful surprises in store that are worthy of master chefs' cuisine! As for the eye, we are already regaled by the harmonious dishes while our taste buds tremble with the successful combination of flavours. We enjoy thus the unmissable frog legs, a snail or homemade tapas assortment, petits farcis niçois or even a crispy warm goat cheese... The chef also puts forward sea specialties with for instance the fishes mix grill or the grilled salmon fillet and its sauce vierge. Meat lovers will choose a thyme and honey duck breast or even a splendid beef tenderloin in Rossini's way. On the terrace or in the beautiful indoor room, the Frog will delight you.

LE GAGLIO
Old Nice – 2, place Saint-François
✆ +33 (0)4 93 85 42 13
www.restaurantgaglio.com
restaurantgaglio@live.fr
♿

«Maître Restaurateur» label. Open all year. Every day from 8am to midnight. Service from 12pm to 2.30pm and from 7pm to 11pm. Booking advised. À la carte: Around €30 (starter + main course + dessert). Lunch menu: €15.50 (starter and main course or main course and dessert). Wine by the glass. Starters from €9, pasta from €17, main courses from €14. American Express, Holiday voucher. Groups welcome (by reservation). Terrace.

Worthy of the greatest parisian brasseries, Le Gaglio has retained the name and the façade of the ancient jewellery where it settled. Ideally located at the entrance of the place Saint-François in the old town, this elegant hotel faces the gardens of the Promenade du Paillon. Its large sunny terrace is the ideal place in the early hours of the morning to have a generous breakfast. On two floors, the elegant dining room reveals powdered colours and chandeliers with pampilles. The cuisine is Mediterranean and reveals nice fresh ingredients: parsley veal liver, mussels marinière, roasted sea bass, risotto with almonds or skate fillet with capers. Also note the various plates of Corsican charcuteries and cheeses, and the Nice tapas to enjoy at the aperitif. A nice gourmet address.

LES GARÇONS (RELAX, EAT, ENJOY)
Old Nice
3, rue Centrale
✆ +33 (0)4 93 80 87 90
www.restaurant-lesgarcons.fr
restaurant.lesgarcons.nice@gmail.com

Open all year Tuesday to Sunday from 7.30pm to 11pm. Price à la carte: €27 (starter + main course + dessert). Wine by the glass. WiFi free. Possibility of privatizing the places. Booking required: first service at 8pm, second from 10pm.

In a very trendy atmosphere, the place offers two styles: on the ground floor, the restaurant displays an industrial furniture where metal blends with red bricks and in the basement, you have a sit in comfortable armchairs to enjoy a drink with friends in a stunning vaulted cellar with exposed stone walls. Les Garçons offers modern French cuisine made with fresh local produce of the terroir, taken from local producers: Italian *burrata* and beefsteak tomatoes on toast of countryside, foie gras terrine with Espelette pepper accompanied by black cherry chutney, burger César *by* Les Garçons and roasted potatoes, creamy risotto with prawns. Gourmets will appreciate the dessert tiramisu *by Manu* or the lemon meringue pie. *Relax, Eat, Enjoy*! Beware, booking is mandatory.

LA GAITÉ NALLINO
Cimiez
72, avenue Cap-de-Croix
✆ +33 (0)4 93 81 91 86

Open all year. Annual closing in August. Closed every Sunday of the year. À la carte: Around €20. Chèque Restaurant. Label Nissarde Kitchen. Terrace. Free Wifi. Pets allowed. Accessibility stroller.

The chef honors the regional nicois products! This neighbourhood restaurant with an authentic charm, since several generations, holds the label Nissarde Cuisine. Stuffed vegetables, salad niçoise, sweet peppers with oil, manjuca plate, gnocchis, onion tart, raviolis, tourta of blea... Tasty and typical recipes of the county of Nice enjoyed in a bright dining room or on the pleasant private terrace. We liked the kindness and the effectiveness of the team which contributes to make this place a little paradise on the hills of Nice.

LE GESÙ
Old Nice
1, place Jésus
✆ +33 (0)4 93 62 26 46

Open all year. Closed from mid-December to mid-January. Open Monday to Saturday from 12pm to 2pm and from 7pm to 11pm. À la carte: Around €27 (starter + main course + dessert). Daily special: €12.50. Groups welcome (by reservation). WiFi. Terrace of 45 places covered and heated in winter.

This emblematic establishment is a real institution in the Old Town of Nice. For over 20 years, the Gesù offers Nice specialities as well as a wide range of pizzas. The owners use their know-how and experience to satisfy you at the highest point and offer you an excellent value for money. Due to its reputation and its affluence, you may sometimes have to have an aperitif on the steps of the neighbouring church while waiting for a table: such also is the conviviality!

LE GRAND BALCON
Old Nice
10, rue Saint-François-de-Paule
✆ +33 (0)4 93 62 60 74
www.legrandbalcon.net
karine@legrandbalcon.net

♿

«Maître Restaurateur» label. Open all year. Except on December 25th. Open 7 days a week day for lunch and dinner. Booking advised. À la carte: Around €65. Wine by the glass. Checks are not accepted. Groups welcome. Terrace. Valet. Activities.

Refinement is not a vain word here, whether for the gastronomy, the decoration or the service! When you step in, you enter the Rembrandt space with numerous paintings that pay tribute to the famous master. Meanwhile, the library in the backroom shares its secrets ... The ideal place for a romantic meal.As for the food, the chef offers a cuisine with seasonal products: the riquette with black truffles chips, the fresh spaghettis with gambas, Alaska king crab tartar with pineapple and mango, gilthead sea bream with acid tangerines and pumpkin cake, sea bass fillet and purple artichokes fricassée, grilled gambas with eggplant mousse with dried tomatoes or duck breast with ceps and foie gras creamy soup. Also a very beautiful outdoor terrace opened in summer and in winter.

HANGOÛT
Old Nice
5, rue du Moulin
✆ +33 (0)4 22 16 99 26
www.hangout-nice.com
hangout@sfr.fr

Open all year. Tuesday to Sunday from 7pm to 10pm. Booking advised. Wine by the glass. Starters from €8.50. Dishes from €13.50 (fish depending on arrival of the moment). Desserts from €6.50. Checks are not accepted. Groups welcome. Terrace.

With its cuisine that looks out into the room with a refined decor, the chef prepares under your eyes and at the minute elaborate Japanese dishes with fresh and seasonal ingredients. The traditional recipes are revisited while the cooking of the meats and fish are perfectly controlled: pork cheek braised with sausage, chorizo and sauce with cider, fish of the day (according to the arrival of the market), pan-fried or in risotto... As for the desserts, the chef prepares himself his ice-creams and sorbets; he also highlights a cheesecake with very delicious exotic fruits. A vegetarian version of the à la carte menu is also available upon request. A smart nice address!

INFLUENCE
Petit Nice Marais
31, rue Bonaparte
✆ +33 (0)9 82 57 39 66
www.influence-nice.fr
influence06300@gmail.com

Open all year. For lunch from 12pm to 2.30pm Monday to Saturday. For dinner from 7pm to 10.30pm Wednesday to Saturday. À la carte: Around €30 (starter + main course + dessert). Fixed rate formula starter and main course: €17.

This is an excellent restaurant managed by a inhabitant of Nice Aurèle Gasperoni. You should know that this young and talented chef has followed a formation at the Institute Paul Bocuse, followed by experiences at Le Doyen ***in Paris, L'Auberge Basque *, at Charles Semeria in Beaulieu-sur-Mer, then by the side of the best blue-collar worker of France, the chef Eric Trochon. Attached to his hometown, it is in Nice that Aurèle decides to settle and to open his own restaurant, a place which enables him to make us discover his cuisine, result of influences from here and elsewhere. All is homemade, with the market products: Tartar of salmon with Korean sauce and a crunchy biscuit of fennel, zucchinis of the country and ricotta, mousse with rosemary, zucchini flower donut, hake with hazelnut butter, raw and cooked fennels, risotto of small German wheat with mushrooms, veal with peas and artichokes... The dishes are generous, the reception is quite as perfect, and the desserts hearty and gourmet! A brilliant address where rigour and know-how combine with wonder culinary techniques.

LE KOUDOU

28, promenade des Anglais
✆ +33 (0)4 93 87 33 74
www.koudou-restaurant.com
koudou@koudou-restaurant.com

«Maître Restaurateur» label. Open all year. Every day except on December 24th. From 12pm to 2.30pm and from 6.30pm to 10.30pm. Booking advised. À la carte: Around €50. Children's menu: €13. Lunch menu: €19.50 (except Sunday and public holidays). Wine by the glass. Menu Promenade at €39. Big Degustation menu €62. Groups welcome (capacity: 150 People). Terrace. Take-away. Masséna public parking at 10 Mr.

Set on the Promenade des Anglais with a sunny terrace and interior rooms in a colonial atmosphere, this brasserie displays a cuisine with regional seasonal products and fresh fish. Some specialties of the house? Olive wood smoked salmon of Label Rouge, homemade foie gras with Sauternes, beautiful rib roast, wild Mediterranean sea bass in a salt crust (for two people), sautéed prawns with persilade, frito-misto from the sea and its tartar sauce, scallops with caramelised pineapples... And to finish on a sweet note: rum baba gratined with champagne sabayon or the fondant chocolate Valrhona, a delight... The service is professional and friendly. An attractive address ongoing for years.

LA LANGOUSTE

Downtown – 7, avenue Georges-Clemenceau
✆ +33 (0)4 93 88 79 23
www.lalangouste.fr
contact@lalangouste.fr

Open all year. Every day from 12pm to 2.30pm and from 7pm to 10.30pm except Sunday. À la carte: Around €55. Menu at €19 including 1 starter + 1 main course or 1 main course + 1 dessert or menu at €24 including 1 starter + 1 main course + 1 dessert.

In a beautiful refined green setting in the heart of Nice, La Langouste welcomes you with its shaded huge garden of 170 m^2 and its two rooms separated by large bay windows. On the programme: fine tart of vegetables from Nice country just candied, lettuce shoots and crisp parmesan; duck fillet stuffed under the skin with olives taggiasche flavours and seasonal vegetables; rack of lamb just grilled, fricassee of vegetables and olives taggiasche; fillet of Charolais beef, mashed potatoes; linguine alle vongole; Mediterranean sea bass baked in foil with basil flavours... Meals can end among others with the half-sphere of white chocolate, red fruits and basil sorbet or baba passionately... An address where the products are enhanced by the chef Patrice Lafon and where lobster is queen in its beautiful fish pond.

LE COMPTOIR

City Center
5, rue Miron
✆ +33 (0)4 93 92 55 94 / +33 (0)6 63 42 12 75
traiteur@le-comptoir-traiteur.fr

Opened Monday to Saturday from 9am to 7pm. Saturdays from 9am to 1pm. Closed on Sunday. Organic Restaurant Certified Ecocert category 2. Formulas 100% Organic. Gluten-free specialties, without Lactose and eggs.

The Comptoir prepares gourmet dishes certified organic by Ecocert category 2, and those intolerant to gluten and lactose will find delicious dishes and desserts: seafood risotto, cod fillet virgin sauce, niçoise stew, casserole of Malaysian chicken and zucchini gratin, lasagne, nicois stuffed vegetables, ratatouille, aioli, minestrone, vegan gratin or trout with almonds... In the afternoon, you will also have the opportunity to enjoy a tea accompanied by a rice pudding with salted butter caramel or raspberry, by stewed apples and cinnamon, crème caramel, a red fruit gratin, chocolate mousse or with a delicious piece of hazelnut cake. An address delightfully healthy.

JAN

Old Nice
12, rue Lascaris
✆ +33 (0)4 97 19 32 23
www.restaurantjan.com
jh@restaurantjan.com

Closed one week with Christmas. 1 Michelin star. Open for dinner Tuesday to Saturday from 6.30pm to 11pm (last order at 10pm) and Friday to lunch from 12pm to 2.30pm. Booking advised. From €30 to €144 for lunch. From €79 to €144 in the evening. American Express. Groups welcome (up to 30 people).

Jan Hendrik, a South African native, has opened his restaurant under his name which reveals a French contemporary cuisine with a touch of South African savours. Elegance blends gracefully with chic, from the navy facade outside to a beautiful stone wall inside going through the tableware to the service. Everything rhymes with refinement. Le Chef offers a gourmet menu with seasonal colours, modern French cuisine inspired by the markets of the South of France, a high-quality cuisine as we like. The bread is homemade. In summer, you can enjoy a vegetable garden on a bed of walnut, marshmallow with carrots, marinated vegetables, grilled sea bass, tomato salsa, roast tomatoes, stock of smoked tomatoes and tapioca of curry, or a stuffed guinea fowl, tart with mushrooms, confit of guinea fowl, marinated and sautéed wild mushrooms, juice of tea with red fruits. For dessert, the Parfait with Malibu, chocolate cake, orange sorbet, orange jelly and toasted meringue are simply delicious. A good address for new gourmet discoveries.

THE ESCALINADA

Old Nice – 22, rue Pairolière
✆ +33 (0)4 93 62 11 71
www.escalinada.fr
restaurant-lescalinada@wanadoo.fr

Open all year. 7 days a week for lunch and dinner. Set menu at €26. Credit card not accepted. Groups welcome (up to 30 people by reservation). Terrace. Label Nissarde Kitchen.

L'Escalinada is the ideal address to taste and enjoy homemade local dishes! You will be accommodated on the lovely terrace, in the small room with exposed beams with an intimate atmosphere with wooden tables or, some staircases higher, in another lovely dining area especially designed for groups. Discover the cannellonis, lasagnas, stuffed squids or the famous supions a la niçoise. As dessert, try the creme brulee or the delicious tarte tatin.

L'ESSENCIEL RESTAURANT

City Centre
50, boulevard Victor-Hugo
✆ +33 (0)4 93 16 41 00
www.splendid-nice.com
info@splendid-nice.com

Open all year round. Open every day. Restaurant from 11am to 2pm and from 7pm to 10pm. Booking recommended. Menus from €22 to €29. A la carte: around €45 (starter, main course and dessert). Lunch menu: €14. Wine by the glass. American express, Diners Club, Holiday voucher, Meal voucher. Groups welcome (upon reservation). Baby chairs. Valet parking service. Panoramic terrace.

L'EssenCiel turns a new page in its history and moves upmarket this year. The chef qualifies his cooking as "gourmet" and his key word is offering pleasure to his clients. Your three senses are awakened: sight, with a beautifully decorated dish, taste, solliciting your gourmet side and smell thanks to the sweet fragrance emanating. No complicated recipes, nor ostentatious luxury here! The cooking is refined, of course, but ingredients remain central, the chef is simply there to sublimate them, and add his personal signature. Niçois food rules the dishes. The menu changes according to theseasons and the inspirtion of the day. This is the new orientation of this Niçois restaurant which also wants to add a noble touch to the pleasure of the art of the table. A new catering manager completes the chef's experience. She makes a point of restoring the elegance of the service, favouring an outstanding welcome. Add an exceptional 360° view over the Promenade des Anglais, over the Alpine peaks, the monuments of the city and the sea, as well as the refined and modern setting. Here is a restaurant where all the conditions to ensure the happiness of the clients meet. As for the Lounge Bar, annual festivities are also celebrated (Valentine's Day, Mother's Day, Father's Day…). You will no doubt find an occasion to come tread the boards of the rooftop terrace!

LE LODGE

Carré d'Or
14, rue Halévy
✆ +33 (0)4 93 88 41 89 / +33 (0)6 15 65 48 38
www.lelodgerestaurant.com
lelodge06@gmail.com

♿

Open all year. Daily for lunch and dinner, Sunday included. Non-stop service from 12pm to 11pm. Booking advised. À la carte: Around €30 (starter + main course + dessert). Children's menu: €9.50. Fixed rate formula: €23 (starter + main course + dessert). Starter from €11. Large salads from €13.50. Pizzas from €9.50. Checks are not accepted. American Express, Holiday voucher, Chèque Restaurant. Groups welcome. Terrace. Activities. Musicians from April to October Friday for dinner.

A comely setting, an external room open on a beautiful terrace in the middle of a sympathetic pedestrian street and a carte with French and Mediterranean flavours. The choice is varied: duck breast of the Southwest, risotto, pizzas, fresh salmon in pastry case, among others. During the fine days, the place is sunny. Every Friday, appreciate the musical evening as from 7pm. Le Lodge is undoubtedly an excellent address, where the price/quantity/quality ratio is unbeatable in the neighbourhood.

LOU BISTROT NISSART

Acropolis
26, boulevard de Risso
✆ +33 (0)4 22 16 25 81

Open all year. From 11am to 11pm nonstop. Closed Wednesday for dinner and Sunday. Service from 11.45am to 2pm and from 6.45pm to 10.30pm. Booking advised. À la carte: Around €28 (starter + main course + dessert). Lunch menu: €17 (starter and main course or main course and dessert). Chèque Restaurant. Groups welcome (up to 35 people). Terrace. Retransmission of games of Ogc Nice. Evening with a guitarist Friday per month (by reservation). Label Nissarde Kitchen.

Lou Bistrot Nissart is undoubtedly a reference in local cuisine. Come and enjoy homemade Nice traditional dishes in a folkloric decor with ancient photos, posters of the Carnival, shirts and flags of the «Gym». On the menu, you can find the classics of the nicoise cuisine, the famous stew, raviolis, pissaladière, Nice salad... and for the more adventurous, the Nice-style tripe, the calf's head with tongue or the breaded mutton testicles! The portions are generous, to enjoy with Bière du Comté, brewed and bottled in Saint-Martin-Vésubie. For dessert, the famous chard pie is honoured and the pear and rum cake allows you to finish your meal on a sweet and pleasant touch. Labelled «cuisine nissarte» in 2014, this establishment is a real favourite!

MAÏDO

Centre ville
29, rue Tonduti-de-l'Escarène
✆ +33 (0)4 93 87 97 28
www.restaurant-maido.fr

Open all year. Tuesday to Friday from 12pm to 3pm and from 7.30pm to midnight; Saturday from 6pm to midnight; Sunday from 6pm to 10pm. Lunch menu: €12 (range of starters + daily special). Tapas from €5 to €10. Dish: €12. Wine by the glass: €4. Terrace.

Seated behind a large central bar, or on a quiet terrace at the back, here is a very charming *izakaya* (translated as Japanese bistro) that offers a discovery of a very nice selection of natural and organic wines while enjoying Japanese tapas and other homemade dishes, prepared with fresh market products: marinated raw fish soy sauce, Japanese omelette, Beef tataki, Japanese pot au feu, tempura of camembert, duck breast in yakitori style with teryaki sauce... So, it is here that work together in a colourful and warm atmosphere, the very pleasant Kanako – sommelier and Japanese chef – and her companion who has lived with her in the land of the rising sun. A good address for lovers of Asian cuisine and culinary innovations.

LA MAISON DE MARIE

Pedestrian area
5, rue Massena
✆ +33 (0)4 93 82 15 93
www.lamaisondemarie.com
lamaisondemarie@wanadoo.fr

«Maître Restaurateur» label. Open all year. Every day from 12pm to 2.30pm and from 7pm to 11pm. Booking advised. À la carte: Around €25 (main course and dessert). Children's menu: €12.50. Lunch menu: €15.50 (starter and main course or main course and dessert). Wine by the glass. Menu Niçois: €23.50 (starter + main course + dessert). Garden. Terrace.

There is a place out of time at the beginning of the pedestrian area. After crossing the porch with red walls, the paved floor and the flowered patio, you end up in this peace haven, a must of Mediterranean cuisine. You will enjoy the excellent fish tartar as starter, the famous stuffed vegetables of Nice, the mushrooms and artichoke salad, the crispy socca or the stuffed beef fillet with truffle sauce. We also recommend trying the rack of lamb or the fisherman's stew. A pastry chef also offers delicious sweet desserts. It is a restaurant to be remembered for its intimate atmosphere and its beautiful dinning room with nicely set tables or on the terrace for sweet summer nights.

LE MARCEL

Old Nice
11, rue de l'Abbaye
✆ +33 (0)4 97 20 14 84
www.marcelbistrochic.com
karine@marcelbistrochic.com

Open all year. Every day except Sunday for lunch. Possibility of organizing your private events by reservation. Booking advised. À la carte: Around €25. Lunch menu: €17. Menu €14 child. Terrace.

In a refined setting that perfectly combines elegance and romance of the beautiful Parisian brasseries of the 20s, Karine and Marcel Marro open their third restaurant after the unmissable Le Moorea in Saint-Laurent-du-Var and Le Grand Balcon in Nice. The menu prepared by the Chef reveals local and seasonal dishes: carpaccio of purple artichokes and Parmesan chips, and calf sweetbreads with cashew nuts and green pepper, grilled swordfish, virgin sauce and vegetables or risotto of alphabet and pérugines… Authenticity and flavours are the keywords of this restaurant where the fresh products are worked with passion. A fine wine list completes the whole for a perfect moment.

LE MARLIN

The Port
13, quai des Deux-Emmanuel
✆ +33 (0)4 93 62 27 35
www.lemarlin.fr
amandine_surinach@hotmail.com
♿

From April to November: closed on Wednesday and Thursday. Winter: check to know the opening hours. Booking advised. À la carte: Around €40 (starter + main course + dessert). Children's menu: €14. Wine by the glass. Daily special between €12 and €14. Lunch menu only €24. Lunch menu and evening and Sunday: €28 (starter + main course + dessert). Checks are not accepted. Chèque Restaurant. Groups welcome (up to 40 people). Terrace. Activities.

You wish to enjoy delicious fish coming from the local fish or from the Breton fish ponds: Le Marlin is the restaurant for you! From fresh ingredients delicately selected near the local market-gardeners, Amandine, in cuisine, concocts a homemade cooking which evolves according to the seasons. She respects the products, controls cookings, proposes generous dishes. On the carte, one can find as starter: the salad niçoise improved of semi cooked tuna and fresh anchovy, the raw fish marinated in carpaccio, the brouillade with poutargue. As main course, steak of swordfish roasted with mango, marine mussels and their homemade chips, but also of a pretty choice of selected meats. For dessert, Amandine offers fondant with spéculos, heart running chocolate, roasted pineapple vervain and sorbet coconut or the creme brulee with citrus fruits. As for the service, its mom, Ode, cordially accommodates you with a smile and good mood. And to perfect the whole, the restaurant is ideally installed vis-a-vis the boats and the pretty green hill of the Castle. An address to be discovered very quickly, seated on the terrace or in the room furnished with an aquarium and exposed stones. You will return there, undoubtedly, regularly, to enjoy the delicious main courses of Amandine and to appreciate the conviviality of Ode.

MELODYNICE

Downtown
12, rue Dante
✆ +33 (0)4 83 55 29 15
www.melodynice.com

Open all year. Tuesday to Saturday from 12pm to 2pm; Tuesday to Friday and Sunday from 7pm to 10pm. Booking advised. À la carte: Around €32 (main course and dessert). Lunch menu: €18. Wine by the glass. Menu discovery €38. Gourmet menu €47.

MelodyNice promotes the French culinary heritage: seasonal ingredients for a creative and careful cuisine. Hot goat cheese with honey on gingerbread with fig jam, salad of crunchy vegetables with raspberry vinegar or marbled duck foie gras puts you in appetite while the gigolette of stuffed poultry with vegetables cream sauce and gratin Dauphinois, the fish stew and spring vegetables or the fillet of bar beurre blanc anisated wild rice will finish convincing you. Desserts are true wonders like the soufflé with chocolate or the crunchy mousse with seasonal fruits. A contemporary and timeless address which recalls how much we are attached to the French lifestyle.

LE MILLESIME

Port
17, rue Smolett
✆ +33 (0)4 93 56 00 13
www.restaurant-millesime.fr
aurelien.restocuis@hotmail.fr

Open all year Tuesday to Saturday from 12pm to 2pm and from 7pm to 10.30pm except Saturday for lunch. Daily special around €11.90. Set menu (starter + main course + dessert at €17.90). Menu around €37. Average price à la carte: €41 (starter + main course + dessert). Wine by the glass. Accepted luncheon vouchers. Groups accepted up to 24 people. Booking advised.

Native of Brittany, Aurélien Nourry, the young Chef owner of this restaurant beginned with great chefs like Jacques Maximin and Joël Garault. His menu is very appetising. His fine cuisine is prepared with fresh, local and seasonal ingredients. He elegantly and skillfully combines flavours. You can enjoy as a starter the duo of foie gras with his French toast and stewed figs, organic honey and pine nuts. As main dish, you can choose the duck breast blazed with Ricard, mashed sweet potatoes with cumin, iced fresh peas with poultry stock and roasted asparagus with veal jus, or the John Dory with fevette mousseline with mint, grilled fennel with organic honey and strong gravy with fish fumet or the delicious Norman prime rib with new potatoes and mild garlic which is a real success. For dessert, you will love the gourmet, hearty, pretty and delicious coffee or the French toast with figs and salted butter caramel or the millesime crème brûlée. You'll have understood, this Chef puts a Breton touch in his Mediterranean cuisine.

MONKEY

10, avenue Felix-Faure
✆ +33 (0)9 54 03 45 27
www.lemonkey.fr

Open all year. Continuous service from 11.30am to 5.30pm. À la carte: Around €18 (dish). Groups welcome (by reservation). Terrace.

Facing the Promenade du Paillon, discover Le Monkey! Trendy address and fresh cuisine, you can find simple and gourmet dishes on the menu: linguine with pesto; duo of salmon and tuna tartares; risotto with parmesan cream, goat cheese and zucchinis; beef tartare with a knife; chorizo apples; roasted salmon with champagne cream, rice and spring vegetables... The dishes hearty, colorful and well presented. We also like the indoor room, dominated by a pretty turquoise blue where some bright cheeky monkeys watch over the back wall and the pleasant sunny terrace. Without forgetting the very friendly welcome of the team. A sybarite address to (re) discover.

MT KAFÉ
City Center – 23, avenue Villermont
✆ +33 (0)9 80 34 45 81 – www.mt-kafe.fr
mtkafe@gmail.com
Tram: stop Liberation

Open all year. Monday to Friday from 7am to 10.30pm; Saturday from 7am to 3pm. À la carte: Around €32 (starter + main course + dessert). Slate of the day from €12.50. Chèque Restaurant. Groups welcome (by reservation). Terrace.

In room with a warm atmosphere, or an outside heated terrace, a pretty modern decor sets the tone. Le Chef offers a seasonal cuisine prepared with fresh ingredients like the sea bass fillets with artichokes, fresh vegetables of the market or rabbit with rosemary and tagliatelle. The dishes are generous at reasonable prices. An excellent address with a friendly and authentic atmosphere.

NISS' ART BURGER
13, rue du Commandant Raffali
Pedestrian area
✆ +33 (0)4 93 80 45 25

Gluten-free friendly. Open all year. Tuesday to Saturday from 12pm to 10.30pm. À la carte: Around €25 (main course and dessert). Children's menu: €13. Burger from €11. Salad from €14. Dessert from €2. Extra bacon, chorizo, cheese €2. Foie gras €6.

This address is a must if you want to enjoy a hamburger! It has a countryside-chic terrace in the privacy of the pedestrian area, and offers a friendly and relaxed service. The burgers are delicious: they are homemade, the beef meat is 100% from Aubrac or Salers. The recipes are varied, for all tastes: gluten-free, vegetarian, végan, south west of France... Without forgetting famous Niss'Art Burger with roasted veal and goat cheese on a bed of tapenade and homemade red pesto, rocket, dried tomatoes, pine nuts, zucchinis, eggplants and grilled peppers with olive oil. A must that goes with fresh French fries peeled and cut just before the service, crusty and tender, to dip in the homemade aïoli. A delight!

MA NOLAN'S IRISH PUB VIEUX-NICE
Old Nice – 2, rue Saint-François-de-Paule
✆ +33 (0)4 93 80 23 87
www.ma-nolans.com
info@ma-nolans.com

Open all year. From 11am to 2am with a non-stop service until 11pm. Happy hours from 5am to 8am. Breakfast from €4.90. Salad from €9.90. Sandwich from €8.90. Burger from €10.90. Dish from €11.90. Concerts.

Irish pub with a warm atmosphere that brings together the Anglo-Saxon communities and their friends, Ma Nolan' S serves some gourmet specialties like the English love eating: burgers, tarts (chicken or beef marinated in Guinness), unmissable Fish' Chips, Sunday Roast including a series of salads at affordable prices. A very nice place where you can always watch all the largest games of Rugby, football or attend *live* music every night of the week; you can even take part in the quiz every monday at 20: 00 and attempt to win a Ma Nolan's voucher up to €100.

NOORI' S
Carré d'Or 1, place Grimaldi
✆ +33 (0)4 93 88 80 87 – www.nooris.com

Open all year. Daily for lunch from 12pm to 2.30pm and for dinner from 7pm to 11pm. À la carte: Around €25 (starter + main course + dessert). Groups welcome (by reservation. Upstairs dining room for the reception up to 50 people). Terrace. Take-away. Caterer.

Le Noori's is a delight for Indian cuisine lovers in a sober and relaxing setting. Its large terrace and the room which can be privatized give a lot of charm to the place whose dishes come from all the provinces of India. You can choose between sweet flavours or more spicy ones, between the traditional tandooris, the Borthons, the Birianies, the Indian breads and the homemade pastries. The «Jaipur» catering service offers spicy dishes and menus on request, to take-away or to be delivered at home.

LE PANIER
Old Nice – 5, rue Barillerie
✆ +33 (0)4 89 97 14 37

Open all year. Open Thursday to Tuesday, for lunch and dinner. Booking advised. À la carte: Around €23 (dish). Menu €45 starter + main course + dessert. Terrace.

Le Panier prepares fresh cuisine in a very simple way! The mediterranean inspired dishes are divinely prepared: sea bass and its braised vegetables; scallops carpaccio; shrimp raviolis with lemon grass, ginger and cumbawa on a light bisque; risotto with chestnuts and truffle oil; squash soup with truffle oil and organic cream; cod fillet, lemon white butter and summer vegetables; lamb leg mashed potatoes and olives, pan-fried chanterelles; cold soup of zucchinis, croutons, Parmesan and olive oil... The menu is reduced: a will of the chef who testifies the freshness of the products presented. The setting is also nice between outdoor terrace, cuisine and bar on the ground floor, and mezzanine dining room upstairs. As for the service, it is both friendly and professional. Fantastic!

LOU PANTAIL
Nice Nord – 107, avenue Saint-Lambert
✆ +33 (0)4 93 52 02 51
www.loupantail.com
contact@loupantail.com

Open all year. Wednesday to Sunday for lunch and dinner. À la carte: Around €33 (starter + main course + dessert). Checks are not accepted. Groups welcome (organization of all types of events. Cake prepared especially for the birthdays and musical atmosphere). Terrace. Take-away. Free shipping on Nice center and northern Nice of all the main courses of the dishes on the carte during the opening hours of the restaurant. Retransmission of football match and the live sporting events.

This family nicois business since 1990 became over the years a real institution. With a simple, rustic and original decor, a warm and friendly welcome, an impeccable service, this place will completely make you change air. Lovers of local and Italian cuisine will love it. You will find on the carte sumptuous mixed salads, fresh pasta with different sauces- Bolognese, carbonara, stew… – including a whole range of traditional pizzas cooked in a wood fire. Without forgetting the particularly tasty grills. Regularly, cannellonis, stuffed vegetables, onion tart and other local specialities are prepared on the spot in a traditional way by this family attached to the niçoises culinary traditions.

PASTRY PLAISIRS

City Centre – 11, rue Delille
✆ +33 (0)4 93 87 92 32
www.pastryplaisirs.com
pastryplaisirs06@yahoo.fr

Open all year round. From Monday to Thursday from 12 am to 3 pm, on Friday from 12am to 3pm and from 7:30pm to 10:45 pm. Closed 15 days during winter and 15 days during summer. Booking recommended. A la carte: around €35 (starter, main course and dessert). Menu: €17. Wine by the glass. Menu including starter, main course and dessert : €22 at lunch and €32 at dinner. Cheques not accepted. Meal voucher. Louis Dubois Master Restorer. Groups welcome (up to 25 people upon reservation. Possibility of privatizing the restaurant during the week). Terrace. Shop. Takeaway pastries upon order. Parking Marshal nearby

Restaurant, boutique, pastry shop... Nothing's missing in this charming address! Behind a pearl grey façade, inside the walls are white and covered with paintings, with a raspberry red section, exposed stones and a few hanging lamps. At lunch, in the evening, during the weekend and the afternoon, you can sit in front of dishes inspired by southern flavours and delight in sweet treats also available for take away. Organic wines and teas imported from London accompany meals or gourmet pauses during the afternoon. It is possible to privatize the restaurant from Monday to Thursday evening for groups from 8 people and during the weekend (minimum 20 people). A choice of birthday or wedding cakes is available upon request. Here, you will find delight everywhere, and it's available for take away!

LE PASSE PLAT

Port – 4 bis, quai Papacino
✆ +33 (0)4 93 26 05 80
www.lepasseplat.com
Tram stop: Place Garibaldi - Parking of the port

Open all year. Closed from end of December to beginning of January. Monday to Friday for lunch and dinner. Booking advised. À la carte: Around €55 (starter + main course + dessert). Daily special: €13. Luncheon voucher only for lunch. Checks are not accepted. Terrace only in summer.

This restaurant has a modern cuisine based on fresh ingredients enhanced by the chef who prepares his dishes according to his desires and seasons around a creative and gourmet ephemeral menu: foie gras and prawns maki way honey and soy sauce, shoulder of lamb with its spicy gravy and vegetables from the market. For dessert, the half cooked chocolate heart with speculoos and passion fruit chantilly. The dishes are inventive, generous and colourful. A tasty address that wakes up the taste buds.

PASSION 'ELLE

City Center – 14, rue Maccarani
✆ +33 (0)4 93 82 24 12
www.restaurant-passionelle.fr

Open all year. Every evening except Wednesday from 6.30pm to 10.30pm. Booking advised. À la carte: Around €45 (starter + main course + dessert). Wine by the glass. Tastings €65 à la carte: starter €16, main course €26 and dessert €10. Checks are not accepted. Groups welcome. Baby chairs. Terrace. Take-away. Tray meals at disposal.

Laurie is passionate. She began working with grand chefs: Yannick Franques, Jacques Chibois, at the Jules Verne restaurant of Alain Ducasse and Luc Salsedo from whom she just has bought the restaurant. It is now the big Chef . She offers mediterranean cuisine according to the seasons and the market in a monthly menu with several formulas in which you can choose between the nicois stuffed vegetables, rocket salad, the cod in hazlnut and savory crust, celery cream and iced turnip, vinaigrette with herbs, fig and mangoe crumble, exotic coulis. Entirely homemade and delicious dishes.

PAPAYOU

Old Nice
35, rue de la Préfecture
✆ +33 (0)4 93 80 15 97 / +33 (0)6 73 01 04 39
www.lepapayou.fr
♿

Open all year. From March to end of October. Monday to Saturday from 12pm to 2.30pm and from 7pm to 10.30pm; Sunday from 12pm to 2.30pm. Without reservation. À la carte: Around €25 (main course and dessert). Shop: gift voucher cooking classes, aprons "workshops of Papayou", knives Thai. Terrace. Activities. Cooking classes niçoise, Morrocan, nicoise and Thai (duration: 2.30hour). Rates: workshop of the morning or the afternoon €80, workshop the evening €50.

The yellow façade of this establishment set in a corner of the heart of the old town echoes its sunny cuisine: nice dishes made in the rules of art with Asian touches punctuates a menu where herbs, spices and flavours mix for a tasty gourmet break. Onion tart, stew with mushrooms and Thai dishes such as chicken with coconut milk and lemongrass or the beef wok with vegetables promise beautiful pure moments of escape. You can also please your friends by offering a voucher gift, cooking workshop, «workshop of Papayou», spiced razorfish and other woks. A surprising place!

PATOCH'S FAMILY

Cessole 9, avenue Cyrille-Besset
✆ +33 (0)4 93 41 69 21
♿

Open all year. Tuesday to Saturday for lunch; Thursday to Saturday for dinner. Open Sunday for lunch only by reservation. Booking advised. Lunch menu: €15 (starter of the day, daily special, coffee or daily special, dessert of the day, coffee). Garden. Terrace.

The name of this restaurant perfectly expresses the philosophy of the house where the family spirit and good mood prevails. The charm of the terrace and the garden that shelters a petanque field and a table tennis table are also seducing. As for the cuisine, you'll enjoy seasonal products of the market and the desires of Patoch like the candied duck leg, a fillet John Dory fish in virgin sauce or a veal sautéed with olives. You can come with your lovers, your family or your friends, and even to celebrate events.

LES PÊCHEURS

Port – 18, quai des Docks
✆ +33 (0)4 93 89 59 61
www.lespecheurs.com
lespecheurs@aliceadsl.fr

«Maître Restaurateur» label. Closed on Monday and Tuesday for lunch. Open from 12.15pm to 2pm and from 7.15pm to 10pm. Booking advised. Menu from €31 to €41. À la carte: Around €55 (starter + main course + dessert). Wine by the glass. American Express. No disabled accesses to the toilets. Groups welcome. Terrace. Take-away. Parking.

The chef prepares sea dishes with Asian touches. Fresh and seasonal ingredients are highly favoured on a well-stuffed à la carte menu: seafood platters, salad of octopus with the condiments of Nice, Thai crab with Granny Smith apple crumble, lobster on its tomato tartar and coriander without forgetting the excellent Thai soup, scented poultry raviolis. The rougail of monkfish and its rice coconut will recall you the flavours of the cuisine of Réunion. The roasted whole fish are perfectly cooked. An address where you can feast while admiring the view of the port and the hill of the castle.

PEIXES

2, rue de l'Opéra ✆ +33 (0)4 93 85 96 15

Open all year. Every day from 12pm to 10pm. À la carte: Around €25 (main course and dessert).

Armand Crespo signs here a new concept that highlights the ceviches, various range of seafood marinades served cold or raw. Peixes, which name means "fish" in Portuguese, is a restaurant based on sea flavours. Comfortably installed in the small room with the tiled floor surprising by the originality or on the terrace, discover a menu composed of scallops, white fish, squids, clams, shrimps or mackerels. The products are fresh, all freshly prepared in a cuisine that can be admired from the bar. The recipes are daring and tasty. You can continue the discovery with nice and delicious desserts: fruit salad, financier, carrot with verbena.

LA PETITE LOGE

Vieux Nice – 10, rue de la Loge
✆ +33 (0)4 93 01 63 28
www.lapetiteloge.com
Parking of Arts. Tram stop: Jean Jaurès

Restaurant open from 6pm to 10.30pm. Cellar open Thursday to Saturday from 6pm to midnight. Wine cellar on request. Wine by the glass from €5. WiFi free.

La Petite Loge gathers lovers of wines and eating well. Jérémy and Lauriane are in charge of this trendy establishment of the Old Nice with an unique decor, where the bar and the shelves were in particular made with a floor of a 150 years old train! Homemade recipes are served here, as the eggs in red wine sauce, breaded camembert and candied onion or the desserts (cheesecake coulis of raspberry and chocolate mousse with nuggets). Other very tasty main courses complete the carte, like the terrine in old-fashioned way, stuffed sausage with Parmesan, basket of crudities and the boards of Frères Marchand cheese or charcuterie. You willl taste these dishes in the pretty vaulted cellar, while you can discover also the wine cellar at controlled temperature, which presents more than 1,400 bottles for more than 200 references. Jérémy and Lauriane share with you their passion while making you discover their wines, from the most accessible to the rarest ones, with a preference for those of the regions of Burgundy, Loire and Provence. Note also the very fine selection of champagne.

LE PETIT CHALET DE NICE

Downtown – 1, rue Maccarani
✆ +33 (0)9 81 20 11 53

Open all year. Every day except Sunday from breakfast to dinner. À la carte: Around €15 (dish). Groups welcome (by reservation). Take-away. Delivery.

A dynamic and very friendly young couple offers a very gourmet stopover in this cave. Here, everything is homemade with deliciously selected products. Ideal to awaken your taste buds around an amazing culinary journey: spinach cream, smoked salmon, apples and mascarpone; onion soup; spinach cream soup; vegetables with curry; parsnip cream, carrots, goat, ricotta; goat's cheese, fresh figs confit with honey, roasted almonds and mushrooms; leek soup and kiwi tart, apples, litchees for dessert, among others. The light and original recipes are nicely presented. To (Re) discover without delay!

LA PETITE COCOTTE

Old Nice – 11, rue Saint-Augustin
✆ +33 (0)4 97 08 48 61
www.la-ptitecocotte.fr

Open all year. Thursday to Monday from 12pm to 2pm and from 7pm (last sitting at 9pm). Lunch menu: €19 (starter + main course + dessert except Sunday and public holidays. Also Fixed formula starter and main course or main course and dessert at €15.50). For dinner menu €28 (starter + main course + dessert) or fixed formula (starter and main course or main course and dessert) €23.50. Checks are not accepted.

This restaurant with authentic flavours of the farmhouse accommodates you in a charming room with stone walls and wooden furniture and local dishes: medallion of pork with whole-grain mustard, cauliflowers with Emmentaler and ham, cod loin with crust of chorizo, poêlée of seasonal vegetables and juice of bouillabaisse or artichoke risotto and sauteed Saint-Jacques. As for the desserts, cream puffs, Suzette pancake and Alsatian apple pie. The menus change every week and are elaborated with fresh ingredients.

LA PICCOLA CAPRI

Downtown – 16, rue Delille
✆ +33 (0)4 22 16 49 63

Open all year. Lunch menu: €15 (dish + drink + coffee).

A nice and delicious Neapolitan wind blows now in the city centre: welcome to La Piccola Capri. On the menu of this young and dynamic address with an elegant setting: octopus salad, eggplant parmigiana, salmon tartare, homemade lasagnas, risotto with ceps without forgetting the unconditional pizzas... A treat. Also discover a fine wine list. Friendly atmosphere for this establishment which is perfect. No need to go to Naples to satisfy your gourmet desires of transalpine escapes: La Piccola Capri is great!

PINXCHO

Petit marais niçois
7, rue Bonaparte
✆ +33 (0)4 93 89 81 83
www.pinxcho.com
contact@pinxcho.com

♿

Open all year. Monday, Tuesday, Thursday and Friday for lunch; Thursday to Tuesday. Booking advised. À la carte: Around €35 (starter + main course + dessert). Lunch menu: €14 (mini starter and main course of the day or daily special + dessert). Wine by the glass. Daily special: €9.50. Luncheon vouchers only for lunch. Checks are not accepted. Groups welcome (jusquà 40 people By reservation). Terrace. Terrace in summer.

Discover a slate located at the crossroads of the Mediterranean and remote regions that changes regularly. The choice is difficult because every dish makes us want to try. *Petit Futé* chose the roasted Marcellin with pine nuts and crunchy vegetables, shoulder of lamb and mashed potatoes and a pastilla Toblerone with ice cream. The service is professional and friendly. A furiously trendy address to try quickly.

LA PLAGE BY THIERRY MARX

Terminal 1
Nice Côte d'azur airport

Children's menu: €10. Lunch menu starting from €20. Brunch from €15.

This establishment is run by the starred chef Thierry Marx, President of the Fondation des Disciples d'Escoffier and enthusiast defender of Nice cuisine. From the hearty breakfast to the chic savory and sweet snacks', via griddled dishes and a whole range of drinks, this address located in the middle of the Nice-Côte d'Azur Airport Terminal 1 displays holidays and escape. Club sandwiches, mixed salads, arancini (small risotto ball with stuffed with cherry tomato and its mozza di bufala), sardines in cartridge with "chuncky rissoles", meat and fish of the day every lunchtime, Corsican meats from Moracchini and its cheese... On the carte, you can choose among many dishes prepared in front of you in order to make the best of culinary escape.

LE PLONGEOIR

Port
60, boulevard Franck-Pilatte
✆ +33 (0)4 93 26 53 02
www.leplongeoir.com
contact@leplongeoir.com

«Maître Restaurateur» label. Open all year. Monday, Tuesday and Wednesday from 12pm to 2.30pm. Thursday, Friday, Saturday and Sunday from 12pm to 2.30pm and from 7pm to 9.30pm. Services of reception: a dock of reception is available for the boats. À la carte: Around €45 (starter + main course + dessert). Lunch menu: €29 (starter and main course or main course and dessert or at €34 in full version). Groups welcome. Terrace. Valet.

It is one of the emblematic places of Nice. A rock almost as famous as that of Monaco, deeply rooted in the heart of Nice. It was also here that the famous Brice de Nice planted his set and practised surfing, at the entrance of the harbour, while waiting for the wave... The setting of Le Plongeoir reveals a charming set. The restaurant seems indeed to lie on the water, divided into two spaces: the diving board and the rock. On the first level, a lounge bar Le Vivier is located feet in the water and welcomes you in a trendy atmosphere for a drink with some tasting dishes to share with friends. The restaurant menu is, when it comes to it, resolutely Mediterranean and gourmet. The dishes are beautifully prepared and hearty. We like the Yellowfin tuna tartar, the Buratta, the fresh-tomato gazpacho or the half-cooked foie gras, the griddled sea bream fillet or the roasted lamb with polenta with grapes and dried fruits. Finish with a tiramusi of Le Plongeoir or the panacotta with figs, crumble with pine nuts. A beautiful address!

POUPON ET MARINETTE

La Madeleine
102, boulevard de la Madeleine
✆ +33 (0)4 93 86 21 39

♿

Open all year. Every day except Sunday for dinner. À la carte: Around €20. Chèque Restaurant. Label Nissarde Kitchen. Take-away. Air conditioning. Pets allowed.

The cuisine of Poupon and Marinette is familial and generous. Typically niçois, the restaurant has a very rustic decoration and is labeled Nissarde Cuisine. Discover traditional dishes, sunny, authentic and tasty, copiously served: capoun, bagnat cauda, onion tart, pan bagnat... A restaurant to (Re) discover, which already enjoys all the neighborhood of La Madeleine.

LE RAJA

Port
24, quai Lunel
✆ +33 (0)4 93 89 57 36
www.leraja-nice.fr

Open all year. For lunch Monday to Sunday from 11.30am to 2.30pm and for dinner from 7pm to 11pm. Lunch menu €11. Salad of the day €10. Lunch menu and evening €13.50 (starter and main course) or €22 (starter + not + main course and dessert + coffee). Free home delivery. Catering. Room rental for weddings. 100 places interior and outside. Checks are not accepted. Groups welcome (by reservation).

This restaurant promises a most pleasant change of scenery. The stylish and elegant decoration – colourful walls, backlit paintings telling Indian mythological stories, pictures of grandiose scenery or monuments, huge sculpted wooden doors – which reminds the Indian culture is a first getaway. The invitation to travel goes on in the plate with copious portions of various refined gourmet dishes which embrace the rich Indian cuisine of Kashmir, Punjab, Sikkim, Manipur, Bihar going through Delhi, Pondicherry, Kerala or Rajastan amonst others. The excellent meats and fish are indeed cooked in the traditional Indian oven (tandoor) while the curry specialities are all so delicious. Besides, they welcome you with a smile and kindly inform you of the dishes with professionalism. You have to (re)discover this restaurant! A clever information is that Le Raja prepares meals on order for your private events.

RÂMEN KUMANO

Centre ville
15, rue Biscarra
✆ +33 (0)4 93 04 58 92
satoshi.yokoya@gmail.com

Open all year. Tuesday to Saturday from 12pm to 2.30pm and 7pm at 9pm. À la carte: Around €20 (dish).

A gourmet escape in the Japanese universe! The name of the restaurant sets the tone with a carte which honors these famous Japanese noodles called "ramen" eaten cold or hot accompanied by a stock of your choice (soy sauce, spices...). But that's not all, other typically Japanese dishes supplement this offer: tonkatsu (dish containing breaded and fried pork), karaage (pieces of fried chicken or fish covered with a fine scented topping), jiǎozi and dumpling (kinds of raviolis vapor or fried), ebis fry (Japanese shrimp donuts) or edamamés (immature broad beans of soy sauce). It is original and the reception is nice. Don't wait to discover this simple and generous cooking?

THE RATAPIGNATA

Ray
63, avenue du Ray
✆ +33 (0)4 92 15 06 39

Open all year. Open from 12pm to 3pm and from 7pm to 11.30pm. Closed on Monday and Sunday all day like Tuesday for dinner. À la carte: Around €20. Evenings accordions regularly organized. Chèque Restaurant. Label Nissarde Kitchen. Terrace. Activities.

La Ratapignata is a restaurant labeled Cuisine Nissarde run by three brothers from the French Riviera capital. Here, no bat but typical dishes, full of sunshine, served in a friendly atmosphere where a resolutely family atmosphere is displayed from the door. On the menu? Stockfish, tripe, homemade gnocchi, beef cheek stew, squid, pissaladière, stuffed, pistou soup, snails... A very charming place, which reputation extends beyond the borders of Ray district where this pleasant restaurant continues now for years. Note: accordion «evenings» are regularly organised throughout the year, friendly atmosphere 100% guaranteed!

REGENCY BEACH BY RADISSON BLU

223, promenade des Anglais
✆ +33 (0)4 97 07 03 09

See page 42.

LA RÉSERVE

Port
60, boulevard Franck-Pilatte
✆ +33 (0)4 97 08 14 80
www.lareservedenice.fr
contact@lareservedenice.fr

«Maître Restaurateur» label. Open all year. Open every day from 12.15pm to 2pm and from 7.15pm to 10pm. Booking advised. Menu from €55 to €85 (approximately). À la carte: Around €95 (starter + main course + dessert). Wine by the glass. American Express. Groups welcome. Terrace. Valet. Parking.

The Chef of this mythical address prepares a resolutely Mediterranean, modern, light and subtle cuisine: cannelloni «Riviera» with ricotta, Parmesan stock, roasted hazelnuts of Piedmont, Parmesan chips with rocket, the roasted Saint Pierre fillet with fennel with its tomato Tartar and cucumber with basil and vervain, barigoule of purple artichokes and fennel with the citrus fruits juice, and exquisite desserts like the Panna cotta with sweet almond cream, crusty with toasted almonds, roasted bricot with foaming honey and rosemary, apricot sorbet. In season, take advantage of the roof terrace which overlooks the sea; its like being on a boat. A privileged moment for a glass of champagne.

ROLANCY' S RESTAURANT

Downtown
22, rue Alphonse-Karr
✆ +33 (0)4 93 16 00 48
www.les-viviers-nice.fr/fr
viviers.bretons@wanadoo.fr

«Maîtres Cuisiniers of France» label. Open all year. Monday to Saturday from 12pm to 2pm and from 7.30pm to 10pm. Booking advised. Menu from €44 to €69. À la carte: Around €65 (starter + main course + dessert). Lunch menu: €29 (except Saturday and public holidays). Checks are not accepted. American Express. Groups welcome. Baby chairs. Terrace. Take-away. Terrace in season. Seminar room up to 25 people

Better blue-collar worker of France like were his father and his mother (first woman MOF in the food trades in 1982), Jacques Rolancy is a chef whom one likes to find. Here, the fish and the shellfish hold the star even if the meats, the poultries, the offal or the risotto have also an important place. Roasted loin of lamb, vegetable bayaldi of the south and salad of fresh herbs, european lobster risotto, escalope of foie gras poêlée on a marinated salmon bed, ginger and turnips candied, fillet of red mullet stove to the condiments, zucchinis with the Parmesan chips, Roman in ravioli... The dishes are concocted for the pleasure of the tastebuds. Refined and generous, the dishes are exceptional! The desserts carte is also tasty: very famous Paris-Brest the house speciality, the exceptional soufflé Grand - Marnier or the tart with creme brulee scented with thyme, raspberries and sorbet cottage cheese. To accompany these dishes, a fine wine list is presented. The service is discrete and friendly, the atmosphere felted. This address is definitively a true moment of happiness where we like to return.

LE SAFARI

Old Nice
1, cours Saleya
✆ +33 (0)4 93 80 18 44
www.restaurantsafari.fr
sarl.safari@wanadoo.fr

«Maître Restaurateur» label. Open all year. 7 days a week from 12pm to 11pm. Non-stop service all day. Booking advised. À la carte: Around €35. Menu from €29. American Express, Diners Club, Holiday voucher, Chèque Restaurant. Groups welcome (up to 40 people. By reservation). Terrace. Label Nissarde Kitchen. Label Home Made.

With its privileged location, on the Cours Saleya, Le Safari displays many beautiful well-laid tables, warm atmosphere, sunny beautiful terrace and local carte labeled Cuisine Nissarde! This timeless address in the old town since 1973 offers a variation of fresh pastas everyday, enjoy also the grilled fishes; the squid with artichokes; the typical bagna cauda – raw vegetables served with an anchovy sauce - and all the other local specialities like the stuffed vegetables, the accras, the grilled peppers or niçoise salad or the various char-baked pizzas. As for the wine, the references mainly come from the south served by a discreet, rapid, efficient and friendly staff.

■ LE SAINT-PAUL

Port – 29, boulevard Franck-Pilatte
✆ +33 (0)4 93 89 39 57
www.lesaintpaul-hotel.com
reservation@lesaintpaul-hotel.com
♿

Open all year. Closed diner of Christmas and New year. Monday to Sunday from 12pm to 2pm and from 7.30pm to 9.30pm. Booking advised. À la carte: Around €45 (starter + main course + dessert). Lunch menu: €22 (starter and main course or main course and dessert, only on weekdays). Wine by the glass. Menu Gourmand €42. Free parking. Chèque Restaurant. Groups welcome. Garden. Terrace.

This building – a Church's house – has many assets: 80 parking places, a clear and breastaking view, 5 conference rooms covering 500 m^2, a bar and a restaurant transformed with a contemporary decor mixing leather, wood and brushed aluminium open onto a vast terrace overlooking the Mediterranean. The Chef offers a menu changing with the seasons and Mediterranean: roasted aglets of Saint Pierre, brocolis mousse, asparagus and shellfish juice; cod loin with chorizo, artichoke stew; lamb carre in herb crust, candied and gratineed eggplants; paned veal, candied shallots, and coco beans mousse; carnoli risotto with shellfish. Gourmands will end with a candied orange tart, or the Toblerone pastilla, cream and ice cream. An address to (re)discover urgently!

■ SARAO

7, promenade des Anglais
✆ +33 (0)4 92 00 50 90
www.sarao-restaurant.com
info@sarao-restaurant.com
♿

Open all year. Every day. Nonstop catering facilities. Breakfast from 8am to 12pm. Lunch from 12pm to 5pm. Dinner from 5pm to 11pm. Bar open from 8am to midnight. Products and dishes 100% home made. Daily special: €10.50. Wine by the glass. Monday to Friday (except public holidays and festivities): €14.50 (starter and main course or main course and dessert), €18.50 (starter + main course + dessert). Breakfast: continental €8.50, English €11.50. Chèque Restaurant. Groups welcome (up to 150 people). Terrace.

Sarao enjoys a privileged location on the famous Promenade de Anglais and offers you a stunning view of the seaside from its sunny terrace. With a capacity of 150 people, the restaurant offers homemade dishes with the Italian and Nice accents. As starter, we chose the eggplants with the parmigiana, the soup of the day, the cured ham of Parma and mozzarella di bufala or the Salade Niçoise. As main course, let yourself be tempted by the succulent spaghetti with the seafood in papillotte, the whole sea bass in slat crust and steamed potatoes or with the tasty loin of lamb with herbs of Provence and gratin. The restaurant invested in a top quality oven so as to prepare a wide variety of pizzas with most authentic flavours! As for dessert, we find the fashionable tiramisu dessert and the pretty pallet Sarao that presents a selection of desserts in miniature.

■ SIEU D'AQUI

Lepante corner – 1, rue Biscarra
✆ +33 (0)9 80 83 68 97
www.sieudaqui.blogspot.fr
sieudaqui@outlook.com

Open all year.

Here, we are proud to be Niçois! Also, the chef highlights the culinary wealth of the Côte d'Azur capital: gnocchis with stew, raviolis niçois sauce with ceps, small stuffed vegetables, polenta with spring vegetables, pan bagnat, zucchini flowers fritters... We also like the reception, as friendly as charming, which adds to the sympathy of this place already very authentic. Finally, generosity is found in the dishes that are also available around some tasty recipes with Italian touches. There is something to delight the whole family. An address that already has its regulars, and which continues to seduce all those who walk through its doors. Sieu d'Aqui, a name that finally means «I am from here» in niçois.

LA SOCCA D'OR
Petit marais niçois
45, rue Bonaparte
✆ +33 (0)4 93 56 52 93

Open all year. From 10.30am to 2pm and from 6pm to 10pm. In summer, closed on Sunday and Wednesday. In winter, Tuesday for dinner, Wednesday and Sunday. Annual closing: two weeks in September and two weeks at Christmas. Booking advised. Wine by the glass. Average bill between €10 and €12. Pan Bagna €5.50. Restaurant Tickets accepted. Credit card not accepted. Groups welcome (up to 20 people. By reservation). Take-away. Label Nissarde Kitchen. Terraces.

Labeled «Cuisine Nissarde», here is an unmissable address to enjoy the true Nice socca! Golden and crispy, it is eaten immediately after being cooked in the oven. And if this chickpea flour pancake is the queen of this establishment run by Valérie, Frédéric and Jean-Aimé, all the other specialities of the area are also available on the spot or take-away: pissaladière, pizzas, pan bagnat with homemade bread, various salads including the famous salade niçoise, or even chard pies... You will also discover the tasting plate and the pan panisse. As for homemade desserts, they change with the seasons: traditional rum baba or lemon cream shortbreads delight the most gourmet ones. Finally, a strong emphasis is given to wines including Côtes-de-Provence and Pays du Var. The welcome is smiling and friendly.

LA TABLE ALZIARI
Old Nice
4, rue François-Zanin
✆ +33 (0)4 93 80 34 03

Open all year. Tuesday to Saturday from 12pm to 2pm and from 7.30pm to 10pm. Closed on Monday and Sunday. À la carte: Around €25. Chèque Restaurant. Groups welcome (only by reservation). Terrace. Air conditioning. Label Nissarde Kitchen. Pets allowed. Free Wifi.

Stuffed sardines, pasta with pistou, small stuffed vegetables, stew from Nice, raviolis, cod dish a la niçoise, stuffed veal pocket... Here, local products are sublimated. A friendly atmosphere, a traditional décor, it is a nice place to discover the cuisine niçoise in this charming labeled restaurant Nissarde Cuisine nested in the middle of the historic quarters. The dishes are generous, like the owner. A real pleasure!

SPAGGIARI
Liberation
60, rue Dabray
✆ +33 (0)4 93 41 83 12

Open all year. Open Monday to Saturday; Friday and Saturday for dinner. À la carte: Around €15 (dish). Terrace.

Niçoise cuisine based on fresh ingredients, vegans dishes, gluten-free, healthy recipes, organic dishes, meat and fish from the neighboring local market... Discover the Spaggiari cuisine. Pumpkin soup; vegetables samoussa, yoghurt soy sauce, dill, lemon, scallion and mixed green salad; gratin of gluten-free pasta with vegetables and scamorza; niçoise tuna stew and gnocchis; vegan burger... Here, you are welcomed «without weapon, violence, hatred» as specified with great humour by the owner of the establishment. The service is welcoming with helpful advices. You can sit at the table on the pleasant terrace or in the bright interior room with the decoration which recalls not without derision the «heist of the century» of which the Société Générale was victim in 1976. An excellent address in the heart of Liberation area.

LA STORIA
Old Nice
3, cours Saleya
✆ +33 (0)4 93 80 95 07
www.restaurantlastoria.com
contact@restaurantlastoria.com

Open all year. Closed December 24th and 25th. Every day from 12pm to 11pm. Label Kitchen nissarde. À la carte: Around €25 (starter + main course + dessert). Children's menu: €10. Wine by the glass. Lunch menu Monday to Friday €13.90 (starter and main course or main course and dessert) and €17.90 (starter + main course + dessert). Menu niçois at €20. Pizza from €9, Pasta from €11. American Express, Chèque Restaurant. Groups welcome (by reservation). Terrace. Paying public parking Cours Saleya.

Located on the authentic cours Saleya, here is an ideal place to discover the local and Italian specialties. Here, the walls are with warm colours and the paved floor refers directly to the Sardinian cities... Enough to immerse us in a typical, perfect atmosphere to enjoy delicious penne carbonara or homemade lasagna cooked in oven. The typically Nice menu honours the products of the region and you will enjoy gnocchi with a stew and rabbit porchetta. As for wine, the regional trade names are well represented with wines from Provence and Corsica, by the glass and bottle. The welcome is very pleasant and the price are very low.

TEMPLE BAR
Centre-ville
12, rue Halévy
✆ +33 (0)4 93 87 80 60
templebar06@sfr.fr

Open all year. 7 days a week. Non-stop service. Low season: Tuesday to Sunday from 10am to 3pm and from 6pm to midnight. High season: every day from 10am and until 2am. The low season gets along from mid-November to beginning of April. Daily special: €10.50. Wine by the glass. Lunch menu and evening: starter and main course or main course and dessert €16. Menu €20: starter + main course + dessert. Chèque Restaurant. Groups welcome (up to 45 people By reservation). Terrace. Take-away.

The Temple Bar has a pleasant terrace and the dining room has a simple grey and red decor. The bar and furniture create an elegant brasserie atmosphere with table runners on the square tables. The presentation of the generous dishes sets the tone of a Provençal

French cuisine the whole presented with an attention to detail, especially in the dishes presentation even for the nicely furnished hamburgers.

LA TERRASSE DU PLAZA
12, avenue de Verdun
Carré d'or- Hôtel Plaza
✆ +33 (0)4 93 16 75 92 / +33 (0)4 93 16 75 73
www.laterrasseduplaza.fr
contact@laterrasseduplaza.fr
Massena and Ruhl public car parks nearby.

Open all year. Every day. From October to April: from 12pm to 2.30pm, the lounge bar from 10.30am to 9pm, only dinner for groups by reservation. From May to September from 10.30am to 00.30am, lunch from 12pm to 3pm, dinner from 7pm to 10.30pm. Booking advised. À la carte: Around €37 (starter + main course + dessert). Children's menu: €12. Wine by the glass. Served only for lunch: daily special €16.90 (Monday to Friday, except public holidays). Daily menu €23 (main dish and dessert coffee). Menu business €36 (starter main course and dessert coffee). Daily specials from €16. Brunch Sunday per month. Checks are not accepted. American Express, Diners Club, Chèque Restaurant. Groups welcome (up to 120 people, 250 in cocktail). Baby chairs. Terrace. Activities.

This restaurant located on the 6th floor of the roof of Hôtel Plaza, offers a stunning view of the Promenade Des Anglais. For lunch, dinner, breakfast in summer, aperitif or *afterworks*, the hotel offers fresh and delicate cuisine. The menu offers captivating touches such as the niçoise salad revisited with half-cooked tuna, the fish tariada or the simenthal beef fillet. In the evening, you can enjoy a fresh algae salad with crab meat and combawa with a citrus vinaigrette and caviar. More gourmet, the burgers – including the one with foie gras – or the risotto of the day. The place is also perfect for beautiful summer evenings, the head in the stars, wit ha musical atmosphere and the presence of a super bartender, king of the mojito and colourful cocktails to be enjoyed with a plate of tapas. At every hour of the day, La Terrasse du Plaza offers nice surprises in a dream setting between sky and sea!

TIGELLABELLA
City Center
54, boulevard Jean-Jaurès
✆ +33 (0)9 82 41 28 38
www.tigellabella.fr
nice@tigellabellafrance.fr

Open all year. Daily for lunch and dinner. Menu from €8 to €10 (tigellona + drink + tigelle sweetened). À la carte: Around €6. Sweetened Tigellona: €3. Aperitivo between €19 and €30 depending on drink. Groups welcome (by reservation).

Are you looking for Italian specialities? TigellaBella is the ideal place to taste the famous tigelles, small breads from Modene that you can garnish according to your tastes to become Tigellonas. You'll also find typically Italian products, like the must-have ham from Parma, the bresaola, the calabrese spianata or the fese di tacchino. Also a large choice of cheeses, fontina, gorgonzola, or scarmoza affumicata; you'll also find sauces with artichokes, tuna, bacon, roquette, and fresh tomatoes. Fancy a sweetness? You can also garnish your tigelles with nut almond or pistachio cream, or Amaretto! For an Italian apertitif, try a charcuterie plate with tigelle with Italian wine or Spritz. The location on place Massena is pleasant and the welcome is warm.

LA TETE AILLEURS
Downtown
35, boulevard Dubouchage
ltaresto@gmail.com

Open all year. À la carte: Around €15 (dish). Groups welcome (by reservation). Terrace. Pets allowed.

In the heart of Nice centre, La Tête Ailleurs invites you for a beautiful gourmet escape: salmon tart, cod loin crumble-style with raw ham and iced carrots, zucchini tart... You can settle agreeably on the charming terrace or in the warm and cozy indoor room for a sweetest culinary journey.

TRADISWISS
The carré d'or
11, rue Massenet
✆ +33 (0)4 93 53 62 90
www.tradiswiss-nice.fr
info@tradiswiss-nice.fr

Open all year. Closed on Monday. Open Tuesday to Saturday from 9am to midnight. Sunday from 4pm to midnight. Slate and salad from €11. Dish from €17. Rösti from €11. Dessert from €5.50.

Once you pass the door of this charming establishment you dive into the decor of an authentic Swiss mountain chalet. The cuisine is tasty and gourmet with Swiss traditional dishes. Discover the röstis, potato pancakes, test the formulas on the blackboard like the Valaisan dish prepared with dried meat, raw ham, slices of dried sausage, slices of dry bacon, Valaisan cheese and rye bread. Without forgetting the variations of fondues, Raclettes and crusts or hearty salads. The portions are generous and well presented. The greediest will finish this gargantuan feast with a sweet touch like Ovomaltine mousse or carac, a pastry with chocolate, between others. Guaranteed change of scenery!

L'UZINE RESTAURANT
Port
18, rue François-Guizol
✆ +33 (0)4 93 56 42 39

Open Tuesday noon to Saturday evening. Advance booking advised. Groups accepted by reservation. Terrace. Activities. Rates: à la carte for lunch €29. À la carte evening: €46 (dish). Accepted visa and Mastercard.

Uzine Restaurant offers mediterranean cuisine in an unusual and friendly setting in the heart of the port of Nice. On the large terrace, sitting around a table or nestling in a sofa for an aperitif with friends, or in the indoor room with industrial and minimalist decor, you can enjoy the chef's specialities in a trendy and musical atmosphere: burrata, salad of artichokes octopus, Tomahawk prime rib... An excellent address with prices sometimes high and and an efficient service.

VEGAN GORILLA
City Center
7, rue du Lycée
✆ +33 (0)4 93 81 32 98
www.vegan-gorilla.fr
veggiesociety@outlook.fr

Open all year. Monday, Tuesday and Thursday to Saturday from 12pm to 2.30pm and from 7.30pm to 10.30pm. À la carte: Around €18 (dish). The dishes change every week. Starter around €8. Dessert around €7. Juice €6.

This restaurant with an organic decoration honours vegan cuisine and doesn't use any animal products. Real haven of peace, experts but also the curious ones and epicureans will be charmed to go in a vegan and crudivore restaurant worthy of this name! The carte offers a choice of dishes which is renewed every week: chickpea pancakes with a home-grown vegetables sautée; black rice noodles, carrots mangos, avocado and sauce with peanut butter; quinoa and chickpeas with roasted eggplants, rocket salad, grenade and dragon sauce, stuffed zucchini, tomato juice and zucchini flower donuts... As for the desserts, according to the inspiration of the week, you will be able to choose a chocolate mousse or a raw tart. Lastly, for a little freshness, the house also created a green mojito and other vitaminized juices. The products used are fresh and organic, and all is home-made. A gourmet and healthy address. An excellent way to discover new healthy flavours!

VIA LATINA
Downtown
12, boulevard Jean-Jaurès
✆ +33 (0)4 93 62 87 21
www.vialatina.fr
contact@vialatina.fr

Open all year. Tuesday to Saturday from 9am to 7pm (service continuous). Sunday from 9am to 12.30pm. Closed public holidays. À la carte: Around €14 (dish). Fixed rate formula from €19. Terrace. Shop. Caterer.

La Boutique offers a tasting space where the greatest classics of the cheese factory and Italian charcuterie are represented. Compose your dish among a range of antipasti, ham, cheese or the must-eat focaccia. The most gourmands will be tempted by a small tour in Italy with a fine selection of best products. Pana Cotta or tiramisu or rum baba or Limoncello will bring the final touch for a perfectly successful stopover. As in any travel, it is necessary to bring home some souvenirs: go through the shop where you will undoubtedly succumb to the gourmet products which highlight the purest Italian artisanal tradition.

VILLA PARADIS
The carré d'or
5, impasse Longchamp
✆ +33 (0)9 67 38 85 31

Open all year. Restaurant open for lunch only. Bar in the evening. Tea room. Breakfast. Booking advised. À la carte: Around €25 (main course and dessert). Groups welcome (by reservation). Terrace.

Breakfast to start the day, lunch or tea time to enjoy some delicacies, or the bar, open in the evening for nice aperitifs, Villa Paradis will seduce you with its cosy atmosphere and warm welcome. Nestled in a dead-end, in the heart of the city centre, in a preserved, refined and rare setting, Villa Paradis has a relaxing appearance. Lunch will be colorful and tasty: Chinese salad with chicken, risotto with truffles and linguine carbonara, tuna steak with Asian sauce... At 4 pm, you can enjoy a Kusmi Tea Blue detox accompanied by Mesiano pastries... A bucolic, pleasant and culinary escape. To (Re) discover!

LE VINGT 4
Centre-ville
24, rue Alphonse-Karr
✆ +33 (0)4 93 88 45 49
www.levingt4.fr
contact@levingt4.fr

Open Monday to Saturday for lunch from 12pm to 3pm (last sitting at 2pm) and for dinner from 6pm (last sitting at 10pm). Closed on Sunday and Monday for dinner. For lunch: à la carte and daily specials. For dinner: menu, gourmet bistro, wine bar, apéritives slates & finger food. À la carte: Around €35 (starter + main course + dessert). Wine by the glass. Terrace.

Vingt4 shows two environments and thus offers two gustatory experiences. With its bright decor with white tones and lilacs at lunchtime midday, come to discover a seasonal menu that changes regularly: carpaccio of tomato pineapple, hearts of lettuce and serrano ham, Nice raviolis with ricotta and spinaches, crunchy vegetables, tagliata of beef fillet or even casserole of supreme of poultry from the Gers farm Label Rouge. In the evening, the atmosphere becomes more intimate when it is the bistronomy time at Vingt4, which offers appetizing slates and a worked gourmet carte: hot camembert casserole, flambéed with Calvados, pan-fried snails in Provence way, fillet of plaice in lasagnas, roasted cod with crust citrus and its emulsion of fava beans with Espelette pepper served with its fresh seasonal vegetables. For dessert, the gourmet ones will enjoy the sumptuous homemade chocolate fondant. To accompany these dishes, ask for the wine list (some are organic), which is almost available by glass. A little very Futé plus; some dishes are *gluten free*. And if you do not have time to sit down at the table for lunch, order before 11am, then pick up your dish of the day in an appropriate and disposable packaging.

VINI MUNDO
East Nice
32, avenue de la République
✆ +33 (0)4 93 56 34 13
riquette.sarl@sfr.fr

♿

Open all year. Monday to Friday for lunch and dinner; Saturday for lunch. Booking advised. Wine by the glass. Single dishes from €12. Wine by the glass from €4. Tickets restaurants only for lunch. Checks are not accepted. Groups welcome (up to 40 people By reservation. Banquet). Terrace. Wine to take away.

In a contemporary and uncluttered bistro wine cellar setting, the daily suggestions on the board are available according to the fresh market products: veal sauté with varied sauces, bœuf bourguignon, salmon in foil, pear-frangipane tart, chocolate fondant... Everything is homemade. As for the wine, the connoisseurs will find a wide range of classic or local vintages for a pre-dinner break as from 6 pm with charcuterie or selected cheeses plates.

VINIVORE LE BISTROT
Vieux Nice
10, rue Lascaris
✆ +33 (0)4 93 14 68 09
www.vinivore.fr
contact@vinivore.fr

Open all year. Closed on December 25th and on January 1st. Tuesday to Friday from 12pm to 2pm and from 7.30pm to 10.30pm; Saturday from 7.30pm to 10.30pm. Until 23: 00 in summer. Booking advised. Fixed rate formula starter + main course + dessert at €32. À la carte: Around €37 (starter + main course + dessert) €.12 (approximately). Wine by the glass. Luncheon vouchers only for lunch. Chèque Restaurant. Groups welcome (up to 30 people). Terrace.

In a cozy interior setting, the atmosphere echoes the menu by including neat dishes displayed on a large wall slate. The Chef offers his inspiration according to the market. You will enjoy the homemade fish soup, fresh scallop carpaccio with hazelnut juice vinaigrette and crab, Tartare of mushrooms and speck bacon or the catch of the day with wild rice with fresh mango, coconut milk lime emulsion. Refinement and respect of flavours will enchant the gourmets in an atmosphere that favours attention and conviviality.

SLEEPING

The team of le Petit Futé has travelled across the city and has put together a selection of establishments that stand out for their hospitality, their services and their quality/price ratio. Whatever your budget you will always be happy there. Feel free to contact them on behalf of le Petit Futé to have a privileged welcome or special tariff conditions. If you are staying in winter, the availability is great but be careful during the peak season (July and August): plan to book in advance.

ARMENONVILLE
Gambetta
20, avenue des Fleurs
✆ +33 (0)4 93 96 86 00
www.hotel-armenonville.com
nice@hotel-armenonville.com

Open all year. Hotel 100% non smoker. Front desk open from 7am to midnight. 17 rooms (including 8 rooms giving on the garden and the outdoor pool). Breakfast: €12 (buffet). Extra bed: €10 (cot available on request). Parking (free). Room from €73 per night for 2 people. American Express, Holiday voucher. Room n°8 adapted to the physically disabled people. Pets allowed (under certain conditions €20 per day). Free Wifi. Satellite TV. Safe and minibar in the rooms.

Hôtel Armenonville mixes contemporaneity with the charm of this former host house of the beginning of the 20th century. The rooms – including one specially designed and arranged for disabled people – are perfectly equipped and very comfortable: wi-fi, private safe, mini-bar, TV or air conditonning. Some rooms open onto the wonderful tree-lined garden where you can take your breakfasts on sunny days, as well as onto the swimming pool, real asset of this address oasis of peace and greenery in the city centre, only 10-minute walk from the beaches and the famous Promenade des Anglais. Big smart plus: private secure and free car park. We also appreciate the flawless reception of Yamina, the hostess.

AJOUPA APART'HÔTEL
Carré d'Or
4, rue Masséna
Reception on the 5th floor
✆ +33 (0)4 93 82 10 05
www.ajoupa.fr

Open all year. Reception 24/24. 39 rooms. Individual from €51. Studio Standard Double from €62 per night. Studio Higher Double from €75 per night. Studio Suite Junior from €87. Apartment Suite 2 rooms from €97 per night. Studios available from 2pm. Wifi. Dishwasher. Satellite TV.

Ajoupa offers rentals of studios and apartment. Its location in the city centre and within walking distance from the Promenade du Paillon makes it an ideal place of residence. If the front is not visible from the street, the reason is that the rooms are spread in a residential building. They are spacious and the style is contemporary and enjoy a quality comfort. All apartments are equipped with kitchenette, bathroom, adjustable air-conditioning and high-speed internet access. Bed linens and towels are provided. Managers are at the disposal of guests and they can also advise you on your holidays. Ajoupa? An ideal solution for a short or a long stay.

BOUTIQUE HÔTEL GOUNOD***
Quartier des Musiciens
3, rue Gounod
✆ +33 (0)4 93 16 42 00
www.gounod-nice.com
info@gounod-nice.com

Open all year. 43 rooms (9 suites). From €69 to €160. Breakfast: €14 (continental breakfast: €16). Parking: €18. Pets allowed (free). Catering facilities. Spa.

This beautiful hotel is in the heart of downtown near place Masséna and the beach. Rooms are air conditioned and equipped with Satellite TV. The bar is very pleasant, the reception and service beyond reproach. The hotel is very professional with excellent value for money.

HÔTEL ACANTHE

City Center
2, rue Chauvain
✆ +33 (0)4 93 62 22 44
www.hotel-acanthe.com

Open all year. Reception 24/24. 50 rooms (100% non smoker). Single room from €52; double room from €56 to €93; triple room from €76. Breakfast: €6. Spoken languages: English, German, Italian, Spanish, Arabic, Russian, Croatian. American Express, Diners Club. Free Wifi. Cleaning service.

With its family and charming welcome, Hôtel Acanthe is a good address with excellent quality/price ratio which offers comfort of good level in its category. Renovated, thermally and acoustically isolated thanks to double glazing, the bright rooms are small but equipped with perfect bedding, a flat-screen TV, toilet and a telephone. All rooms have a shower in modern bathrooms with hairdryer. Some even have a pleasant balcony with a wonderful view across the leafy gardens of the very pleasant Promenade du Paillon. A highly recommended address!

HÔTEL COMTÉ DE NICE

City Center
29, rue de Dijon
✆ +33 (0)4 93 88 94 56
www.hotelcomtedenice.com
info@hotelcomtedenice.com

Open all year. Reception 24/24 (spoken languages: German, English, Italian, Spanish, French). 55 rooms and 12 apartments. 100% non smoker. Single room from €48 to €73; double room from €61 to €86; triple room from €75 to €105. Full-board. Half-board (by reservation). Buffet breakfast: €7.50. Parking (private paying in basement). Small room of meeting for 40 people. American Express. Pets allowed. Free Wifi. Cleaning service. Satellite TV. Excursions.

Here is a charming hotel. Carefully run by Claudia and her team, you can stay in a classic room or in a studio equipped with a kitchenette made up of a fridge, electric hotplates, microwaves, a dining area and air conditioning. No matter what your choice is, everything is well maintained and tastefully decorated. The equipment is of good comfort: beds adorned with white duvets, satellite TV, telephone and complete bathroom... The apartments open onto a very calm inner courtyard. What more can be said? A pleasing staff which speaks any languages, a reception open 24 hours a day and a very good value for money.

HÔTEL CRONSTADT

Centre Ville
3, rue Cronstadt
✆ +33 (0)4 93 82 00 30
www.hotelcronstadt.com
reservation@hotelcronstadt.com

Open all year. Single room €80. Double room €100. Triple room €130. 10 rooms. Breakfast: €10. The reception or the information can be done at the reception, open from 10am to 10pm. Continental breakfast between 8.30am and 10am. Pets allowed.

Here is a charming and unusual and small hotel located in the heart of Nice. It is wonderfully located just a stone's throw away from the Promenade des Anglais (near the Negresco hotel); the beach is accessible on foot in a few minutes. Sheltered from city noise, this hotel is nestled in a flowered courtyard, in a residential building. The 10 rooms are furnished in a rather old-fashioned style, harmony reigns and it has lots of charm. One feels like in a cosy little nest. The rooms are spacious with high ceilings, specific to old buildings. They all offer modern comfort: air conditioning, bathroom... Add to this the warm welcome of the owner and you are guaranteed a pleasant stay.

HÔTEL EXCELSIOR

City Center
19, avenue Durante
✆ +33 (0)4 93 88 18 05
www.excelsiornice.com
contact@excelsiornice.com

Chateaux & Hôtels Collection. Open all year. Reception 24/24. 42 rooms. Double room from €109 to €369. Buffet breakfast: €15. Room business, classical, higher, deluxe, family and junior. Consult the special offers on the website. 2 adapted rooms. Free Wifi. Satellite TV.

This hotel built in 1898 in a Belle Époque style was renovated in 2014 by the atmosphere designer Sandrine Alouf who based the concept upon the invitation to travel: plane, train, cars and boat are equally represented by decorative objects. The setting is refined with modern comfort. The facilities are flawless: air conditioning, wi-fi, flat screen TV, telephone... An interior flower garden where ivy climb along the facade with a bay, as well as a beautiful terrace with teak tables; ideal for sunbathing, complete the services. An outdoor bar located in the middle of the garden opens between April and September whereas thematic evenings and other *after-work* parties are organised there. It is a charming «boutique hotel» just the way we like them.

LE PANORAMIC HOTEL

The Grande Corniche
107, boulevard Bischoffsheim
✆ +33 (0)4 93 89 12 46
www.hotellepanoramic.com
info@hotellepanoramic.com

Logis (2 cheminées). Open from February to November. Front desk open every day from 7am to 2pm and from 5.30pm to 8.30pm except Sunday from 7.30am to 1.30pm. 11 rooms. Half-board (from €68 per person). Room rate low and high season on the basis of double room from €68. Breakfast per person: €8 and €11.50. Rate half-board low and high season, on the basis of double room. No pets. Free Wifi. Catering facilities (Closed for dinner Sundays, during August and weekend of July. Seasonal menu 3 main courses: €26 (excluding drinks), €14 children's menu up to 12 years).

With its enchanting views of Nice and the Mediterranean, Le Panoramic hotel and restaurant offers beautifully decorated rooms, bright and very comfortable, with free direct telephone, hairdryer, Flat-screen tv, wi-fi and a bathroom with toilets. On site you will also enjoy the restaurant 360° which also offers a splendid view of the city. A good place to stay.

HÔTEL LOGIS VILLA VICTORINE**

Nice Ouest
11, rue du Docteur-Émile-Roux
✆ +33 (0)4 93 83 10 51
www.hotel-villa-victorine.com
info@hotel-villa-victorine.com

Logis (2 cheminées). Open all year. Hotel not smoker. Reception until 8pm (spoken languages: French, Italian, German and a little English). 8 rooms (5 doubles, 2 singles and 1 triple with separated beds not smokers). Half-board: €36. Buffet breakfast: €11. Extra bed: €20. Parking: €15 (depending on availability and by reservation). Single room from €50, double room comfort from €69, double room superior from €79, triple room from €99. Rate raised at the time of great events (GP F1 in Monaco, Cannes Film Festival...). Rate raised at the time of great events (GP F1 in Monaco, Cannes Film Festival...). Spoken languages: French, Italian, German and a little English. Pets allowed (€7/day). Free Wifi.

Charming charming hotel located in a residential area at the quiet, Hôtel Logis Villa Victorine is located near to the airport, the beach and the Promenade de Anglais (accessible on foot). This charming house of the years 1930 shelters very vain tastefully decorated rooms. The Raphaël owner is impassioned of gardening: he arranged besides the outdoor terrace in a true oasis of freshness where plants and fruit trees open out marvelously with the sun. The guests adore there to have the breakfast or to stroll after the beach. A small cosy nest where one remains «as at the house». Strongly advised booking.

HOTEL MONSIGNY

Malausséna
17, avenue Malausséna
✆ +33 (0)4 93 88 27 35
www.hotelmonsignynice.com
info@hotelmonsignynice.com

Open all year. Reception 24/24 (spoken languages: French, English, German). 55 rooms (100% non smoker). Breakfast included (all-you-can-eat buffet). Parking (private and made safe on request). Rooms from €90. 3 accessible rooms for disabled guests. Free Wifi. Catering facilities. Tea room. Lift. Reservation of guided tours on request.

Entirely renovated, Hôtel Monsigny has rooms with a cosy decoration, equipped with a small balcony. Air-conditioned and soundproofed, they all have a private bathroom. All are equipped with all the necessary comfort for an excellent stay: air conditioning, duvet, hairdryer, private toilet, shower, cable TV... Ideally located in the heart of the city centre at 250 m from the railway station and in front of the tram stop, you will particularly enjoy the view of the roof from the terrace. You will also enjoy the flavours of the local market typically Nice which is held in front of the hotel every morning. Professional and friendly reception.

HOTEL NICE RIVIERA

City Center
45, rue Pastorelli
✆ +33 (0)4 93 92 69 60
www.hotel-nice-riviera.com
info@nr.com.fr

Open all year. Reception 24/24. Buffet breakfast: €18. Parking: €19 (private). Tourist tax from €1.70 per person and per day. Congress and events: increase of 25% of applicable seasonal rate. Classic room from €193. Superior room from €217. Executive room from €239. Pets allowed (€10 per day by animal). Whirlpool, sauna.

Perfectly integrated in the urban landscape of Nice, this building with Art Déco architecture has just been beautifully renovated. All the rooms as well as the public areas have been redesigned and refurbished for a more contemporary and brighter decor. With a beautiful space of more than 20m², the bright coloured rooms are equipped with quality bedding. As for the lobby, library and bar, the decor is more mineral with dominant tones of grey and white. The wellbeing space is appropriate for relaxation with its indoor swimming pool, hot tub and sauna. A new Decléor spa is open 7days a week from 10 am to 8 pm: massages, scrubs and facials will complete your relaxation moment. The hotel is equipped with Internet access wi-fi.

HÔTEL LE SEIZE

City Center – 16, rue Chauvain
✆ +33 (0)4 93 80 76 11 – www.hotelseize.fr
contact@hotelseize.fr

Open all year. Reception 24/24. 34 rooms (non smoker). Breakfast: €9.50 (continental buffet). Double room from €70. Triple from €89. Small animals allowed (€10 per night). For the disabled guests: telephone for reservation. Free Wifi.

Beautiful establishment located in the heart of Nice just a few steps away from the Promenade du Paillon, Le Seize Hotel is placed under the theme of the Nice Artists. If the facade dates from the beginning of the 20th century, the interior is decidedly contemporary with warm colours such as beige and light – brown. The facilities are of good quality: excellent bedding, free wi-fi throughout the hotel, individual air conditioning, TNT TV ... You can book directly on line from the website and enjoy the numerous «*early booking*» special offers.

HOTEL VILLA LA TOUR

Old Nice – 4, rue de la Tour
✆ +33 (0)4 93 80 08 15
www.villa-la-tour.com
reservation@villa-la-tour.com

Open all year. Reception 24/24 (spoken languages: English, German, Italian, French). 17 rooms (non smoker). Buffet breakfast: €12.50. Extra bed: €20 (per day and per person. Cot €10 per day). 4 room categories: economic from €70 to €80 per night, tradition from €98 to €170, privilege from €130 to €188 and Junior suite from €180 to €240. American Express, Diners Club. Free Wifi. Cleaning service. Satellite TV.

This is a real romantic stopover in the heart of old Nice. Designed like a guestroom, this villa, built in the walls of an 18th century convent, has been bought by a hotelier couple. Jerome and Chimene come straight from the Mauritius island where they worked in luxury hotels. They now put their experiences into their own business. They have completely renovated this little pearl where each room is henceforth decorated on the theme of an artist. The rooms offer views of the old town and some have a balcony. They have quality equipments like: television, air conditioning, safe, wi-fi, hairdryer... It has a lot of charm and thumbs up for this little hotel. A restaurant will open soon on the theme of world food. A nice terrace to enjoy the sweetness of old Nice.

IBIS STYLES NICE VIEUX-PORT

Port
8, rue Emmanuel-Philibert
✆ +33 (0)4 92 00 59 00
www.ibisstyleshotels.com
H6991@accor.com

Open all year. Accor group. Reception 24/24 (spoken languages: French, English, German, Italian, Spanish). 114 rooms (100% non smoker). Double room from €89. Breakfast included. Garage: €14. Room for luggage free and secure. Family room (3 or 4). Checks are not accepted. American Express, Diners Club. Individual air conditioning. Corner games for children. WiFi unlimited. Internet corner in the living room. Sale of Fragonard products. Cleaning service. Catering facilities. Product sales. Excursions.

Ideally located near the port and the old town, this 3 star hotel has an ideal location in the heart of this active district. It has a private garage and 113 newly renovated rooms in a contemporary and electric style. Spacious and comfortable, they are provided with flat television screen, a safe (fee), flexible furniture and a bright bathroom. All have special connections for Ipod, MP3... They have a beautiful space, between 25 and 30 m². We also love the hotel lobby for a drink at the bar or read quietly in a sofa. Moreover, the management of the establishment organizes activities to make the place lively. It's a hotel with vitality, with a good mood, playful, a friendly decoration, a good price/quality ratio for this young and trendy address.

LA MALMAISON NICE

City centre
48, boulevard Victor-Hugo
✆ +33 (0)4 93 87 62 56
www.lamalmaisonnice.com
contact@lamalmaisonnice.com

Open all year. Reception 24/24. Buffet breakfast: €19 (hot buffet and cold). Free breakfast for children -3 years. Double room from €290. Triple room from €319. Public parking nearby: special rates on presentation of the card of the

hotel. Pets allowed (supplement €10/day). Free Wifi. Catering facilities (room service on request). Lounge bar. Business Corner. Bag shop.
In a splendid historic building, La Malmaison displays a trendy style where the charm of the contemporary art mingles with that of the Twenties. We like the bright spaces of the lobby and particularly its seating area. The rooms are carefully decorated. They are divided into 5 categories, from higher to premium with terrace. All of them are equipped with very comfortable bedding. As for the services and technologies, nothing has been forgotten: WiFi and VOD available in the rooms. Very nice address.

THE NEGRESCO
37, promenade des Anglais
✆ +33 (0)4 93 16 64 00
www.hotel-negresco-nice.com
reservations@lenegresco.com

Open all year. Reception 24/24. 96 rooms (and 21 suites). Double room from €245 to €2,500. Breakfast: €30. Extra bed: €85. Garage: €28. Member of The Leading Hôtels of the World. Checks are not accepted. American Express, Diners Club. Pets allowed. Seminars. Receptions and weddings. Internet corner. Free Internet access. Free Wifi. Cleaning service. Catering facilities (Chantecler and the Rotonde). Sale. Satellite TV. Excursions.
How can we mention the palaces of the French Riviera without mentioning the Negresco? Opened on January 8th, 1913 on the famous Baie des Anges and classified as a Historical Monument, it is now a real living museum. With the general renewal, the restoration of the facade, the repair of the entrance hall, and the royal lounge, the restoration of the Gustave Eiffel glass roof, the creation of an «executive floor» on the 5th floor with 9 suites and 6 rooms both fully domotized, the embellishment of the tables of the Chantecler gourmet restaurant and the creation of a terrace at La Rotonde, Jeanne Augier's prestigious hotel with an immaculate facade keeps moving onwards and has found a new youth.

RIVIERA HOLIDAY HOMES
City Center
23, avenue Jean-Médecin
✆ +33 (0)4 93 16 03 44
www.rivieraholidayhomes.com
helena@rivieraholidayhomes.com
Open all year. Rental of villas and apartments in Nice, in the back-country and in Villefranche-sur-Mer. Rates can be viewed on line and are variable depending on the type of accommodation and the season.
Riviera Holidays Homes is a seasonal rentals agency born from the passion Lucienne and Helena. This human-sized structure has for many years offered furnished apartments or independant villas for rent. Lucienne and Helena has no less than twenty years experience and master seven languages! The properties for rent are of great quality: beautiful well appointed apartments in Nice downtown and Villefranche-sur-Mer or villas with pool in the Alpes-Maritimes. You can make search on the Internet and directly book online. Then, the agency handles your transfer at your convenience, linen is provided (with welcome products like in hotels), beds are made at your arrival and even your groceries can be managed. Rental is possible from 4 nights whatever the day of your arrival. Professionalism and cheerfulness as a bonus: you may rent in peace here, there is no problem!

The Negresco.

LE SAINT-PAUL

Port – 29, boulevard Franck-Pilatte
✆ +33 (0)4 93 89 39 57
www.lesaintpaul-hotel.com
reservation@lesaintpaul-hotel.com

Open all year. 50 rooms. (Including 31 completely renovated in June 2017). Reception 24/24. Buffet breakfast: €11. Parking included (free, 80 places). Double room from €76 to €116 in low season; from €86 to €136 on average season and from €116 to €176 in high season. Suite deluxe from €236 to €296; apartment « view mer» from €136€ to €176. The difference in rates is related on the classification of the rooms and the orientation of the room: sea sight or garden. Rooms with beds doubles or twin beds. Possibility of apartment with supplement. Wifi. Catering facilities.

Saint-Paul is an atypical address. Formerly called La Maison du Séminaire, it housed formerly a religious education college then the Grand Séminaire, a hidden treasure on one of the most beautiful sites of the city... Thus, the building towers proudly facing the Mediterranean sea: you simply cross the street to take a swim. The setting is ideal and combines calm neighbourhood and the proximity to the heart of Nice is easy to reach even on foot. The rooms which benefit from a sea view are obviously the most charming. And the more you climb upstairs, the more the wider is the view you have. We also love the breakfast in the sun on the lovely terrace overlooking the sea where a hearty buffet is served every morning. Note that 5 equipped meeting rooms host conferences, workshop days or seminars from 5 to 200 people: the opening onto the chapel patio or the view on the Big Blue sea adds to the comfort of the working sessions. 2017 will be a renewal year for Saint Paul which has undertaken full renovation work for a few months. It will last over 2 years (with a break during the summer season). Thus, during June 2017, 31 completely reinvented rooms will be offered as a "luxury" formula. The second delivery will be done in May 2018. In addition to its geographical location, Saint Paul will enjoy a high quality standards worthy of the upscale Azur's hotels.

LE SLENDID HOTEL & SPA

City Center – 50, boulevard Victor Hugo
✆ +33 (0)4 93 16 41 00 / +33 (0)4 93 16 41 57
www.splendid-nice.com

European Ecolabel. Open all year. Reception 24/24 (online booking). 128 rooms. From €250 to €395. Hot buffet breakfast: €19. Garage: €24 for 24 hours, 2 €/1hour. Menu at €22 and at €29, children's menu at €12. American Express, Diners Club, Holiday voucher. Spoken languages: French, English, Italian, Spanish, Russian, Japanese, Chinese, German. Pets allowed. Seminars. Receptions and weddings. Free Wifi. Cleaning service. Catering facilities. Sale (product sales spa, foie gras and homemade jams). Satellite TV. Hammam, whirlpool. Activities.

The rooms are comfortable and the services worthy of the classification. Many have an individual outdoor terrace. 7th, 5th and 4th floors have just been renovated in a contemporary style which combines charm and traditional comfort. The 7th offers from now on a new presidential suite. Lifts were also changed and widened. On the eighth floor, the restaurant honors organic and local products in original and inventive creations. The outdoor pool is located finally on the roof of the hotel. As for Spa Splendid, it expects you for moments of relaxation. It should be noted that an extra cabin in duo with natural light should come out at the dawn of summer 2017 just as a new fitness space on the ground level. Smart information: a private car park exists under the hotel, extremely useful in the neighborhood!

VILLA BOUGAINVILLE BY HAPPYCULTURE™

29, avenue Thiers – Downtown
✆ +33 (0)4 93 88 96 81
www.villa-bougainville.fr

Open all year. Reception 24/24. Breakfast: €14 (from 7am to 10.30am). Parking: €20. Single room, standard or triple from €70 to €300 depending on the season. Free -2 years. Pets are not allowed. Free Wifi.

We are here plunged in the wild beauty of the tropical expeditions of the 19th century. Louis-Antoine de Bougainville, browser-explorer and fond of botany, brought back straight from Brazil this splendid plant which decorates today the gardens of the Mediterranean basin and which bears from now on its name: the Bougainvillea. Here, it isn't the plant but beautiful wall lining: butterflies, equatorial palms, hummingbirds in flights as well as beautiful botanical illustrations. The bright colors of the rooms, the rattan and exotic tree furniture as well as the Belle Epoque knick-knacks invite us to travel in time. You can go to the very intimate lobby lounge every day between 2 and 7pm at the Odysee Gourmande: a moment of frivolous relaxation between iced tea and exotic dried fruit and fresh exotic fruits. La Villa Bougainville? A pleasant jump in time and space.

VILLA OTERO BY HAPPYCULTURE™

Musicians district – 58, rue Hérold
✆ +33 (0)4 93 88 96 73
www.villa-otero.com
38 rooms. Rooms from €70 to €300 depending on the season. Reception 24/24. Buffet breakfast: €14. Parking: €25. Free Wifi.

A tribute to Caroline Otéro, dancer, actress and first movie star who settled in Nice in 1915 until the end of her life. In this boutique hotel of the musicians district, the Belle Epoque style is honoured. Rooms are comfortable and warm, with a retro furniture and a refined decoration. Some rooms have a balcony and others a large terrace offering the opportunity to enjoy a drink on sunny days. The restaurant has an elegant *vintage* furniture in shades of blue where every day during the afternoon guests are invited to share the Large Afternoon snack, a friendly moment of pleasure that offers apetizers, pastries, pies, macaroons and other colourful sweets. The cozy charm of this hotel is a jewel in the heart of Nice.

LEISURE

CAIRN-EXPE

54, chemin du Mont-Gros – East Nice
✆ +33 (0)6 70 65 25 88
www.cairn-expe.com
contact@cairn-expe.com
Quotation on request.

Want to discover the region differently? This is the address! The travel and event agency, Expe Cairn is specialized in unusual and exclusive excursions on the French Riviera. The team is charming and answers all your wishes while making you discover the Alpes-Maritimes in a surprising way. True impassioned, they will transmit their knowledge with happiness: sporting tourism, cultural discovery, history, heritage and nature, they will concoct you custom-tailored stays and excursions. Top-of-the-range services and an organization without fault will ensure you an unique experience. Discover hikes in the mountains with themes or in 4-wheel drive, paraglide over stunning landscapes, venture in canyons, land in helicopter at the top of a mountain for an aperitif with champagne at sunset. Also possibility to make your proposal in an incredible magic moment. The juniors are also offered singular activities. To (Re) discover urgently!

CANYON CIANS

Daniel Crulli
3, place Général-de-Gaulle
Liberation
✆ +33 (0)6 87 56 49 41
www.canyoncians.fr
daniel.crulli@gmail.com
Canyoning, climbing, via ferrata, alpinism around Nice and its region. From April to October, half-day or for a day. Initiation and improvement for canyoning (from April 1st to October 30th): from €40 to €55. Climbing (all year): from €35 to €400. Via Ferrata and course venture (all year): from €40 to €55. Alpinism (all year): from €280 to €550. Hikings.Canyon.

The club Canyon Cians invites you to discover the region as you never have! Whether you are alone, with friends, family, beginner or experienced, initiate yourself to the practice of canyoning, via ferrata, climbing or water hiking in the Alpes-Maritimes, ideal destination for these activities! The lessons, games, sports are adapted to your level very safely by instructors and qualified guides of State.

© VIRGIL PRUDHOMME

Beach in Nice.

INTERNATIONAL DIVING CENTRE – CIP
Manager: Aurélien Mathieu
2, ruelle des Moulins – The Port
✆ +33 (0)4 93 55 59 50 / +33 (0)6 09 52 55 57
www.cip-nice.com
info@cip-nice.com

Open all year. Low season (consult planning on website): outings 7 days a week from 9am to 12pm and from 2.30pm to 5.30pm. Baptisms €50, long version (40 minutes) €95. Discovery pack €150. Exploration €36. Formation FFESSM and PADI, rates available on website CIP. Group outings 10 divers min. Holiday vouchers accepted.

The CIP Nice takes you aboard his 14 feet long ship approved by Marine Marchande, the «Rene- Madeleine», to make you enjoy the unique experience of diving. On board, you will get equipped without problem thanks to the large space on the deck. As for the material, the club has 45 complete equipments and a capacity of 140 m³ of air inflation. Once equipped, three destinations are offered: port and Cape of Nice, Villefranche bay and Cap Ferrat, Cap Ferrat Est and Cap Estel. For children and adults, an introduction to all types of dives framed by experienced instructors. The club also offers diving for groups or themed around photo or biodiversity.

HOLLAND BIKES
Downtown
2, rue Blacas
✆ +33 (0)9 63 06 00 76
www.hollandbikes.com
nice@hollandbikes.com

Open Tuesday to Saturday from 9.30am to 7pm non stop. City bike rental day €19, week €100. Electric bike rental: day €35, week €200.

Feel like visiting Nice and its neighbourhoods differently? At Holland Bikes Nice, you can rent authentic Dutch bicycles (city or electric) famous for their comfort. Borrow the cycle tracks of the French Riviera and discover the coastline in a sportive and amusing way in family or between friends but also in full safety. A guide ensures in French or English the outing and the framing (3 hours duration from 10am to 1pm). But attention because if you are interested by this formula, don't forget to book! The shop also sells bicycles (city, electric, hiking) Batavus brands, Gazelle, Koga, Sparta as well as accessories and equipment. Holland Bikes ensures also bicycle repairs whatever the brand. Profit from subsidies for the purchase of an electric bicycle by the Urban community Nice Côte d' Azur, get more information at the Nice Town Hall.

NICE DIVING
Port District
13, quai des Deux-Emmanuel
✆ +33 (0)6 14 46 04 06
www.nicediving.com
nicediving@gmail.com

Open every day except Sunday afternoon in low season. 1 diving €55 (if equipped 35€). Package 3, 5 and 10 divings respectively at €100, €170 and €330 if equipped and €160, €265 and €500 without equipment. Technical diving €70 or €85. Formation in collective progress FFESSM level 1 at €315, level 2 and 3: €495 or €550. Semi-private and private classes possibility. Possible formation PADI OWSI. Equipment rental. Special formula « Discover Nice Diving»: €145

Do you wish to explore the wonderful diving sites of Nice and surroundings? Discover the underwater world, very rich in fauna and flora? Nice Diving invites you to share their trainers' passion. Exploration diving to technical diving, or a simple baptism in Discover Nice Diving, a kind of «improved» baptism which includes your first diving course, 15 min of exercises with a monitor which allows the 30 min of free stroll (although accompanied), diving formations framed 20 m and 40 m, to autonomous diver 20 m, with PADI divers. This underwater diving center enables you to enjoy privileged moments in an exceptional environment. Classroom with computers and video projector for the briefing, material top-of-the-range renewed each year, showers and store equipment, shop to buy or rent equipment, workshop for repairs and the maintenance of the equipment and inflation station to 300 bars... but also, and especially, the reception is cordial, the after diving aperitif is musical, and a good atmosphere and professionalism reigns on board!

TRANS COTE D'AZUR
Port
Quai Lunel
✆ +33 (0)4 92 98 71 30
www.trans-cote-azur.com
croisieres@trans-cote-azur.com

Other destinations and outings detailed on the website. Rate (S) on request. Possibility of buying the online tickets on the website. Iles de Lerins (1hour) €40 from end of May to beginning of July and from beginning of September to beginning of October Tuesday, Thursday, Saturday and Sunday and from beginning of July to end of August every day (except Monday).

Trans Cote d'Azur is a navigation company specialist in cruises, excursions, freightings and shuttles with departures from Cannes and Nice. You can discover the coastline during the seafront promenade, take a crossing to Cannes and the lerins islands, stroll along the Corniche d'or or go to Monaco or Saint-Tropez! The company also offers its services during special events such as the fireworks in Cannes or Grand Prix F1 in Monaco. You can also create your own day with lunch, a cocktail or a dinner on the boat.

Relaxation & Fitness

ESPACE HI BODY
Gambetta – 3, avenue des Fleurs
✆ +33 (0)4 97 07 26 26
www.hi-hotel.net
hi@hi-hotel.net
Inside the Hi hotel

Open every day from 10am to 11pm.

Hi is engaged in well being in its Hi-Body Space, all the cosmetics are from the REN brand, organic products combining techniques of treatments and the respect of the skin. On the programme: hammam and Swedish, Californian, Chinese, shiatsu and Thai massages, reflexology and ayurvedic. Contemporary bath in resin, the true Moorish hammam with two areas of warmth and two adjacent rooms, one with musical relaxation on sofas, the other with massages and treatments. Essential oil scents. Infusions and organic green tea available.

NYRVANA HAMMAM
Western Nice
7, avenue de Fabron
Résidence Les Grands Cêdres
✆ +33 (0)4 92 10 96 35
www.nyrvana.fr
nyrvana@orange.fr

Open Monday to Saturday from 10am to 7pm. On appointment only. Ancestral modelling with scented natural oils from €45. Oriental modelling: Modelling of the body, the face, and the scalp with Shea butter: €75. Modelling with volcanic stones, Shea butter and scented oils: €95. Traditional hammam + scrub and space of rest: €40.

This beautiful hammam with shades of colour promises you hours of relaxation combining cares and well-being. Here, the soft treatments for the body optimise the benefits of the humid heat of the hammam. A range of treatments such as Californian massages, body scrubs, ancestral massage with fragrant natural oils (jasmine, orange blossom, white musc), massage with volcanic stones with shea butter and perfumed oils and beauty treatments. Each hammam session can be followed by, facial treatments, oriental hands care, treatments of the feet or a wrap with rassoul... After the treatment enjoy the relaxation room with a cup of tea.

INSTITUTE SPA PATRICIA LAURENS
Gambetta – 93, boulevard Gambetta
✆ +33 (0)4 93 37 95 95
www.institut-spa-nice.com
contact@patricia-laurens.fr

Open Tuesday to Saturday from 10am to 7pm. Face care from €42. Body treatments from €45. Spa treatments from €65. ½ legs + underarms + bikini line: €27 Special rates for subscribed. Tuesday to Saturday from 10am to 7pm. Idea for a gift.

A need or a desire to escape from everydays life? Then go to the Institut Spa Patricia Laurens for a moment of pure relaxation and well-being. Professionals are here at your disposal to take care about your body. In this space dedicated to beauty, you will be pampered: personalized treatments for the face and body, especially for you. You will also find a range of beauty products that come from all around the world. Each week, very good treatments at attractive prices are offered.

MASS' OASIS
Old Nice – 3, rue de l'Opéra
✆ +33 (0)4 93 87 06 70 / +33 (0)6 32 23 41 58
www.massoasis.net

Open every day from 10.30am to 7.30pm.

Relax in this Asian urban spa that offers well-being massages and other relaxation techniques for you to get rid of tensions and stress. Thanks to the expert hands of the Mass'Oasis team, find your energy balance and your interior harmony. You can also enjoy a private hammam, and a relaxation area is at your disposal to relax with a tea selected for its relaxing qualities. Away from the stress of daily life, escape!

GOING OUT

ROOFTOP 17
17, avenue Malaussena
✆ +33 (0)4 93 88 27 35 / +33 (0)4 89 74 91 61
www.hotelmonsignynice.com

Open April 29th to October 15th. Open from 10am to 8pm 7 days a week except Tuesday. Hot tub access + towel €10 (external guest). Softs, fruit juice from €4. Mocktails and smoothies from €7/8; cocktails from €10 to €15. Fixed rate formula Plates to be shared (Nordic, Cheese, Italian) €15 - with 2 glasses of wine €22. Tapas of the moment from €10. Breakfast at €6 in express version and €12 in american buffet at will. Parking Gare du Sud and Libération.

It is the youngest in the family of the rooftops of the city... The Rooftop 17 is perched on the roof of the hotel Monsigny, recently renovated in 2016. It has a stunning 360° view over the roof tops of Nice.

The establishment is in Liberation area: it is a really pleasant part of the city, refreshed by the arrival of the Tram and the renovation of the former railway station of the south, with its covered market, its cinema, its parking... You are close to all (shops, beach, Promenade de Anglais), in a true atmosphere of neighborhood, with its colourful market and its regulars. The bar is on the roof terrace. You can come in the morning to enjoy the view, to have a hot tub break or for breakfast... Day time is rather reserved to deckchair lovers and sunbathing safe from glances... But it is for the aperitif that the setting is most beautiful... You'll enjoy a good cocktail or of a glass of wine, with tapas, in a musical atmosphere. A cosy place to discover!

Tea Rooms

AU GOUT THE D'ANTAN
Valrose – 31, avenue Borriglione
✆ +33 (0)6 09 61 00 59
www.au-gout-the-d-antan.fr

Open Tuesday to Friday from 12pm to 7pm. Terrace. Take-away. Accepted groups. No cheques.

Au Goût Thé d'Antan welcomes you throughout the week in a warm and friendly atmosphere, and in an old-style decoration rather *girly*. Here, enjoy grand cru of teas, coffees variations (natural, coffee of the month, or with a syrup of your choice) and other milk or chocolate drinks, accompanied by homemade and gourmet pastries and cakes as good as grandmas! Everything is delicious, the service is friendly and in a very cosy place.

MANDISE'S COFFEE

City Center
14, rue Defly
✆ +33 (0)4 93 27 98 80
mandises.coffee@gmail.com
Parking Marshall

Open Tuesday to Friday from 7.15am to 6pm, Saturday from 8.30am to 6pm. Espresso €1.50. Tea €3.50. Smoothies 4€. Fresh juice €3.50. Milk shake from €4. Sodas €2. Fixed breakfast formulas from €2.80. Sweeties from €1.80. Bagels from €5.50, toasted slices of bread: €5.90. Salads: from €6.90. Lunch formulas from €8.50.

A sweet corner of paradise in the angle of rue Gioffredo and rue Defly: the Mandise'S Coffee. Amandine and her mom Nathalie welcome you with kindness in a pretty turquoise and gray decor like a Scandinavian bistro. Here, businessmen come for a peaceful break, families for moment of delicacy, students, friends... all in search of a cordial place «like at home». The mistresses of the place love to take special care of their guests. They also offer freshly prepared dishes such as the delicious cheese and vegetable cake, the home made fries, or simple *brownies* and *cookies*. Quality ingredients such as the wonderful fruit juice «Les Chemins de Verger», the Ben & Jerry's ice creams, the Palais des Thés teas... at very soft prices. Whether seated on the terrace or inside, or that you just pass by to take away, the nice smiles of Amandine and Nathalie do not lie: tenderness and delicacy are there for you. Regulars are not misled!

SALON DE THÉ MIEL D'OCHUN

Old Nice
5, rue de la Loge
✆ 07 87 32 44 79
Tram: Jean Jaurès - Parking des Arts

Open all year Tuesday to Saturday from noon to 5.30pm. Organic tea and iced tea: €3.60. Tea of the day: €1.90. Cakes: €3.70 the share.

Miel d'Ochun (pronounced ochon) is a small jewel located in the middle of the old Nice. Leydis, a nice cuban settled here to accommodate and treat us with a smile. We chose the specialty: the Mojithé iced tea, a natural tea with lime, sugar, fresh mint and mojito syrup. We accompanied it with one of the homemade cakes, the lemon-raspberry cake. Leydis also offers daily specials served all day long.

Bars & Pubs

APOTHEKA

Old Nice
2, rue de la Préfecture
✆ +33 (0)6 85 47 13 96

Open from Monday to Saturday from 7pm to 2am. Wine by the glass €5. Aperitifs (Ricard, Martini, Campari) €5. Bottled beers €8. Softs €4.50.

Trendy address at the entrance of the old town, the place is charming. Evenings are regularly organised animated by trendy DJ's, and the menu of cocktails is varied. You can also order a board or a salad to start the night. All the ingredients are there to spend a good evening with friends, only failing: the prices are a little high ... Cloakroom obligatory.

BIG BEN

City Center
9, rue Alberti
✆ +33 (0)4 93 80 09 74
pubbigben@hotmail.fr

Open Monday to Saturday from 5.30pm to 2.30am. Closed on Sunday.Drinks from €3.80, plancha from €6.80/pers.

We love the atmosphere of this very *british* pub: quiet and subdued setting, impeccable service, comfortable sofas and armchairs, wide range of beers, whiskys and varied cocktails on a *rock, pop, jazz* or *blues musical atmosphere*. It is the ideal English pub tor enjoy moments of real relaxation between *gentlemen* or friends. In the family of English pubs, it is definitely the nicest. Possibility of snacks during the evening.

BOSTON BAR

Port
11, place Île-de-Beauté
✆ +33 (0)6 11 75 14 62

Open Monday to Saturday from 5pm to 00.30am. Cocktails, wines and tapas. Booking advised.

For an aperitif or for a pleasant evening with friends, Boston Bar is the ideal place: vintage decor with industrial accents, idyllic view under the arches of the Port facing the sea, intimate atmosphere, list of varied cocktails, tapas snacks (plates of charcuterie, cheese, salmon)... all on a trendy music background! We also love the warm friendliness of the team. A nice address with good humour.

CAFÉ PAULETTE

Petit Marais Nicois
15, rue Bonaparte
✆ +33 (0)4 92 04 74 48

Open all year. Monday to Wednesday from 8am to 7pm as from Thursday from 8am to midnight in low season. Tuesday to Saturday from 7.30am to 00.30am in high season. Terrace. Catering facilities. Activities.

At Café Paulette, the atmosphere changes with the hours. In the morning, you can settle to have your breakfast. At lunchtime, discover a fresh carte and dishes products of the market. For tea time, the place is transformed into tea room just before the aperitif which continues from 7.30pm with delicious bistronomic tapas (Iberian charcuterie plate, trilogy of the sea, hummus, homemade foie gras, dish of cheeses...). We also liked the decoration which recalls these former breweries with an insane charm: a lovely dining area with exposed stones, a canopy opening on a very appreciable terrace covered in any season and some tables posed outside in the middle of Petit Marais niçois. The friendly atmosphere adds to the quality of this place with coloured dishes.

LES CAVES DU BUBBLES

Carré d'or
7, avenue de Suède
✆ +33 (0)4 93 27 97 76

Open Monday to Saturday from 7pm to 1am. American Express. Wifi. Terrace. Catering facilities. Concerts. Bar. Wine cellar. Air conditioning. Parking. Non-stop service. Tea room. Private rooms.

The «Bubbles» is both a wine cellar, a champagne bar and a restaurant with terrace. The decor is modern, stylish and uncluttered. The welcome is warm and relaxed without forgetting the atmosphere, festive and punctuated by the selection of the DJ. At the end of the day for an aperitif, try the refined and copious dishes that go with a wine tasting. Check the musical program and events on their Facebook page. A place not to miss, where you can spend a great time for a drink or dinner.

COMPTOIR CENTRAL ÉLECTRIQUE

Petit Marais
10, rue Bonaparte
✆ +33 (0)4 93 14 09 62
Open Monday to Saturday from 8.30am to 00.30am. Sunday brunch around €25.
In a felted and cosy atmosphere, the Comptoir Central Electrique (CCE) invites you at any time of day to relax around a hot chocolate or a fresh fruit juice. Seetled in an old electricity shop, the CEC is also a restaurant at midday and in the evening for gourmet dishes, and a hearty Sunday brunch (booking strongly advised). The friendly and cheerful welcome of the team adds to the conviviality of this very bright place!

DISTILLERIES IDÉALES

Old Nice
24, rue de la Prefecture
✆ +33 (0)4 93 62 10 66
www.lesdistilleriesideales.fr
lesdistilleriesideales@gmail.com
Open all year. Every day from 9am to midnight. Happy Hour from 6pm to 8pm. Wifi.
Just for a fresh beer or to nibble a good charcuterie or cheese plate, or simply for a coffee break in a nice place... Les Distilleries Idéales are worth the detour. It is at the same time a lounge and a tasting bar which brings us back a few centuries ago. Decoration is splendid: old style, mingling in an original way coppered metal and wood panelling. The prices are very reasonable and the atmosphere extremely pleasant. A true bistro as we like them.

THE FOLIE'S

City Center
18, rue du Congres
✆ +33 (0)6 26 84 21 02
www.lefolies-nice.com
lefolies06@gmail.com
Open from 7pm to 2.30am. Afterwork every Tuesday and Wednesday on the private terrace from 7pm.
Chic, elegance and trend, all the assets are put together here for you to start your gourmet evenings with a cocktail prepared by the chef bartender with delicious finger food. An early evening which you can continue in the festive atmosphere that continues. . .

AU FUR ET A MESURE

Old Nice – 2, rue Jules-Gilly
✆ +33 (0)4 93 55 29 75
www.aufutetamesure.com
nice@aufut.fr
Open Monday to Sunday from 5pm to 00.30am
Beer lovers have found their address. Concept coming from Spain, enjoy trappist, abbey, flavoured, white beers, lager, ales... On each table, a beer pump is installed allowing guests to do the waiter's job: with a card, you can therefore without getting up directly (re) fill your glass in an rocky atmosphere. Four pumps are also directly set up on the bar. In the evening, the giant screen allows you to watch sporting events. Note that cocktails and homemade tapas complement the menu. A friendly place.

GOSSIP BAR

Port
7, rue Bonaparte
✆ +33 (0)4 93 45 72 15
gossip.bar06@gmail.com
Open every day from 5pm to 2.30am. Restaurant until midnight. Wines and cocktails. Terrace.
This cosy and relaxing place, ideally located in the Petit Marais area of Nice and close to the Garibaldi Square, is perfect for a drink with friends after work. Nestled in the sofas, a place to gossip, while sipping the speciality of the bar, the mojito. The intimate moments change to more electric rhythms as the hours go by: here we go for a great party in a gay-friendly atmosphere which we love! Note that the Gossip is also open during the day and offers a great restaurant menu to be enjoyed on the terrace in summer.

JAM

Carré d'Or
8-10, rue Commandant Raffalli
✆ 07 86 21 25 29
www.jam-bar-nice.com
Open all year. Open until 2.30am Tuesday to Sunday. Happy hours (from 6pm to 9pm). Beers from €4. Cocktails from €8. Organization of events. Premises rental. Coffee philosophy. Jam Session. Wine bar. Tapas. Private club. Creative bar. Concerts (every day. Programming available on the website).
This scenic space with its cosy and intimate decor is the perfect place for a drink and to discover the future artistic talents. A real open stage for all forms of artistic expression, the programming is eclectic (comedy, classical music, circus, music, improvisations) and changes every evening following the different themes (visual and/or sound shows, mini concerts...). Bring your musical instrument, get on stage and start your jam – improvisation session, in case you are wondering! Between 5: 00 and 8: 00 pm, you can also have meal within an acoustic atmosphere and share a stimulating aperitif with a varied programme: slams and poetry, café philosophique, café litéraire... If you are a lovers of cultural innovations, it is your new address! You will also appreciate the dynamic and smiling welcome of the team as well as the à la carte menu that offers Nice's dishes, vegetarian dishes, hearty dishes of tapas on blackboard or charcuterie and cheeses, the burgers, a French local cuisine or the dishes of the world for a guaranteed escape moment! Starting from 1st of May, profit from a breakfast service from 8: 00 in the morning and lunches and dinners shows as well.
Guided tours service on foot with a national guide speaker, by bicycle, electric bicycle and on board of a minivan in partnership with Nice Azur Visit – Creative Tourism. Information on www.nice-azur-visit.com

JUKE HOUSE CAFÉ

City Center – 8, rue Defly
✆ +33 (0)4 93 80 02 22
jukehousecafe@yahoo.fr
Tram: Garibaldi stop

Open all year. Tuesday to Saturday from 5pm to midnight. Nonstop catering facilities. Burger from €11.50. Tapas around €5. Salad around €13. Terrace. Air conditioning. Wifi.

This tapas and cocktail bar comes straight from the USA. Between old vinyls, Coca-Cola vintage posters and photos of New York around the Juke Box which stands in the main dining room, guests can choose tunes of their choice between the hundred pieces of pop, rock, soul and jazz. Bright walls, bar, black leather chairs, comfortable armchairs and dark wooden tables on the chocolate floor make the decor where you enjoy your drink chosen among forty cocktails, beers and aperitifs. You can also enjoy hearty tapas dishes, burgers and desserts on the terrace on sunny days.

KOSMA PIANO-BAR

Old Nice – 8, rue Sacha-Guitry
✆ +33 (0)4 89 03 47 46
www.kosmapiano-bar.fr

Open all year Tuesday to Sunday from 11pm to 5am. Thursday to Saturday, afterworks aperitifs shows from 6pm to 11pm with Live Music.

Want to start with a relaxation evening in the heart of the Old Nice? Le Kosma offers *live* music jam sessions, scenes open to music, or theater and cabaret shows... It is an aperitif show! A friendly setting, an atmosphere given by the resident pianists with rich and varied repertoires, here is the ambiance of the place so that you can take good advantage of theese important moments of decompression.

MOVIDA

Promenade des Anglais – 37-39, quai des Etats-Unis ✆ +33 (0)4 93 80 48 04

Open all year. Open 7j7 from 10am to 2.30 in the morning.
Latino bar with a 100% friendly atmosphere, Movida displays a beautiful atmosphere bodega type! Nestled at the bottom of the Castle hill, you'll appreciate either the terrace overlooking the sea or the nicely decorated interior elegant dining room. La Movida is the perfect place for homemade tapas, on a pleasant musical background. The carte proposes inter alia, bravas potatoes with salsa and aïoli, small nems with shrimps and squids a la niçoise... It is beautiful and it is good.

MA NOLAN'S IRISH PUB NICE PORT

Port – 5, quai des Deux-Emmanuel
✆ +33 (0)4 92 27 07 88 – www.ma-nolans.com

Open all year. From 11am to 2am with a non-stop service until 11pm. Breakfast from €4.90. Snack from €4.90. Salad from €11.90. Sandwich from €5.50. Burger from €10.90. Daily special €9.90. Children's menu €6. Concerts.
There is no longer any need to prove Ma Nolan's reputation in the old nice, which is now world-wide. Now discover the eponymous pub located on the pier of the port. A stylish and elegant décor mixes harmoniously wood, steel and leather giving it a friendly atmosphere. This address is the ideal place for a drink with friends and have fun. There are also live groups every Friday, Saturday and Sunday evening, and sporting retransmissions of all the largest football, rugby and gaelic games. . . You can even try to win €100 at the Ma Nolan's quiz every Thursday at 8pm. The choice of drinks is varied and everyone finds happiness. Also note the beautiful terrace which offers both an extraordinary view of the fishing boats as well as the moored yachts but also on the castle hill.

MA NOLAN'S IRISH PUB VIEUX-NICE

Old Nice – 2, rue Saint-François-de-Paule
✆ +33 (0)4 93 80 23 87 – www.ma-nolans.com

Open all year. From 11am to 2am. Breakfast from €4.90. Snack from €4.90. Salad from €11.90. Sandwich from €5.50. Burger from €10.90. Daily special €9.90. Children's menu €6. Concerts.
Ma Nolan's is an irish pub with a friendly atmosphere and a decoration from the beginning of the 20th century with a large wooden room. It is here in the cool and jovial atmosphere that the Anglo-Saxon communities and their friends get together to listen to pop-rock sound and to sip a whisky, a cocktail but above all a good Irish beer! From 12.00 p.m. to 11.00 p.m. a large carte offers dishes like the english like eating: burgers, chicken pie, mushrooms and peas, beef and Guiness pie, a good irish T-bone steak and a series of salads at reasonable prices.Take part in the quiz every monday at 20: 00 pm and attempt to win a Ma Nolan's €100 voucher. You can also watch all the biggest football or rugby matches and even gaelic sports. Those who prefer listening to music can attend live music sessions every evening of the week from 10:00 or 11:00 pm.

PER LEI
7, rue Emmanuel-Philibert
✆ +33 (0)4 93 07 50 24
Open Monday to Saturday from 9am to 12pm and from 2pm to 6pm. Breakfast from €3.50. Snacking from €3.90. Cocktails from €6.
It is in the heart of the Bonaparte area, in the middle of the Nicois Marais that Café Per Lei was established. In spite of the multitude of bars and restaurants present in this smart and trendy area, this Lounge café distinguished itself with a refined and purified decoration. Here, the dominant colours are white and felted gray. As soon as you pass the door of this establishment, you'll feel the warmth of this place which counts a good amount of tables. The room is spacious and bright thanks to a huge bay window. In Per Lei, you can come for a French or English breakfast, for a drink during the day or to enjoy a bruschetta.

POOL BAR & LOUNGE-RADISSON BLU
223, promenade des Anglais
Radisson Blu Hotel ✆ +33 (0)4 97 17 71 77
www.radissonblu.com
info.nice@radissonblu.com
Opening of the bar from 10am to 5pm every day, from 9am to midnight in summer.
One of the most beautiful views of Nice, with a perspective on the Promenade de Anglais, the Pool Bar & Lounge of the Radisson Blu Hotel became one of the places impossible to circumvent for the trendy nicois evenings, in particular during the Jazz festival and in high season. The atmosphere is smart and relaxed and the service is worthy of the place: staff takes good care and all is done for you to pass a pleasant evening.

PUZZLE BAR
1, rue de la Préfecture
✆ +33 (0)6 43 17 99 26 / +33 (0)6 32 39 27 39
www.puzzlebar-nice.com
contact@puzzlebar-nice.com
Open all year Monday to Sunday from 6pm to 2.30am.
In a modern and elegant ambiance, where some works of art are regularly exposed, the barmen behind the bar excel for the greatest happiness of the guests. On a trendy musical background, cocktails – that can go with a beautiful dish of tapas – display daring and original names, who leave in your mouth various astonishing and even surprising flavours! Taste the Hey Farfadet des Iles, La Belle rencontre, Ramon la Fraise, Jet lag... We loved it, and the team is pleasant, professional and dynamic. Indeed, each barman already has a brillant course: departmental gold medal for Better Apprentice of France and regional Silver medal of France for Maxime; the Chef Barman Matthieu – ancient bartender of the Hôtel Métropole in Monaco, the Grand Hotel of St-Jean Cap Ferrat and Fred's Bar in Nice – also worked for prestigious spirit brands in the region PACA; Anthony was crowned Better Apprentice of France «tableware and the service» and Jeune Talent restaurateur 2013 (inter alia). Puzzle Bar? A know-how to awake you tastebuds, quality ingredients, a rich and varied carte, and a top atmosphere for unforgettable evenings. What more?

STARBUCKS
City centre
30, avenue Jean Medecin
Nice Etoile shopping centre NO
✆ +33 (0)4 93 80 11 10
www.starbucks.com
Open Monday to Saturday from 8.30am to 7.30pm. Take-away.
The coffee specialist is very succesfull in the azurean capital: hot drinks containing coffee (cappuccino, mochaccino...) and a range of hot chocolates are offered on the spot or take-away. (Re) discover the frappés with or without coffee but also the fruit juices or the various pastries (cheese-cake, bones, muffins, cookies...) in a modern and contemporary atmosphere. A pure pleasure!

THE STAGE
Old Nice
4, rue du Pont-Vieux
✆ +33 (0)9 81 47 77 70 / +33 (0)6 84 68 64 74
www.thestage-nice.com
info@thestage-nice.com
Tram stop: Cathédrale-Vielle Ville - Parking: Palais de Justice
Open Wednesday to Sunday from 6pm to 0h30. Happy hours (aper' hour from 6pm to 8.30pm: antipasti buffet included in the price of your consumption). Wednesday: open scenes, Thursday: concert, Friday: all around theater, Saturday: concert.
An "Aperitif factory" with *live* music or theatre workshops! The Stage is the place to discover, the place where there is always something going on. As for discoveries, you will be delighted every evening, The Stage offers, after his *aper 'hour*, the famous Italian aperitif declined a la nicoise from 6pm to 8.30pm with live music with future talents and also with its nursery of jazz, rock, classical music and open mics talents without forgetting their theatrical discoveries... Everyone can find their pleasure. A nice program to be discovered on their website.

WAREHOUSE
Promenade des Anglais
73, quai des Etats-Unis
✆ +33 (0)6 16 24 45 27
www.warehouse-nice.com
contact@warehouse-nice.com
Open all year. From 6pm to 8pm: aperitif, board, tapas. From 7pm to 11pm: bistronomic restaurant. From 11pm to 2am: live music and DJ.
This chic and modern bistro with a decoration which reminds us a New Yorkean atmosphere offers a revisited french cuisine: homemade foie gras, Burgundy snails, frogs' leg with pastis, cassolette of Scallops and crayfish with mashed sweet potatoes, mountain pork chop and its potatoes. Most gourmet will choose the excellent tiramisu dessert or the homemade tarte tatin. At the end of the day or in the evening, you can enjoy homemade tapas with friends: nachos and guacamole, crustys of goat cheese with curry, *pan con* tomatos and raw ham or hearts of stuffed artichokes! A very nice address.

WAYNE' S BAR

Old Nice
15, rue de la Préfecture
✆ +33 (0)4 93 13 46 99
www.waynes.fr
info@waynes.fr

Open every day from 10am to 2am. Terrace. Concerts (live music and DJ).

This pub has a very good atmosphere and the two rooms are often bursting with people. Here, we speak English on all floors, winter and summer. In the first room, you can enjoy a good burger while watching a sports match on the TV while in the backroom, you will be seated for a drink while listening to live music playing pop-rock sounds. As the hours go by, the temperature rises: as a result, everyone ends up dancing on the tables at the end of the evening in a boosted atmosphere!

WORKHOUSE CAFÉ

Facing the MAMAC
64, Boulevard Risso
✆ +33 (0)4 93 01 27 25
www.workhousecafe.com
info@workhousecafe.com

Coffee. Possibility of privatizing the place on request. WiFi optical fiber. Printer. Scan. Secure lockers. Terrace exceptionally accessible to all on Sunday.

Are you a nomad worker or a freelance, and you want to work from a warm and welcoming place? Direction the Workhouse Cafe where you can share, exchange and extend your network thanks to a beautiful space of 400 m ^{2} which can accommodate up to 32 people. You can also combine business with pleasure, by tasting a pastry, a salad, a sandwich or even a brunch on site.

Nightclubs

THE 6

Old Nice
6, rue Raoul-Bosio
✆ +33 (0)4 93 62 66 64
www.le6.fr

Open all year. Tuesday to Saturday 10.30pm at 5am. Téléphone Bar Club. Special disco and jazz funk evening each Wednesday. Evening Erotic Harder Show each month. Live DJ and artists every evening. Free admission, compulsory consumption. Animations. Concerts.

Unmissable place for colourful rainbow birds of the night, Le 6 stands out for its resident DJ with large repertoires (electro, house, disco and Oriental) but also by its talented artists performing every evening. Without forgetting its modern decor with neon lights that create a very successful clubbing atmosphere and its erotic-show under the shower where guys – very sensual gogos – are rubbing to lather. The team is also top and will leave you with unforgettable memories! Disco and funky evenings on Wednesday. A reference on the French Riviera.

CALYPSO CLUB

Old Nice
8, descente Crotti
✆ +33 (0)4 93 62 59 60

Open all year Thursday to Saturday from 11pm to 5am. Friday and Saturday: entrance + consumption + cloakroom: €16. Free for the girls with glass offered Friday until 1am. Free for all until 0h30.

Afro-Caribbean atmosphere: afro beat, kizomba, naija and zouk with themed evenings, nights prestige, hip-hop, R'n'b, DJ or latina feeling. Special program for St. Valentine's day, Halloween or New Year's Eve. Different theme every weekend with a RESIDENT DJ and guest: Afro beat, girl credit twice a month with a bottle offered for 4 girls or more.

THE FEELING

City Center
14, rue Pertinax ✆ +33 (0)6 18 44 43 45
www.discotheque-lefeeling.com
wilfried_06@live.fr

Open all year. Thursday to Saturday from 8.30pm to 5am.

Le Feeling is both a restaurant and a nightclub with a friendly atmosphere in a revisited modern déco: hardwood floor, white sofas, exposed rough stones, silver plated footstoles, backlighted dance floor and black and white tonalities. The place organizes many themed evenings like karaokés or single evenings, dance, disco or candies without forgetting the DJ's evenings which revisit all the sounds of the 1980s to our days. Each week, you will also be able to discover the musical news of the world thanks to the DJ Club. Good mood and good atmosphere guaranteed! Smart information: the place can be privatized for your tennagers birthdays, ideal when you want to organize a great festival without disturbing your neighbors.

L'ÉTOILE CLUB

City Center
8, passage Emile-Négrin
✆ +33 (0)6 24 48 61 11

Open on Thursday, Friday and Saturday from 11pm to 5am. Cloakroom €2 per article.

With its minimalist décor and warm atmosphere, this place has become *the place to be* for the partygoers of Nice. The room is not very big but the atmosphere is boosted: perfect for a memorable evening with the most popular resident DJs of the time but also international stars like Nikki Bellucci or even David Vendetta. Caution: do not forget to bring a chic and trendy dress, passage required to enter this party temple!

SHOPPING

ANTHROPOSAGE

Old Nice
Rue Rossetti
✆ +33 (0)6 66 83 02 88
Open Tuesday to Sunday from 10am to 7pm.
In the heart of the Old Nice, embark on an exotic journey and discover the works of artists of nice, Balinese, Papuan, Timoriens or African. The common point of the collections of Anthroposage? primitive arts. You will discover the creations made with shells or wood but also ornaments, paintings, statues and totems.

ATELIER GALERIE SYLVIE T

City Center
14, rue Droite
✆ +33 (0)4 93 62 59 15 / +33 (0)6 82 29 90 07
www.sylvie-t.com
Open Tuesday to Saturday from 10.30am to 6pm non stop. Possibility of carrying out courses and workshops from 4 to 12 years old children on the theme of art and architecture.
Sylvie is a passionate artist who takes her inspiration in the narrow winding streets of the old Nice, in the majestic and impressive monuments of the City, in its unusual places and unavoidable, in its sometimes soft colours sometimes more intense or in its particular vegetation. Child of the country, she offers therefore in her workshop gallery drawings made with the watercolour or Indian ink sublimating the capital of the Riviera but also sometimes other destinations.

BABALUX

Port – 7, rue Emmanuel-Philibert
✆ +33 (0)6 62 55 55 14
www.babalux.fr
info@babalux.fr
Artisanal factory of lamps. Open all year. Open on Monday from 10am to 2pm and from 2pm to 7pm, Tuesday from 10am to 7pm, Wednesday from 9am to 12pm, Thursday from 10am to 12pm andfrom 2pm to 7pm and Friday and Saturday from 2pm to 7pm.
This shop with a felted atmosphere is an Ali Baba cave for those seeking for the ideal lamp able to perfect your interior decoration: lamps on foot, mural brackets, vaporous suspensions, lamp-shades with seams or wandering lamps are made here with rare and original materials. The pieces are unique or carried out in small quantities. Creations are very original: colourfull, simple and romantic, glamour, inspired by Japanese art or rock... Here you can find hte rare pearl. An inspiring address!

THE CHATELARD 1802

Old Nice – 2, rue du Pont-Vieux
www.le-chatelard-1802.com
contact@le-chatelard-1802.com
Every day from 10am to 7pm. Sunday, public holidays and summer: call them.
The history of the Châtelard began in 1802 with the Montaud family who produces essential oil from wild lavender. At the end of the 1990's, the company defines its own products line based on their history, their experience, their love for lavender and their perfect knowledge of this symbolic plant. Find the full products range – fragrance bags, perfumes, soaps and toilet waters – in their shop. There are ideal products to give your house or your clothes a natural perfumes but also for gifts.

CREUTZ AND SON

City Center
19, rue Hôtel-des-Postes
✆ +33 (0)4 93 85 35 13
www.creutz.fr
Open Tuesday to Saturday from 9am to 12.30pm and from 2pm to 7pm.
True family institution, the Creutz et Fils house is well-known in Nice. Since 1896, lovers and collectors have frequented this temple of fountain pens to admire the most beautiful pieces, offer a gift or bring their fetiche pen repaired. This specialist also offers a wide choice of brands and models, and also offers diaries, repertoires or calendars.

DÉZIRDÉZARTS

Old Nice – 5, rue de la Prefecture
✆ +33 (0)4 93 85 40 69
Open every day from 10am to 7pm.
Whatever the occasion is, this small shop next to Palais de Justice is the perfect place to find a card for a birthday, an early retirement, birth or a baptism. You'll find all colours, all shapes and all sizes! The shop also offers a whole range of very original bookmarks and calendars with very artistic artwork. The miniature fans of cars will also be happy with about fifty models displayed.

GALLERY ALTMANN

Port
19, rue Emmanuel-Philibert
✆ +33 (0)6 08 76 17 53 / +33 (0)4 93 56 08 85
www.altmann-antiquites.com
lazore@ymail.com
Open every day except Sunday. Trilingual expertise. Antique restoration
Specialized in the catering and export of antiques, the Altmann Gallery also sells, purchases and expertises objects of art. On 200 m^2, we escape through an artistic and aesthetic journey with quality paintings, furnitures and rare antiques, it takes us into an old, modern or more contemporary world.

GALLERY DE LA MARINE

Promenade des Anglais
59, quai des Etats-Unis
✆ +33 (0)4 93 91 92 92
Open Monday to Friday from 8.30am to 5pm.
The Galerie de la Marine displays contemporary creations of emerging artists on the national and international stage. It is in 1967 that this former fish market was transformed into an art gallery with exclusive vocation for the presentation of temporary exhibitions.

GALERIE DES PONCHETTES

Promenade des Anglais
77, quai des Etats-Unis
✆ +33 (0)4 93 62 31 24

Open Tuesday to Sunday from 10am to 6pm.

This gallery where Matisse presented his first exhibition in Nice has now temporary exhibitions dedicated to contemporary creations. Each year dozens of more or less famous artists national or international present their latest creations: sculptures, photographs, mobiles, paintings, ceramics...

GALLERY EVA VAUTIER

Liberation
2, rue Vernier
✆ +33 (0)9 80 84 96 73
✆ +33 (0)6 07 25 14 08
www.eva-vautier.com
galerie@eva-vautier.com

Tuesday to Saturday from 2pm to 7pm.

Daughter of the famous artist Ben, Eva Vautier opened a beautiful exhibition space of contemporary art, where her father held his own gallery «Espace à Débattre» a few years ago. Several major annual exhibitions highlight the work of young emergent artists or experienced artists from the Fluxus group or the Figuration Libre.

Performances, concerts, evenings videos, dance, debates or poetry readings regularly come to punctuate these events. Note the presence of a reading corner for those wishing to take the time to discover catalogues of artists and videos.

KARTELL

La Buffa
21, rue de la Buffa
✆ +33 (0)4 93 87 94 69
www.kartell-boutique.fr
nice@kartellflag.com

Open Tuesday to Saturday. From 10am to 12.30pm and from 2.30pm to 7pm.

In this shop of the famous Italian publisher of contemporary *design*, you will find more than 500 references created by some of the biggest: Philippe Starck, Ron Arad, Patricia Urquiola, Antonio Citterio, Marteen von Severen, Anna Castelli Ferrieri, Patrick Jouin... This brand has managed to democratise the *design* while working on plastics to make the furniture more accessible. The most famous example is the armchair in Louis XVI style in transparent polycarbonate plastic «Louis Ghost» revisited by Philippe Starck.

MOLINARD

Old Nice
20, rue Saint-François-de-Paule
✆ +33 (0)4 93 62 90 50
www.molinard.com
france@molinard.com

Open every day from 10am to 6pm; closed between 1pm and 2pm as well as Sundays from October to March included except school holidays. December open every day from 10am to 6.30pm. From April to September from 10am to 7pm every day.

A family-owned business for five generations founded in 1849, Molinard creates perfumes sold in elegant Baccarat crystal bottles. In 1891, Queen Victoria bought her colognes from there. The success was confirmed in 1921 with the inimitable fragrance Habanita which success has never stopped! In the early 1930s, Lalique and Viard signed splendid bottles. In the shop nestled in the heart of the old city of Nice, you will find a range of perfumes, toilet waters and colognes and also cosmetics and others scents for the house with sweet, enchanting and delicate fragrances. Highly skilled consultants guide you according to your needs and tastes. Do not miss to visit and discover this boutique-studio with its authentic and timeless products without forgetting the small museum and workshops where to create your own perfume. A friendly and ideal place for gifts ideas or to please yourself!

THE NARCISSIO

Downtown – 16, rue Parmentier
✆ +33 (0)4 93 84 81 30
www.le-narcissio.fr
communication@de-lart.org

Open from 2pm to 6pm Monday to Friday.

Narcissio is a new space dedicated to contemporary creation. Managed by the Association DEL'ART, several art exhibitions mark the calendar of events of this unique place, anchored in its time and combining culture and artistic reflection.

POPART

Old Nice
3, rue Saint-François-de-Paule
✆ +33 (0)4 93 80 42 62
www.popart.fr
info@popart.fr

Open Monday to Saturday from 10am to 7pm.

This workshop is dedicated to the original concept of paintings in Andy Warhol way: from personal photos, the team creates pop art paintings, objects, clothes (t-shirts, caps, sweat shirts, shirts, leggings) or stickers, posters and business cards. All the supports are printable on request. The *showroom* displays a bunch of declinable and trendy products.

RÊVE D'ANGE

Old Nice
4, rue Francis-Gallo
✆ +33 (0)4 93 62 22 64

Welcome to the magic kingdom of Rue Gallo. Here, they sell dreams with a concept around angels and fairies. Enter this dream world for a gift idea which will delight children or adults. Magic has no age: figurines, postcards, decorative objects... There is something for all budgets and all tastes.

YANN OBJETS DE MARINE

Port
38, rue Ségurane
✆ +33 (0)4 89 14 85 21
www.la-palmeraie.com
yann.lods@gmail.com

Open Tuesday to Saturday from 10.30am to 6.30pm.

Several times a year, this enthusiast sails the seas to India to find unusual objects found on ships at the end of their life. In his shop in the antiquarian district, you will find all sorts of treasures: oriental cabin lamps, compass, fine-copper compass of the 19th century, cabin furniture made of mahogany or cane shark vertebrae... There is something for all budgets.

Gourmet Basket

APÉRITIV

Port
4, rue Cassini
✆ +33 (0)4 83 55 37 09
www.aperitiv.fr
contact@aperitiv.fr

Monday to Saturday from 9.30am to 8pm. Closed on Sunday.

Are you planning a drink with friends but the idea to run in the butcher, the cheese, wine merchant and baker discourage you? Meet at Apéritiv'! New *concept store* in France located steps from Place Garibaldi, you can find food here (Bayonne and Parma ham, sausage from Arles, tapenades, olives, popcorn, chips with chorizo, organic chips...)drinks, with and without alcohol (rosé with printer, fruit juice, chablis, sparkling wine, champagne, beers, spirits, banana cream...) including a range of accessories (glass of champagne, paper napkins, shakers, giraffes and beers, corkscrew bottle openers, pailles, peaks aperitifs...) more traditional to the most original but always rigorously selected, especially with small producers. *Must* undoubtedly remains the range of boxes *apéritiv*: elegant ecrins and practices which you can make your own (wines, spirits, champagnes, tapenades, crackers, sausages, foie gras...) for an original and gourmet souvenir. Also note, bar area and its selection of boxes "cocktails key-in- hand" allowing to realise home and easily cocktails at the bar of a Grand Hotel. To eat, without moderation!

BERNARDI & CO

Borriglione
91, avenue Alfred-Borriglione
✆ +33 (0)4 93 84 62 76

Open all year Tuesday to Friday from 9.30am to 7pm; Saturday from 8am to 1pm. Closed on Monday. Bakery. Caterer.

Discover the Bernardi & Co know-how! A large choice of breads and pastries and also a caterer section with cooked meats and prepared dishes (paella, beef wok with pepper, couscous, salads, chicken wok with spinache and peanuts, coasts of lamb with figs coriander and ginger, roast of lamb with herb crust...) will give to your evenings, barbecues and family picnics or with friends another dimension. We also liked the kindness of the team, their service and advises. We loved this tasty delicatessen-caterer shop!

BIOMAN

7, avenue de la République
✆ +33 (0)4 93 26 72 68
biomanfood@gmail.com

Open all year. Friday and Saturday evenings, possibility of enjoying good meals on the premises.

In a bright setting, Bioman exhibits with elegance its products, as beautiful as organic. On site, a young and dynamic team welcome you and advise you seriously with a smile. According to the stores , you'll find seasonal fruits and vegetables but also a caterer part very appetizing. An invitation to travel and emotions of flavours and textures. Also note the possibility to enjoy every Friday and Saturday evenings to eat on the spot good dishes in a cosy atmosphere.

BREAD

Gare thiers – 44, boulevard Gambetta
✆ +33 (0)4 93 53 14 96
contact@breadfrance.com

Open all year Tuesday to Sunday from 7am to 2pm. Responsible bakery. Gluten-free bread. Country bread. Pissaladière. Brownie.

Here is an eco-responsible address that advocates gluten-free authentic bread made with yeast using the best organic flours. The recipes are original with flour of millet, almond, buckwheat, rice, adormidera, linen, coconut or chestnut including bread R.M.S (with brown rice, manioc, full buckwheat and honey) or Grindato (using sunflower, sesame and linseed). The pastries are not less surprising including the cake of pila almond mom made and seasonal fruit with an olive oil tip. The shop is pretty and the service cheerful. Chez Bread, fill the tank of vitamins and good humour.

THE DAILY-RIC

City Center – 32, rue de l'Hôtel-des-Postes
✆ +33 (0)4 89 03 72 71

Open all year from 7am to 6pm.

Gourmet pastries, muffins, cookies, smoothies and desserts await you behind the attractive windows of this address with a modern decoration and a resolutely fashionable mindset. The products are fresh, good and homemade. On the spot or to take away, the pleasure of taste is always there in this new address that is also declined in restaurant for lunch.

GIROFLE & CANNELLE

Old Nice
4, rue Pairolière
✆ +33 (0)4 93 54 43 13
www.girofle-et-cannelle.com

Open every day from 9.30am to 7pm.

A true treasure cave, this brand displays colours, scents and flavours by thousands. There is a large selection of spices, salts and peppers from all around the world, authentic balsamic vinegars of Modena, vintage versions, precious oils, gourmet boxes, a choice of rigorously selected teas... It is a fun getaway for the eyes dedicated to the delight of taste. The owner passionately hunts flavours and products of delicatessen dedicated all over the world and invites us to travel in the very heart of the old town.

LES GOURMANDISES D'ANGEA

Old Nice
5, rue de la Poissonnerie
✆ +33 (0)4 93 80 92 69

Open all year from 10am to 1.30pm and from 3.30pm to 7pm. Closed on Wednesdays all day. Macaroon €1.20 the unit. Travel box: €18. Chocolates. Brioches. Confectioneries. Wedding cakes and other creations personalized on request.

In a charming place which reminds us a doll's house, Catherine and Nathalie expect you in their gourmet cave. Discover their local specialties: nicois macaroons with almonds and a fruit heart, macaroons with natural flavours, flower candy pearls "Les Coquettes", chocolate sardines, brioche with crystallized flowers and candied fruit without forgetting the surprising MaGlagla, a giant macaroon filled with ice cream... You can also bring back some softnesses in pretty travel boxes and in nice metal boxes. Know-how is there and it is perfect. As for the reception? It is charming.

LA MADONE

City Center – 63, rue de la Buffa
✆ +33 (0)7 81 14 38 24
www.madone.fr
boutique@madone.fr

Open all year. Tuesday to Friday from 9am to 12pm and Saturday from 9am to 12pm and from 2.30pm to 6.30pm

A few years ago, a priest from Nice had this brilliant idea to create La Madone, a monastic delicatessen allowing him to generate incomes at a time when donations and resources for his parish became increasingly rare... Discover a selection of artisanal products manufactured by the monks themselves. Here, French products are offered: cosmetics (creams and lotions), herbal teas and delicatessen (jams, honeies, terrines, condiments, but also liquors) created by monks from all over France. A selection of products manufactured by monasteries and abbeys of France and Europe in this pretty address which cultivates wellness and health.

MAMA BAKER

City Center – 13, rue Lepante

Open all year. Monday, Tuesday, Thursday, Friday and Saturday from 7.30am to 7.30pm. Wednesday from 7.30am to 1.30pm. Closed on Sunday.

This epicurean bakery has nothing ordinary. Certified 100% organic by Ecocert, the choice of the suppliers is done on producers working according to the principles of a responsible agriculture. The raw materials are seasonal, the flours of grinding stone are resulting from French organic wheat, the AOP butter and salt come from Guérande. Here, the flours are diversified (wheat, German wheat, khorasan, buckwheat, corn, rye and rice) accompanied by flax seeds, pumpkin, sunflower and sesame. Just like their composition, the presentation of the products is neat. The bakery also offers some *snacks* for the students and has a small organic delicatessen with the sale of flours, teas, compotes and artisanal fruit juice manufactured in an organic farmhouse. Inspired by their experiments abroad and in France, Celine and Bastien manufacture original products: bread with cocoa for the gourmands, Norwegian bread with seeds and fruits for the curious ones... More classical but also delicious, the gingerbread and the Vendean braided brioche. Quality and flavour guaranteed for a fashionable bakery!

PÂTISSERIE CAPPA SERAIN

Place Garibaldi – 7 et 9, place Garibaldi
✆ +33 (0)4 93 62 30 83 / +33 (0)4 92 10 09 65
serainpatissier@free.fr

Open Tuesday to Sunday from 7.30am to 7.30pm. Open for Christmas on December 25th from 7.30am to 1pm. Catering. Possible delivery.

Welcome in the cave of delicacies and artisanal know-how! For more than ten years Serge Serain, grand master pastry and chef-chocolate maker, and his team enjoy you with their many delights home-made with fresh and quality ingredients. You will find for midday a rapid fixed rate formula proposing omelettes and savory pies for an excellent balanced lunch. Without forgetting the desserts: orangettes, almonds with chocolate, truffles, delicious macaroons and other sweetened petit four. A nice address where you can stop at any time of the day for a tea or café. It should be noted that the establishment also offers a catering with combinations of salted and sweetened cold buffet. There is no minimum of quantity to make an order. Possible delivery.

LE PECHE MIGNON

The Port – 41, rue Bonaparte
✆ +33 (0)4 93 89 75 56
www.peche-mignon-nice.com
contact@peche-mignon-nice.com

Open Tuesday to Saturday from 7.30am to 12.30pm and from 3pm to 7.15pm. Sunday from 7am to 12.30pm. Restaurant tickets accepted. Delivery on Nice and in the department (ask for information).

Péché Mignon is an excellent caterer, confectioner, chocolatier and pastry cook combining quality and quantity. This property has been offering, with talent, a very wide range of products and incessant creations for over forty years for various events. From savoury to sweet, you will find a range of hot dishes such as the duck pâté in crust, the monkfish blanquette, the saddle of lamb or a wide range of salads as well as tasty traditional pastries like the opéra, the saint-honoré or the vacherin. For ice-creams and sorbets, there are about twenty flavours with the possibility of creating your fruit sorbet, upon request. For all your special occasions, the house offers macaroons, pièces montées, homemade chocolate. There is also a caterer section for your cocktails, your buffets and your parties with friends: order mini-sandwiches, pans bagnats, canapé or a stuffed nicois... Here, the presentation is refined, elegant and generous. Everything is prepared each day with carefully selected and extremely fresh products . This Péché Mignon will become yours!

LE VANILLIER

Musicians district – 7, avenue Auber
✆ +33 (0)4 93 88 71 77
www.le-vanillier-nice.com
levanillier@free.fr

Open Tuesday to Saturday from 8am to 7.30pm, public holidays from 8am to 1pm. Public parking Mozart at 50 meters. Présent every morning on the market of Cours Saleya. Checks are not accepted.

Opened in 1940, this pastry- chocolates placed in the heart of the Musicians district is run by Gabriela and François Ducroux since 1993. In tribute to this bourgeois area of the city of Nice, many specialties bear the names of great artists of the world of music, Chopin combines chocolate and praline, Armstrong sublimes black chocolate... Cake with lemon, macaroons, amaretti, fruit and chocolates complete the range of delicacies whose presentation already titillates the palates from the window! Do not forget to discover the inevitable «Macaroon of Nice» declined with violet, lemon, pink, orange gluten-free... or lactose.

LA VERRIERE

Old Nice – 2, rue Pairolière
✆ +33 (0)4 93 54 43 13 / +33 (0)6 63 59 32 14

Open Wednesday to Saturday from 10 am to 7 pm, Sunday from 12 pm to 6 pm. American Express. Tea room. Take-away. Accessories around tea.

The Verrière is a garden of Eden for all lovers of tea and coffee. This cozy and feminine place conceals amazing taste treasures with over 200 large aromatic and natural tea gardens created by Christine Dattner, author of the tea for the hostess. Both have managed to put together teas in perfect balance, unique and delicious. The place also offers grand crus coffees carefully selected. Each week, discover a new variety from Brazil, India or Ethiopia as well as a fine and delicate combination of Brazil and Costa Rica. Without forgetting two other rare and exceptiona coffees, produced in limited quantities. Everything can be eaten in or sold to detail in grain or ground accompanied by homemade pastries and Alsatian biscuits. Accessories and utensils around the tea are also available to purchase: services teapot, porcelain, filters, mugs, solitary... A fascinating and charming boutique you can not miss.

Markets

MARCHÉ AUX FLEURS

Vieux-Nice – Cours Saleya

♿

Open Tuesday to Saturday from 6.30am to 5pm. Sunday from 6.30am to 1.30pm. Closed on Monday and public holidays.

Listed by the National Council of Culinary Arts in the markets of exceptional in France, it is unmissable. Ideal place to rub with authentic life niçoise, the stalls display their colourful flowers and fragrant sheltered from the sun under striped curtains: mimosa, lily, impatiens, dahlias, anemones and succulent plants... bouquets and potted plants, you will be spoilt for choice!

MARCHÉ DE LA LIBÉRATION

Libération
Place du Général-de-Gaulle

Open every day except Monday from 7am to 1pm.

From the place de la Libération, you will find in this neighbourhood market fruits and vegetables, flowers, delicious fish including some local producers of honey, cheeses and oils. . .

MENTON ★★★★

Menton is the last French town before Italy. City of lemons, the town is also that of gardens where nature, culture and art are an exceptional natural and historical heritage.

The Menton Seigniory appeared in the 13th century. It has become one of the 120 French cities with the label City of Art and History. It is a city of dreams where every step is a journey through six centuries of history and heritage. The Italian architectural influence is present everywhere, but it is mainly the Belle Époque luxury hotels, the baroque heritage, perfumes, colours and tranquillity of the place which give a special touch to the *«la Perle de la France»* as named by the geographer Elisée Reclus. An exceptional microclimate gives birth here to gardens and rare varieties such as the mythical tree of Easter Island. Beautiful and original plants thrive in these sumptuous frames of seven unique and beautiful gardens spread out in the town; Carnolès, the Val Rahmeh, Maria Serena, Fontana Rosa, Serre de la Madone, the Colombières, the Clos du Peyronnet. This incomparable wealth is especially highlighted in June and September, during the month of gardens and Mediterranean garden days.

As concerns arts, visits are not lacking with the Cocteau Museum, Collection Séverin Wunderman, the wedding room of the town hall, painted by the same artist, le Bastion, the Museum of Fine Arts, the Museum of Regional Prehistory without forgetting the art galleries complementing the richness of this place, now a tourist destination in all seasons.

Do not miss the great events that put Menton in honour starting with the Fête du Citron, known worldwide or the Festival of chamber music, musical evenings of the Annonciade...

Menton and lemons

For nearly a century, thousands of spectators from around the world attend in February, the Lemon Festival, which as the Nice Carnival, is the biggest winter event on the French Riviera. According to the legend, Eve would have planted on these lands of Menton a lemon that had been stolen from paradise... The municipality then decided to make this citrus be the emblem of the City which accompanies the motto "Menton, my city is a garden." The originality of the parades is the exclusive use of citrus (oranges and lemons). Within the Biovès gardens, giant motifs tell through eleven panels a different story every year.

TOURIST OFFICE OF MENTON
Palais de l'Europe – 8, avenue Boyer
✆ +33 (0)4 92 41 76 76
www.tourisme-menton.fr
tourisme@menton.fr
Qualité Tourisme label. From mid-September to end of June: open Monday to Saturday from 9am to 12.30pm and from 2pm to 6pm. From July to mid-September: every day from 9am to 7pm.
The Tourism Office of Menton is the perfect place to find all the necessary information for visiting the town: maps, booklets, activities...

Knife & Fork

ALKENA
8, promenade de la Mer
✆ +33 (0)4 93 41 58 13
www.restaurant-alkena-menton.fr
Open all year. Service nonstop at any hour. Open every day from July to September from 9am to end of the evening. From October to June from 9am to 7pm Mondays, Wednesday, Thursday and Sunday, and from 9am to end of evening Friday and Saturday. Starter from €11. Salmon from €16. Meats from €12.50. Pasta from €10. Dessert €4. À la carte: Around €35. Vegetarian menu: €14 (single starter, main course and dessert + coffee). Menu of festivals: €22. Menu birthday €27. Mediterranean cuisine. Organization of theme parties. Activities. Bar. Daily specials.
This dynamic team warmly welcomes you all year round in an exotic setting decorated in the shades of turquoise and chocolate colors with a sea view. As for the bar, Yannick treats you with his homemade cocktails with amazing colours and also with more surprising exotic flavours. As for the cuisine, the menu is typically Mediterranean and the dishes are prepared exclusively with fresh products and homemade toppings (except the french fries): red mullet, Provencal prawns, pesto penne, tagliatelle carbonara, escalope with cream or a steak with pepper sauce, among others. Alkena also offers an entirely vegetarian menu. The «extra» of this establishment is its excellent value for money. It also organizes regularly theme evenings.

LE BISTROT DES JARDINS
14, avenue Boyer ✆ +33 (0)4 93 28 28 09
www.le-bistrot-des-jardins.fr
lebistrotdesjardins@orange.fr
Open all year. Open Tuesday to Sunday for lunch from 12pm to 2pm and from 7.30pm to 9.30pm. Closed Sunday for dinner and Monday. À la carte: Around €17.50 (dish). Starter + main course + dessert: €31 Tuesday to Saturday.

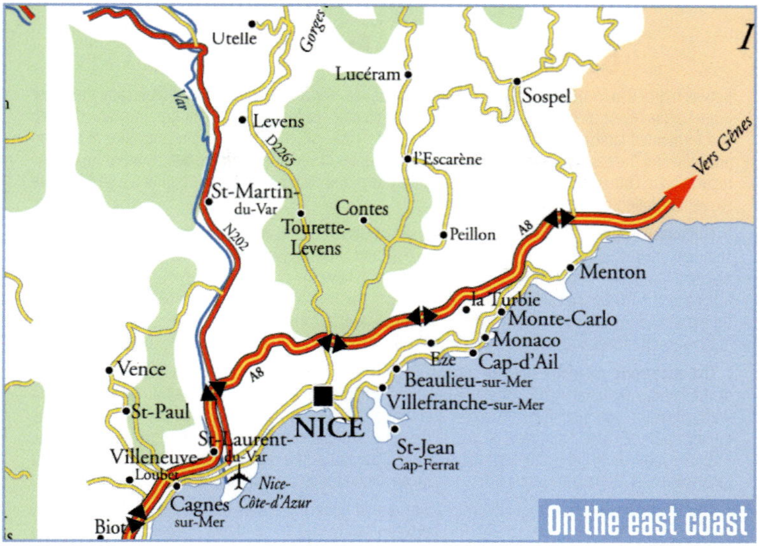

Starter and main course or Main course and dessert: €22 Tuesday to Saturday except public holidays. Menu from €38 Sunday for lunch.

Less than 500 m from the city centre you will find a hidden haven of peace with a lush garden. It is Mr. Delserre's den who delights his guests with simple dishes, a tasty and authentic cuisine that he cooks according to his desires and market supply. You will enjoy crunchy vegetables, the meat of crab and fresh shrimps or the avocado mousse in guacamole way without forgetting the casserole of scallops and blue lobster tail with fisherman sauce or the pan-fried veal morel cream. Finish on a sweet gourmet touch by choosing the delicious pear Charlotte with chocolate sauce or rum baba vanilla cream duo of fresh pineapple comfit with spices. A love at first sight for this address in a peaceful atmosphere that you should absolutely share.

LE BRUIT QUI COURT

31, quai Bonaparte ✆ +33 (0)4 93 35 94 64
www.lebruitquicourt.fr
contact@lebruitquicourt.fr

♿

Open for lunch and dinner Wednesday to Sunday evening. Open for lunch from 12pm to 2pm and for dinner from 7pm to 9.30pm. Booking advised. Menu from €24 to €39 (menu of Festival from €47). À la carte: Around €23 (main course). Children's menu: €12. Wine by the glass. Starter from €14. Risotto from €23. Meat from €19. Fish from €21. American Express. Groups welcome. Terrace. Parking.

At the foot of the old town of Menton and facing the sea, Xavier Raymakers and Sylvie Dias, from Belgium, have made this restaurant, which celebrated its 10 years anniversary in 2014, a must in the city. The reception is warm and professional and the tables are nicely set. The gourmet menu offers an interesting culinary journey: semi-cooked foie gras terrine with Corsican black cherries and thyme compote and its glass of Rivesaltes wine; Scottish beech wood smoked salmon, goat cheese mousse, tomatoes and yuzu tartar, and sesame Alrette, grilled fresh tuna slice in Rossini's way, scampis and saffron risotto or even the grilled duck breast and its truffle cream... Rumour says that these raffined dishes will make you want to come back. An excellent address!

CARNIVAL

29, quai Monléon ✆ +33 (0)4 93 35 99 95
www.restaurantcarnival.com
riki.carnival@orange.fr

Closed 2 weeks in January. Open every week day except Thursday for lunch from 12pm to 2.30pm and every evening from 7pm to 10pm. Booking advised. Menu of the market at €19.50: starter + main course + dessert. Menu at €32 every day with a choice of 7 starters, 4 choices of main dishes and 4 choices of desserts. À la carte: Around €40. Starter from €10. Pasta from €15. Main courses from €18. Dessert €7. Terrace.

Carnival accommodates you in a family atmosphere in a shaded spacious dining room, nicely decorated or on the flowered pergola for a gourmet break. The Chef Riccardo will enjoy you with his specialties cooked with attention and simplicity, and prepared with fresh ingredients of high-quality like organic vegetables or wild fish: salad of hot goat cheese and honey, tuna carpaccio, stuffed vegetables, raviolis with artichokes, artisanal spaghetti with half-lobster from the tank, roasted wild prawns, or beef romsteak with pepper sauce. To finish on a sweet touch, let yourself be tempted by the delicious tiramisu. In summer, you can also appreciate thai specialties, with sweetened, acidulous and spiced flavours.

Cornices of the French Riviera

Between Nice and Menton, the mountain falls into the sea. Rocks and indomitable cliffs despite the dense urbanization give a spectacular meeting with the deep blue sea for our great pleasure. This carved, steep and tormented landscape is crossed by three cornices: three different roads connecting Nice to Menton and allowing the travelers to admire, from three balconies of varied height, the beauty which made the reputation of Côte d'Azur(French Riviera). On sunny days and clear blue skies, the higher we go, the more we will be delighted with this magic setting.

The basse corniche (low cornice) along the sea follows all the meanders and the outlines of the Coast. The road crosses all the municipalities of the coast and therefore, remains the most crowded. In some places, in particular, between Beaulieu and Eze, you will have the cliff on one side of the road, and on the other the sea. The **basse cornice** was briefly drawn in the 18th century, by a Prince of Monaco. For a long time it was only used as a bridleway where carts circulated, its construction was resumed at the beginning of the Second Empire and accelerated as from the incorporation in 1860. The work was completed in 1881.

The moyenne corniche (middle cornice) is situated a little higher. Opened in 1927, it is the route of the famous National 7 (N7). Built with major mechanical and modern engineering techniques, it is wide, pleasant, ponctuated by structures and tunnels. It has remarkable view-points since it is a little higher from the coast. From Nice, it crosses the col of Villefranche, by-passes the Saint Michel plateau, links the road connecting Eze with the col of Eze, by-passes the massif of the Tête de Chien, crosses Beausoleil over Monaco and comes down again on Roquebrune-Cap-Martin.

The grande corniche (higher cornice) was drawn upon the orders of Napoleon I. It is the most impressive and the most spectacular. It is between 300 m and 500m above sea-level, and spreads in harmonious but often dizzying curves. It largely takes back the route of the ancient Aurelian road, built by Romain who wanted to channel their legions by the heights, more easily defensible, rather than at the water's edge where the troops would have been more vulnerable. It crosses the Col des Quatre-Chemins, connects the belvedere of Eze, the col of Eze from 512m above sea-level, passes near the mount Bastide, former Roman oppidum which both allowed to watch and to lock the Coast and the valley of Paillon. It then crosses Turbie, offers an exceptional view on the Principality of Monaco that it dominates and goes down on Roquebrune -Cap- Martin. Be careful if you go there in winter: it is often icy.

For the impatient, there is a fourth way: the A8. From behind the hills, the passenger will not be able to have a sea-view but, it offers between Italy and Monaco, the infinite viaduct-tunnel-viaduct adventure. Drawn above the other three, due to a lack of space, its construction has been very expensive because it necessitated numerous art works, construction of bridges and tunnels' openings that take place practically without interruption to climb over ravines and cross the rocky spurs that are perpendicular to the coast. By car, you can enjoy the show of striking gaps – that are short-lived when driving at 130 km/h – on the creeks and coves located below. Some rest areas have stunning view-points, especially in the direction Nice-Ventimiglia (in Italy) and deserve a few staging areas to admire one of the most beautiful views in the world.

Between the three cornices and at several places along the whole path, small connection roads allow to switch from one road to another. The cornices start as from the suburbs of Nice.

LA CAZ'AMIS

11, rue Trenca
✆ +33 (0)4 22 16 23 85
lacazamis@gmail.com

Open all year. For lunch only. Exceptional openings in the evening for themed events: disguised evenings, karaoké… À la carte: Around €15 (dish). Luncheon vouchers. Cheques lunch.

Ambiance 100% familial for this sympathetic mentonnaise address. On the programme of this very warm establishement, a traditional Southern cuisine prepared with fresh market products: gnocchi with leeks, mixed fries, blanquette, pot au feu, risotto with asparagus and small shrimps, Tartare, hot goat cheese salad… Colourful and hearty dishes, for a very pleasant time.

GUSTO E SAPORI DEL VICOLETO

40, rue Partouneaux
✆ +33 (0)6 23 50 31 62
www.gustoesaporidelvicoletto.com
gustoesaporidelvicoletto@gmail.com

Open all year. Monday to Saturday from 11.30am to 2.30pm and from 7pm to 10pm. Possibility of privatizing the restaurant for your private events. À la carte: Around €15 (main course and dessert). Menu pizza €15. Groups welcome (by reservation). Terrace. Take-away.

Taste and Flavours... The tone of this charming restaurant with a gracious reception is set! The carte offers transalpine specialties but also typically Mediterranean dishes that regularly change according to the seasons and the Chefs lucky finds at the market: tagliatelle tirolese, sauce with walnuts and speck; carpaccio of fresh salmon with citrus fruits; spaghetti with pesto sauce; fillet of sea bass in the Mediterranean way; taglioni candelese; fritto misto; gnocchi alla Sorentina; Mantecato risotto; escalope Viennese and French fries; grilled fish duo and vegetables; cavatelli with fish stew; spaghetti alla puttanesca dello Chef or guazzetto of mussels and clams without forgetting the impossible to circumvent and delicious pizzas! The pleasure of the tastebuds continues with homemade desserts like the panna cotta or the tiramisu. A very nice address with a friendly atmosphere.

IL ETAIT UNE FOIS

884, promenade du Soleil
✆ +33 (0)4 92 10 30 33

Open all year. Open Tuesday to Sunday from 8.30am to 10pm. Snacking service in the afternoon. À la carte: Around €35 (approximately). Menu of the market (valid only weekday lunchtime) from €16 (starter and main course or main course and dessert, glass of wine) or from €19 (starter + main course + dessert + glass of wine). Suggestions and fishing of the day. Checks are not accepted. Holiday voucher, Chèque Restaurant. Groups welcome (up to 200 people). WiFi. Terrace with panoramic view. Artisanal and local products.

The chef offers a menu wisely prepared with locally caught fish and fresh market vegetables. You will find original delicacies with Mediterranean accents: lobster of the day with garlic and parsley butter with candied tomatoes, zucchini flowers with fresh farm goat cheese from Castellar, home-made foie gras with local pickled lemons... The atmosphere is warm and pleasant with a rapid service offered by an incredible team makes this place exceptional. The Cousteau family welcomes you «as you have known them for years» with humor and conviviality. This chic bistro is a great tribute to freshness.

LITTLE ITALY

7, rue Piéta
✆ +33 (0)9 67 19 15 44

Open all year. On the spot and take-away (salads and pizzas). Reception of groups. Terrace. À la carte between €10 and €30 approximately. Chèque Restaurant. Open every day from 12pm to 2pm and from 7pm to 9pm. Closed on Tuesday. Open public holidays. Groups welcome (up to 40 people. Possible group menus). Organization all types of events.

This family-run restaurant decorated in an Italian *trattoria* style offers mediterranean cuisine. Discover various suggestions cooked and prepared with fresh local products. Specialized in seafood, choose the large assortment composed of octopus salad, homemade salmon carpaccio, small mussel and clams sauté or a shrimps minicocktail or even the fish mixed-grill with vegetables and potatoes. Meats (beef ribs, grilled lamb and veal a la Milanese, beef tartare in two ways...), pizzas (fifteen varieties) and a large choice of fresh pasta with all sauces - pistou, lobster and cep mushrooms – are also in the menu. A friendly and warm place where you will feel good. To be rapidly discovered!

MAISON MARTIN ET FILS

7, rue des Marins
✆ +33 (0)4 93 35 74 67
www.maison-martin-et-fils.com
info@maison-martin-et-fils.com

♿

Closed on Sunday and Monday all day. Lunchtime service: from 12pm to 2pm, for dinner from 7pm to 9pm. Booking advised. Daily special: €11.90. Wine by the glass. Lunch menu: €20 (starter of the day + daily special + dessert of the day). Lunch menu at €15 (starter of the day + daily special or daily special + dessert of the day). American Express, Holiday voucher, Chèque Restaurant. Groups welcome. Terrace. Take-away.

In a trendy decor with mocked and purple colour tones, and a family atmosphere, this lively and friendly brasserie serves niçoises and mentonnaises specialities: zucchini flower fritters, chard pie, mentonnaise plate, nicois stuffed vegetables, truffle raviolis, barbajuans, *merda di can* (kind of green gnocchi) or even raviolis "sans chemise" and lots of other specialitys. As for the location, you can choose between the most spacious room, a smaller and quieter one or the lovely terrace facing the market of Menton.

Old port de Menton

LA MANDIBULE
1014, promenade du Soleil
✆ +33 (0)4 93 28 41 95
www.lamandibule.com
mandi@infonie.fr

Closed from mid-December to February. Closed on Wednesday all day and Sunday evening except in season. From end of June to beginning of September: open every day, for Brazilian show dinner with Brazilian dancers and capoierists from 7.30am to 2.30am. Off-season opening from 7.30am to midnight. Menu from €24 to €46. Children's menu: €10.50. Creole specialties from €12.50. Salad from €11. Pasta from €12.50. Attention, the evenings of Brazilian shows, prices increase of one euro.

A warm and sincere welcome with Caribbean flavours. The atmosphere of this restaurant is wildly tropical with a new cheerful decoration and a terrace facing the sea which is simply beautiful. The specialties of the house will make you travel with balls of cod a la Creole, salade Bourbon (pineapple, shrimps, mango, avocado, cocktail sauce) or the dish of the Lagoon (shrimp fritters, creole rolls, samoussas, cod balls, vegetable achards) between others. It also offers salads, from the classical nicoise, to the surprising coral with marinated shrimps in lime, avocado, cherry tomatoes, red oignons, and an avocado vinaigrette. In summer, don't miss every evening, the Bresilian show with dancers and capoierists. A total change of scenery guaranteed!

LE PETIT PRINCE
69, promenade du Soleil
✆ +33 (0)4 93 41 66 05
www.lepetitprince-06.com
rest.lepetitprince06@gmail.com

Open all year. Every day from 12pm to 1.30pm and from 7pm to 9.30pm. Booking advised. Set menu at €19.50 (starter, main course or main course, dessert). À la carte: Around €45 (main course). Children's menu: €12.50. Wine by the glass. Daily special €12.50. Menu from €24. Holiday voucher, Chèque Restaurant. Groups welcome (up to 60 people). Terrace.

Located on the ground floor of Hôtel Prince de Galles, you'll enjoy in the garden shaded by palm trees a traditional mediterranean cuisine that will delight your eyes and surprise your tastebuds. The menu of this address changes every day. Try the crunchy salad with prawns, the foie gras terrine half-cooked and Chartreuse ice-cream, Saint Jacques and prawns duo with a creamy sea food risotto or the fillet of sea bream a la plancha with citrus butter and fennel. A beautiful menu where flavours and ingredients are punctuated according to the seasons and the market. To be consumed deliciously!

LE VINTAGE
25, rue de la République
✆ +33 (0)4 93 57 63 68

Open all year. Monday to Saturday from 9am to 8pm. À la carte: Around €15. Aperitif plate Friday for dinner: €10. Groups welcome.

Le Vintage is a concept of snack bar, restaurant and tea room which pays tribute to King Elvis! The owner, also creator of the National Fan Club in Italy, is among the world's 10 biggest collectors of objects related directly or indirectly to the world of rock and roll legend: unreleased recording reels, shirts and scarves, plectrums, concert tickets, records and posters of the time are then exhibited here in an American decor where the retro seats echo the chequered floor and the juke boxes. The place brings together fans of the King of rock and also lovers of good atmosphere who meet to enjoy gnocchis with prawns and courgettes, tagliatelles with mushrooms and perugina sausages, fried sardines and mixed salad, grilled ribs or the dish of courgette-flower fritters and stick of mozzarella. During the day, we are tempted by some sweets: milk shakes, smoothies, hot chocolate in the Italian way... Every Friday evening, consider booking your place for the aperitif evening. Note that charitable nights are also regularly organized.

Sleeping

HOTEL AIGLON
7, avenue de la Madone
✆ +33 (0)4 93 57 55 55
www.hotelaiglon.net
jacquesaiglon@hotmail.com

Open all year. 24 rooms (5 suites). Breakfast: €10. Parking: €9. Single room from €63. Double from €76. Suite from €156. Package « Culture and Patrimoine» from €347 to €764 per person or « Festival du Citron» from €536 to €776 for 2 people. Pets allowed (€6 per day). Wifi. Catering facilities (on the premises). Satellite TV.

In a villa of the last century, this former mansion of the 1880 managed by the family Servoin since 1950 seduces you at first glance by the charm of its architecture. Inside, the charm continues with classic and warm décor with a beautiful staircase, antique furniture weathered by the time and a beautiful lounge style Belle Epoque with an intimate atmosphere. As for equipment, the rooms have satellite TV, a minibar, a safe and a hairdryer. On the ground floor, the garden invites you to relax. You will also enjoy the heated swimming pool and solarium before enjoying a cocktail at the bar. The restaurant – offering a breathtaking view on a beautiful relaxing atmosphere garden - will allow you to enjoy a cuisine with Mediterranean accents. A good address which guarantees peace and serenity.

HÔTEL CLARIDGE' S
39, avenue de Verdun
✆ +33 (0)4 93 35 72 53
www.claridges-menton.com
hotelclaridges@wanadoo.fr

Open all year. Reception 24/24. 39 rooms. Breakfast: €7.80. Extra bed: €10. Parking: €6.90. High season rate: room 1 person from €54.20; small room 2 people from €63.40; triple room from €73.40. Possibility parking cars, motorbikes and commercial vehicles from €7.80. Lift. Watcher 24/24. American Express,

Diners Club. Pets allowed. Free Wifi. Satellite TV. Ideally located in the heart of Menton at 200 m from the beaches and the Casino, Hôtel Claridge's offers nicely decorated soundproofed and air-conditioned rooms. All of them are equipped with bath or shower, a toilet, a telephone and satellite TV. Claude Rodde, the owner, is very concerned to ensure a quality accommodation to his guests: he will nicely inform you for example about the activities to discover around. Finally, back from a walk, you can relax in the hotel and enjoy the terrace, lounge or bar on site.

HÔTEL DE LONDRES

15, avenue Carnot
✆ +33 (0)4 93 35 74 62
www.hotel-de-londres.com
info@hotel-de-londres.com

Closed from December 31st to beginning of February. Reception 24/24. 27 rooms; ; Buffet breakfast: €12. Garage: €9 (closed). Comfort room from €79. Room Junior Suite from €115. Pets allowed. Receptions and weddings. Free Internet access. Free Wifi. Cleaning service. Satellite TV, Canal+.
In the centre of Menton, this charming building with an ochre façade and a garden full of flowers has rooms in a modern decor, warm and cosy where bright colours match with beautiful materials. The hotel has all the necessary comfort for a pacefull and pleasant stay. In summer, you will especially enjoy the greeny and fragrant garden the time of a refreshing break. And for your afternoon at the sea, it is possible to rent mattresses and parasols on the spot.

HOTEL MENTON RIVIERA

57, avenue de Sospel
✆ +33 (0)4 93 28 28 38

Logis (3 cheminées). Open all year. Reception 24/24 (spoken languages: French, English and Italian). 40 rooms (100% non smoker). Breakfast: €9.80. Extra bed (paying on request). Garage closed and supervised by reservation. Room from €65 to €120. 2 accessible rooms for the physically disabled. Pets allowed (the dogs should not remain alone in the rooms). Free Wifi. Night watchman. Calm and shaded terrace. Relaxation area with TV (Canal+). Table football and games for children. Race carpet. Lift. Free newspapers in the lobby.
Ideally located a few minutes on foot of the City Center and beaches, this address of charm with a modern decor is a promise of beautiful holidays in a warm and friendly atmosphere. Very attentive are carefull staff adds to the quality of this place which is spread on three floors, and at the same time bright and comfortable rooms. Soundproofed, the majority of them have a view on the inner courtyard of the hotel. You will be able to choose between three room categories being able to accommodate from 1 to 4 people: double with a double bed, double with two separate beds or triple room. All are equipped with a bathroom, air conditioning, a safe, free wifi, a TV and a telephone. An address which combines perfectly authencity, relaxation and serenity.

HOTEL PRINCESS ET RICHMOND

617, promenade du Soleil
✆ +33 (0)4 93 35 80 20
www.princess-richmond.com
reservation@princess-richmond.com

Closed from beginning of November to mid-December. Reception 24/24. Breakfast: €12 (buffet or continental served in room. Express €6.50. Free -6 years. From 6 to 12 years old child: €5). Extra bed: €20 (- 6 years free. From 6 to 12 years old: €10). Room mountain and street side from €80 to €135. Room standard mountain side from €90 to €145. Room mountain side comfort from €95 to €155. Room higher mountain side from €105 to €165. Room view on the sea side from €105 to €165. Room facing the sea from €115 to €190. Room premium facing the sea from €130 to €210. Suites facing the sea from €200 to €310. Indoor garage (7 places): €11. Parking in the alley of the hotel (2 places): €8. Outdoor parking (5 places): free. Pets allowed (€7 per day). Free Wifi. Whirlpool. Provision of sport equipment. Solarium.
Perfectly located a few minutes away from the SNCF train station, the city centre and the bus station, Hôtel Princess & Richmond is an excellent pied-a-terre to enjoy the peacefull azure of your stay! Run by the friendly Caravelli family, the helpful and professional welcome from all the staff is very pleasant. With their magnificent views of the surrounding mountains or Mediterranean facing the hotel, the rooms are spacious, soundproofed and comfortable. You can have your breakfast there unless you choose the terrace or in the common room with a serene and calm atmosphere. To complete your day, enjoy the hot tub and the gym equipment at your disposal. A very nice place where you can also be recommended on the things to do around. Bonus: wi-fi is free throughout the hotel.

HÔTEL RICHELIEU

26, rue Partouneaux ✆ +33 (0)4 93 35 74 71
www.richelieu-menton.com

Open all year. Reception from 7 to 9pm. Spoken languages: English, Italian, German, French. 29 rooms (15% smokers). Single room from €39 to €85; double room from €49 to €95; triple room from €55 to €115. Buffet breakfast or in room: €7. Extra bed: €15. Garage €9.25/day. American Express, Diners Club. Pets allowed (free). Free Wifi. Cleaning service. Satellite TV.
This beautiful 19th century building located in the city centre offers comfortable and pleasant rooms with both simple and warm decor. Some even have chimneys and have balconies with views on the orange trees in rue des Partouneaux. They are all equipped with bathroom, shower, WC and free wi-fi. Guy offers very good prices and a warm and high quality reception; you will also take advantage of his expert advice about outings. Note that he can also arrange your stay and facilitate accesses to such or such activities or visits. An exceptional welcome and personalised services are appreciable. The offers along the year also allow you to enjoy at any time the charm of Menton and of the hotel at affordable prices. You have understood, it's a good plan!

■ **NAREV' S HOTEL**
12 bis, rue Lorédan-Larchey
✆ +33 (0)4 93 35 21 31
www.hotel-narevs.com

Open all year. Reception from 7.30am to 8pm. Spoken languages: English, Italian, German. Including 2 accessible to disabled guests. Single room from €55.70 to €86.70; double room from €72.40 to €122.40; triple room from €110 to €146.10. Half-board (for groups). Breakfast: €8 (in room or €9 in room. Fixed rate formula coffee-croissant €4). Garage: €10 (closed). American Express, Diners Club. Pets allowed (€8). Seminars. Free Internet access. Free Wifi. Cleaning service. Individual safe €3.50. Narev's Club facing the hotel open for all (special rate for the guests of the hotel) from 8am to 9pm on weekdays, from 9am to 3pm Saturday and from 9am to 12pm Sundays and public holidays.

In a listed, quiet and residential district, Hôtel Narev's with the typical architecture of Menton is in front of the regional Musée de Préhistoire. New and soundproofed, rooms of this small charming hotel all have air conditioning and all have the necessary comfort for a pleasant stay: direct phone, modem machine, TV and minibar. The hotel also has a meeting room, a small bar with musical ambience and a closed garage. Le Narev's is suitable both for a tourist or a business clientele. Charming welcome from Pascale, the owner. Little extra: sportsmen will appreciate the presence of the Narev Club facing the hotel open to all but with a special rate for guests of the hotel.

Going Out

■ **CAFÉ DES SPORTS**
Casino Barrière de Menton
Avenue Félix-Faure ✆ +33 (0)4 92 10 16 16
www.lucienbarriere.com

Open all year. Open every day from 10am until the closing of the casino. Possible access without ID. Cocktails, cold and hot drinks, ice creams. Catering facilities.

The old Le Brummell nightclub was transformed into a sports bar with a design decor that changes colours when the night comes for a soft and trendy atmosphere. In a chic and relaxed atmosphere where the rosace on the ceiling remains which once marked the dance floor, enjoy a cocktail at the circular bar or sit comfortably in the room for a refreshing and gourmet break.

In the surroundings

Castellar ★★

Good walkers can reach the village of Castellar from the center of Menton via the Ciappes Castellar path: you should have good walking shoes. The road is approximately 4 km and the slope is quite steep. On the spot, after visiting the village, there is another trail: discover the seven chapels that go to the Valley of Razet while following the D2566, by car this time.

Sainte-Agnès

■ **LE RIGHI**
1, place du Fort ✆ +33 (0)4 92 10 90 88
www.restaurant-lerighi.fr

Open from September to June from 9am to 6pm. Catering service from 12pm to 2pm. July and August from 9am to 10pm: catering service from 12pm to 2pm and from 7pm to 9pm. Closed on Wednesday. Tea room the afternoon. Menu from €18 to €23. Children's menu: €10. Wine by the glass. American Express, Diners Club, Holiday voucher. Groups welcome. Terrace. Parking. Free shuttle service event evenings and weekends.

Restaurant, bar, glacier and tea room, Righi has many assets starting with its incredible location, perched on the rocks of the beautiful village of Sainte-Agnès at more than 780 m high. With a stunning view on all the Riviera, you can even see Corsica on nice days! You can enjoy a meal in the dining room or on one of the two panoramic terraces. But beyond its spectacular view, it is for the menu that

The Castillon pass

The D2566 follows the valley of Carei up to Sospel. The Castillon hill pass perched at 707 m altitude is the gateway to the Grand Alps route that climbs up to the Mercantour. The landscape and tree species change very quickly. There are lemon and mimosas and also olive and pine trees. On the left bank of Carei, we can see the Franco-Italian border which follows the line of ridges. The road goes through the beautiful forest of Menton and passes by the viaduct of Caramel, art-work built in the nineteenth century for the tram Menton-Sospel which remained in service until the previous war. The village of Castillon situated on the road at 1 km before the hill, was destroyed twice without mentioning the past wars and conflicts such as the 1887 earthquake that nearly completly destroyed it and the powerful bombing in 1944. The new village, modern, dates from 1951. It now houses artists' and craftspeople. From the hill of Castillon, you can enjoy a beautiful view over the valley of Bévéra and the Italian Alps. The D2566 leads to Sospel 7 km to the north.

you will return there with a traditional and family cuisine: ravioli, gnocchi and fresh pasta, suckling pig, roasted lamb, Aveyron products, fish cooked in tinfoil without forgetting homemade desserts and homemade bread. Hikers, tourists or families, come to make a gourmet stop in the kitchens of Franck Dujardin for a meal on the heigths outside the bustle of the coastline.

LE SAINT-YVES

76, rue des Sarrasins
✆ +33 (0)4 93 35 91 45
www.restaurant-saint-yves.com/fr

Open all year. For lunch and dinner, all the week except Friday. Booking is essential Sunday. Menu from €19 to €42. Rooms 2 people €46 per night. Half-board €48 per person and per day. Breakfast €8. Extra bed €18. Full-board €57. Holiday voucher, Chèque Restaurant.

Set in the village of Sainte-Agnès, this beautiful stone building has an exceptional view at more than 700 meters above the sea. Between sea and mountain, you can relax in a warm atmosphere for a meal in the corner of a fire or for a stopover for a few days because this friendly address also offers rooms at affordable rates. The menu showcases regional specialities: trout with almonds, squash tart, rabbit with herbs, wild boar stew, cappellettis or borage raviolis. Starters to the desserts, the dishes are hearty with an excellent value for money.

Sospel ★★★

LA CABRAÏA

1, place de la Cabraïa ✆ +33 (0)4 93 04 00 54
www.la-cabraia.com

♿

Open daily for lunch and dinner except Thursday in low season. Closed during All Saints holidays. Service Monday to Friday from 9am to 1pm and from 2pm to 7pm. Booking advised. À la carte: Around €25. Lunch menu: €15.50. Wine by the glass. Fixed rate formula Snack €12. Daily menu €22. American Express, Holiday voucher, Chèque Restaurant. Groups welcome. Terrace. Parking opposite the restaurant.

In a delightful setting, halfway between the mountain and the Côte d'Azur coastline, the menu of this charming hotel displays traditional french cuisine: rabbit with beer, tagliatelles with asparagus, sole meunière, omelette with morels, grilled veal breast, ravioli and homemade gnocchis... These dishes tastefully and copiously prepared by the Chef are served in the bright dining room with rustic decor or on the beautiful terrace very appreciated in the summertime. This is without forgetting the friendly and dynamic welcome of Marjorie who works in the dining room. A friendly atmosphere and a perfect decor for a beautiful gourmet getaway.

General view of Sainte-Agnès.

BEAULIEU-SUR-MER ★★★

Bearing such a name (Beau Lieu) (beautifull place), the town could accommodate only beautiful and famous people! And it's all about this in this small fishing village destined to become known due to the enthusiasm of royalties and the most illustrious businessmen of the nineteenth and twentieth centuries. For examples: Queen Margherita of Italy, The Empress Sissi, and the Tsars of Russia, Queen Victoria, Sir Winston Churchill or Sir Thomas Lipton. All have left their mark: sumptuous villas, high standard hotels, trains with several wagons stop at the station of Beaulieu in order to bring down an army of servants and baggage without forgetting the terrific yachts anchored in the harbour, the tennis courts made of clay then frequented by Suzanne Lenglen, the first international star tennis woman star, and the monarchs... Founded by Peter Lautier from Nice, the Reserve (now a luxury hotel) at the beginning was a restaurant bearing such a name due to the stock of fish and shellfish that were in its concrete tanks fed by seawater. At that time, a steamer then was used regularly to connect the port of Nice and the Bay of foumis. Very quickly, the place becomes the restaurant of the kings! The palace will be attended by the global elite as Mistinguett, Rita Hayworth, Clark Gable and Charlie Chaplin. Today, Beaulieu-sur-Mer still charm those who take time to visit it: narrow streets, small coves and stunning heritage. From the Greek Villa Kérylos, to the Rotunda of the Residence Bristol, do not forget to take a look at the half-timbered façade of the Eiffel Residence, a house rented during winter season by the Grand Duke Peter of Russia then in 1895 by Gustave Eiffel himself. In short, Beaulieu conceals treasures.

Sightseeing

VILLA GRECQUE KÉRYLOS ★★★
Impasse Gustave-Eiffel
✆ +33 (0)4 93 01 01 44
www.villakerylos.fr
villa.kerylos@wanadoo.fr
♿

The villa is closed on January 1st, on May 1st, 1st and November 11 as well as on December 25th. Open every

Itinerary Beaulieu Belle Epoque

Get your free map from the Tourist Office at Clemenceau Square and go and discover the Belle Epoque heritage of Beaulieu-sur-Mer in a 2h30 walk. The walk starts from the Palace des Anglais from 1885, former hotel dating from Queen Victoria's period. Take the Avenue Foch at the right then right again Boulevard Marinoni towards the market square: every morning (except Sundays during off season), you will discover the flavours and scents of Provence. Then discover on top of that square a beautiful Musical kiosk from 1904 made by the architect Bovis, ironworkers Gianetto and Fassio. At the back of the square is a bust of Hippolyte Marinoni, the inventor of the printing press and the first mayor of the town. Head to the left behind the statue of Marinoni and take the path of the Myrtes: 100 m you will find on your left the Anglican Church St. Michael built in 1893 and designed by the architects Temple Moore and Aron Messiah. Go down again Marinoni Square; towards the stairs of the street of the Market then take those which go under the railway. Take Gallieni Street along the Sacrée Coeur church built in 1899 by the architect Joseph Berlugan Bovis: on its side is the Romanesque chapel Sancta Maria Olivo dedicated to Virgin Mary dating from the ninth century and houses exhibitions all year round. Facing these two religious buildings, you will find the superb luxury hotel La Réserve (1880). Go down the boulevard Maréchal Leclerc towards the marina located under the Townhall, taking small stairs on the right which will take you directly to the Whitechurch dock: you will then walk along the docks near which you can admire the beautiful boats of this 800 rings port and its mall that houses many restaurants and various shops. Behind that, the beach of Little Africa invites you for a swim. Then go up the road again using the car way-out of the port and cross the two sections towards the Olivaie garden in the street of Jean Bracco (visible by the magnificent portal that adorns its entrance). Away from the hubbub of the city, enjoy the pleasures of relaxation in the middle of the park with more than 100 olive trees. The entrance is at the top of Jean Bracco Street, just before the railway bridge: a small gate leads to the garden. Take back the direction of the Sacrée Coeur Church to Le Metropole hotel built in 1891 and then to the Eiffel residence where lived the constructor of the most worldly famous tour! Finally, at the end of Gustave Eiffel Street, the "Greek Villa Kérylos» ancient Greek model villa inspired by Delos built between 1902 and 1908 according to Emmanuel Pontremoli's plans for Theodore Reinach, awaits you for a wonderful visit (2 hours). Then you head to the Casino located avenue Fernand Dunan. While going along Verdun square, do not forget to admire the beautiful architecture of the old palace «Le Bristol» and its reception hall «La Rotonde» built in 1899 by the architect Tersling which was used as a hospital during the war. For the more adventurous, the Promenade Maurice Rouvier (1.2 km) enables you to reach Saint-Jean Cap Ferrat by the seafront starting from the promenade overlooking the beach of the Bay des Fourmis.

day from 10am to 5pm from January 2nd to April 30th and from November 1st to December 31st. Open every day from 10am to 6pm from May 2nd to May 31st and from October 1st to October 31st. Open every day from 10am to 7pm From June 1st to September 30th. Free for under 7-year-olds (journalists on presentation of a written proof). Adult: €11.50 (reduced rate €8). Bookstore-shop is open same hours as the villa. National Monument Label. Shop. No pets allowed.

This villa is one of the most incredible monuments of the Riviera as it has been built in the early 20th century by the archaeologist patron Theodore Reinach and the architect Emmanuel Pontremoli to recreate in a unique way an antique Greek residence of great luxury and beauty. Inspired by the noble houses of the Delos island in the 2nd century BC, the place invites you to discover its extraordinary setting and its marble, bronze or ivory furniture which adorn the lounges and the garden.

Knife & Fork

AFRICAN QUEEN

Marina
✆ +33 (0)4 93 01 10 85
www.africanqueen.fr

♿

«Maître Restaurateur» label. Open all year. Every day from 12pm to midnight. Booking advised. À la carte: Around €30 (dish). Children's menu: €12. Wine by the glass. Sushi Master Wednesday to Sunday. Menu from €64. Groups welcome. Baby chairs. Terrace. Take-away. Shop. Parking. Valet in summer.

The menu enjoys you with the daily arrivals of fish and seafood, the daily suggestions depend on the market, without forgetting the delicious and gourmet generous desserts! The odyssey of the African Queen with her beautiful cozy room completed with a lounge for friends and extended with a pleasant terrace with a stunning view on the harbour and the moored yachts begin and ends with an impeccable service, that VIPs and many English-speaking customers appreciate.

CAFÉ DE LA PAIX

7, boulevard Maréchal-Joffre
✆ +33 (0)4 93 01 04 18
cafedelapaix06310@gmail.com

Open all year. Restaurant open from 12pm to 3.30pm Monday to Saturday. In the evening from 7pm to 10pm Monday and Thursday to Saturday evening. Bar open from 6.15am to 11pm Monday to Saturday evening. À la carte: Around €25 (starter and main course or main course and dessert. Excluding drinks). Lunch menu: daily special + gourmet coffee €15; with glass of wine €17.50. Groups welcome (only by reservation). Terrace. Take-away.

Pascal and Laure cordially welcome you in Café de la Paix around a simple traditional, tasty and seasonal cooking. The dishes are authentic and are carefully prepared with fresh products: scampi and saffroned rice, tournedos Rossini and its vanilla sauce white truffle, semi-cooked tuna, lamb shank, calf's head, fish couscous or salad of hot goat cheese. The desserts vary according to the mood of the Chef, apple pie, brownie and rum baba, between others... You sit at table here in a friendly and family atmosphere in a pleasant room with a decor in wooden red tonalities, or on the terrace. A nice address.

LA CHICORÉE

5, rue du lieutenant Colonelli
✆ +33 (0)4 93 01 01 27
www.restaurantlachicoree.online.fr
contact@lachicoree-bistrot.com

Open all year. Monday to Saturday from 8am to 10.30pm. À la carte: Around €18 (dish). Wine by the glass. Groups welcome.

Chicorée is a family-run restaurant opened since 1964 with a friendly atmosphere which reminds us of a Parisian bistro: red bench seats, paintings on the walls with exposed stones, Belle Epoque-style decor... Here, the dynamic Ludovic Ducani (who was formed at La Réserve of Beaulieu-sur-Mer and the Marriot in Cap D'ail) accompanied by his sparkling sister Caroline (herself having had a beautiful experience at the Louis XV in Monaco) welcome you with courtesy and professionalism. Their cuisine is prepared with passion and simplicity and the delicious dishes are prepared with fresh ingredients that let all their flavours explode in your mouth. An excellent address with very good ratio quality/price for all those who want to have a good time with friends.

LE FABULEUX DESTIN

Port de Plaisance
✆ +33 (0)4 93 01 13 23
auberge.du.port@orange.fr

Open all year. In winter 7 days a week for lunch. In summer 7 days a week days for lunch and dinner. Menu from €16 to €18.50. À la carte: Around €30. Daily specials: €12 (to €18). Events on Facebook page: Le-Fabuleux-Destin.

Le Fabuleux has a beautiful outdoor terrace with view on the yachts. Shaded in summer and sheltered in winter, it is a real pleasure eating there as soon as the sun comes out...almost 365 days in the year! The indoor room is very bright, carefully decorated in black and white tonalities with some colourful touches. A *lounge* space shelters *cosy* sofas and also an outdoor terrace. As for the cuisine, the Chef offers suggestions which come in different forms on the blackboard: sea mixed grill, pepper steack, beef tagliata. It is good, simple and without fuss. On the menu, you can choose between fish and griddled seafood (prepared in front of you in the open kitchen), burgers, pasta and Nice raviolis. For lunch, the snacking formula offers toasted foccacias for an excellent value/price ratio. The bistro formula also offers a dish (carpaccio, tartare or burger) and a gourmet coffee at a more than reasonable price. In the evening, the atmosphere is more discrete with pretty individual lighting at each table. Every Thursday evening, in season, you'll have diner in a musical atmosphere with live singers. Check information on the Facebook page of the address. A very pleasant address run by the owner Yves who is a true restaurant professional.

LA TABLE DE LA RÉSERVE

5, boulevard Général-Leclerc
✆ +33 (0)4 93 01 00 01
www.reservebeaulieu.fr
reservation@reservebeaulieu.com

Open Tuesday to Sunday for dinner from 7.30pm to 10pm; Friday to Sunday for lunch from 12pm to 2.30pm. Formal dress code required. Booking advised. À la carte: Around €55. WiFi. Private parking (daily rate). Pets allowed. Fixed rate formula starter and main course + drink €32. Garden. Terrace.

Have a culinary stopover in a magical place where luxury, calm and refinement mix: La Table de la Réserve offers an elegant cuisine enhanced by the Chef Anne-Sophie Sabini who honours Mediterranean and local flavours. A charming address in an unusual and very relaxing setting.

L'ESCENTIEL

26, boulevard Maréchal-Leclerc
✆ +33 (0)4 93 01 17 33 / +33 (0)6 13 03 18 99
www.lescentielbeaulieu.com
info@lescentielbeaulieu.com

Closed Tuesday for dinner, Wednesday for dinner, Thursday and Sunday for lunch. Open from 11.45am to 2.30pm and from 7pm to 10pm. Booking is essential. À la carte: Around €28 (starter, main course, dessert). Lunch menu: €19 (main course and dessert, except Saturday and public holidays). Wine by the glass. Holiday voucher, Chèque Restaurant. Terrace. Parking opposite.

After having spent about thirty years in the largest cuisine brigades of luxury hotels in the French Riviera and Europe, Charles Séméria wanted to rediscover his hometown and live serenely his professional life at his own pace. He now works with products bought early in the morning from the market in Beaulieu-sur-Mer then warmly welcomes guests in his "berlugan bouchon" in a setting where you feel like at home. He elaborates simple and delicious dishes, displayed on the blackboard on the wall. The guideline is Mediterranean and inspired by the morning discoveries at the market.

Sleeping

LA RÉSERVE DE BEAULIEU HÔTEL & SPA

5, boulevard Maréchal-Leclerc
✆ +33 (0)4 93 01 00 01
www.reservebeaulieu.com
reservation@reservebeaulieu.com

Closed from mid-October to mid-December. Reception 24/24 (spoken languages: English, Italian, German, French). 39 rooms (100% non smoker). Double room from €150 approximately. Buffet breakfast or in room: €20. In high season. Garage (€33 low season and €36 high season). American Express, Diners Club. Pets allowed. Seminars. Receptions and weddings. Internet corner. Free Internet access. Free Wifi. Cleaning service. Catering facilities. Sale. Satellite TV, Canal+. Hammam, whirlpool.

The Réserve de Beaulieu Hotel & Spa is a mythical place in a beautiful Renaissance Villa with thirty-nine rooms and suites softened with frescoes, decorated with bright and warm colours, without forgetting the very peaceful and magic patio, a dining room reminding the main deck of a boat and the Spa – Maria Galland. Here you are in a peaceful, pleasant and noble haven where a real change of scenery is guaranteed, whether for the setting, the panorama or the talents of the Chef who delights all those who pass the door of this idyllic place!

Going Out

CASINO DE BEAULIEU-SUR-MER

4, avenue Fernand-Dunan
✆ +33 (0)4 92 00 60 00
www.casinodebeaulieu.com

Open all year. Slot machines: open Sunday to Thursday from 10am to 3am in the morning. Friday and Saturday from 10am to 4am in the morning. Access for people over 18 only, nonprohibited of games and on presentation of an ID. Catering facilities.

This historic casino located in front of the sea mixes former glory and modernity with elegance and refinement: monumental marble staircase, crystal chandeliers, purple and gold carpets, glass room, milky cream paintings, mirror games... Stroll through the four connecting lounges where you'll find 75 slot machines of the latest generation equipped with «full tito» without touching money and 12 tables of traditional games: traditional roulette, punto banco, stud poker, blackjack, Texas hold'em... Also on the spot, the restaurant Le 4 with a Parisian brasserie atmosphere which offers a top level traditional French cuisine that you can enjoy in a cosy dining room or outside in semi outdoor. Don't forget the bar Le Baccara. Feel like having a drink? Head for Les Jardins du Casino: cocktails, giant mojitos, tapas, grills, giant salads... The atmosphere is very festive! The Gala room meanwhile offers concerts, shows or private meals.

BEAUSOLEIL

The town of Beausoleil was created in 1904 by Camille Blanc , taking a small territory from the town of La Turbie located not far. The exceptional location of Beausoleil – very near indeed to the principality of Monaco – was worth the nickname of «Monte-Carlo Supérieur». Its position offers a great highlight: a panoramic view which extends from Cap Ferrat to Italy. This very favorable geographical location enables the city to maintain a very strong attractivity while developing dynamism and its own highlights. Having celebrated the centenary of its creation in 2004, Beausoleil is one of the most recent cities of the French Riviera.

The origins of its territory begin in Antiquity as witness the remains of the Oppidum Mont des Mules listed Historic. But it is the birth of Monte Carlo that the city will truly thrive and know its economic, demographic and touristic growth.

The town gathers today more than 12 different communities from around the world which bring to the city a great cultural wealth.

TOURIST OFFICE OF BEAUSOLEIL

32, boulevard de la République
✆ +33 (0)4 93 78 01 55
www.beausoleil-tourisme.com
info@beausoleil-tourisme.com

From October to April open Monday to Friday from 9am to 12pm and from 2pm to 6pm. Saturdays and Sunday from 10am to 2pm depending on events. From May to September open Monday to Friday from 9am to 12pm and from 2pm to 6pm. Saturdays from 10am to 2pm. Sunday from 10am to 2pm depending on events except July and August open every Sunday from 10am to 2pm.
Find all the news of Beausoleil at the Tourist Office where you can ask for a cultural visit of the city but also on outings and activities.

RIVIERA PALACE

✆ +33 (0)4 93 78 01 55
www.beausoleil-tourisme.com
info@beausoleil-tourisme.com

Guided tour organized by the Tourist Office of Beausoleil throughout the year. Booking required. Number of places limited. Free.
The Tourist Office offers a discovery tour from the city centre to the Riviera Palace around the theme "Belle Epoque". Discover the majestic Riviera Palace, former luxury hotel whose facade is listed Historic Monument since 1989. It is the Société Internationale des Grands Hôtels et Wagons-Lits, the owner of the legendary Orient Express, which initiated the construction of the luxurious Riviera Palace in 1898. This important holiday resort of the Russian, Austro-Hungarian and English aristocracy of the begining of the 20th century has become the symbol of the splendor of the Belle Epoque. The building has been transformed into flats between the two wars. It also has on its premises a real gem: a winter garden and a splendid canopy which was conceived in Gustave Eiffel's workshops (900 m² and 27 m high) where sumptuous parties took place.

Sightseeing

LE FOYER DU POILU ★★

9, avenue Maréchal-Foch

Open all year. For all visits contact the ✆+33 (0)4 93 41 99 29.
Memorial created by the Association of soldiers and veterans of Beausoleil to help soldiers and their families, this museum was inaugurated by Marechal Foch in 1928. A visit that allows you to discover many military objects and which plunges you into the souvenirs of the two world wars and the war of Algeria.

GUSTAVE-EIFFEL MARKET ★★

Rue du Marché
Boulevard de la République

Open all year. Every day from 7am to 1pm. Free access.
Partially covered by an architecture attributed to Gustave Eiffel, discover the stalls of this typically local colourful market with fresh ingredients of first quality: fruit, vegetables, cheese, etc., in a very friendly atmosphere.

TRAIL OF THE TROPHY OF AUGUSTUS FROM BEAUSOLEIL TO LA TURBIE ★★

This hiking starting from Beausoleil enables you to join the village of La Turbie and the famous Trophy of Augustus. At the exit of Monacos train station, take direction Beausoleil and on the left, the small avenue d'Alsace. Continue going up, then take on your right a small passage which skirts a small waterway «Moneghetti». At the top of the staircases take on the left to Place des Moneghetti and go up the homonymous boulevard on the right. You will be able to then join the departure for La Turbie in the direction of the Moyenne Corniche (staircases) and take the opposite road La Turbie Supérieur. Arrived at a crossing under the allotment «Les Hauts de Monte-Carlo», follow towards the right the itinerary which dominates Beausoleil to reach the pine forest of La Turbie by a ground track. You will be able to join the center of the village (avenue de la Pinède then via Julia) and reach the Trophy of Augustus, the park, and the museum.

Sleeping

ADAGIO MONACO MONTE CRISTO

2 a, rue des Martyrs-de-la-Résistance
✆ +33 (0)4 92 10 52 50
www.adagio-city.com
h6799@adagio-city.com

European Ecolabel. Reception 24/24 (7 days a week). 78 rooms (39 apartments non smoker). Parking. Cheaper rates depending on duration of the stay. Group rates. Apply for information directly by phone. 6 apartments accessible to physically disabled people. Pets allowed (paying). Free Wifi. Satellite TV.

Located a few minutes on foot from the famous Casino de Monte-Carlo square and the SNCF train station of Monaco, spacious studios and apartments can accommodate up to six people. They all have necessary comfort: TV, mini equipped kitchen, air conditioning... It is the perfect place for your family holidays or your business trips. Rates vary according to the season, the number of people and nights. Offers are also proposed all year on the website.

HÔTEL FORUM

16, avenue d'Alsace ✆ +33 (0)4 93 78 96 36

See page 30.

HÔTEL OLYMPIA

17 bis, boulevard Général-Leclerc
✆ +33 (0)4 93 78 12 70
www.olympiahotel.fr

European Ecolabel. Open all year. Reception 24/24 (spoken languages: French, Italian, English). 33 rooms. Breakfast: €10 (€15 in room). Extra bed: €40 (cot €15 per day). Parking: €15. Price per night. Single room deluxe from €85. Double room from €100. Superior double room from €120. Triple room from €140. Suite from €160. 2 accessible rooms for physically disabled people. No pets allowed. Free Wifi. Close to the Principality of Monaco, this Belle Epoque-style hotel offers classically decorated rooms, including two that are specially arranged for people with reduced mobility. All rooms are equipped with private baths, with tubs or showers, LED screen televisions, landline telephones, WiFi, mini-bars, safes, air conditioning and double-glazed windows.

CAP D'AIL ★★★

When you arrive from Nice via the Basse Corniche, the town of Cap-d'Ail is the last town before entering the principality of Monaco. Former neighbourhood of La Turbie which became a popular resort in the early 20th century, Cap-d'Ail has very beautiful sheltered beaches. You can admire many façades dating from Belle Époque like Château des Terrasses built at the end of the 19th century, Château de l'Hermitage where Queen Victoria stayed in 1897, Hôtel Éden or Villa Le Roc Fleuri, an Italian-style building dating back to 1900. Cap-d'ail also has about ten parks and gardens that shelter the whole Mediterranean flora but also some rare species: do not miss the Sacha Guitry park, the Bellando de Castro and the Beaverbrook squares or Balcon des Salines where the view of Monaco is sublime. Finally, take a look at Amphithéatre Jean Cocteau where many shows are held during the summer season.

TOURIST OFFICE OF CAP-D'AIL

87 bis, avenue du 3-Septembre
✆ +33 (0)4 93 78 02 33
www.cap-dail.fr – tourisme@cap-dail.com

July and August Monday to Saturday from 9.30am to 1pm and from 2.30pm to 6pm and Sunday from 9am to 1pm. Tourism label & Disability. From January to May and from October to December Monday to Friday from 9.30am to 12.30pm and from 1.30pm to 5.30pm and Saturday from 9am to 1pm. In June and September Monday to Friday from 9am to 1pm and from 2.30pm to 6pm and Saturday from 9am to 1pm.

Cap d'Ail is located on the outskirts of the Principality of Monaco. Its coastline offers wild landscapes that can easily be explored on foot. Its amazing beaches are lined with pine trees. The tourist office offers charged guided tours around plural themes. Inquire for prices and schedules.

THE CASTLE OF THE TERRACES ★★★

1, avenue du Général-de-Gaulle
✆ +33 (0)4 93 78 02 33 – www.cap-dail.com
tourisme@cap-dail.com

Guided tours ensured by the Tourisme office on appointment. Possibility of privatizing the place. Lift.

Built around 1890 for British banker William Mendel, Château des Terrasses knows his glory when in 1895 the grand duke Georges Alexandrovitch, brother of Tsar Nicholas II, rents the villa for winter to cure his tuberculosis there. He is quickly rejoined by his mother, Empress Maria Feodorovna accompanied by Prince Michel and Princesse Olga. The Président Félix Faure visited them as well as a cousin, the Queen Victoria herself, who stayed at Cap D'ail for the occasion. The residence then became the property of an opera prima donna of St Petersbourg before going in the 1930s to the hands of the Vice-consul of England, M. Buckingham. Then, transferred by his son in 2001 to the town of Cap D'ail, the site has been restored identically: its comfort and its beauty of rare perfection give this place the impression to discover a precious stone patinated and forged by time. A central elevator provides now access from the ground floor to the people with reduced mobility. In a green park of 2000 m² with shaded and flowery alleys, this place offers an exceptional view of the sea. Le Château also allows the organization of various events while the terraces, the garden and the two function rooms accommodate conferences or private parties in its bright and modern Belle Epoque style.

Beausoleil.

Sightseeing

VILLA LES CAMÉLIAS
17, avenue Raymond-Gramaglia
✆ +33 (0)4 93 98 36 57
www.villalescamelias.com
contacts@villalescamelias.com

Open all year. From November 1st to March 31st the museum is open on Sunday from 10am to 4pm; Tuesday, Wednesday, Thursday, Friday from 9.30am to 12:00 and from 1.30pm to 4.30pm. From April 2nd, 2017 to October 31st, 2017, the museum is open on Sunday from 11am to 6pm; Tuesday, Wednesday, Thursday, Friday from 9.30am to 12.30pm and from 2pm to 4pm. Free for under 12-year-olds. Adult: €9. Group (10 people): €5. Reduced: €5 (students, +60 years and from 12 to 18 years old). Guided tour (group by reservation). Shop. Free Audioguide in 3 languages (French, English, Italian).

In a beautiful villa Belle Epoque style recently converted into a private museum, visitors will discover on the ground- floor of the building the history of the town Cap D'ail (formerly Turbie-sur-Mer) through archives, photographs and various documents of the 19th century which testify the expansion of the city and the arrival of the english and international high society (Churchill, Paul Doumer, Jean Cocteau...) whereas on the first floor a temporary exhibition with a unique collection of paintings, drawings and enamels of the Basque painter Ramiro Arrue (20th century) is presented thematically. After the visit, don't forget to go strolling through the beautiful and luxurious garden surrounding the house.

Knife & Fork

LE BISTROT GOURMAND
16, avenue du 3-Septembre
✆ +33 (0)4 93 86 15 94
marechalantoine@wanadoo.fr

Open all year. Tuesday to Saturday from 12pm to 2pm and from 7.30pm to 9pm. Sundays and Monday from 12pm to 2pm. Closed Monday for dinner. Label Nissarde Kitchen. Label Chaine des Rotisseurs. À la carte: Around €35 (dish). Daily special: €13. Menus only weekday lunchtime: €16.50 starter and main course of the day or daily special + dessert or €20 starter and main course of the day + dessert. Chèque Restaurant. Groups welcome (up to 60 people. Possible custom-tailored menu). wi-fi.

Le Bistrot Gourmand welcomes you with its innovative revisited traditional French cuisine. The menu bears semi-gourmet creative and tasty dishes prepared by the Chef Antoine Marechal (ex Chef of Bec Rouge in Monaco, Orangeraie in Montpellier and the Bistrot Loumiri in Eze) with fresh local products changing according to the seasons: caramelized piglet tenderloin, mashed apples, or marinated Vendôme beef steak, croutons, poultry liver stuffing in Armagnac and marrow, red wine sauce marinade, caramelised currant jelly and deglazed mixed vegetables. As for desserts, you will also be surprised by the creativity: caramelized apple puff pie, vanilla ice cream with Armagnac sauce, homemade profiteroles, baked alaska... We also appreciated the atmosphere of the room, bright and carefully decorated, as well as the view on the sea and the quality of the service, always gracious. A family restaurant which will delig ht the gourmets.

LA CAMBUSE
4-6, Front-de-Mer pier
Port de Cap d\'Ail
✆ +33 (0)4 93 78 03 11
restaurantlacambuse@gmail.com

Open all year. You can reach it by entering the port of Cap d'Ail. Located at the end of the dock on the left after the barrier. Open every day from 9.30am to 11am for breakfast, from 12 to 3pm for lunch and from 7.30 pm to 10pm for diner. À la carte: around €28 (dish + dessert). Lunch formula: 15€ (daily special+daily dessert). Complete formula of the harbour: 20€. Credit card not accepted. Terrace. Parking on the port offered to the guests of the restaurant.

Beautifully located on the port of Cap D'ail facing the yachts. An unrivalled location with its sunset orientation warms the beautiful terrace on sunny days. The attractive and refined contemporary decor and beautiful bright terrace overlooking the port is an extra to the friendly and charming atmosphere of the place. It is a convenient meeting point for a lunch or after work to sip a glass in a fairy decor with music in the background. If the menu is traditional at lunch leaving the spotlight to beef tartar or fish that can be accompanied with a good wine with suggestions from all appellations, it is more elaborate for dinner. Atmosphere guaranteed!

LE COMPTOIR

11, avenue du 3-Septembre
✆ +33 (0)4 93 35 27 54

Open all year. À la carte: Around €20 (dish). Live music. Retransmission of sporting events. Groups welcome (by reservation). Terrace.

The Comptoir menu is renewed every season and according to the Chef's desires: here, only fresh market products are cooked! Snacked scallops and creamy risotto, risotto with mushrooms and truffle cream, flank steak shallots sauce, sea mixed grill, chestnut cappucino with hazelnut oil, vegetable rings, Comptoir burger, homemade foie gras with sweet spices, beef fillet, Comptoirs board... The welcome and service are excellent; the dishes are colourful and delicious, and the atmosphere in «bistro» way is attractive. An excellent address.

Leisure

SUNSATION

Port de Plaisance ✆ 07 85 22 92 17
www.sunsationboat.com

Open in summer season. Wake surfing, wake board, buoy, doughnut, snorkeling. On request, Taxi-Boat service from Monaco to Menton, Cannes to Saint-Tropez. Boat Trip 10 people max 1hour €180, 1/2 day €550, 1 day €850 (included skipper, petrol, services on board). Possibility of organizing private events.

Strong sensations by practising water sports with Sunsation! For over 10 years, this company offers different formulas: wakesurfing, wakeboarding, waterskiing, buoy or snorkeling. The Mediterranean becomes your new playground during your stay on the French Riviera. You can also try the *supra boat*, a unique boat imported straight from the United States. Sunsation also organizes your birthdays or aperitifs without forgetting the taxi-boat services, perfect to avoid the traffic jams.

EZE ★★★★

Eze is one of the most beautifull villages in the department. This spectacular village perched high above the sea, is one of the major attractions of the French Riviera, offering visitors a sublime viewpoint. From the sea to the grande corniche, the village stands at 700 meters. Access to the village is provided by the three cornices. A poet said: «Eze has its feet in the Mediterranean, the head in the sky and the mountains as crown». Without forgetting the nature that is well preserved. With different districts, the most important being Eze village, the old historical village and Eze seafront on the basse corniche. Eze village exudes an atmosphere of authenticity and traditions, the other Eze facing the sea, sheltered by Saint-Jean-Cap-Ferrat swell, offers all seaside pleasures. The old village is perched 429 feet above the sea. Its narrow streets are dominated by the ruins of a medieval castle. The stone used to build and pave the streets, comes from La Turbie and its extreme white gives an exceptional brightness to the village. Many artists and craftsmen are today in the former cellars or ground floor, which were once stables or sheepfolds. The location of the village was occupied from classical Antiquity, first by a ligurian celto oppidum, then by the phoenicians, the Romans, Saracens, then by a private medieval fortress whose ramparts were dismantled by Louis XIV, as he did in the castle of Nice. You can access the old village by a double fortified gate of the 14th century. From the top of the village, you can see a small cemetery, also perched between heaven and earth.

TOURIST OFFICE OF ÈZE

Place Général-de-Gaulle
✆ +33 (0)4 93 41 26 00
www.eze-tourisme.com/fr
office-tourisme-deze@wanadoo.fr

Open January, March, November, December from 9am to 4pm, closed on Sunday. February, April, May October from 9am to 6pm, open Sunday and public holidays. June, July, August, September from 9am to 7pm open every day.

Three cornices – the lower, the middle and the high one – cross Eze, revealing different views and different histories. The tourist office offers several activities (boules balls rental, guided tours...) to discover the charm and assets of the village. Note that the town has the label «classified tourism station» which guarantees a certain level of hospitality ans equipments.

Discover Eze on the steps of Nietzsche

The Tourist Office of Eze village organizes regular guided tours to discover the village in the footsteps of Friedrich Nietzsche. The circuit is within the medieval walls with the visit of the streets, squares, baroque church and chapel of the White Penitents without forgetting the discovery of the Botanical Garden and its exceptional scenery, as well as sculptures of Jean Philippe Richard. About 2 hours duration. Information: ✆+33 (0)4 93 41 26 00.

Sightseeing

★★★★

EXOTIC GARDEN
Rue du Château
✆ +33 (0)4 93 41 10 30
www.jardinexotique-eze.fr
eze@webstore.fr

Remarkable garden. Closed from December 19th to December 25th. October, November, December, January, February and March: open from 9am to 5pm. April, May and June from 9am to 7pm. July, August and September from 9am to 8pm. The garden accepts the last visitors up to 30 mn before closing. Free tour or guided tour. The Tourist Office proposes paying guided tours of the medieval village coupled with the exotic garden: 1.30hour approximately by reservation. Free for under 12-year-olds (and for Ezasques). Adult: €6 (from March to November). Group (12 people): €3.50. Adult €4 from December to February (covered cacti). -18 years, groups starting from 12 people: €1 / personne. Combined rate with the visit of the villa Ephrussi de Rothschild.

Located at an altitude of 429 m and at the foot of the ruins of the former medieval fortress (12th century), the site joins beauty of art and nature since 65 years. True terrestrial paradise, you will enjoy an exceptional view of the azure coastline, from Saint-Tropez to Italy. Fifteen "land goddesses" signed by the sculptor Jean-Philippe Richard will be your guests for an artistic journey between botany and poetry. The garden has been divided in two areas since summer 2014: the south slope (3 500 m^2) and the north slope (2 500 m^2).

- **The part located to the south of the garden** is a hot and dry area arranged in 1949 presenting a collection of cacti and succulent plants including some rare species on this level of development on the French Riviera: cacti, aloe, opuntias, agave mainly from South America and Africa.
- **The north part** is more Mediterranean and subtropical. Shaded and humid, this area has undergone major renovations allowing its reopening in July 2015. Visitors walk here between interlacing stairs, walkways, vegetable pockets, rocks and small courtyards while discovering myrtle, cistus or arbutus, among others. You will also be seduced by the caves with stalactites from which flows a thin trickle and little cascade whose noise can be heard from the church square below and invites visitors to this oasis after the tiring climb of the village in summer.

Alone, with family or friends, this visit promises a beautiful change of scenery! You should note that Jardin Exotique is also labelled *Jardin Remarquable* since 2015!

Knife & Fork

L'ALCHIMIE
197, avenue de Verdun
✆ +33 (0)4 93 41 12 79
✆ +33 (0)6 09 38 61 94
www.restaurant-lalchimie.com
alchimie.loicsiino@gmail.com

Open all year. Summer schedule from July 1st to the end of October: Open Monday to Saturday from 12pm to 2pm and from 7pm to 10.30pm. Closed on Sunday. Winter

© P. MASSON

Place du Planet.

schedules from November 1st to the end of June: Open Mondays, Tuesday, Thursday, Friday, Saturday from 12pm to 2pm and from 7pm to 10pm Closed Wednesdays and Sunday. À la carte: Around €25 (dish). Children's menu: €8. Evening menu €41. Terrace.

Loïc Siino is a passionate Chef who shares his love of beauty and good. After his beginnings at the best tables (in Royal Riviera in Beaulieu-sur-Mer, in Vista Palace in Roquebrune- Cap-Martin and L'Atelier de Joël Robuchon in Monaco), a meeting disrupts his course, the one with the michelin-starred Chef Mauro Colagreco of the Mizarur in Menton, with whom he excelled for three years as under chief. An enriching experience that will allow him to become second Chef at La Réserve in Beaulieu-sur-Mer before opening his own restaurant, «L'Alchimie» in the charming village of Eze, his native land. Creative cuisine, tasty and colourful inspired by his travels, Japan via Argentina, Belgium or Gers: Bresse of crab with melissa, avocado fricassee and ginger vinaigrette; creamy risotto with chanterelles; grilled tuna steak, roasted ceps and black sesame sauce; chocolate fondant and passion fruit sauce or the strawberry soup and white chocolate espuma....His love for plants – which nearly could have made him become gardener! – also allows him to know edibles in herbs and flowers that he collects carefully and that he uses to highlight his dishes which are prepared with quality and seasonal ingredients. A perfect alchemy for this surprising place that offers an incredible culinary stop.

ANJUNA BEACH
Eze Seafront – Avenue de la Liberté
Basse Corniche RD 698 ✆ +33 (0)4 93 01 58 21
See page 45.

LA CHÈVRE D'OR
Rue du Barri ✆ +33 (0)4 92 10 66 61
www.chevredor.com
Open from March 4th to November 5th, 2016. Lunch from 12.30pm to 1.30pm and dinner from 7.30pm to 9.30pm. Open every day except in March Monday. In July and August: closed for lunch Mondays, Tuesday and Wednesday except in November: closed for dinner Sunday; Monday and Tuesday; Wednesday only for lunch. Booking is essential. Wine by the glass. À la carte and menu at €85 and €110 with the wines in accordance, €145 for lunch, €205 and €240 for dinner. American Express, Diners Club. Groups welcome. Valet. Shop. 2 Michelin stars. Parking. Dress code: smart elegant (no jeans, shorts, open shoes for men).

Dream in front of the panoramic dining room overlooking the Villefranche-sur-Mer harbour where every detail seems to have been worked to make the moment unforgettable until the prices which are rather aristocratic. Three other catering places are also to be discovered on the spot: Les Remparts for lunch outside at noon; L'Eden for dinner facing the Mediterranean Sea and the Café des Jardins for a light meal. Excellent meals, right and controlled cooking and perfectly presented dishes. This culinary getaway is only waiting for you!

LA TABLE DE PATRICK RAINGEARD

Cap Estel – 1312, avenue Raymond-Poincaré
✆ +33 (0)4 93 76 29 29 – www.capestel.com
contact@capestel.com

Closed from beginning of January to beginning of March. Open Tuesday to Saturday from 7pm to 10.30pm; Wednesday to Sunday from 12pm to 2.30pm. Booking advised. Menu from €125 to €150. From €79 to €150. Wine by the glass. €45 menu 2 main courses or €55 menu 3 main courses only for lunch, except weekend and public holidays. Degustation menu from €115 for lunch and dinner. Menu inspiration from €150 only for dinner. Brunch every Sunday. American Express. Groups welcome (up to 50 people). Garden. Terrace. Valet. 1 Michelin star. 3 toques and favorites in Gault and Millau. Golden Gault and Millau PACA 2013. Parking.

The chef Patrick Raingeard cooks with fresh local products which he takes from his vegetable garden or from the local farmers. His dishes in a geometric composition are well controlled both in terms of precision of cooking and of the savours: butternut soup with caviar of esturgeonniere, egg tempura with chorizo; roasted scallops with autumn truffles and star anise; carrots à l'orange; croque monsieur with summer truffle.... As for the desserts, they remain in the same light and fresh spirit: Menton lemon meringue sphere, cottage cheese mousse, vanilla lemon ice cream. Do not miss the Sunday brunch made up of pastries, freshly squeezed juices, ham on the bone, seafood, verrines, homemade pastries, the whole with unlimited champagne.

Sleeping

LA CHEVRE D'OR

Rue du Barri ✆ +33 (0)4 92 10 66 61
www.chevredor.com

Relais & Châteaux. Closed from the last weekend of November to first Thursday of March. In november, open from Wednesday at 3pm to Sunday after lunch. Reception 24/24. 38 rooms. Breakfast: €35 (continental and €45 American). Extra bed: €70 (free baby bed and bed for child of more than 6 years: €65). Parking (external non covered €15 per day). Classic room from €310. Traditional room from €320. Elegance room from €520. Panoramic suite from €2,600. American Express, Diners Club. Pets allowed (€25/day). Seminars. Receptions and weddings. Internet corner. Free Internet access. Free Wifi. 4 restaurants: La Chèvre d'Or, 2 Michelin stars, Les Remparts (open every day depending on the weather), L'Eden (open every evening, depending on weather) and Le Café du Jardin (open every day). Shop. Satellite TV, Canal+. Hammam, bubblebath, sauna. Excursions (via the concierge: concierge@chevredor.com).

La Chèvre d'Or is a luxury hotel like no other. The thirty rooms and eight suites are charming while having modern equipment, an old romantic insolent setting or proud for some – in particular the one where the large bathtub of the bathroom is fitted under the rock and the presidential suite with its private heated swimming pool. Each room is unique and offers an individual decoration and charm. It is a real gem where refinement rhymes with sweet life. A swimming pool, a gym, a sauna and massage rooms are available for you to relax.

EZE HERMITAGE HOTEL

1951, avenue des Diables-Bleus
Grande Corniche ✆ +33 (0)4 93 41 00 68
www.ezehermitage.com

Logis (3 cheminées). Open all year. Reception 24/24. 24 rooms (100% not smoker). Buffet breakfast. Extra bed: €20. Parking (free). Rate room low and high season on the basis of double room between €80 and €160. Breakfast per person: €15. Rate half-board low and high season on the basis of double room: €40 per day and per person besides the price of the room. Tourist tax €1.50 per day and per person. VIP reception €25 per day and per room with dressing gowns, slippers, fruit basket, bottle of water as well as a varied range of body products. Spoken languages: French, English, Italian, German. Checks are not accepted. 1 room arranged for wheel chair, access to the restaurant, the lounge and the garden. Pets allowed (€8/day). Receptions and weddings. Free Internet access. Free Wifi. Cleaning service. Catering facilities (menu €40. Wines by the glass. Children's menu €15. Average price à la carte (main course): €23). Organization of all types of events: banquets, weddings, communions, receptions professional... satellite TV. Activities. Excursions.

Imagine a peace haven in a beautiful flower garden. Eze Hermitage Hotel is a small charming and calm hotel with a breathtaking view of the Mediterranean Sea and the mountains of the Mercantour National Park. Its 24 cute rooms of provençal style bear flawless comfort. The reception and service are the same and at a reasonable price. The swimming pool of the hotel offers all the fun of bathing in summer and you can enjoy the splendid strolls in the park of the Grande Corniche and on the Plateau de la Justice nearby all year round. Eze Hermitage also has a restaurant whose menu is oriented towards Provence: thyme lamb confit ravioli, ceps and parmesan cream, warped sea bass filet in aioli style and vegetables, bitter chocolate teardrops with pear mousse. You will enjoy this very tasty cuisine in the restaurant or in the garden near the swimming pool with a view on Nice backland. The lounge bar offers delicious homemade cocktails. Possibility of organizing receptions on site: the staff listens to each of your desires.

Shopping

L'EPICURIEN

34, avenue de la Liberte
✆ +33 (0)4 93 13 01 01– www.l-epicurien.fr

Open in summer non stop from 11am to 9pm.

It is an Ali Baba cave, Epicurus version... You will find everything that delights gourmets: foie gras, smoked salmon, caviar, chocolate, honey, terrines, mustard, vinegars, oils, jams and especially a beautiful range of wines, champagnes and spirits. The shop is transformed into a wine and champagne bar every evening at aperitif time. Lovely outdoor terrace.

THE DIGITAL VERSION OF THIS GUIDE BOOK IS FREE

ZLG95EJB

The code can only be used once.

1. Go to the Petit Futé online shop: http://boutique.petitfute.com/
2. Type the promotion code in the banner « **La version numérique de votre guide offerte** » and click on OK.
3. Click on « **Continuer le paiement** » with a global amount of 0€.
4. Sign in by clicking on « **S'identifier** » and select your billing address and click on « **Continuer** ».
5. Or create your online account by clicking on « **S'inscrire** », fill in the fields and click on « **S'inscrire** », complete your billing address and click on « **Continuer** ».
6. Check your billing address.
7. Click on « **Continuer** » / « **Pas d'information de paiement nécessaire** » / « **Passer la commande** ».
8. Simply click on « **Mes produits téléchargeables** » link, or click on the « **Mon compte** » link at the top and then below « **Mes produits téléchargeables** » link in the « **Mon compte** », and on the right select your digital version.

Offre valable jusqu'au 31/12/2017 sous réserve de l'arrêt de commercialisation de certains titres en France métropolitaine et dans le monde et sous réserve que le nombre de téléchargements soit inférieur ou égal au nombre d'exemplaires de guides papier imprimés. Formats disponibles pour smartphones, tablettes, liseuses et ordinateurs PC ou MAC.

■ **LYSAND CRÉATIONS**
Rue Carriera-Plana ✆ +33 (0)4 93 97 85 42
www.lysandcreations.com
Open from 10am to 7pm. Former interior decorator, this artist opened a shop in Eze village a few years ago to devote herself to her first passion: painting. Her work has then quickly evolved into creating decoration objects for the house and female accessories where each piece is unique and made from images of her paintings. Friendly welcome.

LA TURBIE ★★★

La Turbie is famous for the presence of the one of the two only Roman trophies still remaining built to honour Auguste – the second is at Adamklissi at 150 km from Bucharest. Located 500 m above the sea, La Turbie is the highest point of the Via Julia Augusta which connected Cimiez, capital of the Roman province in the Alpes-Maritimes, to Genoa in Italy. It is on this remarkable site that the Roman decided to raise a trophy to the glory of emperor Auguste, conqueror of the Alp-Ligurians and forty-three other regional tribes, that he submited to the authority of the roman Empire. This trophy was strongly mistreated during centuries: ransacked at the end of the Roman Empire, transformed into fortress in the Middle Ages, denounced by the monks of Lérins like an impious and pagan monument, dismantled on the order of Louis XIV, it was used as stone quarry for the construction of several monuments of the region, of which the church of La Turbie. It was finally partially restored at the beginning of the 20th century, partly under the impulse and with the contribution of an American patron, Edward Tuck, which entrusted restoration works to the architect Jules Formigé.

Sightseeing

■ **TROPHÉE D'AUGUSTE** ★★
Avenue Albert 1er ✆ +33 (0)4 93 41 20 84
la-turbie@monuments-nationaux.fr

Closed on January 1st, May 1st, 1st and 11th November and December 25th. From January 2nd to May 18th, open Tuesday to Sunday from 10am to 1.30pm and from 2.30pm to 5pm. From May 19th to September 20th, every day except Monday from 9.30am to 1pm and from 2.30pm to 6.30pm. From September 21st to end of December, every day except Monday from 10am to 1.30pm and from 2.30pm to 5pm. Free for under 18-year-olds (and also disabled person and her guide. Unemployed, on presentation of a certificate of less than 6 months. Card Culture – Card ICOM. Pass Education). Adult: €5.50. Group (20 people): €4.50. Last admission one hour before closing. The evacuation of the shop takes place 15 minutes before closing. Model of the trophy with instructions in Braille on tablets, film, audioguide. Guided tour (1.15hour approximately). Shop. No pets allowed except guide-dogs.
Although it was partially destroyed, the size of this monument remains very impressive: it was originally 50 m high (against 35 m today) and 38 m long. You can access all the levels by the stairs. A circular Doric colonnade initially included recessed nests where statues of all the illustrious generals during the campaigns of Augustus had been placed. In a museum set in the trophy, we can see a model of the reconstitution of the monument and numerous mouldings, documents and objects from excavations carried out in the region.

Knife & Fork

■ **LA CAVE TURBIASQUE**
Place Théodore de Banville
✆ +33 (0)4 93 41 15 02
www.caveturbiasque.com
caveturbiasque@orange.fr
Open all year. Open 8am to the evening after the service. Closed Sunday for dinner and Monday all day. Annual closing between February 15th and on March 15 during 3 weeks (telephone for information). Booking advised. From €9 to €15 for the starters. From €14 to €20 for the dishes. Desserts €7.
Here is a very nice place that offers simple, varied, authentic, tasty, fresh and seasonal cuisine, where everything is homemade: tartare of tomatoes and mozzarella di bufala, shortbread with Parmesan; risottino with artichokes and speck; cassolette of scallops with Noilly Prat; beef cheek stew and gnocchi; Charolais steak and homemade fries... The delicious menu changes every week depending on the mood of the Chef and the market. Pleasant surprises in the plate, a cosy decor and a generous welcome.

■ **HOSTELLERIE JÉRÔME**
20, rue Comte-de-Cessole
✆ +33 (0)4 92 41 51 51
www.hostelleriejerome.com
Open for dinner only. Closed weekly: Monday and Tuesday. In July and August, open every evening. Possibility of rooms on the premises. Booking advised. Menu from €78 to €138. American Express. Free wi-fi. Terrace.
In this wonderful 13th century house erected in the old village of La Turbie, a large vaulted room where you can enjoy a nice fresh Mediterranean cuisine and the result is a menu full of flavours, constantly renewed, largely open on seasonal products and orchestrated by the talented Bruno Cirino: grilled raw lobster mirabelle plum brandy and brioche, roasted squab; sea bass escalope, peas, mandarines; red rock mullet, saffroned stock, artichokes; raviolis with bufflone milk, meadow and forest mushrooms, crayfish; Roasted Saint Pierre, potatoes compote with olive oil... An absolutely exceptional moment if you are lucky enough to occupy one of the few tables on the terrace open onto the sea. As for the desserts, you'll enjoy the Tainori chocolat, small wild plums, brandy, mountain angelica, hot croquettes and sorbet. A beautiful wine cellar with 20,000 bottles and 1,400 references.

THE STEAK HOUSE

7, avenue de la Victoire
✆ +33 (0)4 93 51 53 54
www.steakhouse-laturbie.webself.net
le-napoleon@orange.fr

♿

Open all year. From 12pm to 2.30pm and from 7pm to 10pm. Booking advised. Wine by the glass. Lunch menu at €12: all-you-can-eat buffet + 1 daily special. Menu at €16 including starter and main course or main course and dessert. Menu at €19 starter + main course + dessert. Slate from €14. Holiday voucher, Chèque Restaurant. Groups welcome (up to 80 people. By reservation). Terrace.

Come and discover a friendly cuisine with Mediterranean accents within a contemporary setting. In the bistro-chic room or comfortably seated on the terrace, enjoy the grilled meats and fish. The buffet is worthy at midday, associated with the daily special. The chef supplements the carte with daily specials, declined on the blackboard according to the arrivals of the market. Regulars like getting together to enjoy traditional dishes: prawn skewers, bœuf bourguignon, calf's kidneys with whole-grain mustard, salad of gizzard confits or Atlantic smoked salmon plate, between others. The dishes are nicely presented, and the team has a warm welcome.

LA TABLE GOURMET BARBERA- 1902

13, avenue de la Victoire
✆ +33 (0)4 93 41 58 49
http://latablegourmande-laturbie.fr
barbera.laturbie@orange.fr

Open all year. Tuesday to Saturday from 12pm to 3pm and from 6pm to 10pm. Sushi, temakis, makis and sashimis from €4.20. Booking advised. À la carte: Around €18 (dish). Fixed rate formula only weekday lunchtime: €16 (starter + main course + dessert). Suggestions for a week. Starter from €14. Checks are not accepted. Chèque Restaurant. Groups welcome (up to 23 people). Terrace.

Since 1902, the recipes are prepared with fresh seasonal quality products, while the know-how is passed along from generation to generation. The various and generous dishes combine tradition with local flavours: beef burger and homemade lasagna, veal osso bucco and lamb parmentier, veal liver and homemade mashed potatoes, mariniere mussels, linguine alle vongole, rabbit with green olives sauce polenta, papardelles with tuna peppers oignons, beef burger with comté cheese and sauce tartare, beef burger with eggplants alla parmigiana.... Also discover the very nice sushis, temakis, makis ans sahimis carte. The welcome is warm, with a smile and humour. *A smart place!*

Sleeping

HOSTELLERIE JÉRÔME

20, rue Comte de Cessole
✆ +33 (0)4 92 41 51 51
www.hostelleriejerome.com
hostellerie.jerome@wanadoo.fr

Open all year. 5 rooms. Room for 2 people from €98 per night. Free Wifi. Catering facilities (the Hostellerie Jérôme and Le Café de La Place).

Hostellerie Jérôme offers rooms with refined decoration, simple and elegant, combining modernity and authenticity. You can choose between those with a nice view of the village or those revealing an exceptional view on the sea. All rooms are equipped with modern and comfortable bathrooms. On the spot you can enjoy the delightfull gourmet dishes signed by Bruno Cirino or sit at Café de la Place, the other gourmet address of Hostellerie Jérôme.

© GIANLIGUORI – ISTOCKPHOTO

Views of La Turbie and Trophée d 'Auguste.

HÔTEL RESTAURANT LE NAPOLÉON
7, avenue Victoire ✆ +33 (0)4 93 51 62 66
http://hotel-napoleon.com
reservation@hotel-napoleon.com

Open all year. Spoken languages: French, Italian, English. 24 rooms (with bathroom). Half-board: €22 (including starter, main course, dessert, drink soft or ¼ of wine and coffee). Champagne offered (or any other drink of your choice) for any reservation made via the site or by telephone. A motorbike private and free location is reserved for the guests of the hotel. A public and free parking is located within walking distance of the hotel. Room rate on request only. Free Wifi. Catering facilities (the Steack House).
Next to the historic center and medieval village, Hotel Napoleon*** allows you to discover the beautiful village of La Turbie. With a bright décor, the rooms are warm and comfortable, they all have a private bathroom. On site, enjoy the Steak House restaurant which has a contemporary atmosphere and a menu with Mediterranean flavours.

ROQUEBRUNE-CAP-MARTIN ★★★

Natural extension of Roquebrune, Cap Martin peninsula is comparable to that of Antibes. This highly residential site is dotted with beautiful and majestic villas in parks with century old trees. It is possible to make the tour of it by walking along the coastal path called Le Corbusier path, in memory of the famous architect who had a shed on the cape that you can visit (registration at the Tourist Office). The path goes along beautiful beaches and flowery gardens. Sometimes, you will glimpse a semi-palace or a sumptuous 19th century villa, true vestige of the Belle Epoque. Also discover the Aleppo pine trees, palm trees and other Mediterranean species offering freshness and shades, in a typical local decor.

LE CABANON OF LE CORBUSIER ★★★
Sentier du littoral des Douaniers
✆ +33 (0)6 48 72 90 53
www.capmoderne.com
contact@capmoderne.com
Guided tour only on appointment. Take good shoes for walking. Prohibited strollers. No pets allowed.
This small wooden hut, secret castle of the architect Le Corbusier, stands at the foot of a carob tree. Designed as a minimal habitat model, it is in 1952 that this unit was created on the site. Today, it is the testimony of a place of life rich in anecdotes. Sparsely furnished, it allowed the architect to make frequent summer trips on the banks of the Mediterranean. The entrance to this hut is authorized but only for groups of 4 people accompagnied by the guide, and not more than 2 or 3 minutes on the spot.

VILLA E-1027 EILEEN GRAY ★★★★
Esplanade of the station
Avenue Le Corbusier
✆ +33 (0)6 48 72 90 53
www.capmoderne.com
contact@capmoderne.com
Access by train: stop at the station of Roquebrune Cap-Martin. Access by car: follow the indications to Gare de Cabbé.
Guided tour by appointment only. Take shoes adapted to walk. Prohibited strollers. No pets allowed. Two visits per day Tuesday to Sunday. Departures at 10am and the afternoon at 3pm in July and August. The rest of the year, departure at 2pm. Free for under 7-year-olds. Adult: €18. Group (15 people): €200. Reduced rate: €10 (from 7 to 17 years old child, families starting from 4 people, students, unemployed people on presentation of a valid written proof). Guided tour (duration 2.30 hours. Up to 12 people).
After important restorations, this beautiful seaside house classified as an historical monument in 2000 is now opened to public. It was owned by the designer and architect Eileen Gray, accompanied by Jean Badovici. The place combines modernity and science of climatic comfort since 1929. The name of the house is a code for its owners: E for Eileen, 10 for J of Jean, 2 for B of Badovici, 7 for G of Gray. Inside, superb frescoes were painted by Le Corbusier.

THE CAP MARTIN FORTRESS ★★★
Avenue de Montléon
www.roquebrune-cap-martin.fr
From March 1st to May 30th: visit Saturday at 2pm, from June 1st to September 30th: visits Saturday at 2pm and Wednesday at3pm, from October 1st to November 30th: Saturday at 2pm. Free for under 6-year-olds h. Adult: €5. Child, student or group: 3 €. Guided tour (by appointment only. Assured visit starting from 5 people). Take good shoes.
Work of the Maginot Line built in 1930, this fort played an important role during the battles opposing the French and Italian in June 1940, allowing a subterranean life in perfect autarky. Its crew consisted of 11 officers and 343 soldiers.

THE MEDIEVAL VILLAGE AND ITS CASTLE ★★
www.roquebrune-cap-martin.fr
Open all year. By appointment only. Assured visit starting from 5 people. Opening hours: from October 1st to January 31st from 10am to 12.30pm and from 2pm to 5pm, from February 1st to May 31st from 10am to 12.30pm and from 2pm to 6pm. From June 1st to September 30th from 10am to 1pm and from 2.30pm to 7pm. Castle closed on May 1st, 1st and on November 11th, on December 25th and on January 1 as well as Fridays between November 1st and January 31st. Free for under 6-year-olds. Adult: €5. Child: 3 €. These rates understand the entrance to the castle. Registrations for the visit at least one day before at the Tourist Office.
The tour includes the visit of the village, the narrow streets, the ancient olive tree, the chapels and the castle. It is also an opportunity to enjoy the magnificent panoramas that are offered to contemplation, especially on sunny days. The castle was built in 970 by Conrad I, count of

Ventimiglia, with the aim of defending the western border of its feudal estate and preventing a renewed attack of the sarrasines. The fortress then included the entire village. In the 15th century, Grimaldi enlarged the military power of this keep. Sold as national property in 1808, it was sold in 1911 to a rich British tourist who donated it to the city in 1921. Since 1927, it is listed in the Inventory of Historical monuments.

Knife & Fork

LE BOUCHE A OREILLE

8, avenue de France
✆ +33 (0)4 93 17 55 17
www.restaurantleboucheaoreille.com
contact@restaurantleboucheaoreille.com

Closed on Sunday and Monday. Open from 11.30am to 1.30pm and from 7.30pm to 9.30pm. Homemade dishes and the menu changes every day. Set menu at €27.50 (starter + main course + dessert). À la carte: Around €24 (main course). Children's menu: €10. Wine by the glass. Organization of custom-tailored private events.

Nicely presented original and colourful dishes, homemade and enhanced by the Chef Joël Metony, the French cuisine of Bouche à Oreille (*BO* for the regulars) is revisited with talent and flavour according to the seasons: shellfish cream cappuccino way, sardine rillettes and marinated pieces, lightly seared turbot with asparagus, sea bream tartar, pork cheek with ginger and candied lemon, pintadeau supreme with foie gras sauce, roasted sea bass steak, black Angus Rossini beef fillet without forgetting the unmissable beef tartar and foie gras homemade fries and sucrine that wine lovers will accompany with an excellent French vintage rigorously selected. You will also be charmed by the modern setting of this restaurant with warm atmosphere that offers a magnificent view on the Mediterranean. Little smart extra: the BO also organises your customised private events!

LE DECK

Monte-Carlo Beach
Avenue Princesse-Grace
✆ +37 (0)7 98 06 51 00
www.monte-carlo-beach.com
bh@sbm.mc

♿

Open from mid-April to end of October every day from 12.30pm to 3.30pm (4pm in July and August). Every Wednesday, seasonal barbecue with meat selection in poolside. Each Sunday, between 12.30pm and 3.30pm, the Market of Flavours: an organic buffet full of sun and with freshness presented like a stall of market, where the local produce has the star. €75/person (excluding drinks). Booking advised. À la carte: Around €72 (starter €25, main course €35, dessert around €12). Children's menu: €25. Daily special: €29. Wine by the glass. American Express, Diners Club. Groups welcome. Garden. Terrace. Valet. Shop. Activities. Free outdoor parking. No pets allowed.

An air of holidays blows on this terrace where you have lunch in all relaxation facing the magnificent pool-mirror of Monte-carlo Beach. The italian chef, Paolo Sari offers here clear dishes and quality: tomatoes and mozzarella di bufala with basil of Riviera; salmon ceviche and avocado, coconut vinaigrette with lime and ginger; crab salad with citrus fruit, quinoa colours; lé minestrone gumes parfumé with pesto of Levante; trofie di Gragnano with langoustines and tomatoes épicé es; dory fillet à anise, eggplant caviar and candied fennel or chicken wok to satay and sour- soft lé gumes to sé same, among others. A good address Chimes perfectly luxury, calm and pleasure.

LA DIFFÉRANCE

Parking at the country club
Sentier des Douaniers
✆ +33 (0)4 92 07 35 51
www.ladifferance.com
contact@ladifferance.com

♿

Open every day except Wednesday. Booking advised. À la carte: Around €20. Wine by the glass. Credit card not accepted. Groups welcome. Terrace. Take-away. Parking Monte-Carlo Country Club.

The A of La DifférAnce (stands for Amour) is the key word because here, everything is done with love in this restaurant perched on the rocks below the Tennis courts of the Monte-Carlo Country Club. Its large terrace overlooks the sea and the Cap Martin for you to settle and spend a nice time. Add to this a warm and familial welcome. The dishes confirm all the rest: quality, fresh products with daily suggestions according to the market copiously served. The menu offers beside the fish of the day: warm octopus salad, traditional beef tartar, beef tagliatta, stuffed sea bass and chocolate fondant. Please note, the restaurant does not have a private beach, but a path which leads to a beach a little further on the Sentier des Douaniers.

LE PICCADILLY

16, avenue François-de-Monléon
✆ +33 (0)4 93 35 87 16
www.lepiccadilly.com
contact@lepiccadilly.com

Open all year. Every day of the week from 8am to 2 in the morning except Wednesday. À la carte: Around €20. Starters from €4.50. Pasta from €7. Pizza from €8. Meats from €10.50. Fish from €11.50. Snack.

Family-run, this café-restaurant- bar has a friendly atmosphere where good humour and understanding are the keywords. If the room is decorated in an English-style, if the menu is in the way of the London subway and if the presentation of the team on the website does not lack humour, the cuisine is resolutely Mediterranean: spaghetti, tagliatelli and cappelleti are available here with classic and original tasty sauces. Also discover the freshness of the carpaccio with Parmesan or that of steak tartare without forgetting the traditional lamb chops or the range of pizzas. Lovers of seafood will choose the mussels in white wine or a salmon cooked in foil, among others. The main courses and suggestions change regularly, but the smile and good humour remain. A very smart address!

RESTAURANT ELSA
Monte Carlo Beach
Avenue Princesse-Grace
✆ +33 (0)4 93 28 66 66
www.monte-carlo-beach.com
restaurantelsa@sbm.mc

Relais & Chateaux. Open from beginning of March to end of October. Open daily for lunch from 12.30pm to 2.30pm and for dinner from 7.30pm to 10pm. Breakfast from 7.30am to 10.30am. 1 Michelin star. Relaxation package: €200 from mid-April to end of October. Booking is essential. À la carte from €104 to €144. Wine by the glass. Lunch from €45 Monday to Friday, except public holidays. Dinner from €98 every evening and for lunch Saturday, Sunday and public holidays. Menu Inspiration: 9 main courses around the Mediterranean, €125, only for dinner. American Express, Diners Club. Groups welcome. Garden. Terrace. Valet. Shop. Free outdoor parking.

The Italian chef, Paolo Sari, charms the gourmets with a cuisine made up of local and regional organic products. His menus reflects his natural approch which we find in products certified as organic in most of the preparations from the bread made twice a day with organic flour to the first seasonal red berries associated to the zabaglione gratin, the raw San Remo red prawn tail steak, minifennels, fragrant bergamot and Provence herbs, mountain early potato gnocchis, flowers, herbs and gourmet vegetables, roasted lamb chops with homemade bacon and acacia honey, celeriac and liquorice puree, with a crispy spiral of potatoes. You can enjoy in summer, the elegant white terrace and one of the most beautiful view of the Principality which seems to hang over the water.

RESTAURANT L' HIPPOCAMPE
44, avenue Winston-Churchill
✆ +33 (0)4 93 35 81 91
www.hippocampe-restaurant.com

Annual closing: from mid-November to end of December included. Closed weekly Monday. Open Tuesday to Sunday from 12pm to 2.30pm. Open in the evening Thursday, Friday and Saturday in May and June; from July to September Tuesday to Saturday evening; in October Friday and Saturday for dinner. Lunch menu. Menu from €35 to €48. À la carte around €25 main course. Deckchair rental €14 per day and €9 half-day.

The family-run restaurant L'Hippocampe does everything since 1963 to satisfy you! A breathtaking view of Menton and its surroundings, an idyllic setting between sea and mountains, the smell of the sea air and finally the taste of a good traditional and inventive cuisine: shrimps tartar with chives, sea bass fillet and candied pears, gambas skewers pineapple and curry, goose liver aspic with homemade jelly, sole fillets with hollandaise sauce, coq au vin, crayfish tagliatelles...In summer you can rent a deck chair to relax on the private beach located below the restaurant.

Sleeping

HOTEL AND RESTAURANT LES DEUX FRÈRES
1, place des Deux-Frères
✆ +33 (0)4 93 28 99 00 / +33 (0)6 80 86 22 41
www.lesdeuxfreres.com
info@lesdeuxfreres.com

Open all year. Every day. 10 rooms. Breakfast: €9. Room from €75/night. Catering facilities (menu from €28 to €48. Closed on Sunday evening, Monday all day and Tuesday lunchtime).

Set in an old school of 1854, the Les Deux Frères hotel and restaurant is an excellent address. Each room has a unique decoration and you can choose between those with a stunning view of the Sea or the ones offering a view on the mountain. Each has air conditioning, tv with satellite connection as well as a bathroom with toilet. Just next door, enjoy the delicious cuisine of the restaurant seated on the lovely terrace, near the fireplace or in the veranda.

HÔTEL VICTORIA
7, promenade du Cap
✆ +33 (0)4 93 35 65 90
www.hotel-victoria.fr

Open all year. Reception 24/24. 32 rooms (including 17 with diving view on the sea and 15 with view on mountain). Buffet breakfast or in room: €14 (Express breakfast: €6). Extra bed: €20 (free extra bed for children under 10 years old). Garage (parking (booking advised) in front of the hotel: €15/night or municipal garage 300 m from the hotel: €10/night). Room « Classique» from €89 to €275 flexible rate. Room Sea sight from €99 to €345 flexible rate. Prepaid rate 12% off: see conditions on the website. American Express, Holiday voucher. 2 rooms adapted to disabled guests: book according to your specific needs. Parking reserved at the entrance of the hotel with a ramp to reach the reception. Toilets adapted installed on the ground floor. Pets allowed (€20 per night). Seminars. Internet corner. Free Internet access. Free Wifi. Cleaning service. Light snacks from 12pm to 9pm (omelette, pasta, paninis, sandwiches, charcuterie or cheese plates). Lounge bar open 24/24. Satellite TV. Tourist information point and digital tablet at disposal at the reception. Meeting room with multi-media facility (10 people). Terrace external and covered with panoramic view on the Sea.

Twin of the Hôtel Napoléon in Menton, you can easily

imagine the beauty and quality of Hôtel Victoria! From the reception, it is a pleasant surprise with a contemporary design, bright, refined and warm. Delicate and refined decor was created by the talented designer Philippe Nuel around a theme: artists of the Riviera in the 1950s. Le Corbusier, Eileen Gray, Picasso, Matisse and Chagall are therefore the references of this charming hotel. On one floor, 32 rooms follow one another along a large corridor: 17 have a pleasant balcony with sea view and 15 others offer beautiful mountain views. An elevator provides access to the places for people who can enjoy two specially designed rooms. The deep and striking blue of the Mediterranean is found tastefully everywhere in the Hotel: furniture, wall and room. A place designed for all lovers of life on the Riviera. Hotel Victoria is the perfect place to explore local cultural heritage.

MONTE CARLO BEACH

Avenue Princesse-Grace
✆ +33 (0)4 93 28 66 66
www.monte-carlo-beach.com

Open from beginning of March to end of October. Reception 24/24. 40 rooms (spoken languages: Italian, French, Russian, English, German. Possibility of smoking in the rooms). Breakfast: €40. Parking (external free if not €15 per day). Double room from €158. American Express, Diners Club. Seminars. Receptions and weddings. Internet access. Free Wifi. Cleaning service. Catering facilities (restaurant Elsa, 1 Michelin star). Product sales. Spa. Satellite TV, Canal+. Hammam. From 3 to 8 years old children's club open July and August. Swimming pool of 50 m sea water, with ozone, heated, in open air and swimming pool for children. Bike rental with electric assistance.

The Monte Carlo Beach Hotel was created at the dawn of the roaring twenties to accommodate all the elite in a palace «on the waterfront». Located on an exceptional listed site, it is an unique place beyond time. It is the architect and designer India Mahdavi who has redesigned the place in the spirit of a romantic break of the 1930s. The forty rooms and suites are equipped with high technology but this does not diminish the poetic charms of the lit-up spaces with the sea on the horizon. The mural frescoes – relics of Matisse – are a poetic ode and the light-toned decoration faithful to the seaside spirit is an invitation to relaxation.

LE ROQUEBRUNE

Lower corniche
100, avenue Jean-Jaurès
✆ +33 (0)4 93 35 00 16
✆ +33 (0)9 61 35 53 32
www.le-roquebrune.com
leroquebrune@orange.fr

European Ecolabel. Open all year. Reception until 7.30pm (then call them). 6 rooms (100% not smoker). Double room from €120 to €220. Breakfast: €13 (express breakfast: €5.50, breakfast américan €24.50). Extra bed: €20. Six locations of parking to be reserved. Spoken languages: French, German, English, Italian, Spanish and Portuguese. American Express, Diners Club, Holiday voucher. Tourism label & Disability. Pets allowed (€10 per night). Free Wifi. Catering facilities.

Overhanging the Golfe Bleu and the Cap Martin, at only 1. 5 km from the Principality of Monaco, on the lower cornice, the Roquebrune offers 6 charming rooms, including a small suite, all with balconies facing the sea. Clear tones add to the brightness of the rooms opened on the sea. Breakfasts are served on sunny days on the terrace of the dining room, you feel like being on the top deck of an ocean line! As for the restaurant , booking is essential: the menu is prepared with local products and fresh-caught fish. A very attractive restaurant.

SAINT-JEAN-CAP-FERRAT ★★★★

There is a reason if the greatest fortunes in the world in search of tranquility and beauty are settled on this peninsula connected to the mainland by an isthmus: thus, the place is dotted with luxury villas hidden in sumptuous and highly secure parks. You must visit the site to understand why Somerset Maugham, F. Scott Fitzgerald, King Leopold II of Belgium or Gregory Peck (among many others) have found refuge in this land of choice. You can go around the Cap Ferrat by sea, by road or by the 10 km tourist trail in 3 hours without hurrying with a few stops to admire the landscape: you will discover the Ganivette peak, Coisse peak, the Crau de Nao to Malalongue peak that bears a lighthouse of 33 m with a 50 km range. The tourist trail then goes through the most jagged part of the peninsula bypassing Fosses bay and the Saint-Hospice peak, port of the Maurice Rouvier promenade up to the Baratier peak at the entrance of Beaulieu-sur-Mer. Of all the sea-side promenades, it is the most spectacular for the scenic beauty and the diversity of the landscape. Warning: the days of high winds, waves can be violent and access to the promenade is highly inadvisable.

TOURIST OFFICE OF SAINT JEAN CAP FERRAT

59, avenue Denis-Séméria
✆ +33 (0)4 93 76 08 90
www.saintjeancapferrat.fr
office-tourisme@saintjeancapferrat.fr

From May to September: Monday to Friday from 9am to 6pm, Saturday from 9am to 5pm. Closed on Sunday. From October to April: Monday to Friday from 9am to 5pm. Closed on Saturday and Sunday.

Saint-Jean-Cap-Ferrat is one of the gems of the French Rviera. It is a wild peninsula connected to the world by a tiny isthmus. This very beautiful rocky ground was and still is the home of crowned heads or show business stars. Whether it is by the sea, by the road or along the footpath, the ride is charming.

Sightseeing

VILLA & GARDEN EPHRUSSI OF ROTHSCHILD ★★★★

1, avenue Ephrussi-de-Rothchild
✆ +33 (0)4 93 01 33 09
www.villa-ephrussi.com
message@villa-ephrussi.com

Open all year. The villa is open every day from 10am to 6pm. In July and August from 10am to 7pm. From November to February on weekdays from 2pm to 6pm, weekends and school holidays from 10am to 6pm. Last admission half an hour before closing. The bookstore-shop as well as the tea room are open at the same opening times as the villa. Adult: €14. Reduced rate: €11 (from 7 to 17 years old children, students, teachers and unemployed people on presentation of a written proof). Guided tour. Shop.

This villa is one of the most beautiful residences of the French Riviera and the evidence of the grandiose Belle Epoque which initiated the Riviera. The house which was inspired by great Renaissance buildings of Venice and Florence presents around twelve lounges and flats with furniture and decorations of great refinement as well as an extraordinary collection of artworks which the Baroness Béatrice Ephrussi de Rothschild, the daughter of the Governor of Banque de France gathered throughout her life. She nourrished a passion for arts, travels and great projects. She conceived nine different thematic gardens: while strolling from one garden to another, we roam from one continent to the other, from a century to another, from a civilisation to another.

We therefore travel through the French, Japanese, Spanish, Florentine, Provence, exotic and oriental gardens. We end up on the promontory of Saint-Jean-Cap-Ferrat overlooking the sea from all sides with the sweet whisper of a small fountain as only sound.

At her death, the baroness left the property to the Institut de France so as to make a museum.

Knife & Fork

LA CABANE DE L'ÉCAILLER

New marina
✆ +33 (0)4 93 87 39 31
www.lacabanedelecailler.com
contact@lacabanedelecailler.com

«Maître Restaurateur» label. Open all year. Open every day from February to October from 9am to 11pm. Booking advised. À la carte: Around €40. Lunch menu: €17 (starter and main course or main course and dessert. Starter + main course + dessert €22). Wine by the glass. Take-away seafood platters. Terrace.

Based on the concept of fresh wild fish cuisine (daily arrival from different French fishing ports), of shellfish and seafood, the brand created by Sami Ben Slama and located on the Saint-Jean-Cap-Ferrat harbor, offers continuous service. The seafood products are showcased with originality and expertise by the chef who prepares a homemade quality cuisine with fresh products. Add to that a beautiful decor, a pleasant terrace facing the sea and a very pleasant welcome.

LE CAP – GRAND HÔTEL DU CAP FERRAT

71, boulevard Général-de-Gaulle
✆ +33 (0)4 93 76 50 50
www.fourseasons.com/fr/capferrat

Open in June, July and August for dinner exclusively from 7.30pm to 9.30pm. Open every day from 7.45pm to 9.45pm. Booking advised. Menu from €158 to €248 (excluding drinks). Wine by the glass. Average price à la carte between €180 and €300. Smart casual oufit recommended. American Express, Diners Club. Groups welcome (on request and depending on availabilities). Garden. Terrace. Valet. Shop. Parking of the Hotel. Musical entertainments in summer evenings.

At Le Cap du Grand Hôtel restaurant in Cap-Ferrat, the Chef offers a gourmet cuisine which aspires to be simple, tasty, sober and elegant. How can you not surrender to the warm Norway lobster, taragon condiments, green apple and sesame daïkon, the Allaiton Lamb from Aveyron skewer-grilled with rosemary, ceps, aubergines, figs and fresh goat cheese, the Mediterranean John Dory roasted with Canadian salt, burratina, lemon caviar, avocado and borage? Finish with lemon soufflé or the coca and verbena sorbet orchestrated by Damien Gendron, sacred in March 2016 as Champion of France in senior category dessert! The dish is expressive thanks to the quality of the products and a refined service in a charming setting. Le Grand Hôtel has two other restaurants: the Véranda for a continuous service during the whole season and, the restaurant Club Le Dauphin for lunch and snacks until 5.30 p.m.

LA GOELETTE

Port Saint-Jean ✆ +33 (0)4 93 76 14 38

Open all year. 7 days a week from 12pm to 11pm uninterrupted. From €17 to €45. Children's menu: €9.80. Menu from €22.50. American Express, Chèque Restaurant. Terrace. WiFi free.

In an intimate setting opposite the moored yachts, you can enjoy a varied cuisine that showcases the specialities like zarzuela with half lobster, bouillabaisse with half lobster, imperial paella with half lobster or aioli. The entire team of La Goélette offer a pleasant welcome and makes every effort to prepare all these flavours that will delight you.

LA MAMMA DU PACHA

Terre-plein du nouveau port
✆ +33 (0)4 93 54 98 36
lepacha06@orange.fr

Closed Monday, Tuesday, Thursday and Sunday for dinner, and Wednesday all day. Booking advised. Menu from €18 to €50 (approximately). À la carte: Around €20 (main course). Wine by the glass. Groups welcome. Terrace. Pets allowed. Air conditioning.

Ideally located on the small Saint-Jean-Cap-Ferrat marina, Le Pacha is an address to be remembered for all seafood lovers, between others! The restaurant has just expanded and changed name. The menu showcases fresh fish (depending on the arrival), and also offers tasty dishes like fish soup and its rouille, homemade foie gras with muscat, beef fillet with truffle cream and Provençal prawns. A table where we like coming for its attentive, warm and friendly hospitality all year round, and also on sunny days for its beautiful terrace.

LE PACHA DU SLOOP

Port Plaisance
✆ +33 (0)4 93 01 48 63
lepacha06@orange.fr

Open all year. Possibility of privatizing the restaurant for private events. Daily special: €15. Every day: 2 formulas Land and Sea €18 including starter + main course and dessert. Groups welcome (by reservation). Terrace. Take-away.

Settled on the harbor of Saint Jean Cap Ferrat, Le Pacha du Sloop displays a good atmosphere and a very cordial reception. You'll discover the carte comfortably seated on the very beautiful terrace of this charming redesigned establishment. The interior large room is very friendly. The cuisine is traditional and tasty: the dishes are prepared with fresh seasonal ingredients. A nice address to (Re) discover!

THE PIRATE

New Port de Plaisance
✆ +33 (0)4 93 76 12 97
www.restaurant-le-pirate.com

Open all year. Low season: daily for lunch. High season: daily for lunch and dinner. À la carte: Around €18 (dish). Children's menu: €12. Menu from €28. Checks are not accepted. American Express, Holiday voucher, Chèque Restaurant. Terrace.

The black flag floats over this pleasant restaurant where the terrace is among the yachts of the marina of Saint-Jean. A traditional cuisine directed towards fish and seafood - delivery possible for the yachtmen wanting a seafood platter without leaving their boat. For the others, discover the bouillabaisse, the royal with lobster for two people, fish and shellfish paella, the declined fresh fish (roasted, a la plancha, in curlpapers...), spaghettis, raviolis and risotto without forgetting the bisque, the marine mussels, the onion tart or mixed salads. Meet lovers will also enjoy the duck with honey, fillet of beef with Gorgonzola or the lamb shank with five spices. Without forgetting the homemade desserts like the millefeuille gingerbread and apples with honey and its cracking scoop of ice-cream.

LA TABLE DU ROYAL

Royal Riviera hotel
3, avenue Jean-Monnet
✆ +33 (0)4 93 76 31 00
www.royal-riviera.com
info@royal-riviera.com

Breakfast from 7am to 11am. Lunch from October to April from 12.30pm to 2pm. Dinner from 7.30pm to 10pm (10.30pm in July and August). Free parking and valet service. Booking advised. Menu Bistrot €39. Intemporel menu, Menu Without-Gluten and Vegetarian menu €63. Tasting menu €95. À la carte: Around €70 (main course). Children's menu: €26. Wine by the glass. Brunch Sunday. Checks are not accepted. American Express, Diners Club. Groups welcome (on request). Garden. Terrace. Musical entertainment in summer for dinner.

La Table du Royal offers a contemporary approach of gastronomy to this magnificient five-star Royal Riviera hotel: raw cut red prawns with lemon and shellfish lemongrass ginger broth, risotto in paella way, squids, octopus and mussels, creamy pea sweets, chorizo emulsion, wild sea bass roasted in casserole, salsifies, turnip pulp with rice vinegar, leek and shellfish cream soup, root chips, squabs and market vegetables roasted in casserole with toasted bread in béatille and for the dessert, JM «XO» rum baba and whipped cream, the hot Grand Marnier soufflé and the marmalade sorbet. Every Sunday, a brunch formula to be discovered.

LA VOILE D'OR

7, avenue Jean-Mermoz
Port de Saint-Jean
✆ +33 (0)4 93 01 13 13
www.lavoiledor.fr
reservation@lavoiledor.fr

Opening of the beach of the hotel of mid-May 2017 until September 24th from 12.30pm to 2pm and from 7.30pm to 10pm. From end of May to September from 8pm to 10.30pm. From September to beginning of October from 12.30pm to 2pm and from 7.30pm to 10pm. Hotel open of May 5th until the beginning of October 2017. À la carte: Around €50. Terrace.

In a setting who combines with wonder tranquillité and confidentialité, the cuisine respects the traditions and the seasons. The restaurant of La Voile d'Or is a gourmet address with (Re) discovering in a decor of dreamed vis-a-vis the port, just like the restaurant of the private beach and its intimate decor which proposes as for him a simple cooking, summer and Mediterranean: salad niçoise, fish roasted, daily specials and desserts traditional. The building created in 1925 by the Captain Powell, an English champion of golf and billiards, knew to preserve at the access of the centuries its size and its elegance.

Sleeping

GRAND HOTEL OF CAP-FERRAT

71, boulevard Général-de-Gaulle
✆ +33 (0)4 93 76 50 50
www.fourseasons.com

Open all year. Reception 24/24 (spoken languages: English, Spanish, Italian, Dutch, French). 73 rooms (including 24 suites and among them 8 with private pool). Possibility of parking formula weekly, monthly, quarterly and annual. Kid's Club & Amenities on the premises. Rates available on request. American Express, Diners Club. Seminars. Receptions and weddings. Free Wifi. Catering facilities (3 restaurants including one gourmet, the Cap). Satellite TV. Hammam, whirlpool, sauna. Activities. Spa of 750m² with its private garden and possible treatments outside.

It is certainly one of the most beautiful luxury hotels of the French Riviera! Imagine an entirely white building nestled in the middle of gardens covering 7 hectares, with a view over the sea... Some spacious suites have their own pool and a 30 m² terrace. A 750 m² spa offers a full range of cares. As for the catering, La Véranda (open at any time of the day) offers a relaxed atmosphere and a light cuisine. For formel evenings, you can choose the gastronomical Michelin starred restaurant, Le Cap. At last, for lunch by the pool while admiring the sea, the restaurant Le Club Dauphin is the ideal option.

HOTEL ROYAL-RIVIERA

3, avenue Jean-Monnet ✆ +33 (0)4 93 76 31 00
www.royal-riviera.com
info@royal-riviera.com

Closed from end of November to beginning of February. Reception 24/24 (spoken languages: French, Italian, German, English, Russian). 94 rooms. Buffet breakfast or in room: €38. Extra bed: €85. Closed parking (external, free). Rates available on request. Pets allowed (up to 6 kg). Seminars. Receptions and weddings. Internet corner. Free Internet access. Free Wifi. Cleaning service. La Table du Royal restaurant. Musical entertainment evenings in summer in the gourmet restaurant. Product sales. Spa. Sandy private beach from May to September. Satellite TV, Canal+. Hammam, sauna. Excursions (on request).

This palace of the Leading Hotels of the World chain still stands proudly for more than one century after its construction along Baie des Fourmis opposite Villa Kérylos. The Art Deco and neo-hellenic spirit of the decoration brings elegance and serenity. The spacious and bright rooms open onto the lush gardens, the Mediterranean Sea or on the mountains. The large sunny terraces, the infinity pool and the private sandy beach bring some additional happiness to your stay. The «Table du Royal» is the perfect culinary complement to this splendid 5-star hotel.

VILLEFRANCHE-SUR-MER ★★★★

Nestled in the heart of one of the most beautiful natural ports in the world, Villefranche-sur-Mer has kept its picturesque charm over the centuries and since its antique creation 130 years B.C. The town owes its name to the count of Provence which endowed it with a special status exemption from trade. From the 16th century, the dukes of Savoy began to fortify the beautiful natural port to make it a shelter against incursions of Barbaric and a base of mooring for the armed galleys. It made the dig port of the darse and built the citadel. Until the 18th century, Villefranche was the main port of the Sardinian State. Then attached to Savoy, it declined when Nice obtained in his turn a port. Fishing port in the beginning, Villefranche can also boast a long past dedicated to the marine. Lent to the Russian imperial navy after 1856, they made it a base of maintenance and stock to the First World War, the harbour housed the American Life fleet for several years after the Second World War till the exit of France from NATO in 1962. Today, it is now a fishing port and marina for one of the most important stages of all cruises in the Mediterranean.

Vue sur la ville.

Knife & Fork

LA BELLE ETOILE

1, rue Baron de Brès ✆ +33 (0)4 97 08 09 41
www.labelleetoile-villefranche.com
labelleetoilevillefranche@gmail.com

«Maître Restaurateur» label. Open all year. Open Monday to Saturday in June and September, every day in high season. Closed Sunday and Monday in low season. Booking advised. À la carte: Around €27 (dish). Terrace.

Nestled in the historic area just a few metres from the docks this ancient house, with a contemporary, intimate and refined decor makes this restaurant a friendly place with a warm atmosphere. In the *cosy* dining room or on the beautiful terrace, discover the tasty seasonal cuisine of Chef Didier Hostein who offers a new menu every evening as well as fresh dishes and quality lunch and diners, rigorously selected and accompanied by fine wines. A charming address, a promise of a delightful moment.

LOU BANTRY

13, quai Amiral-Courbet
✆ +33 (0)4 93 91 87 68
www.loubantry.com

Open all year. Every day from 7am to 11pm. Accept reservations and groups. Terrace. Room.

With its exceptional setting on the seaside, Lou Bantry enjoys regulars as well as passage visitors. For breakfast on the terrace, or for a sunny cuisine for lunch or dinner. Here fresh and local seasonal ingredients are honoured all year round. On the carte you'll find fine and tasty traditional dishes: stuffed vegetables, salad niçoise, panisses, troucchia (omelette with blettes) or fresh fish (according to arrivals) like the fillet of bar with fennel. The desserts are also hearty like the tiramisù which punctuates this meal with fresh and coloured dishes. A very nice address to (Re) discover with pleasure!

L'OURSIN BLEU

11, quai de l'Amiral-Courbet
✆ +33 (0)4 93 01 90 12
www.restaurant-oursin-bleu.com

♿

«Maître Restaurateur» label. Open all year. Every day from 12pm to 2.30pm and from 7pm to 10.30pm. Booking advised. À la carte: Around €55. Wine by the glass. Menu from €43. New: fine confectionery shop open 7 days a week. American Express. Groups welcome. Terrace. Valet. Take-away. Shop. Public parking nearby. Skipper and valet at disposal.

Seated in the sun on the harbour, facing the bay of Villefranche or in the room evoking the large cabins of the transatlantics, Jérôme Deloncle and Hervé Lelu – from the most prestigious Parisian houses - will make you discover a fresh and tasty cuisine: tiramisu of goat cheese with green peppers and smoked salmon with lychee dulcé, grilled prawns nougatine with garlic celery and granny tartar, rock octopus marinated lime passion crunchy salad, bouillabaisse (chic and simple), lamb loin of Provence, beef fillet of Limousin with morels, roasted turbot and prawns hull juice of shells gnocchi... This medley of gourmet dishes ends on a sweet note with the dynamite crunchy caramel with vanilla ice-cream or the liquid guanaja chocolate with frozen heart of red cherrys. Hervé, also passionate about jazz and sea, is inexhaustible on the magnificent aquariums that give an air of lagoon of the South Seas in the spacious dining room of the restaurant. After your meal, take a look at the shop of L'Oursin Bleu next to the restaurant where you can make a gourmet and bacchic shopping: fine macaroons, pastries, wines, spirits...

LE MAYSSA

Place Wilson ✆ +33 (0)4 93 01 75 08
www.lemayssa.fr – mayssa@mayssabeach.fr

«Maître Restaurateur» label. Low season: closed Sunday for dinner, Monday for dinner, Tuesday all day. High season: open daily for lunch and dinner uninterrupted. À la carte: Around €50 (starter + main course + dessert). Starters from €15.50 to €18. Main courses from €15 to €72. Desserts from €9 to €11.50. Groups welcome (up to 200 people).

The Vanini family who already manages Paloma beach operates one of the most beautiful places in Villefranche. This small gem out of sight overlooks the port and has a breathtaking view from the roofs of the cruise terminal. As for food, we appreciate the freshness of the products and the fish of the day cooked with precision and creativity: John Dory fish fillet, tomatoes and fresh herbs vinaigrette and creamy polenta, pan-fried pluma de pata negra steak, rosemary stock and white beans with chorizo and for the dessert, the passion-fruit tiramisu and the coconut crumble. The professional and flawless reception and service take part in making this place one of the most beautiful addresses of the area.

Rade de Villefranche-sur-Mer.

LA MÈRE GERMAINE

7-9, quai Amiral-Courbet
✆ +33 (0)4 93 01 71 39
www.meregermaine.com
contact@meregermaine.com

♿

Closed 1st Sunday of November after the lunch service until Friday included before December 25th. Open every day from 12pm to 2.30pm and from 7pm to 9.30pm. Booking advised. Menu €46 excluding drinks (starter, specialty, cheese or dessert). À la carte: Around €55. Wine by the glass. American Express. Groups welcome (up to 120 people interior + outdoor terrace). Terrace. Valet. Public parking nearby.

The history begins in 1938 when the sailors of the 6th North-American fleet went to eat at Germaine. Indeed, Germaine Halap and her husband Louis Brau had just opened their small restaurant opposite the sea when the USS Salem anchored in the port of Villefranche. The owner – known as «mom» Germaine – became a real mother for these sailors, officers and non-commissioned officers who found comfort of the heart and...stomach! Since then, the history goes on. And even if Germaine is no longer here, the restaurant still belongs to the family: after Josiane, the youngest daughter and her husband Rémy Blouin, it now belongs to Thierry, their son helped by his bigger brother. Their first concern is the quality of the food which makes of this already renowned place a gastronomic destination. Even if some meats are on the carte like the roasted beef fillet of Bavaria with grilled petals of garlic, most of it is dedicated to fish and seafood: bouillabaisse (2 people minimum), Saint Pierre a la plancha, roasted shrimps risotto paella way, chorizo chips with parsley and garlic sauce. Finish with the poached pear with Bourbon vanilla, light chestnut heart and crumble.

PALM

17, promenade des Marinières
✆ +33 (0)4 93 01 72 97
www.restaurant-palm.com
contact@restaurant-palm.com

Open all year. Tuesday to Sunday from 12pm to 2.30pm and from 7.30pm to 11.30pm. Lunch menu: €23 (starter and main course or main course and dessert; €32 starter + main course + dessert). Diner menu: €44 (starter + main course + dessert). Mediterranean cuisine. Terrace. Valet. Boat service.

Nested in one of most beautiful bays of the world, the decoration of Palm restaurant is inspired by the Balinese universe: wooden exotic furniture, turquoise like the sea, plants, mixed colors... Expatriation is assured! A nice cuisine opens onto the room and an external lovely terrace opens on the port for our pure pleasure. As for the cuisine, they are accustomed in choosing noble products of first choice, then cooked with a certain simplicity and a great professionalism. It is simply divine. The reception of the team is friendly, smiling and effective. A beautiful elegant table.

LE SERRE

16, rue de May ✆ +33 (0)4 93 76 79 91

Open all year. Every evening from 6.30pm to 11.30pm. À la carte: Around €20. Menu at €18. Groups welcome. Baby chairs. Terrace. Pets allowed.

This is a small authentic and charming address in the heart of the old town of Villefranche-sur-Mer. In a friendly atmosphere with a dynamic and effective team, discover a simple and family cooking with Mediterranean accents. Here, from the starters to the desserts, everything is homemade. Hearty dishes, a pleasant atmosphere, a warm décor and a lovely terrace in the pedestrian street... A canteen where to eat that you should (re) discover urgently!

LA TRINQUETTE

Port de la darse
30, avenue Général-de-Gaulle
✆ +33 (0)4 93 16 92 48
la.trinquette@orange.fr

Open every day except Wednesday from 10am to 10pm. Booking advised. Average price à la carte starter + main course + dessert: Around €25. Wine by the glass. Entertainment. Reception of groups. Terrace. Take-away.

On the way down towards the dock of Villefranche-sur-Mer, discover this original space which combines the pleasures of taste and hearing. La Trinquette is a restaurant which will make you discover the house specialities like the nicoise stew, roasted fresh sea bass, raviolis a la provencale, fish soup without forgetting the delicious pieces of charcuterie and cheeses of the Mercantour. This charming space is also a place of dynamic entertainments which regularly organizes a sciences or a literary café, culinary classes or oenology, shows and rock or pop folk, jazz, samba, bossa nova, rhythm & blues or instrumental music of the world concerts. Change of scenery guaranteed with a view on the sailing ships anchored in this serene port of the Mediterranean.

Sleeping

LA FIANCÉE DU PIRATE

Moyenne Corniche
8, boulevard de la Corne-d'Or
✆ +33 (0)4 93 76 67 40
www.fianceedupirate.com
info@fianceedupirate.com

Open all year. Check in from 2pm to 10pm. Out Check before midday. Spoken languages: English, Italian, French. 15 rooms (100 % non smoker). Buffet breakfast: €12 (per day and per person; €9 -12 years). Extra bed: €30 (package cot €10). Parking (free in front of the hotel). Double rooms sea side garden from €76, triple from €101. American Express, Holiday voucher. Pets allowed (€10). Free Wifi. Cleaning service. Satellite TV.
Although the building – in red coating outside – is easily recognisable from the road, once you get inside, light and warm Mediteranean colours take over. The tastefully decorated rooms offer stunning views of Saint-Jean-Cap-Ferrat and bay of Villefranche-sur-Mer. Facing the sea, the environment is calm and relaxing. All rooms have a flat-screen television, individual air conditioning, a telephone, wi-fi and a bathroom or a private shower. Those upstairs are spacious while those on the ground floor, are very cosy but smaller. Some also have a small private garden overlooking the swimming pool with a panoramic view of the bay. La Fiancée du Pirate is a haven of peace located less than 5 minutes from the port of Villefranche. The owners live on site and brought a new impetus to this address that can be described as delightful.

HOTEL WELCOME

3, quai Amiral-Courbet
✆ +33 (0)4 93 76 27 62
www.welcomehotel.com
resa@welcomehotel.com

Closed from November 15th to December 25th. Reception 24/24 (spoken languages: English, Italian, Spanish, German, French). 35 rooms (100% not smoker). Buffet breakfast or in room: €18. Extra bed: €28 (in low season. €46 on average and tourist seasons). All the rooms have a balcony and a sea sight. Service concierge 24/24. Senior Suite from €480. Suite travels from €311. Suite Boat from €226. Deluxe from €223. Superior room from €195. Comfort room from €169. Classic room from €149. Garage with valet service booking compulsory: €30 per day in low season and €46 per day on average and tourist seasons. Tourist tax: €1.20 per adult and per day. American Express, Diners Club. 2 accessible rooms to PMK of higher category. Pets allowed (dog 17,50€ per day). Free Wifi. Cleaning service. Satellite TV. Sauna. Wine Pier open every day all year except on December 24th.
This charming hotel faces the sea, a short distance from the old town and a few metres from the public beach. The poet Jean Cocteau is said to have stayed here: he affirmed on a drawing left at the hotel that he had spent the best days of his life there. All the rooms have a different style. They are functional, air conditioned: they are very comfortable with internet and ADSL access. Free Wi Fi, a minibar, satellite TV, WC and a bathroom with a bathtub are available in the rooms. All the rooms – comfort, superior and suites – overlook the sea. The Wine Pier, an excellent wine bar is present on the spot open on a exterior terrace facing the sea, offering beautiful sunsets with a an excellent glass of wine and live music evenings every Friday and Saturday evening. On Sundays, you can enjoy an excellent brunch until early afternoon. We particularly appreciate the fabulous welcome of the attentive and warm staff.

Shopping

THE BOUTIQUE OF THE OURSIN BLEU

Quai de l'Amiral-Courbet
✆ +33 (0)4 93 01 90 12
www.restaurant-oursin-bleu.com
oursinbleu@club-internet.fr

Open 7 days a week at the opening times of the restaurant.
Just beside the unmissable gastronomic restaurant L'Oursin Bleu, a shop of the same name run by the same team will delight fine gourmets! Lovers of upscale macaroons and chocolates, discover the delicate sweets such as the vanilla ice bars crunchy caramel in cake version or the lemon basil tiramisu with its light Mascarpone Lemoncello mousse... For yourself or for someone else, refinement and sweetness in this address.

© VALÉRY TRILLAUD

Old town of Villefranche.

ANTIBES ★★★★

The history of Antibes-Juan-les-Pins is that of an exceptional site that has been inhabited for 2000 years. Founded in the 5th century BC under the name of Antipolis – which probably means the city opposite.. from Nice - the city was often attacked and ravaged by the Ligurians. The Roman occupation brought safety and a relative prosperity. In the 2nd century AD, the city became a bishopric and took the name Antiboul. Its proximity to Italy makes it a stronghold. In the middle Ages, it went through incessant attacks of the Barbarians. In the 12th century, Antibes became a Major component of the fortifications of the Provence County. It is the only town on the coast to have been surrounded by ramparts. But in 1244, the episcopal seat was transferred to Grasse, again for safety reasons, given that the fortified town of Grasse was less exposed as compared to the coast which experienced barbaric attacks on its shores. In the 14th century, Queen Marie of Anjou confiscates the Antibes fiefdom from the Grasse Bishop and entrusted it to the Pope of Avignon. In 1482, finally united to Provence, Antibes will experience a new period of prosperity. The Fort Carré was built a hundred years later in 1588. It was so well designed and so well armed that it was never fully conquered. In 1746, the city was besieged by the Austrian army. Louis XIV entrusted the development of the city to Vauban who completed the fortifications of the city. They will be demolished at the end of the 19th century under the pressure of the growth of the city beyond its walls. Remains of these remarkable fortifications are the Fort Carré, Antibes pride. Napoleon 1 had a stay there. Indeed, after the fall of Robespierre, he will be held some time in Fort Carré. Finally, in March 1815, after his landing at Golfe-Juan -les cent jours- the city of Antibes as well as that of Cannes, refused to receive him and he directly went to Grasse, starting point of the famous route Napoléon. The seaside resort of Juan-les-Pins was created in 1882. Antibes continued to thrive after the First World War. Many artists have succumbed to its charm: Prévert, Audiberti, Greene, Picasso or Monet. Between heritage (archaeological museum), cultural events (jazz) and luxury tourism (palaces, Cap d'Antibes) the city preserves its environment and thus its identity. Antibes was one of the first towns in the county to sign the States environment charter.

■ **TOURIST OFFICE OF ANTIBES-JUAN-LES-PINS**
42, avenue Robert-Soleau
✆ +33 (0)4 22 10 60 10
www.antibesjuanlespins.com

From September 1st to June 30th Monday to Saturday from 9am to 12pm and from 2pm to 6pm. Sunday from 9am to 1pm. From July 1st to August 31st Monday to Sunday from 9am to 7pm. Tourism label & Disability. Assistance system for hearing.
A 4 star structure in charge of the entertainment and promotion of the city. Free brochures and multilingual information.

Sightseeing

■ **FORT CARRE** ★★★
avenue du 11 Novembre
✆ +33 (0)4 92 90 52 13 / +33 (0)6 14 89 17 45
www.antibes-juanlespins.com
Open all year. Tuesday to Saturday, from 9.30am to 12.30pm and from 1.30pm to 5pm (last admission 30 minutes before closing). Closed on January 1st, May 1st, on November 1st and on December 25th. Tuesday to Saturday. Free for under 18-year-olds. Adult: €3. Large families, students, retired €1.50. Guided tour (by reservation – Duration: 1.30hour). Cards of assistance to the visit available in several languages in reception.
Located on the Saint-Roch peninsula, the fort is built on a rock, 26 m above sea level. It was built on the orders of King Henry II to serve as sentinel and defence

Antibes.

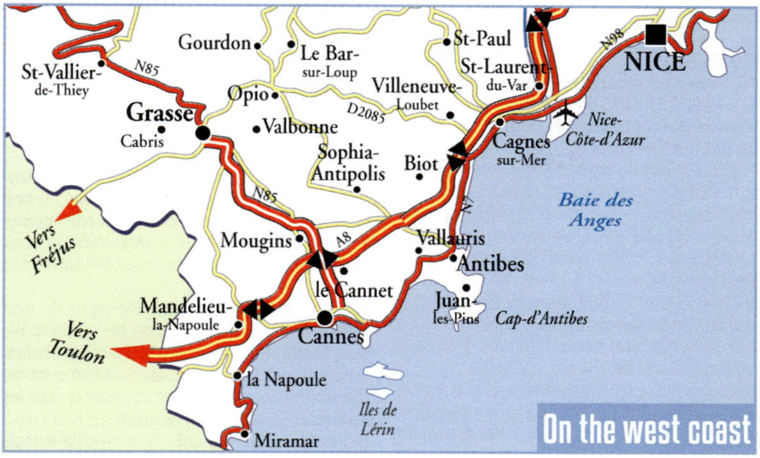

post of Antibes, last French port before the border with the county of Nice. Surrounded by a protected park of 4 hectares, it is now the property of the Conservatoire du Littoral. The watchpath goes up to 43 m high and offers a 360 degrees panoramic view. It was built at different periods: the central tower in 1550, then four bastions in 1570. The fort was invaded partially once in 1592 by the army of the Duke of Savoy. Vauban finished the ring of defences and the site remained a strategic one until the 19th century. When Nice was annexed to France, it became unsuitable for military use. The army installed a high – level military barracks and sports training centre at the foot of the fort which was then handed over to the Ministry of Sports in 1967. The abandoned fort was restored by volunteers between 1979 and 1985. The city of Antibes bought it again in 1997 and opened it to the public in 1998.

PICASSO MUSEUM ANTIBES ★★★★
Château Grimaldi – Place Mariejol
✆ +33 (0)4 92 90 54 20 / +33 (0)4 92 90 54 26

Closed on Monday as well as on January 1st, on May 1st, on November 1st and on December 25th. Open from September 16th to June 14th from 10am to 1pm and from 2pm to 6pm. From June 15th to September 15th: from 10am to 6pm. Night in July and August, Wednesday and Free for under 18-year-olds Friday until 8pm (and for certain public). Adult: €6. Large families, students, retired €3. Tourism label & Disability. Guided tour. Shop. Activities. Le Café du Jardin proposes drinks in the garden facing the sea.

This museum is set in a superb place. The Grimaldi castle was the residence of a branch of the family in the Middle Ages before being turned into a town hall during the French revolution. From 1820 to 1924, it was used as barracks. The castle was then bought by the city of Antibes in 1925 to host a historical and regional archaeological museum. Twenty years later, Romuald Dor of La Souchère, its conservator, invited Pablo Picasso to set up his workshop there: the artist, who loved the French Riviera and its backcountry, accepted this great offer and started to work enthusiatically. When he moved, Picasso left some of his works – drawings and paintings – created on site: *La Joie De Vivre, Satyre, faune et centaure au trident*, Le *Gobeur d'oursins, La Femme aux oursins, Nature morte à la chouette et aux trois oursins, La Chèvre*... During the following years, other creations of the brilliant artist, including ceramics designed in the workshop Madoura de Vallauris came to enrich the collections of the museum. In 1966, the site was named Musée Picasso, it was the first institution of France to bear such a name. Another collection of the museum is devoted to Nicolas de Staël. This painter of Russian origin was a tormented man who committed suicide in Antibes in 1955. Halfway between figuration and abstraction, this great master of colours created paintings with an unusual intensity. Thanks to a donation of his widow then to purchases, the museum can today present a fine selection of his works. Finally, the modern art holds an important place in this beautiful museum, particularly represented by workpieces from a donation made by the Foundation Hans Hartung and Anna-Eva Bergman as well as paintings or sculptures of other artists. Most of the trends covering the last hundred years are present through creations by Arman, Jean-Michel Atlan, Balthus, Ben, Vincent Bioulès, Pierre Buraglio, Pol Bury, Alexander Calder, Louis Cane, Denis Castellas, César, Eduardo Chillida, Antoni Clavé, Robert Combas, Olivier Debré, Daniel Dezeuze, Max Ernst, Albert Gleizes, Henri Goetz, Simon Hantaï, Christian Jaccard, Yves Klein, Jean Leppien, Alberto Magnelli, Robert Malaval, Paul Mansouroff, Georges Mathieu, Amedeo Modigliani, Zoran Mušič, Francis Picabia, Jean-Pierre Pincemin, Martial Raysse, Sarkis, Daniel Spoerri, Claude Viallat... After your visit, you will certainly enjoy a drink at the café of the museum located in the middle of a shady garden that offers a superb view of the Cap d'Antibes. Note that the association of friends of the Picasso museum of Antibes regularly organises projections and conferences devoted to modern artists in different places of the city.

Knife & Fork

ALBERT 1ER
46, boulevard Albert-1st – Sea side corner
✆ +33 (0)4 93 34 33 54
www.restaurant-albert-1er.com
Open all year. Every day from 12pm to 10pm. 10.30pm in summer. Booking advised. Menu from €28.50 to €34.50. À la carte: Around €45. Children's menu: €12. Lunch menu Monday to Friday: €16.90 (daily special + dessert + ½ water or 1 glass of wine or 1 beer 15 Cl + 1 coffee) and €18.90 (6 oysters or 6 prawns or Joël' S small fries + daily special + ½ water or 1 glass of wine or 1 beer 15 Cl + 1 coffee). American Express, Holiday voucher, Chèque Restaurant. Groups welcome. Terrace. Take-away. Parking of Ilette at 300 meters. Voiturier on request. Seafood stall. Fish shop. Deliveries.
Restaurant Albert 1er: «the best of the sea» in Antibes. Run by Michaël Mô, this great mansion is specialized in wild fish and seafood, and even has its own fish shop «Chez Mô» at the entrance of restaurant. On its à la carte menu, let us quote the homemade fish soup, the snacked fresh scallop with green asparagus cooked au gratin with Parmesan, beurre blanc, the sea bass fillet roasted on skin, marinière shellfish and vegetables scented with star anise, the sea paella (a classic of Albert 1er) without forgetting extra-fresh whole fish wild from the fishing, the blue lobster and crayfish of the fish pond! Some meats will also delight traditional French cuisine lovers like the lamb loin roasted with honey and thyme, vegetables tatin, reduced juice, farmhouse Pountoun duck breast roasted on oven, bitter sauce orange with kumquats, with its rice scented with vegetables, and of course, the must-eat beef tartare... As for the dessert, special mention for homemade chocolate mid-cooked, the famous «Grandmother» pancakes flambéed with Grand Marnier without forgetting the succulent profiteroles with vanilla ice-cream accompanied by hot chocolate and whipped cream. Warm welcome, terrace, large bright and comfortable veranda, all of that is ideally located between the ramparts and the Cap d'Antibes, offering a sea view.

L'APPART DE GÂTEAU
3, avenue Robert-Soleau
2nd floor
✆ +33 (0)6 64 13 74 41
lappartdegateau@gmail.com
Open all year. Closed on Saturday. Monday to Friday from 10am to 3.30pm. Open on Sunday for brunchs on reservation. Booking advised. Wine by the glass. Quiche + dessert: €10. Main course and dessert: €12. Checks are not accepted. Chèque Restaurant. Groups welcome (up to 24 people). Take-away. Shop.
Located in an apartment on the 2nd floor of a building in the city centre, this tea room also offers snacks at lunchtime, to be enjoyed on site or to take away. Everything is organic, fresh, simple and homemade, quiche, savoury crumble, pie, tart, fondant, mousse, clafoutis... by Mathilde Goniot who works in a room with an open kitchen. A second room – a more cosy small lounge – welcomes you for your coffee breaks or tea with delicacies.

L'ART DES METS
30, boulevard James-Wyllie
✆ +33 (0)4 92 93 17 52
www.artdesmets.com
claude.jacques.4@orange.fr
Open all year. Open daily for lunch, Monday to Sunday. Open for dinner, Thursday to Saturday. Advance booking advised. À la carte: Around €25. Fixed rate formula: €13.50 (starter, main course or main course, dessert). Menu at €35. Checks are not accepted. Holiday voucher. Terrace.
Here is a good restaurant facing the sea on the road leading to Cap d'Antibes through the coastline. We really like the red indoor room and of course the terrace overlooking the bay. Claude Jacques is a former starred chef who has just settled down and loves to share his passion for good food with his guests. He offers you a gourmet pause like he usually says so well. The flavours are authentic, and the dishes are nicely decorated, generous and tasty. Every day, you can discover on the slate many suggestions. The wide range pizzas to eat on the spot or to take away will please pizza lovers. In addition to that, you have an almost unrivalled welcome in the corner at very reasonable prices. It is without any hesitation one of the best restaurants in Antibes!

L'AUBERGINE
7, impasse Sade
✆ +33 (0)4 93 34 55 93
Open every day for dinner from 6.30pm to 10.30pm. Also open Sunday for lunch in winter. Menu from €25 to €38 (starter + main course + dessert). À la carte: Around €30.
In a sunny decor dedicated to eggplant, this typical Mediterranean vegetable, a charming couple will warmly welcome you to make you discover their tasty cuisine. All the meat or fish dishes are perfectly prepared. To finish the meal on a sweet note, try the delicious creme brulee. The products are fresh and of quality; by the way all the dishes are homemade. In winter, you can enjoy the Swiss cheese fondue, a real treat!

BRASSERIE FOCH
20, boulevard Gustave-Chancel
✆ +33 (0)4 93 33 69 29
Open for lunch Monday to Saturday from 8am to 4pm and Thursday, Friday and Saturday for dinner from 6.30pm to 10pm. Closed on Sunday. Free Wifi. Booking advised. Daily special: €15 (daily special + dessert). Menu at €25 for dinner including starter + main course + dessert. 3 breakfasts from €2.50 to €7.50. Lunch menu at €15 with starter and main course or daily special + dessert. 1hour parking offered at the library located opposite. Chèque Restaurant. Terrace. Take-away.
A strategic location (facing the library), a modern and cosy decor, a warm atmosphere and welcome, a small outdoor terrace, and a simple and tasty cuisine from the market at reasonable prices make of Brasserie Foch a very good new address in the center of Antibes. Here, all is home made. The carte changes with the seasons:

lasagnas, filet mignon of pork, stew of Provence, poultry escalope, duck Parmentier without forgetting the traditional menu options (beef tartare or of tuna, hearty burgers, eggs, salads...) and succulent desserts... The establishment also proposes an unbeatable breakfast and can accommodate groups on request.

LE BRÛLOT

3, rue Frédéric-Isnard – Old Antibes
✆ +33 (0)4 93 34 17 76
www.brulot.fr
contact@brulot.fr

Open Monday to Saturday for dinner; every day for lunch. Menu from €21.90 to €44.90. À la carte. Children's menu: €8. Lunch menu: €14.90 (starter + main course + dessert or main course and dessert + coffee or main course + drink + coffee). Chèque Restaurant.

For over twenty years, Goran welcomes its clients in all simplicity with his sympathetic team within the ancient walls of this restaurant of the old Antibes which is full of history. When you come visit this place you have the occasion to taste a hearty Provencal cuisine highlighting meats and fresh fish of the day, cooked on wood fire: whole duck breast, prime rib, rib steak, sea bass, red mullets of the country, sea bream, prawns... The studied menus and the daily special are listed in the varied menu which make this authentic and cordial restaurant quite attractive. An excellent value for money.

LE CAFÉ DES CHINEURS

28, rue Aubernon ✆ +33 (0)4 93 34 57 58
♿

Closed from November 15th to December 26th. Open every day from 12pm to 10.30pm. Menu at €24. Children's menu: €9. Lunch menu: €15 (daily special, dessert and coffee). Wine by the glass. Daily special: €12. Checks are not accepted. American Express. Groups welcome (from 20 to 25 people to the maximum). Terrace. Pay car park at 20 meters.

Located on a charming square of the old Antibes, a stone's throw from the port and the beach, this address enjoys the dynamic life of this picturesque area. The menu and the slateboards display various refined daily suggestions and varied traditional dishes: fritters, honey duck breast fillet, panfried scallops flambéed in whiskey, whole gilthead sea bream grilled with olive oil sauce, without forgetting a large choice of pastas and salads, etc. If in summer, the place bathed in light, in summer, the pretty terrace is covered, allowing then to enjoy, all year long, pleasant snack breaks around homemade pastries among which the famous mille-feuille, very popular among the regulars! The authentic atmosphere of the old town at night attracts customers looking for conviviality.

LA CAFETIÈRE FÊLÉE
Antibes

18, rue du Marc
✆ +33 (0)4 93 34 51 86
www.lacafetierefelee.com
fiju@lacafetierefelee.com

«Maître Restaurateur» label. Open all year. Open for lunch Wednesday to Saturday and for dinner Tuesday to Saturday. Closed on Sunday and Monday. Booking advised. À la carte: Around €30. Lunch menu: €29 (starter + main course + dessert. Gourmet plate: €23). Discovery menu: €39 including starter, Thai wok, dessert. Fusion menu: €48 including starter, specialty, dessert. Take-away.

The rue du Marc, nestled in the old Antibes and close to the rue James-Close, inspired the name of this charming restaurant where Julien Fiengo, chef in his thirties and with a rich career in great French Riviera restaurants. He prepares an original and inventive cuisine with Asian tones. Here, the «homemade» is the order of the day! The finely and neatly presented dishes unveil a subtle fusion cuisine Asian-French: the Label Rouge duck breast stuffed with foie gras, sea bream make with tomato confit and tapenad, spiced beef tartare cut with a knife; moriawasé of red tuna tandoori and smoked swordfish or the presa de Iberian Pata Negra lacquered with Aztec honey. A nice variety of Thaï wok and desserts complete the carte menu with dish names which inspires to travel and to exoticism. Fine selection of takeaway dishes.

LE CARNET DE BORD

1, rue James-Closes
✆ +33 (0)6 17 78 46 47
lecarnetdebord@yahoo.fr

Open all year. Every day from 7pm to 10pm. Booking advised. Starter from €16. Dish from €22 approximately. Dessert from €7. Chef's suggestion « Fish & Chips»: €20. Take-away.

Le Carnet de Bord is a small restaurant as large as a pocket handkerchief located in the middle of old Antibes. There are only 14 seats in this cosy room where posters and pictures related to the sea adorn the walls while the whole set opens on an «open space» kitchen. Aline works in the kitchen, Laurence serves the customers. They both come from Belgium with their nice accent and the legendary good humour of our Northern neighbours. The cuisine is very creative and prepared with fresh products only. The plates are nicely decorated and original. Aline prepares passionately revisited recipes... and we love it. The menu often changes so we will only quote a few examples just to get you started: duck breast with rum half-cooked in a cloth, Scallops, pumpkin compotee with ginger, confit fennel and soubressade, caramelized filet mignon of pork, sweet potato creamy, chanterelles and small vegetables, without forgetting the chef's suggestion, the Fish & Chips plate. It is a lair for amateurs of "bistronomy" at affordable prices. You have to discover it absolutely. So, you are advised to book for this non ordinary restaurant.

LE CHAUDRON

18, rue Sade
✆ +33 (0)4 93 34 67 37

Open all year. À la carte: Around €20 (dish).

A room with exposed stones and soft lighting... Installed in the heart of old Antibes, this establishment offers an authentic and traditional cuisine. The carte displays paved beef and mashed potatoes, stew of Provence, duck with ceps, Saint-Jacob flamed forest sauce, gnocchi or rizotto with prawns, between others. Dishes of quality prepared with fresh ingredients and a very kind service; Let yourself be tempted by the tasty dishes of the Chaudron.

LA CLOSERIE
8, boulevard Dugommier
✆ +33 (0)4 93 34 09 92
contact@patisserie-cottard-antibes.fr
Open Monday to Saturday from 11.30am to 2.30pm. Children's menu: €9. Wine by the glass. Starter starting from €7. Main course from €12. Dessert from €5. Groups welcome. Garden. Terrace. Classes of pastry by reservation (program to be consulted on line). Parking Poirier at 50 meters.
La Cour des Thés has changed name and has moved to a house full of charater in the middle of the town. The principle is the same but it is in some way a "fusion" of the know-how of Andréa the hostess and her husband the famous chocolate maker Christian Cottard.The restaurant offers a nice sunny garden where you can eat salmon gravlax, steamed Chinese ravioli, tarine in burger style, raw ham, mushroom and Comté gratin, or even stew with monkfish and shrimp with tarragon. A varied menu where quality is the keyword of the day. The farandole of homemade desserts is enriched with the sweet and chocolate specialties of pastry.

LA COTE A L'OS
28, rue James Close ✆ +33 (0)4 93 34 36 05
www.lacotealos-restaurant.fr
Open all year. Daily for lunch and dinner. Menu from €15.90 to €28.90. Children's menu: €9.90. Lunch menu: €15.90 (starter, main course or main course, dessert). Parking nearby.
The name of the restaurant immediately indicates that you are in a meat kingdom. Here, in the old Antibes, you will enjoy grills presented on board (prime rib, steak, grilled sirloin steak, rack of lamb...), the traditional calf's head with gribiche sauce or a beef bourguignon, marrowbone... Without forgetting the classic dishes, a rock fish soup, a roasted fresh salmon escalope, a fillet of chicken with camembert cream, with good wines carefully chosen by Patrick with wine formula by the glass.

AUBERNON GALLERY
3, rue Aubernon ✆ +33 (0)4 93 74 59 25
Open Thursday to Saturday from 12pm to 10pm and Sunday to Wednesday from 12pm to 6pm. À la carte: Around €15. Dish and daily specials. Terrace.
Here is a place that offers simple but tasty cuisine not far from the Provencal market. They welcome you warmly and serve generous dishes: you can choose pizzas, pancakes and galettes as well as meats or fresh fish of the day. Everything is homemade, from the starter to the dessert. The plates are copious and the prices reasonable. A value for money that is often difficult to find along the coast. In groups or in small groups, everyone is pleased and left satisfied. So, the next time you go to the market, you know where you can stop to eat.

L'ALCYON
13, avenue du 11-Novembre
✆ +33 (0)4 93 34 07 42
www.brasserie-alcyon.fr
brasserie-alcyon@orange.fr
Open all year. Open for lunch and dinner Monday to Saturday from 8am and Sunday from 10am. Closed for dinner Tuesday, Wednesday and Sunday. À la carte: Around €20 (starters around €15, main courses around €20, desserts around €10). Children's menu: €10.50. Lunch menu: €13.90 (starter and main course or main course and dessert). Wine by the glass. American Express, Chèque Restaurant. Groups welcome. Terrace. Take-away. Port Vauban public parking opposite the restaurant. Occasional musical evenings.
Located on the Vauban port, this address is dedicated to seafood with platters among which we find the delicious Marennes-Oléron oysters, carefully chosen shellfish and also cooked fish: sea bream fillet with black truffle cream, tuna steak with Spain flavours, pan-fried fish (tuna, salmon, sea bream, etc.), etc. You can also enjoy brasserie food such as Caesar salad with fresh salmon, a few meat dishes on the menu (grilled rib steak, tartar, lamb shank, etc), pasta and raviolis, without forgetting delicious ice cream cups.

LOU CANCAN
6, avenue Guy-de-Maupassant
✆ +33 (0)4 93 61 12 80
www.loucancan.fr
resa@loucancan.fr
Open all year. Every day from 7am to 3pm and from 6pm to 10pm. Non-stop service in July and August from 12pm to 1am. Pasta around €20. Pizza from €9. Meat and fish around €20. Homemade dessert around €8.
Beautiful dishes served in a typical Provencal decor: wooden beams and furniture, mural frescoes pointing out the Riviera landscapes, room and bar with brick walls... All reminds us the warmth of the South of France: pasta with seafood or pistou, penne with salmon, eggplants alla parmigiana, beef fillet with Provençal herbs, whole duck breast with honey and rosemary, pan-fried scallops and also beautiful pizzas. Classical but very gourmet, the desserts are homemade: chocolate fondant, warm tarte tatin, tiramisu, chocolate mousse, île flottante... You'll leave this restaurant satisfied, and with your heart full of sun!

LA NOCHE
10, rue de Sade
✆ +33 (0)4 93 74 57 06
Open all year. Thursday to Tuesday from 4pm to 2am. Closed on Wednesday. Summer: evenings « After Work» Monday, Tuesday, Thursday and Friday from 5pm. Assortments from €3.50 to €5.50. Plates €16. Dessert €5. Take-away.
Need to escape? Then go to La Noche, the ideal place in the heart of the old Antibes to share some tapas in all conviviality. In a stone decor embellished with beautiful filtered red light, everything is reminiscent of the warmth of Spain, the generous dishes, well stocked cocktails menu and coloured and spiced dishes of tapas. The atmosphere is festive throughout the evenings with guitarist, paella, etc. Everything is there for a *caliente* moment!

L'OURSIN
16, rue de la République
✆ +33 (0)4 93 34 13 46
lorenzo.aurore@yahoo.fr
Open daily for lunch and dinner until 10.30pm. Closed on Monday in winter. Possibilith to take away seafood traysfrom

10am to 11pm. Menu from €24.50 to €29.50 (starter + main course + dessert. On weekdays for dinner). Lunch menu: €16.50 (main course and dessert + coffee). Seafood platter from €22 to €125.
We are on a pleasant voyage in the Mediterranean sea here: portholes, wood panelling, rope, maps... Everything is reminiscent of a ancient boat. You can enjoy hearty seafood platters, a succulent mini-bouillabaisse, largely appreciated by regulars or aioli and whole fish. All is fresh and the service is friendly. An excellent address.

PANE E VINO
2, boulevard Marechal-Leclerc
✆ +33 (0)4 93 34 00 21
www.panevino.fr
contact@panevino.fr
Open all year. Every day. Closed on Sunday and Monday for dinner during winter and Monday from July to August. À la carte: Around €25(main course and dessert). Terrace.
This pleasant restaurant on the seaside offers an enticing carte which declines generous and tasty dishes with transalpine accents: antipasti, pizzas, sea bream tartar, cep risotto, fritto misto, cannelloni ricotta and spinaches, bucatini a la calabrese, Milanese veal cutlet... Colourful dishes from the South that you'll enjoy facing Cap d'Antibes in a very friendly atmosphere.

LES PAPILLES
3, traverse du 24-Août
✆ +33 (0)4 92 91 96 11
Open Monday to Saturday from 9.30am to 3pm and from 7pm to 10pm. À la carte: Around €30. Lunch menu: €16.50 (daily special and dessert). Terrace
A pleasure for our tastebuds in this cosy restaurant of old Antibes with a warm welcome and a relaxed atmosphere. Whether on the lovely terrace or in the beautiful interior room, you'll enjoy French dishes like the duck breast with foie gras, the classical Tartar and its potatoes, the hearty salad of the Chef or the croque gourmand. As regards the desserts, the profiterole is a delight! All is home made and the products are fresh.

LE PERROQUET
La Pinede
9, avenue Gallice
✆ +33 (0)4 93 61 02 20
http://restaurantleperroquet.fr
contact@restaurantleperroquet.fr
Closed from November 3rd to December 26th. Open every day from 12pm to 2pm and from 7pm to 10.30pm. Open until 11.30pm in high season. Menu from €32 to €39.80. À la carte: Around €40 (main course from €22). Children's menu: €14.
In a distinguished setting, enjoy a french cuisine prepared with fresh seasonal ingredients: squid poêlée in schopped parsley, artichoke hearts and dried tomatos, home made rock fish soup and its rust, donuts of zucchini flowers, crab tartar with pink grapefruit and avocado, salmon gravelax, patta negra with morello cherries, mashed potatoes of parsnip and sweet potatoes, kidneys creamed in Porto, duo of fresh duck liver and scallops, seafood risotto as well as beautiful grilled fish portions. An very good address to find authentic flavours.

PLAGE KELLER – RESTAURANT LE CÉSAR
Cap d'Antibes ✆ +33 (0)4 93 61 33 74
See page 50.

POMODORO
11, rue Migrainier
✆ +33 (0)4 93 34 57 12 / +33 (0)6 78 72 73 15 / +33 (0)6 78 72 73 15
www.pomodoro.fr
quymey@hotmail.com
Open Wednesday to Monday from 7pm. À la carte: Around €15. Menu €19.50: starter + main course + dessert. Pizza 13 € approximately. Pasta around €14.
In the heart of old Antibes, this establishment pays tribute to the fruit to which it takes its name: the tomato, (*pomodoro* in Italian), true symbol of the Italian cuisine honored in all its forms here. In the dining room with red walls, you can sit at the table to enjoy pasta or pizza. A simple and unpretentious cuisine that is worth tasting. A home kitchen, a warm welcome, just like in our neighboring country: Italy!

RESTAURANT LE J
17, avenue du Docteur-Dautheville
✆ +33 (0)4 69 00 12 95
www.restaurantlej.fr
Open all year. Closed Sunday and Monday. Open Tuesday to Saturday from 12pm to 2pm and from 7pm to 10pm. Starter from €12 approximately. Dish from €25. Dessert from €9. Main courses from €16 to €22 for lunch. American Express. Parking. WiFi free for the guests. Terrace.
In the line of the bistronomy new generation, the Restaurant Le J restaurant follows the mainstream by offering an authentic and refined cuisine at reasonable prices. The creative and carefully worked dishes, inspired by the many journeys of the owners: mid-cooked tuna, marinated pork ribs, Caesar salad, fish cooked in Tahitian way, quesadillas, foie gras with Tahaa vanilla, creamy white chocolate and passion fruit or guayaquil chocolate coulant. A mouthwatering à la carte menu which will satisfy your tastebuds in a smart and convivial setting. The dishes change over the course of the day and the time. In short, you do not get tired of it!

LA TABLE DE NICOLAS
7, rue James-Close ✆ +33 (0)4 92 94 07 31
www.latabledenicolas.fr
contact@latabledenicolas.fr
Open Tuesday to Sunday for lunch from 12pm to 2.30pm and Thursday to Saturday evening 7pm to 10.30pm. Children's menu: €10. Lunch menu: €15.50 (starter and main course of the day or daily special + dessert). Degustation menu: €27. Parkings nearby.
Nestled in one of the most typical narrow streets of Old Antibes, Table de Nicolas is part of these addresses where sunshine is present everywhere, from the smiling and cordial reception to the dish. In the indoor room with exposed stones, you'll enjoy a generous cuisine of the south which changes according to the seasons: veal medallion, creamy polenta and frozen carrots, fillet of sea bass, crunchy vegetables and espuma of Parmesan, or risotto with pesto sauce and roasted prawns. Also on the carte, perfectly sublimated pizzas and pasta. All is home-made, from the starters to the dessert. A cuisine resolutely sunny!

■ **LE VILLAGE**
31, rue James-Close ✆ +33 (0)4 93 34 19 66
Open all year. Closed on Wednesday all day and Thursday for lunch. From 12pm to 2pm and from 7pm to 10pm. Booking advised. Menu from €20.90 to €26. À la carte: Around €25 (to 30). Wine by the glass. American Express, Holiday voucher, Chèque Restaurant. Groups welcome.
In the «village» atmosphere of the Old Antibes, this restaurant bear well its name. The bright dining room is enlivened by pretty flowers scattered almost everywhere. The cosy little corner at the back with its large table, away from the main dining room, is ideal for dinners with friends. The tables are carefully laid, you can sit to enjoy Chef Thierry Jouve's cuisine, traditional dishes with provencal notes: griddled octopus, beef tartar, half-cooked tuna steak, fillet of red mullet with tapenade oil, homemade foie gras with its seasonal chutney, Nicois raviolis with tomato, basil and olives, rack of lamb with honey and rosemary. Note the excellent fruit tarts in various versions according to the seasons. Daily suggestions on the blackboard complete the menu. Also note a beautiful wine list at reasonable prices and a very warm welcome!

Sleeping

■ **LA PLACE**
1, avenue du 24-Août ✆ +33 (0)4 97 21 03 11
www.la-place-hotel.com
contact@la-place-hotel.com

Open all year. Reception 24/24 (spoken languages: French, English, German, Portuguese). 14 rooms (100% non smoker). Double room from €99 to €180. Buffet breakfast: €13 (gourmet buffet at €8 the afternoon and buffet aperitif at €15 in the evening). Extra bed: €20. Parking: €10 (at the public parking of the Post office). Checks are not accepted. American Express. Internet access. Free Wifi. Cleaning service. Satellite TV.
Completely redesigned, this three floor establishment located at the entrance of the pedestrian streets of the old Antibes and a few steps away from the bus station features air-conditioned and soundproofed rooms with elegant and contemporary setting. Warm and perfectly equipped rooms decline three atmospheres and three colours with an attention to refined detail. The heated terrace of the hotel displays a lounge style. You can have your breakfast there in the morning; you can enjoy coffee, tea and sweet delicacies in the afternoon and sip drinks and cocktails in the early evening. As you can well imagine, this place cultivates the art of living and pleasure in a friendly atmosphere.

© VINCENT FORMICA

Fishing boats at sunrise- Antibes.

LE PONTEIL

11, impasse Jean-Mensier
✆ +33 (0)4 93 34 67 92
www.leponteil.com

Open from February 10th to November 12th. Front desk open from 8.30am to 10pm. 12 rooms. Single room from €70 to €109; double room from €70 to €134; triple room from €113 to €150. Breakfast: €8.(only in the dining room-gluten-free, reservation €+2). Closed parking (private €5). Visa, MasterCard, Maestro, Visa Electron and V Pay accepted. Package night and breakfast on the web site. Holiday voucher. Internet access. Free Wifi. Some rooms are air-conditioned.

A few steps away from the streets of the old Antibes, at the end of a quiet dead end road, at 5 minutes walk from a sandy beach and 10 minutes from the City Center, this provençal villa of the 1920's is surrounded by a lovely garden. The rooms, simply decorated and comfortable, are spread throughout the property. They offer peace and quiet for a guaranteed stay of relaxation. Pascal Gianni and his wife take care with a warm and attentive welcome in this family-run address. Shuttle service, private driver from Nice-Côte d'Azur airport and car rentals (price on request).

Leisure

THALAZUR ANTIBES

770, chemin des Moyennes-Bréguières
✆ +33 (0)4 92 91 82 00
http://antibes.thalazur.fr

Cure 6 days from €576 and 5 days from €462. Stay 1 to 5 days from €136. Price with treatment(S) + night (S) + half-board (S). Other rates available on the website.

The Baies des Anges Thalazur Antibes Thalassothérapie & Spa Hotel has been entirely renovated in 2013 to offer softness, calm and pleasure. Its exceptional view of the Baie des Anges and the massif of the Southern Alps and its bright decoration where wood mingles with transparent material, make it a dream atmosphere ideal for relaxation and for treatments (for a day or over several days). The spa has two indoor pools of heated seawater equipped with goosenecks, spa seats and underwater jets, a whirlpool bath, a sauna, a hammam and outdoor swimming pools to complete your relaxation. The cardio-training area, with free access throughout the day, the René Futerer beauty centre and the By Thalgo centre or the tearoom are the additional services which you can enjoy while combining relaxation and purification of body and spirit. You can also benefit from the advices of professionals on site while the Lounge Bar 770 at lunchtime or L'Angélus in the evening complete the range of services with a generous cuisine. Two chefs, Patrice Demangel and Didier Aniès, Best worker of France, offer a «Five S» concept: Seasonal products, Healthy (Sain in french) with Simplicity, full of Flavours (Saveur in french) in an exceptional geographic Situation.

Going Out

PASTRY COTTARD- LA CLOSERIE

8, boulevard Dugommier
✆ +33 (0)4 93 34 09 92
www.patisserie-cottard-antibes.fr

♿

Pastry-chocolate shop-restaurant. Open Monday to Saturday from 8.30am to 7pm and Sunday from 9am to 1pm. Garden. Terrace. Classes of pastry (planning to be consulted). Parking Poirier at 50 meters. Wifi. Shop.

For over 25 years, the Cottard House has been a real institution in Antibes. The owner, Christian Cottard, master pastry chef, created this magical place with a three in one concept, pastry-restaurant and school. The restaurant has a sunny terrace where you can eat fresh and quality cuisine. The menu varies according to the seasons and the highlight is the medley of homemade desserts that will enjoy your tastebuds.

Shopping

LE COMPTOIR D'EDGAR

4, rue Lacan
✆ +33 (0)4 93 34 54 29

Open all year from 9am. Delicatessen. Coffee shop. Tableware.

Nestled in the heart of old Antibes, this delicatessen and tableware shop will awaken all your senses! The master of the place, Yann accommodates you with smiles and kindness. He will invite you to taste directly in the shop some of the beautiful and quality ingredients. A large choice of olive oils, scented oils, vinegars, a top-of-the-range collection of tin cans, jams, spices or surprising products for aperitifs. Without forgetting the delicious Corsican, Iberian, Italian and French charcuterie with Parmesan, fennel or truffles... In this waltz of flavours, you will also be allured by the authentic déco with some contemporary touches. Le Comptoir d'Edgar also offers for lunch beautiful tasting dishes, fine gourmet sandwiches and, for tea time, some other delicious delicacies.

CUTLERY OF THE OLD ANTIBES

19, place Nationale ✆ +33 (0)4 93 34 81 22
http://coutellerie.pages.free.fr
coutelleriepages@hotmail.com

Tuesday to Saturday from 9.30am to 12.30pm and from 3pm to 7.30pm. Sunday from 10am to 1pm in August only. Sharpening and maintenance of the knives.

Passionated for a long time by beautiful blades, Bernard Pagès holds this shop on the main square of old Antibes. In his cave, you will find a vast choice of knives, scissors and swords. However the preference is given to the French products in this place and repairs are also possible. Specialist in old fashionned shaving, you will aso find there shaving brushes, metal razors, traditionnal razor blades and also upscale kitchen knives, pocket knives, katanas, swords, sword-sticks... all under the expert eye of the owner who takes a real pleasure to transmit you his knowledge.

SÔ-SIJ

4, boulevard Gustave-Chancel
✆ +33 (0)6 31 74 28 41 – emma@so-sij.com

Open Tuesday to Friday from 10am to 2pm and from 4pm to 6.30pm; Saturday from 10am to 2pm. Home made English sauces.Prices 10 €/kg. 6 sauces: €5. In this tiny little shop, Emma carefully prepares typical british dishes with sauces. Pork cooked with leeks, apples, black pepper, chives or cumberland. Emma also cooks lamb and beef to perfection, and also offers some gluten-free dishes.

CAP D'ANTIBES

Real peninsula, the cap d'Antibes is a privileged, protected and residential site with a rich Mediterranean vegetation. The tour of the cap by car along the seafront is a delight. Through the greenery natural screen, one can see some of the sumptuous properties, carefully protected.

The palace Eden- Rock, embedded in a 8 acre estate, is undoubtedly the most beautiful jewel of Cap d'Antibes that hosts the stars and the VIP in particular for the International Film Festival in Cannes. Opened in June 1870, American Gordon Benett revived it later by sponsoring automobile races. Extended in 1914 it became, with the Negresco in Nice and the Carlton in Cannes, the archetype of the sumptuous palaces of the French Riviera.

Sightseeing

BOTANICAL GARDEN VILLA THURET ★★★
90, chemin Raymond
✆ +33 (0)4 97 21 25 00 / +33 (0)4 93 61 94 50
www6.sophia.inra.fr/jardin_thuret
thuret@sophia.inra.fr

In summer from 8am to 6pm. In winter from 8.30am to 5.30pm. The garden is closed Saturday, Sunday and holidays. Duration of the visit from 1.30hour to 3 hours to be defined when booking. Guided tour.

This is a botanical acclimatization garden managed by the National Institute of Agronomic Research (INRA) created in 1865 by the botanist Gustave Thuret. Attracted by the climate and the wild nature of Cap d'Antibes, he bought 5 hectares of land, where he studied the acclimatization of exotic plants. So, you can discover a large collection of trees and exotic bushes in the process of experimentation (1600 species) to test their Mediterranean conditions tolerance.

Knife & Fork

RESTAURANT EDEN-ROC
Boulevard J.-F. Kennedy
✆ +33 (0)4 93 61 56 63
www.hotel-du-cap-eden-roc.com
restauration@hdcer.com

Open every day from April 14th to October 15th, 2017 from 12.30pm to 2.30pm and from 7.30pm to 10pm. Booking advised. Wine by the glass. Buffet for lunch: €98. Lunch: Menu of the market at €76 and Menu "the time of a lunch" at €125. Dinner: Discovery Menu at €152 and Tasting menu at €190. Checks are not accepted. American Express, Diners Club. Groups welcome. Terrace. Valet. Parking.

For lunch or dinner, enjoy a place much frequented by VIP's and celebrities in this exceptional luxury hotel and sit on the teak terrace opposite this magical bay highlighted by the Lérins islands. A trio team, Arnaud Poëtte, executive chef, Olivier Gaïatto, head chef, and Lilian Bonnefoi, pastry-chocolate chef, will enjoy your tastebuds with excellent dishes, crusted monkfish with hazelnut of Piedmont, roasted pigeon or roasted venison with Juniper butter... Magical!

RESTAURANT LES PÊCHEURS ET RESTAURANT LE CAP
10, boulevard Maréchal-Juin
✆ +33 (0)4 92 93 13 30
www.ca-beachhotel.com
contact@ca-beachhotel.com

Relais & Chateaux. Open from March 31st to the end of October. Gourmet restaurant Les Pêcheurs open every day from 7.30pm to 0h30 - last sitting at 10.30pm. Le Cap restaurant open only for lunch then every evening in June, July, August and September. Le Cap restaurant open daily for lunch from April 1st to mid-October, and every evening in June, July, August and September. Booking advised. Restaurant Les Pêcheurs, menu from €85 to €125 (average price à la carte €80). Wine by the glass. At the Le Cap beach restaurant, average price à la carte €30 (whole fish roasts up to €120). Checks are not accepted. American Express, Diners Club. Groups welcome. Terrace. Valet. Free outdoor parking. 1 Michelin star.

Native of Nice Nicolas Rondelli, former disciple of Alain Llorca, works in the kitchens at Les Pêcheurs gastronomic restaurant of the hotel Relais & Châteaux Cap d'antibes Beach Hotel and those of the beach restaurant, Le Cap, ideal place for lunch or dinner on the sand facing the Sea. In the gastronomic restaurant, the culinary register is turned to the sea with whole local fish and shellfish on the grill or in the oven.

Sleeping

BEACH HOTEL CAP D'ANTIBES
10, boulevard Maréchal-Juin
✆ +33 (0)4 92 93 13 30
www.ca-beachhotel.com
contact@ca-beachhotel.com

Relais et Chateaux. Closed from October 15th to April 13th. 15 Deluxe Rooms from €390, 13 Privilege rooms from €580, 6 Design Suites from €1500 and 1 Executive suite from €1900. Two rooms are arranged for the disabled guests. Reception 24/24 (spoken languages: French, English, Spanish, Italian, German); Breakfast included (continental). Extra bed: €25. Garage: €25 (by car and per day). Free outdoor parking. American Express, Diners Club. Pets allowed. Seminars. Receptions and weddings. Internet corner. Free Internet access. Free Wifi. Cleaning service. Restaurants Les Pêcheurs and Le Cap. Product sales. Spa Summer Beach Wellness. Heated external sensory pool. Beach. Satellite TV, Canal+. Whirlpool. Excursions.

The contemporary architecture of this hotel merges marvellously with the vegetation and the garden edged by a fine sandy beach which dims in the sea. It offers luxurious and comfortable rooms which open on terraces or private gardens. Two gourmet stops are available: the gourmet restaurant and the beautiful terrace of Les Pêcheurs and Le Cap, the restaurant of the private beach.

HÔTEL LA JABOTTE
13, avenue Max-Maurey
✆ +33 (0)4 93 61 45 89
www.jabotte.com

Open all year. Spoken languages: French, English, Italian. 10 rooms (100% non smoker). Double room from €80; suite from €129. Breakfast: €10. Parking (on reservation). Bike rental. Loan of kayak and tuk-tuk service. Checks are not accepted. Holiday voucher. Pets allowed (an extra charge 10€). Seminars. Internet corner. Free Internet access. Free Wifi. Cleaning service. Catering facilities (snack). Product sales. Canal+. Activities.

Located at the beginning of Cap d'Antibes at 60 m from the beach and away from the bustle, this charming boutique hotel has ten rooms in total, including eight opened onto the garden and two upstairs of the villa. The fuchsia and orange illuminate the interior room where breakfasts are served in winter. The outdoor patio proudly boasts a magnificent mimosa and a good number of small plants carefully maintained. The charming and colourful rooms open onto the flower-filled garden and the upstairs suite of the villa deploys a most romantic charm. In summer, a singer with acoustic guitar comes to play once a week. An unusual address highly recommended for a romantic stay!

JUAN-LES-PINS ★★★★

You can not separate Juan les Pins and Jazz that made its great reputation and moved here in the 20's following the American tourists and the blare of the first Charleston.After the Second World War, Juan naturally became the rendezvous for great names of jazz and annually hosted Sydney Bechet who married there in 1951. Also came, Claude Luther, Lionel Hampton, the great Ella Fitzgerald, then, from the creation of the Jazz Festival of Antibes-Juan-les-Pins in 1958, the city hosted Duke Ellington, Dizzy Gillespie, Charly Parker, Stéphane Grappelli, Michel Petrucciani and many others who have rocked the Juan-les-Pins sky with their rhythms and their virtuosity. In July, this festival attracts fans from around the world, all around the Pinède Gould, nightlife is then intense. Groups improvise small concerts, notes invade the city, artists, musicians and the public get together to reveal the intimate and festive spirit of Juan les Pins.

VISIOBULLE ★★★
Pontoon Courbet
Boulevard Do – Guillaumont.
✆ +33 (0)4 93 67 02 11 – www.visiobulle.com
info@visiobulle.com

Open from April to September. Guided tour of 1 hour approximately. Departures every day except bad weather. April, May, June and September: 11am, 1.30pm, 3pm, 4.30pm. July and August from 9: 25 to 6pm. Rates: €14 from 2 to 11 years old adult and child: €7. No reservation.

Visiobulle awaits its passengers at the Courbet pontoon on the juanais seafront. You can sail along Cap d'Antibes and comfortably admire the seabed through a hull glass during the nautical getaway hour, on board of this yellow boat with an amazing appearance. Its bubble glass touches rocks and Posidonia sea grass inhabited with fish, sea urchins and starfish. It also provides an underwater vision of the billionaires bay which on the course, you can admire dream villas hidden in the pine forest and cliffs that surround Eden Roc, palace of stars. After passing the Rascouis shelf and the Ilette lighthouse at the western tip of Cap d'Antibes, the return to Juan-les-Pins offers a wide view of massif de l'Esterel and its red rocks, the Lerins Islands and the Croisette pointe in Cannes. A fun, instructive and original outing!

Knife & Fork

L'AMIRAL
7, avenue de Chaumont-Courbet
✆ +33 (0)4 93 74 29 71
www.restaurant-amiral-antibes.fr
restaurantlamiral7@gmail.com

Closed from January 2nd to January 12th. Open Tuesday to Sunday from 12pm to 2.30pm and from 7pm to 10pm. Closed Sunday for dinner and Monday. Booking advised. Daily menu starter + main course + dessert €29. Daily special: €21. Menu Admiral at €44. Tasting menu €59 and €85 with 4 glasses of wine. Chef's menu €65. Terrace.

A few meters from the sea, in a street away from the seafront agitation of Juan-les-Pins, the Admiral is a small semi-gourmet gem, a moment of softness that will delight your tastebuds! The carte revisits the French and transalpine specialities and is carefully elaborated with fresh, local and seasonal ingredients. The dishes are refined, elegant and are sublimated by a rich and daring wine list. You'll enjoy scallops with mashed topinambours, sauce bagna cauda, sole sauce champagne, steak of deer with bays of juniper sauce or butternut flan, rabbit roll. Le Chef also prepares dishes for vegetarians and people intolerant to gluten. The desserts are also perfect: Belle Helene pears, flambe pancakes «Maitre Alexandre» or orange creme brulee and ice cream with walnuts. The service is impeccable, discrete and cordial. An address to be discovered!

BISTRO TERRACE

Juana Hotel
19, avenue Georges-Gallice
La Pinede
✆ +33 (0)4 93 61 08 70
www.hotel-juana.com
bistrot-terrasse@hotel-juana.com

«Maître Restaurateur» label. Open all year. In low season, open for lunch and dinner Monday, Tuesday, Thursday, Friday and Saturday, and Sunday only at lunchtime. Closed on Wednesday and Sunday for dinner. In high season, open every day from 7am to 10.30pm. Booking advised. Menu from €23 to €39. À la carte: Around €40. Children's menu: €15. Wine by the glass. Vinothèque of more than 25 references. American Express, Diners Club, Holiday voucher, Chèque Restaurant. Groups welcome. Garden. Terrace. Valet. Activities. Take-away pastries. Parking.

The Chef of the group Belles Rives, Yoric Tièche renewed this hotel restaurant with a chic bistro concept and a beautiful menu at affordable rates. Let yourself be seduced by a contemporary cuisine with local and southern flavours without forgetting the large choice of delicacies to be enjoyed on the terrace or inside in the elegant refined dining room.

BRASSERIE DE LA JETÉE

Promenade du soleil
✆ +33 (0)4 92 38 09 67
www.plagelajetee.com
brasseriedelajetee@hotmail.com

Open all year. Daily for lunch and dinner. Until 1am in June, July and August. À la carte: Around €20 (starter around €15, main course around €25, pizza from €11, dessert around €7). Children's menu: €8.

A bright and modern space where metal, wood, brick and glass mix for a fresh and gourmet cuisine signed by the chef Volodymir Polyakov: squids and smelts fritto misto, chicken nems, marinated salmon carpaccio and its tuna tatakis, hearty burger and delicious pizzas, pan-fried scallops and prawns in Provençal way, chicken wok sautéed with lemon grass, etc. The homemade desserts are carried out by the Chef pastry who worked in a starred restaurant. All is set for a beautiful moment in a friendly atmosphere, facing the Mediterranean.

AUX ENFANTS TERRIBLES

5, boulevardd Charles-Guillaumont
✆ +33 (0)4 92 38 05 81
www.auxenfantsterribles.com

Open all year. Open 7 days a week days for lunch and dinner. Kitchen open daily for lunch all year and evenings in weekend; in season from May to October daily for lunch and every evening. À la carte: Around €20 (starter around €15, meat and fish around €20, dessert around €5). Children's menu: €11.50 Terrace.

Aux Enfants terribles is a pretty chic brasserie with bistronomy pattern which stands proudly opposite the sea at the far end of Juan les Pins. This evocative name of Jean Cocteau displays a decoration combining retro and contemporary style. An orchestrated harmony and a decidedly elegant atmosphere. We liked the large outdoor terrace with a roof open on the first ray of the sun. The menu changes every 15 days. Here, only fresh ingredients are used, it is the signature of the house. It must be said that the owner is a real minimalist. We love the excellent Charolais beef tartare, olives, tomatoes, whole south west duck breast with peaches, Beef salad in Thai's way or even the famous "Linguine ale Vongole".

Note also a wine list consisting of wines by the glass on the menu at reasonable prices, thanks to a wine cellar with nitrogen protecting the wine from any oxidation and guarantees optimal conservation). The hotel is also a very nice meeting place during the aperitif time, after beach or after work according to your desires! Aperitifs formulas are offered with wine tasting accompanied by Corsican charcuterie (Lonzu, Coppa & sausage wild boar) or by excellent homemade foie gras. The reception of the whole team is like the owner: same, professional and always smiling.

An excellent address you cannot miss when visiting Juan les Pins.

LE FESTIVAL DE LA MER

146, boulevard Président-Wilson
✆ +33 (0)4 93 61 04 62
www.restaurant-festivaldelamer.com
contact@restaurant-festivaldelamer.com

Open all year. Open daily for lunch and dinner. Booking advised. À la carte: Around €35. Children's menu: €12. Menu Festival: €29.90. Lunch menu: On weekdays, daily special: €12.50; Starter + main course + dessert of the day €22. Sunday: 6 oysters n°3 or starter of the day + main course and dessert of the day €25. Seafood platter for 1 person: €44. Checks are not accepted. American Express, Diners Club, Chèque Restaurant. Terrace. Take-away.

Since 1999, this address ideally located in the heart of Juan-les-Pins has been welcoming lovers of seafood in its air-conditioned room in simple and contemporary setting or on its beautiful outdoor terrace. Lobster, oysters, spinny lobster, camerone, sea cicada, mussels, clams, whelks, prawns and ultra-fresh fish, all bought from rigorously selected producers, are offered on the menu. Richly garnished seafood platters are also prepared on request and to take away.

LA PASSAGÈRE

Belles Rives hotel
33, boulevard Édouard-Baudoin
✆ +33 (0)4 93 61 02 79
www.bellesrives.com
info@bellesrives.com

Closed from January to February. Low season: open Wednesday to Sunday from 12pm to 2pm and from 7.30pm to 9.30pm. Full season: every day from 7.30pm to 10.30pm. Lunch served at the restaurant of the beach in summer. Booking advised. Menus €55 (3 main courses) €85 (6 main courses) and €120 (6 main courses). À la carte: around €90. Lunch menu: €45 (canapés, appetizers, starter, main course or main course, dessert, except Sunday). Wine by the glass. American Express, Diners Club, Holiday voucher, Chèque Restaurant. Groups welcome. Terrace. Car valet. Animations. Parking.

In a renovated setting with always the Sea as background, the chef Yoric Tièche (who has just been appointed «*Grand Chef de Demain*» by Gault & Millau 2016) elaborates a tasty, harmonious and controlled cuisine. He stood apart with his lighthouse menu, the *Grand Bleu*, which sublimates the local underwater treasures. Each product is elaborate so as to extract its quintessence and to emphasize its characteristics: sea-bream scented with the Cap's pine needles, scallops poached in a soup, duck breast fried on a high-sided frying pan... as well as fresh and refined cheeses. The desserts of Steve Moracchini also follow this guiding line which are powdered with exotic tonalities: fine Kalingo chocolate coating accompanied by a passion mango nectar with yesteryear praline and an ice cream with caramel, lemon soufflé refreshed with Kalamansi sorbet, or pineapple with old Rum, and its rice chips and ice cream with black sesame... Enjoy them, during fine days, facing the Lérins islands, on the most beautiful hotel terrace in Europe, awarded at "*Prix Villégiature awards 2012*".

LE PERROQUET
9, avenue Gallice
✆ +33 (0)4 93 61 02 20
www.restaurantleperroquet.fr
leperroquetjuan@hotmail.fr

Closed from November to January. Open every day from 12pm to 2pm and from 7pm to 10.30pm. Last sitting in summer at 11.30pm. Booking advised. Menu from €32 to €44 (menu at €32 with starter, main course and dessert: served until 8.30pm). À la carte: Around €30. Children's menu: €14. Wine by the glass. American Express. Groups welcome. Terrace. Parking.

An institution opened since 1920 which still lives with the seaside, touristic and night life activities of Juan-les-Pins. The address has a neat and bright setting and offers seasonal and traditional food made from fresh market products: duo of fresh foie gras and scallops, duck breast lacquered with spices and mango, decorticated big prawns, spaghettis with vegetables, dried tomatoes and garlic, lobster gratin, scallops and scampis with saffron, gravlax salmon... are just some examples of the gourmet dishes which are appreciated in the elegant setting of this chic restaurant located opposite the legendary Gould pine forest.

LA TABLE D'ASIE
132, boulevard du Président-Wilson
✆ +33 (0)4 93 65 07 03

Open all year. Every day from 10am to 10pm. À la carte: Around €25. Menu at €15.

This asian family cuisine at reasonable price is still present and offers a wide range of delicious, tasty and quality dishes: soups, noodles, rices, raviolis, Peking duck, nems and vegetarian dishes.

The service is perfect and the dishes are nicely presented.

ULTIMO
2, boulevard Baudoin
✆ +33 (0)4 93 61 22 46

Open all year. 7 days a week for lunch and dinner from 7am to 11pm, even midnight in season; Service uninterrupted all day. Daily special: €14. Wine by the glass. Menu at €15: dish + a glass of wine. Menu at €16: main course + a glass of wine + dessert of the day. Terrace.

The cuisine is traditional. The carte which is declined on the blackboard offers a beautiful salad variation (Caesar, niçoise, Italian.), meats (Milanese escalope, with cream, beef tartare....) but also fish (fillet of sea bass, marine mussels, salmon Tartar to Asian...) and various woks (poultry, vegetarian...). Some pizzas supplement the menu as well as club sandwiches concocted by the Chef. L'Ultimo is also a tapas bar, to share (squids, accras, hipirons, small rolls...) with happy hours every evening from 6 to 8pm. This brasserie also offers Barbarac ice creams – famous on the St Tropez harbor, pancakes and waffles, on the spot or take-away!

Sleeping

GARDEN BEACH HOTEL
15-17, boulevard Édouard-Baudoin
✆ +33 (0)4 92 93 57 57
www.hotel-gardenbeach.com
contact@hotel-gardenbeach.com

Closed from October to April. Reception 24/24. 175 rooms (100% non smoker). Double room from €99. Buffet breakfast: €25 (at the restaurant). Extra bed: €65. Closed parking: €28 (valet service). Le Bonsaï restaurant: carte around €35. Spoken languages: French, Italian, English, Russian, German. Checks are not accepted. American Express, Diners Club. Pets allowed. Seminars. Receptions and weddings. Free Wifi. Cleaning service. Restaurant. Parking offered during the lunch or the dinner. Garden Beach Spa. Heated indoor pool. Satellite TV, Canal+. Hammam, whirlpool, sauna. Excursions.

Garden Beach Hotel remains one of the rare «resorts» of the French Riviera to offer a wealth of activities to his guests. It enjoys a privileged location on the waterfront opening directly on the beach, in the heart of the shopping streets and close to the Gould pine forest. As for accommodation, fairly spacious rooms are divided into 3 categories which differ according to their position (sea view, garden or pine forest). They are all equipped with flat-screen TV, furniture is streamlined and contemporary, and some have a balcony or a terrace. As for leisure, the hotel offers a wide choice: a private beach with a pontoon for water activities from April, a fitness centre on the ground floor with a year-round heated indoor swimming pool. At Le Bonsaï restaurant, opposite the Grande Bleue, the chef offers an inventive and creative menu with Mediterranean flavours. The Eden Casino offers times of game, so many attractions in the same place. Also enjoy the spa, for body or face massages, hands and feet treatment... a moment of pure relaxation not to miss out.

HÔTEL BELLES RIVES
33, boulevard Édouard-Baudoin
✆ +33 (0)4 93 61 02 79
www.bellesrives.com
info@bellesrives.com

Closed from January to March. Small Luxury Hotels. Prize Holiday 2016: Meilleur Hôtel de Charme in Europe. Reception 24/24. 43 rooms (certain smokers). Low season: double room from €135 to €2,500. High season: double room from €315 to €6,000. Breakfast: €27 (to €32). Extra bed: €60 (to €100). Parking: €30 (external closed, per day and per vehicle). Concierge Golden key. Spoken languages: French, English, Italian, German, Russian. American Express, Diners Club. Pets allowed. Seminars. Receptions and weddings. Internet corner. Free Internet access. Free Wifi. Cleaning service. La Passagère restaurant. Product sales. Massages in the room or on the beach, swimming classes, private coach, naturopathy, jogging cards, boat rental. Satellite TV. Activities. Excursions.

Set right above the sea, this superb 1930's building, which was the residence of Scott and Zelda Fitzgerald, offers maximum of charm and comfort: mahogany wood panelling and boat style, Art deco rooms, all with a balcony and luxurious bathrooms. Lounge, Fitzgerald piano bar to start or end the evening in peace, private beach with sand, pier for water activities and the accosting of boats, spacious terrace with panoramic view on the Lérins islands, a multitude of services and a gourmet restaurant La Passagère brilliantly kept by the chef Yoric Tièche, are the assets to spend a dream holiday.

HÔTEL COLBERT
12, rue Bricka
✆ +33 (0)4 93 61 20 08
www.hotelcolbertajuan.fr
contact@hotelcolbertajuan.fr

Closed from November to January. Reception until 9pm. 32 rooms (certain smokers). Single room from €65; double room from €75; triple room from €85. Buffet breakfast: €9. Extra bed (free cot on request). Garage. Spoken languages: French, English. Checks are not accepted. American Express. Pets allowed. Internet corner. Free Wifi. Cleaning service. Catering facilities.

Within hundred metres from the sandy beaches, five minutes from the city centre and its commercial center, near the train station, this small recently renovated hotel has many assets. The atmosphere is family-like and the staff is attentive and discreet. The rooms are simple, comfortable and well equipped. It is also a good start for visiting the region, from Cannes to Nice.

HÔTEL JUANA*****
19, avenue Georges-Gallice
✆ +33 (0)4 93 61 08 70
www.hotel-juana.com
reservation@hotel-juana.com

Closed from November 1st to December 28th. Small Luxury Hotel. Reception 24/24 (spoken languages: French, English, Italian, German). 40 rooms (certain smokers). Double room from €136 to €2,000. Breakfast: €28. Extra bed: €60 (at €100). Parking: €30 (per day and by vehicle – €15 per day and vehicle from January to March). Checks are not accepted. American Express, Diners Club. Pets allowed. Seminars. Receptions and weddings. Internet corner. Free Internet access. Free Wifi. Cleaning service. Bistro terrace. Free access to the Belles Rives Beach. In-room massages. Animated workshops of oenology Saturday per month by Aymerick Verdy, Chef Wine waiter. Satellite TV. Hammam. Excursions.

It is a pure Art deco gem, whose façade, classified as a Historical Monument attracts all fans of architecture. To a luxurious furniture a very upscale facilities with the services of a is added 5 star, in respect of the great French hotel tradition. The beach and all water activities, are just 100 metres (private beach Belles Rives). Whatever the time of the day, enjoy the marble pool from immaculate white, hammam or the fitness room. The restaurant has become a chic bistro where flavours blend with the south and the local.

HÔTEL LE PRÉ CATELAN
27, avenue des Palmiers
✆ +33 (0)4 93 61 05 11
www.precatelan.com
info@precatelan.com

Castles & Hôtels Collection. Open all year. Front desk open from 7.30am to 8pm (9pm in summer). Spoken languages: French, English, Italian, German and Russian. 24 rooms (100% non smoker). Low season: double room from €175 to €235. High season: double room from €115 to €205. Buffet breakfast: €17 (€10 the continental one. In room: €3 extra). Extra bed: €20. Parking: €16 (per day and €9 in low season). Visa, Mastercard, American Express. American Express, Holiday voucher. Pets allowed (€12 per day). Seminars. Free Wifi. Product sales. Terrace. Solarium. Satellite TV. Whirlpool.

It is in the shade of palm trees and 200 metres from the sandy beaches that you can find this lovely Provencal country house dating from 1920. The setting is idyllic and offers renovated rooms with different atmospheres. Colours are soft and warm. You feel a bit like at home and you can even enjoy a whirlpool bath. A real haven of peace in full heart of Juan-les-Pins.

HÔTEL MADEMOISELLE
12, avenue Docteur-Dautheville
✆ +33 (0)4 93 61 31 34
www.hotelmademoisellejuan.com
info@hotelmademoisellejuan.com

Open all year. 14 rooms. Single room from €92 to €157; double room from €102 to €189; triple room from €142 to €229. Breakfast: €15. Extra bed (on request). Terrace. Garden. Babysitting. Pets allowed. Free Wifi. Tea room from 2pm to 7pm with homemade pastries.

The Mademoiselle Hotel, just 50 m away from the beaches in the heart of the town centre, is a colourful stopover which will bring you back to childhood dreams. The owners Alain and Alexandra who come from the advertising sector have renovated the 14 rooms just like in a fairy tale. Three types of rooms of different sizes: standard, superior or suite from 14 to 30 square metres. It also offers high quality equipment: large flat screen LED TV with 24 French and foreign channels, free wi-fi, air conditioning, telephone, minibar, hairdryer and electric towel dryer... Smart information: there is a small and very pleasant patio for breakfast on sunny days. The designer of this place, Alexandra, a young pastry chef, prepares your breakfast with freshly squeezed fruit juices... and the tea room awaits you from 2 p.m. to 7 p.m. for a sweet break, with pastries and other sweets. A totally atypical address. We love!

LA MAISON BLANCHE RESIDENCE HOTEL
6, avenue Alexandre-III
✆ +33 (0)4 22 13 55 61
http://maisonblancheresort.com
contact@maisonblancheresort.com
❄

Open all year. Reception until 8pm. 10 air-conditioned double rooms, 18 studios and 17 apartments. Extra bed: €20 (per week). Garage (€15/day depending on the period and the availability. Depending on the season: room from €497 to €847. Studio from €567 to €1,183. 2 rooms from €777 to €1,554. Free Wifi.

Acidulated colors, clean lines and great bright volumes, this residence hotel combines comfort, modernity and conviviality. La Maison Blanche mixes the privacy of an apartment with the services of a hotel by offering personalized services and a flexible accommodation. The clientele can benefit from a partner restaurant or go easily in one of the establishments of the downtown or the seaside, the residence being located in the middle of Juan-les-Pins. All the apartments ensure a great comfort: large kitchen with full tableware, wi-fi unlimited, cabled LCD TV, spacious bathroom and wall cupboards... Some have even a terrace with view on the Mediterranean. The house also proposes courses and stays with themes (modelling and sculpture, golf, fitness, personal development, yoga...). A haven of peace and serenity.

Leisure

SO SOLEX
✆ +33 (0)6 49 42 52 89
olivier@so-solex.com

½ day (4 hours): €35. Day (10 hours): €50. End of the day (2 hours): €20. Guide 2 hours: €40 and 3 hours €50. Valid on the axis Nice-Cannes, starting from the daily rental and at least 2 Solex. Guarantee requested €400. Home delivery €10, pick up at home €10 or delivery + pick up 15€.

Would the Solex be fashionable again? Why not! Olivier Durin offers in Juan-les-Pins at News Caffé or the Vieux-Nice or the Les Garçons restaurant to rent this machine of pleasure and freedom to discover the region with established tours with or without guides. Went you take your Solex, a member of the So Solex TEAM will take a picture of you in order to immortalize this original moment.

CAGNES-SUR-MER ★★

Le Haut-de-Cagnes, historic district of Cagnes-sur-Mer is for a walker a haven of peace. Its shaded streets, and its covered passages, its view of the sea and Mercantour creates a unique atmosphere. Cagnes is a ligurian original name meaning inhabited place on a round hill (91 feet high). Originally, a position of surveillance and defence for the inhabitants of the site. Occupied by the Celto- Ligurian then by the Gallo-Romen, Cagnes becomes a border-village from 1388. At that time Nice joined the county of Savoy separated to Provence by the river Var. In 1483, Provence is joined to France. Cagnes is then the border village on the only road leading to France from the States of Savoy. Headquarters of many pillaging from the 16th century, it is a time disturbed by the Great European Wars. The golden age of Cagnes is under the reign of Louis XIII. The castle is transformed by Jean-Henri Grimaldi into an aristocratic residence around 1620 and became the busiest palace of the region. At the end of the 18th century, the inhabitants culture vineyards, olive trees, hemp, citrus fruit and vegetables. At the beginning of the 19th century, a distinguished visitor, Auguste Renoir settled in the city. He will stay until his death in 1919. He bought the estate Domaine des Collettes in 1907 and retained the small farmhouse that existed on the property as it was in his eyes a privileged reason for painting (now the shop of the museum is run by the association of Friends of the Renoir museum whose honorary president is Mr. Jacques Renoir, great-grandson of the painter). He built his house nearby (current Renoir museum). His presence attracted a good number of painters who, like the impressionist Master, also settled in Cagnes quickly called «Montmartre of the French Riviera.» Until the 1960s, the celebrities will follow one another: Georges Simenon, Mouloudji, Foujita, Yves Klein, Suzy Solidor, Georges Ulmer... On the coastal stretch, Cros-de-Cagnes offers the charm of a fishing port. During the French Revolution, the place was composed of pebbles and marshes. Some cottages housed fishermen families from Menton who came to fish twice a year. The place is full of fish and sheltered (Cros means hollow). They then decided to settle permanently on this part of the coastline. Cagnois farmers and traders became fishermen. In 1866, the village is placed under the protection of Saint Pierre, owner of abundance and the latter had the church and its bell. Between 1920 and 1930 fishing is at its peak. A hundred boats and about 200 fishermen. The port in 1960 can accommodate pleasure boats and the flotilla of fishing of the Cros. It is an opportunity to admire the cagnois pointu boats, a mix between Genoese and phocaean pointus. The fishing of the putin is still practiced. It is a alevin used as food for tuna fishing. This fishing was originally a privilege granted by the king of Sardinia to fishermen before the annexation of the county of Nice to France.

TOURIST OFFICE OF CAGNES-SUR-MER

6, boulevard Maréchal-Juin
✆ +33 (0)4 93 20 61 64
www.cagnes-tourisme.com
info@cagnes-tourisme.com

Main office: open in July and August, Monday to Saturday from 9am to 1pm and from 2pm to 6pm. From September to June, Monday to Friday from 9am to 12pm and from 2pm to 6pm. Saturdays from 9am to 12pm. Tourism label & Disability. Physical disability: reserved parking. Assistance system with hearing. Documentation available in Braille.

The Tourist Office offers guided tours on various themes: Cros-de-Cagnes, fishermen's village and maritime traditions; Religious heritage; Hippodrome of Côte d'Azur: behind the scenes of the racing world; the square boules: a different game... Under the light of Renoir; Haut-de-Cagnes, the mysteries of the Middle Ages; Haut-de-Cagnes, the small Montmartre of the French Riviera; in the footsteps of Renoir discovering the 5 senses; Haut-de-Cagnes a historical village; L'Olivier: secrets and flavours of Provence or La Côte d'Azur of painters, in the footsteps of the great masters...

Sightseeing

CHÂTEAU-MUSÉE GRIMALDI

Place du Chateau
Haut de Cagnes
✆ +33 (0)4 92 02 47 35

July and August from 10am to 1pm and from 2pm to 6pm. September, April, May and June from 10am to 12pm and from 2pm to 6pm. From October to March from 10am to 12pm and from 2pm to 5pm. Closed on Tuesday and on December 25th and January 1st. Ticket coupled for the castle-museum and the Renoir museum in the same day €8. Free shuttle n°44 from the bus station downtown every 15 minutes 7 days a week until 10.30pm (00.30am from June to September). Free parkings nearby. Guided tours: Wednesday, Saturday and Sunday morning. Several one hour visits are offered in French or English. Rate €4. Free for under 26-year-olds.

Built in 1309 by the lord of Cagnes, Rainier Grimaldi, this fortress remained the home of the Grimaldi family before being acquired by the city of Cagnes-sur-Mer in 1937. The castle was then converted into museum, then classified as Historical Monument in 1948. This fortress from the outside contrasts with the bright and airy interior dating from the embellishment during the Baroque period. Do not miss: the patio surrounded by arches, the Louis XIII's door with marble framing topped with a Balcony of Honour, the fireplace and the Baroque ceiling of the exhibition hall.

RENOIR MUSEUM

Chemin des Collettes
✆ +33 (0)4 93 20 61 07
www.cagnes-tourisme.com

From June to September from 10am to 1pm and from 2pm to 6pm (gardens open from 10am to 6pm). From October to March from 10am to 12pm and from 2pm to 5pm. From April to May from 10am to 12pm and from 2pm to 6pm. Closed on Tuesday and on December 25th, January 1st and May 1st. Free for under 26-year-olds (and for the cagnois). Adult: €6. Ticket coupled for the Renoir museum and the Grimaldi castle-museum in the same day €8. Guided tour. Shop.

Located in the heart of an over 2-ha park planted with olive trees, the house of the painter Auguste Renoir, which was transformed into an outstanding museum, was built in 1908. This beautiful setting, which is a

Château-Musée Grimaldi.

real oasis of greenery, flowers and fruits, inspired the master during the last eleven years of his life. In 1960, Cagnes-sur-Mer town bought the house to transform it into a museum. The former small rustic farmhouse that was the only existing building when Renoir bought the estate now features a projection room today. The house itself includes both living rooms, which preserved their layouts and their original furniture, and showrooms where 14 paintings by Renoir are exhibited, 25 sculptures made with Richard Guino and fifty works by artists who were his close relatives.

Knife & Fork

LA BERGERIE

78, boulevard de la Plage
Cros-de-Cagnes
✆ +33 (0)4 93 31 54 47

Open Wednesday to Sunday for lunch and dinner. Open Tuesday for dinner in July and August. Open Wednesday to Sunday for lunch and dinner. À la carte: Around €20. Lunch menu: €10. Terrace.

The warm atmosphere is set in the long room with exposed beams and vaulted passages. Open kitchen, wooden tables and wall-mounted blackboards add up to the friendliness of the place. Savoury and sweet pancakes classic, original and sometimes local (Nice, Italian) flavours. Other specialties like the Savoyard fondue, raclette and Burgundy fondue warm up the gourmets in winter. The handmade jugs of cider and the Breton beers go along with the meals on the terrace in summer, on the Cagnes-sur-Mer seaside where La Bergerie has been gathering its herds for more than 35 years now.

THE BRASSERIE ET L'ÉCAILLER DU COURS

3 et 5, Cours du 11-Novembre
✆ +33 (0)9 84 23 16 64
loydt@hotmail.fr

«Maître Restaurateur» label. Open all year. Monday to Saturday from 7am to 7pm. Daily special: €11. Suggestion of the day between €14 and €20.

Ideally located in the heart of the town centre of Cagnes-sur-Mer, the address has a beautiful terrace which makes the setting even more pleasant. A car park nearby allows you to park your car withouth any worries. Inside, the dining room is modern and the decoration neat. The menu is diverse with meats, pastas, fish and seafood that you can order as take-away platters. A true brasserie atmosphere and a warm welcome. Our crush goes to the tiramisu which has its lovers and the copious gourmet coffee.

LA CABANE DE L'ÉCAILLER

24, avenue des Oliviers
✆ +33 (0)4 93 31 68 60
www.lacabanedelecailler.com
♿

«Maître Restaurateur» label. Open all year. Tuesday to Saturday from 9am to 3pm and from 7pm to 11pm; Sunday from 9am to 3pm. Booking advised. À la carte: Around €55 (seafood platter from €24 to €145 for 2 people). Children's menu: €15. Lunch menu: €17 (starter and main course or main course and dessert; starter + main course + dessert at €22 except Sunday and public holidays). Wine by the glass. Cocktail bar and aperitif afterwork. Groups welcome. Terrace. Take-away. Shop.

In a chic exotic setting, you can enjoy excellent fresh wild fish, fine seafood platters and a whole panel of first-quality shellfish. Seafood-product specialist, this restaurant has a menu full of surprises: fricassee of warm octopus, shells gratin, bourride de la Cabane, fish parillada and wild prawns, bouillabaisse, a wide choice of seafood platters but also some meat dishes, foie gras from the Southwest, beef fillet or duck breast. The fish, from the daily catch, are prepared in front of you and accompanied by seasonal vegetables. The service is impeccable and the welcome warm. A must-see address to have a friendly, fresh and gourmet moment!

CAFÉ RISTORANTE POURQUOI PAS

60, promenade de la Plage
✆ +33 (0)9 83 54 52 28
✆ +33 (0)6 08 28 93 16
www.cafepourquoipas.com
contact@cafepourquoipas.com
♿

Open all year. Every day from 12pm to 3pm and from 7pm to 10pm. Booking advised. Menu at €29 (Choice of main course on the carte). Starter or Salad + Meat, Pizza or Fish + Dessert). Children's menu: €10. Wine by the glass. Groups welcome. Terrace. Take-away.

This establishment does restaurant, pizzeria and ice-cream shop, and offers a pleasant terrace opened on the sea, the cuisine has a Mediterranean accent. On the menu: a wide choice of pasta (grandmother's penne, gratin of raviolis...), sunny starters (the dish "Amour Italien" with classical raw ham, salami, speck, pancetta and Parmesan), pizzas without forgetting some fresh meats and fish such as the Valdostana escalope or the roasted salmon fillet tartare sauce. The desserts and the ice creams are as good as the rest of the carte: generous, coloured and hearty.

DOMAINE DE COCAGNE

Domaine Cocagne
30, chemin du Pain-de-Sucre
✆ +33 (0)4 92 13 57 77
www.sandton.eu/cagnes
cocagne@sandton.eu

Open every day from 12pm to 3pm and from 7.30pm to 10pm. Booking advised. Menu from €49 to €54. À la carte: Around €40. Lunch menu: €30 (starter, main course, dessert). Wine by the glass. Checks are not accepted. American Express. Groups welcome (minimum 10 people – maximum 25 people). Garden. Terrace. Parking.

Up on the hill, this hotel has a restaurant open to outside customers. Far from the urban noise, you can either have lunch on the terrace near the swimming pool in complete relaxation while enjoying a simple and light cuisine, or dine in a more intimate atmosphere. The Chef Thijs Gelaude has worked in the most beautiful starred restaurants of the Belgian coast. He will surprise you with his creativity with the best products of the Cote d'Azur. An excellent delicious moment!

LE GRILL DU BOUCHER

78, promenade de la Plage
Cros-de-Cagnes ✆ +33 (0)4 93 14 30 06

Open daily for lunch and dinner. Summer, open for dinner until 2am in the morning. Booking advised. À la carte: Around €30. Children's menu: €9.50. Daily special: €11. Lunch menu €14. Chèque Restaurant. Groups welcome. Terrace.

This reference address for all lovers of excellent meats and pastas carefully selects extremely fresh products with clear tracability and certified origin. The meat cooked à la plancha for example goes with a gratin dauphinois or homemade french fries with a variety of selected sauces: pepper, ceps, shallots, roquefort... The minute minced tartare satisfies the lightest appetites and the daily specials go along with the seasonal market products. The numerous mixed salads can be served in summer on the wooden terrace overlooking the sea and the homemade desserts (tiramisu, chocolate fondant, iced nougat...) complete the quality meals carefully and rapidly served.

HÔTEL ET RESTAURANT CHÂTEAU LE CAGNARD

Haut-de-Cagnes 54, rue Sous-Barri
✆ +33 (0)4 93 20 73 22
www.lecagnard.com
contact@lecagnard.com

Closed from January 1st to February 13th, 2017. Open for dinner only Tuesday to Saturday. From April to September open every evening. Booking advised. Menu from €68 to €80 (excluding drinks). Wine by the glass. American Express. Groups welcome. Terrace. Parkings at the bottom of village. Free shuttle for the Top of Cagnes.

This restaurant has a bright room with sliding ceiling of 200 panels hand painted, for lunch or dinner in open air or and on the terrace with a beautiful view on the landscape of Villeneuve-Loubet castle to Cap d'Antibes. The quality of the cuisine is based on the freshness of the products in a short menu: duo of foie gras with mandarin, egg casserole, sweet potato confit and chestnuts, catch of the day, roasted sea bass and crunchy vegetables, Iberian pork and acidulated mushrooms, pineapple sabayon and pabana sorbet, crumble yuzu and meringue, rice pudding with vanilla...

THE MAESTRO

2, avenue de la Gaude
✆ +33 (0)4 93 20 31 92
www.lemaestro.fr
contact@lemaestro.fr

Closed on Sunday and Monday. Open for lunch and dinner Tuesday to Saturday from 12pm to 2pm and from 7pm to 10.30pm. Booking advised. Children's menu: €10. Daily special: €10.50. Pizza from €9. Lunch menu at €16 with starter + main course + dessert. Chèque Restaurant. Take-away.

This family-run restaurant in Cagnes-sur-Mer has a sober decor and a friendly atmosphere. You'll enjoy tasty and generous pizzas cooked in a wooden fire. But also traditional specialities of meats and fish, grilled meats, as well as a menu prepared by the Chef with fresh, seasonal ingredients. The wine list is efficient and unpretentious.

VIVA SOCCA

Downtown, Pedestrian area
Corner rue Giacosa and rue de la Villette
✆ +33 (0)4 92 02 76 75 – www.vivasocca.com
contact@vivasocca.com

Closed from January 1st to January 31st. Open Tuesday to Saturday from 9am to 10pm non stop and Sunday from 9am to 2pm. Booking advised. À la carte: Around €20. Daily special: €13 (at €17). Terrace.

Viva Socca is a small address to be discovered, located in the heart of Cagnes sur Mer. Carole and Raymond left their ancient early vegetable trade (which they exerted for more than 30 years) to open this gourmet establishment, based on nicoise specialties prepared with salt, olive oil and hickpea flour: the famous "socca". Here, it is like at home. All is fresh and the products come from the market. Carole is in the kitchens, Raymond is in room. Besides the socca, you can enjoy all the local gourmet specialties of Comté de Nice: stuffed vegetables, pan bagnat, onion tart, salads, poutine, stew of raviolis... To be enjoyed on the spot or take-away. Note the lovely terrace which opens on the pedestrian street. It is possible to order the dishes for private events like birthdays, evenings...

Sleeping

HÔTEL ET RESTAURANT CHÂTEAU LE CAGNARD

Haut-de-Cagnes – 54, rue Sous-Barri
✆ +33 (0)4 93 20 73 22
www.lecagnard.com
contact@lecagnard.com

Small Luxury Hotels of the World. Closed from January 1st to February 13th, 2017. Reception up to 23 (spoken languages: French, English, Italian, Russian, German). 28 rooms (and suites 100% non smoker). Double room from €150; suite from €290. Breakfast included. Extra bed: €70. Parking (on request parkings at the bottom of village, shuttles free). Valet service. Half-board and pension on request. American Express. A room for the reception of disabled people. Babysitting. Pets allowed. Seminars. Receptions and weddings. Free Internet access. Free Wifi. Cleaning service. Restaurant open only in the evening. Product sales. Satellite TV. Excursions (on request).

The Swedish Ivarsson family, owner of this exceptional residence perched on the heights of the medieval town have decided to write a new chapter in the history of this 13th century building. The suites and rooms, named after personalities from the world of arts, Renoir, Modigliani, Bonnard, Picasso, Fujita…, some of which have private access from one of the streets of the village, were decorated with refinement in the authentic and characteristic spirit of the place, for comfort and modernity. As for the restaurant, whose main dining room is known for its homemade sliding ceiling of 200 panels hand painted, which opens onto the sky, the Chef works a short menu with fresh and seasonal ingredients.

■ **SANDTON HOTEL & RESIDENCE DOMAINE COCAGNE**
33, chemin du Pain de Sucre
✆ +33 (0)4 92 13 57 77
www.sandton.eu/cagnes

Annual closing in winter. Reopening on March 24th, 2017. 30 rooms. Double room from €107 per night. Seminars. Receptions and weddings. Free Wifi. Catering facilities (restaurant Cocagne). Satellite TV. Petanque field. Free parking.

Cagnes-sur-Mer Hill offers the ideal setting for a stay on the French Riviera. The Cogane Hotel and Residence belong to a prestigious hotel chain present especially in the Netherlands and Belgium. You will stay in one of the 30 rooms, suites, flats or residences of great comfort in the green surroundings of a vast protected estate of 5 hectares. Some of the rooms overlooking the garden or the heated outdoor swimming pool has a private terrace. The Cogane Restaurant for its part offers refined food from a chef who began his career in the best restaurants of the Belgian coast. Everything is here to spend a relaxing and replenishing moment. You can all the same leave the estate for some hours to go to the beach only 7 kilometres away.

TIERCE BEACH HOTEL
33, boulevard John-Fitzgerald-Kennedy
✆ +33 (0)4 93 20 02 09
www.hoteltiercebeach.com

Citotel. Open all year. Reception 24/24 (spoken languages: French, English, German, Italian). 23 rooms (100% non smoker). Single room from €73 to €99; double room from €88 to €130; triple room from €99 to €167; suite from €129 to €210. Breakfast: €10 (€5 for the children up to 10 years. €12 in room). Parking: €10. Checks are not accepted. American Express. Internet access. Free Wifi. Cleaning service. Satellite TV, Canal+.

Barbara and Arnaud Lecompte, former hotelkeepers in Nîmes, have renewed the address and redesigned the rooms with views of the sea, the hippodrome, or the courtyard and a balcony. A successful renovation: a contemporary atmosphere with white walls and soft acid colours. Four types of room when it comes to the comfort: standard, superior, privilege and suite. Added to this, a high standard equipment for each category (LCD TV, satellite channels, safe...). The beach is located opposite the hotel by just crossing the promenade. A lounge bar is available with a selection of wines, beers and soft drinks, to enjoy in a very «beach» atmosphere.

Going Out

■ **CASINO TERRAZUR**
421, avenue de la Santoline
✆ +33 (0)4 92 27 14 40
www.casinoterrazur.com

Tranchant group. Open all year. Prohibited – 18 years. Formal dress code required. Sports gear and beach outfit prohibited. Open 7 days a week. Open from 9pm until 4am for the table games and poker rooms. Slot machines 7 days a week. Access bars family/restaurants, concerts/shows, meetings/events. Free parking.

In this casino of 5,000 m^2, you can satisfy your desires for games with the slot machines, English roulettes, blackjack, stud-poker and ball 2000. The restaurant, in a cosy and contemporary decor, offers a moment of relaxation combining local and regional products. Also note the presence of *a snack* in the rooms of table games and slot machines. Terrazur regularly organises diverse activities all year long: musical, gourmet, commercial operations, quizzes, calendar festivals, theme decorative accessible with family or friends for friendly and memorable evenings.

■ **HIPPODROME DE LA CÔTE D'AZUR**
S.C.C.A. (Company of the Races of the French Riviera) – 2, boulevard Kennedy
✆ +33 (0)4 92 02 44 44
www.hippodrome-cotedazur.com

Admission €4.50. Free -18 years. Check the site for the dates of the Meetings winter and summer. Free parking. 3 panoramic restaurants.

Created in 1952 just a few metres from the sea, the racetrack of Cagnes-sur-Mer is one of the most successful in France. It hosts prestigious races like that of the Grand Prix de plat, the Grand Prix de la Côte d'Azur or the big rally speed. You can have lunch at the gourmet restaurant "Le Pesage", at the "Le Paddock" brasserie, at "L'Hippocafet" or nibble a snack at the snack bars. The hippodrome is also the perfect place to stroll in family: tours of the stables to approach the horses, and playground available for children.

FRENCH RIVIERA: THE COASTLINE

Hippodrome de La cote D'azur, Cagnes-sur-Mer.

POLYGONE RIVIERA

This new outdoor shopping centre opened at the end of October in Cagnes sur Mer, on the French Riviera. With its 70,000 square metres of shopping space, Polygone Riviera is a true place of American life-style and shopping.

A concept straight from the United States

This open-air shopping and leisure centre, also called "lifestyle malls" was inspired by the "shopping-villages" of California or Florida such as Bal Harbour Shop. At the centre of this concept, the idea of creating a place of life mixing shopping, leisure, art and entertainment. This is why Polygone Riviera is structured in various districts and walk. The place has preserved an architectural "french touch" since no less than five local businessmen have worked together and co-signed the interior and exterior design of the shopping centre.

A gourmet world tour

Polygone Riviera has 26 areas for refreshments and gourmet breaks to delight everybody's taste buds. The major asset of this gastronomic offer is the diversity of the addresses and cuisines. Among them, you will find local cuisine namely at "Le Comptoir" and "Le Bistrot Nice". "Pavillon Gourmet", the made in France catering *par excellence* is also present and offers, besides its self-mix and take-away menus, fun workshops for children. "Made in USA" burgers with typical Indian cuisine, Asian specialties and gourmet breaks, is a real culinary journey that Polygon Rivera offers its guests. If after your shopping, or your movie at the cinema, you are feeling hungry.... 26 catering and gourmet break spaces will meet your needs.

- **Namaskar**: the reference in indian cuisine
- **Ben Burger**: "Made in USA" burgers, also with delicious self-mix salads, smoothies from fresh fruit cut on the spot.
- **Maotsumy**: a sushi bar and fish teppanyaki. At nightfall, it changes into a cosy and festive lounge.
- **Le Comptoir and Le Bistrot Niçois**: a traditional and tasty cuisine in a modern and refined atmosphere.
- **La Piazza**: the creativity and generosity of Italy with fresh ingredients
- **Coffee or tea breaks**, whatever the time of day: pleasure anytime, art coffee, « café cocotte » ...
- **Gourmet moments** with, namely, Saint Tropez pie, lindt, Emilie's cookies and boon and Fratini ice-cream...
- **Le Pavillon Gourmet**, a delicatessen with the best local products, but also an open and welcoming cuisine from the chefs for "cooking sessions".

Culture and art accessible to all

The region has one of the richest cultural and artistic heritage. Polygone Riviera thus wanted to pay tribute to this wealth by opening its spaces to contemporary art, culture and leisure. Eleven international artists including Ben, Daniel Buren, Caesar or Wang Du among others were chosen to decorate with contemporary touches the walks and places of Polygone Riviera. Among the major works shopping center you will find "Le Guetteur" by Sacha Sosno overlooking the entrance of the site from the top of its 22 metres high and houses a restaurant, an office as well as a panoramic terrace. As for leisure and entertainment, Polygone Riviera houses the Casino Terrazur with a surface of 5,000 square metres as well as the 'multi-screen Cinema Cap. These two places will accommodate many cultural events (concerts, theme nights...) during the summer months.

Exclusive fashion brands

Shopping is of course the main offer of Polygone Riviera. On the 70,000 square metres of the centre it is nearly 150 brands were established, the whose presence of some is completely new in France and in the region. Let us mention in particular the Japanese brand Uniqlo, the French chain Printemps or Forever 21, the American brand which attracts teenagers. Classified according to their characteristics, the different brands are divided into 3 groups: the unmissable brands (Mango, Zara, H& M, Massimo Dutti...) known as "iconic" and designer boutiques (JOTT, American Vintage, Ron Abraham...). Last March the Irish giant PRIMARK specialising in clothing at low prices opened his 4000 square metres shop and made Polygone Riviera an unmissable place for shopaholics!

4 -star service

Polygone Riviera is rated as a 4 -star shopping center thanks to the quality of its services. To facilitate your shopping, to make it more pleasant and qualitative shopping the center is at your service and offers you:

- **a nursery and a baby area** where changing tables, as well as a microwave and baby bottle heaters are available. Strollers are also provided free of charge at the reception.
- **a personal shopper**: a fashion professional of accompanies and advices you for a personalized shopping (upon reservation).
- **a mobile application** of the shopping centre allows you to find friends present at the shopping centre, an audio guide, or to locate your car in the underground parking.
- **free and unlimited wi-fi** as well as an area for recharging your mobile phone.

■ POLYGONE RIVIERA SHOPPING CENTER
119 avenue des Alpes
www.polygone-riviera.fr

Facebook: https://www.facebook.com/PolygoneRiviera/timeline/. Parking of 3000 places. Open Monday to Saturday from 10am to 9pm. Sunday from 10am to 7pm. The restaurants and the cinema remain open until 1am!

What a nice surprise to discover this new temple dedicated to shopping, inspired by the «lifestyle malls» of the United States! A wonderful open-air shopping center where shopping, leisure and Contemporary Art harmoniously mingle. The Centre offers free and unlimited wi-fi, a smartphone app («meet my friends») if you lost your friends or your parents! Also note the great initiative: the child-care for toddlers. As for shopping there are not less than 150 shops, some of which are completely new in the region: Primark, Reiss, UniQlo, Forever21, Anotherstories, Grand Playground, Nue 19.04...

UNEXPECTED
SHOPPING
ANIMATIONS
RESTAURANTS / CINEMA
EVEN ON SUNDAY
POLYGONE
RIVIERA
CAGNES-SUR-MER
BETC SHOPPER ASL POLYGONE RIVIERA – ZAC Sudalparc – Avenue des Alpes – 06800 CAGNES-SUR-MER – SIREN 813 888 476.

Shopping

MIC MAC MACAROON

50, chemin du Val-Fleuri
✆ +33 (0)4 89 14 33 47
www.micmac-macaron.com
boutique@micmac-macaron.com

Open Tuesday to Friday from 10am to 12.30pm and from 2.30pm to 7pm and Saturday from 9.30am to 12.30pm and from 2.30pm to 7pm. Parking. Macaroon classes as of 8 years. Duration 3 hours approximately by group of 7 at the most. Voucher gifts valid 6 months (order form to be downloaded on the site). Rates €85 and – 12 years €70 (...).

This leading shop on the Côte d'Azur is dedicated to the macaroon, this small and fun dessert famous for some years now. Bruno Laffargue created Mic Mac Macaron in 2009. He offers an exceptional range of flavours in more than 40 different creations among which limited seasonal editions like the lime/cactus, the yuzu, the popcorn or the vanilla olive oil versions which you can have as eat-in or take-out. But there is more: the place also offers workshops to learn how to make them and are conducted by the pastry chef. The course is a very convivial moment popular among children; you will leave it with your own creations. Bruno also hosts all your events (weddings, christening or birthdays) and makes pièces montées upon request according to your theme. Hurry up to discover it! Follow them on Facebook.

AUX ENFANTS GÂTÉS

1, cours du 11-Novembre
✆ +33 (0)4 93 22 90 67
contact@aux-enfants-gates.fr

Open Monday to Saturday from 6.30am to 7.30pm, Sunday from 6.30am to 1pm.

Located in the city centre of Cagnes-sur-mer, this bakery and cake shop which produces artisanal bread and viennoiserie will quickly become your daily meeting point. You can come at dawn to enjoy your coffee and pancakes there, buy your bread at lunchtime, or try their homemade burgers, go back there at 4 pm to taste the cookies, cupcakes or muffins, and finally buy your baguette at 6 pm for your evening meal. In addition to the quality of the products, you have a colourful, warm and trendy decor, and the kindness of the owners will conquer you. Beautiful outdoor terrace to relax on sunny days.

CANNES ★★★★

The English nobility discovered it when it was only a village. Movie stars have made it a myth. The biggest brands have set up their shops. Visitors see it as a prime stop. Cannes, dream destination, today continues to reveal its secrets.»The only way to live is to be under the sun doing nothing» wrote Mérimée who loved Cannes so much. A city that has continued to charm its visitors. Adored or criticized, it remains a key destination on the Côte d'Azur. Here, in a unique atmosphere, made of luxury hotels of the Croisette, stones full of history of the old town, the authenticity of the old fishing port, the luminous beauty of the islands, sun-drenched beaches, the excitement of great events of the Palace of festivals and Congress. Located at the edge of a large bay between the Lérins Islands and the Esterel foothills, jewel of the Côte d'Azur sea resorts, Cannes is non the less an ideal place to stay throughout the year and increases attraction points.Such success comes with drawbacks. A welcome not always friendly, an apparent coldness, a glossy image that one has difficulties at first sight to tame, the worship of the appearance ... Yes, Cannes is all that. Victim of its success, the city overhyped portrays an image of the Riviera dolce vita. Between appearance and reality, there is a sort to do, in order to keep just the best. As concerns heritage, a stroll in Cannes often begins from the Old Town. The Suquet, with its picturesque

La Croisette.

pedestrian streets still remains the identity of Provence and the remains of its history. The trip continues to the Forville market where mingles accents, scents and colours of the south. The Meynadier pedestrian street is full of delicatessens, florists and souvenir stalls, recreating the atmosphere of an authentic village. Then comes the famous golden scope: between Croisette and Antibes streets. It is the fashion square of the town. The big brands are alongside shops; from the most elegant to the most trendy- ambassadors of haute couture, of jewellery and luxury trade. A hyper centre where large tables are available with all the flavours of gastronomy, and where palaces in boutique hotels continue the tradition of impeccable hospitality. Intense cultural seasons, a remarkable heritage, the beauty of tradition, a hectic life facing a promising future involved in influence that puts Cannes at the level of large cities.

TOURIST OFFICE OF CANNES

Palais des festivals
1, boulevard de la Croisette
✆ +33 (0)4 92 99 84 22
www.cannes-destination.fr
tourisme@palaisdesfestivals.com

Main office open 7 days a week from 9am to 7pm from March to October, from 10am to 7pm from November to February and from 9am to 8pm in July and August. Desk of Cannes la Bocca: open Tuesday to Saturday from 9am to 12pm and from 2.30pm to 6.30pm. In July and August, open from 9am to 12.30pm then from 3.30pm to 7pm. Tourism label & Disability. Assistance system with hearing. Consultable documentation in Braille. Way to record the conversation.

Located on the esplanade of the palais des festivals on Croisette, in the offices of the Tourist Office where one of the world capitals of cinema lies, there is also a shop where you can purchase T-shirts, books, DVD, bags but also pens, postcards, lighters or key-rings, perfect because there are lots of souvenirs! Note that the branch of Cannes-la Bocca is located opposite the typical market of the same name. They will provide you with important informations, you will find in the Tourist Office everything you need to know in order to discover every assets of Cannes.

- **Guided tours according to various sets of themes**: «Cannes and the Cinema», «In the middle of the myth» and "It was once Cannes". Rate from €4 to €6, for people under the age of 16 years it's free of charge. The duration is approximately 1: 30. Advance reservation is highly advised for each visit in summer. Visits include 5 people and limited to 25.

1834: birth of Cannes

In December 1834, Lord Henry Brougham and Vaux, Lord Chancellor of England, brings his daughter Eleonore Louise to visit Italy. Unfortunately for him and fortunately for Cannes, King of Piedmont had closed its border with France because of a cholera epidemic. Forced to go back, Lord Brougham decided to move to Grasse. At nightfall, he stops at the inn of master Pinchinat in the actual rue du Port in Cannes. Charmed by the place, the welcome, the bouillabaisse and the wine of master Pinchinat, Lord Brougham decided to build a residence in the village. Two years later, the whole high-class society of London urged in Cannes for the opening of a vast and magnificent house: the Villa of Eleonore. Some years later, the small fishing port has become the town of international aristocracy. 1837, the British General Taylor built the castle of St. George. In 1838, the construction of the first port started and the trail that winds along the coast is expanded. Called the chemin de la Petite Croix, it then will be called Promenade de la Croisette. In 1848, Alexandra Feodorovna Skrypitzine, the wife of the Consul of France in Moscow, Eugene Tripet falls in love with Cannes and then will the Russian aristocracy too. In 1858, the first building stands on La Croisette: Hotel Gonnet which later became Hotel Gonnet and of the Queen. Cannes, the mythical city was born.

Climb the steps!

Play the star by following the guided tour of the Palais des Festivals et des Congrès de Cannes. The doors are open to the public 2 to 6 times per month, except in May because of the film festival. We climb the famous steps with the red carpet, we look at the footprints left by the stars on the Esplanade Georges Pompidou, visit the legendary hall that welcomes for example the opening and closing ceremonies of the International Film Festival. There are the Auditoriums, the gala hall «the Ambassadors» and from the terraces, we can admire the view over the old town, the hill of the Suquet, the old port, the Croisette and the Lerins Islands. The tour starts at 2.30pm, it lasts about 1h30. It costs € 3 per person, children under 12 free. Tickets are sold only at the Tourist Office of the Palais des Festivals.

Infos : ✆+33 (0)4 92 99 84 22 or www.palaisdesfestivals.com

HISTORIC VISIT OF THE CITY OF CANNES ★★

Tourist Office of Palais des Festivals et des Congrès
✆ +33 (0)4 92 99 84 22
tourisme@palaisdesfestivals.com

Duration of the visit: approximately 1.30 hour. Visit assured starting from 5 people and limited to up to 25 people. Every Monday at 2.30pm in French and English version. In July and August: every Monday simultaneous departures, at 9.15am, in French and English. Free for under 16-year-olds. Adult: €6.

Let yourself be told the history of Cannes while walking along noticing the modernity of a dynamic city always looking towards the future. Discover the past often ignored of this captivating city following the footsteps of those who marked its soul. Lérins islands to the Old Suquet, it has managed to build in nearly 2 centuries a reputation as a privileged place for the world leaders.

Sightseeing

THE CROISETTE ★★★★

Catering facilities. Shop.

In the early 19th century, the seafront road embellished with a small cross was called "Chemin de la Petite-Croix". In 1838, during the development of the port, most of the streets along the sea were named in memory of this small cross, the new promenade was given the name "Promenade De La Croisette". The most prestigious street in Cannes, it is now lined with luxury hotels renown worldwide whose names evoke the aristocracy, the jet set, the world of arts and cinema: the Intercontinental Carlton, mythical hotel with its 150 meters façade and its 2 domes at the ends inspired by the shape of Belle Otero breasts, the Majestic Barrière and the Grand Hyatt Cannes Hôtel and the hotel Martinez. They all welcome in May the cream of international cinema. At the end of the Croisette, admire the view of the Esterel massif, the gulf of La Napoule, Golfe-Juan, the Cap d'Antibes, the Alps and the Lérins islands. Continue your walk till the Palm Beach with its calm and shaded areas: slightly isolated, here the beaches are more discreet and less populated.

ILES OF THE LERINS ★★★★

Regularly assured departures by maritime shuttles from quai Laubeuf, or from Golfe Juan harbour.

A stone's throw from the famous Croisette, you can find the two islands of Lérins, two sites that offer visitors a beautiful outing combining nature, local, history, legend, spirituality and contemplation. Once well-known of sailors, these islands were a regular and important stop for main marine itineraries from Antiquity.

Saint-Honorat: it is the smallest (1.5 km from the shores and 400 m wide). It tells the story of Cannes. Formerly known as Lerinum, it takes its modern name from ecclesiastic Honorat of Arles, the future saint Honorat, who wanted to find solitude here. But soon joined by many disciples, he founded in the 5th century a monastery and built school throughout Provence owing to its rigorous asceticism. Around 1703, to protect the monks from the raids of pirates, a fortress was built there, constituting one of the rare examples of fortified monastery: the gate was located in height it was necessary to climb down a ladder to enter or to leave! Other amenities came grid the elders during the 19th century. The building faces the sea in an ideal configuration so as to lead to thinking. Monks still live here: praying, meditating and cultivating vines, they produce excellent wines as well as a liqueur became the local speciality: Lérina. Today, the island is a very spiritual place of peace (smart dress compulsory and no smoking) that you can easily go around on foot thanks to the walkway along the coast.

An arm of sea about 700 m long, called the canal of Friuli, separates the two islands.

Sainte-Marguerite: four times larger, sailors are fond of this beautiful place and its very rich sea beds. From Cannes, the bank is very close and the most adventurous people could almost go there by swimming, as only 1 100 m separate the tip of the Palm Beach of the Royal fort to the island! The Mediterranean scents of pine and eucalyptus come to tickle immediately your nostrils when you arrive: the particularity of the Sainte-Marguerite island is indeed in the forest, the only coastal forest of the Alpes-Maritimes department. Migratory birds, crystal clear water, rare species... . The setting is idyllic. A botanical trail designed by the ONF (National Forests Office) allows you to discover the site, bordered to the west by the pond of Batéguier and equipped with natural observatory to observe wildlife and other natural riches. To the north stands the royal fort built by Richelieu then reinforced by Vauban in the early 18th century. Former State prison, the site has a poor reputation of having kept prisoner for 11 years the Iron Mask. Transformed into a military gaol, now the place hosts the Musée de la Mer. No matter on which island you are, the view of the surrounding mountain ranges is spectacular with in the west the contours of the Maures Massif or Esterel, and on the other side, the back country of Grasse with the bare chain of Cheiron topped by the Mercantour mountain tops. There are several maritime companies insuring regular round trips on average every 20 minutes during the summer period to get there.

Knife & Fork

THE 1331
14,rue Venizelos
✆ +33 (0)9 83 24 87 53
www.le1331.fr – info@le1331.fr

Open Monday to Saturday from 8am to 0h30. Lunch menu: €13 (daily special + coffee). Diner menu: starter and main course €31. À la carte for lunch around €33. À la carte the evening around €40.

An original concept based on figure 13 and its opposite 31. Here, all the products are fresh and are worked in two different ways, a simple, quick and classical service at midday "13" and one second more gourmet and refined in the evening "31". In this restaurant and bar *lounge* with an industrial déco inspired by New York, you'll enjoy the dishes comfortably seated on the banquette while the cocktails can be drunk directly at the bar. Assured conviviality!

LA BRASSERIE DU MARCHÉ
17, place du Marché-Forville
✆ +33 (0)4 93 99 15 96

♿

Open all year. Tuesday to Sunday from 12pm to 2.30pm. Booking advised. Menu of the market at €15 (1 choice of main course, 1 choice of desserts) on the à la carte or panel suggestions. Chef's suggestion around €15. Breakfast €5, continental fixed rate formula €12. Checks are not accepted. Chèque Restaurant. Groups welcome (up to 20 people). Terrace. Parkings Ferrage and Forville in the vicinity (first hour free).

After a stroll between the stalls of the producers and the food traders, take a break in this brasserie next to this large covered market to enjoy a coffee and croissants, or a good meal at lunchtime. You will love the simple and homemade traditional cuisine: the niçoise salad, Italian style tartar, the gourmet plate, the aioli (every third Thursday of the month), chocolate fondant.

LA CABANE DE L'ÉCAILLER
2, rue Felix-Faure ✆ +33 (0)4 93 68 74 33
www.lacabanedelecailler.com

Open all year. Every day from 9am to 11pm in continuous service. Possible privatization, private events, business meal, groups. Set menu at €28 (for lunch and dinner). À la carte: Around €60. Children's menu: €15. Lunch menu: €17 (starter and main course or main course and dessert; €22 starter + main course + dessert). Free shipping from €50 of purchase.

An intimate atmosphere, hot colours and inspiring dishes... Cabane de l'Écailler is a sophisticated place offering fresh, quality and seasonal ingredients: beautiful sea fruit plates, cooked shellfish, a reserve of oysters rigorously selected and delivered directly by the oyster culturists, wild fresh fish but also foie gras poeleed and scallops, cod fillet and its creamy polenta with almond milk and veal fillet with cep gravy. For the sushi unconditionals, a selection on the carte with special creations with scallops or oysters. The desserts and the pastries are made daily. La Cabane has also a beautiful range of cocktails and invite you to try their creation «Cabane Passion» with vodka, pineapple, cranberry juice, mashed passion fruit, mashed raspberry and lemon juice. A hut of luxury for gourmets!

L'ANTIDOTE
60, boulevard d'Alsace
✆ +33 (0)4 93 43 32 19
www.lantidote-christopheferre.fr

Closed from December 24th to January 31st, 2017. Open Monday for dinner; Tuesday to Saturday for lunch and dinner. Booking advised. Menu from €31 to €39. À la carte: Around €30 (starter around €20, main course around €35, dessert around €10). À la carte for lunch around €20. American Express, Diners Club. Groups welcome. Garden. Terrace.

It is a family work here! The chef Christophe Ferré assisted by his younger brother Alexis in the kitchen, his spouse Karin and his sister take care of this charming restaurant with a most beautiful terrace, set in a house full of character located below the expressway. As for the menu, the cuisine with Mediterranean accents is heartily and beautifully defended and offered with an excellent value for money; smoked salmon pancake, crab meat and ricotta on potatoes blinis, crispy panfried line-caught bass, thyme and lemon emulsion, linguine, stuffed guinea-fowl supreme, puréed parsnips, vanilla crème brûlée, fig compote and old-fashioned wafer...

The movie stars alley

As in Los Angeles near the famous Chinese Theatre on Hollywood Boulevard, directors, actors, writers and other celebrities of the 7th art leave the imprint of their hands and their signatures during the International Film Festival or during their visit to Cannes. This Star of the Cinema alley, located at the foot of the Palais des Festivals, on the Pompidou esplanade and the adjacent gardens has more than 400 handprints and signatures of the most famous people of national and international cinema.

LE CABANON
Boulevard du Midi
✆ +33 (0)6 21 56 26 09
www.lecabanoncannes.com
fred@lecabanoncannes.com

7 days a week for lunch and for dinner in July and August. Closed on Sunday evening. Valet service in season. À la carte: Around €40 (starter up to €15. Dish up to €32. Dessert up to €12). Daily special: €16. Suggestions between €18 and €30 - Rental of deckchair €20 / jour. Credit card not accepted.

A real favourite for this private beach hidden almost at the end of the Boulevard du Midi... Here, guests are regulars getting together in this little paradise throughout the year.

Cabanon is a true fresh gustatory haven for whoever wishes to enjoy an authentic and tasty cuisine. The dishes are elaborated with fresh and seasonal ingredients, a regional gastronomy inspired by the sea and land. The fish are from local fishing (fish label of «mer de Lérins»). On the carte menu, we like for example the homemade duck terrine, the crab rillettes, the tartare with smoked duck breast, the pollack fillet, the double burger with truffle, or even the pork simmered at low temperature... The desserts are appetising: macaroon with raspberry praline, Japanese finger food, fresh fruit basket, rum baba... The whole served in an enchanting setting of a Cannes beach facing the Mediterranean.

During the fine days, you can enjoy a deckchair on the beach. Always in the same spirit of service, the deckchair is rented only for a day with the parasol, the bath sheet and the small bottle of water. And then, there is the teak wood bar installed on the beach: champagne and tapas! An excellent price-quality ratio and an always regular reception and charming whatever the season. Well done!

BISTRO LES CANAILLES
12, rue Jean-Daumas
✆ +33 (0)4 93 68 12 10
www.bistrolescanailles.com
bistrolescanailles@orange.fr

Open all year. Tuesday to Saturday from 12pm to 2.30pm and from 7pm to 1am. Booking advised. À la carte: Around €20 (starter around €14, main course around €20, dessert around €7). Wine by the glass. Checks are not accepted. American Express, Diners Club. Groups welcome. Terrace. Shop. Parkings nearby.

The people named here «the scoundrels» (Les Canailles) who created this cosy restaurant are real professionals in gastronomy with experiences in great restaurants. Lysiane Levivier and Carole Peretti have combined their know-how with the experience of the chef Michel Cortesi to offer a gourmet place whose chalk board changes regularly. They offer traditional dishes like the pan-fried foie gras with red berries, the beef cheek in stew style, the duck breast with orange and ginger sauce, red mullet fillet with olive oil sauce, old-fashioned custard, the rum baba... The exposed stone walls, the suspended lamps, the chocolate brown furniture, the large Baroque mirror, the armchairs and sofas give to the place a contemporary look with a bistro atmosphere at lunch time and a more relaxed setting for dinner. The glasses of wine go with gourmet delicatessen dishes early in the evening for a «wine bar» version.

LA BROUETTE DE GRAND'MÈRE
9 bis, rue d'Oran
✆ +33 (0)4 93 39 12 10
www.labrouettedegrandmere.fr
labrouettedegrandmere@yahoo.fr

Closed from January 8th to February 13th, 2017. Open Monday to Saturday from 7pm to 10.30pm; Sunday for lunch. Booking advised. Set menu at €42 (including wine, half-bottle, several starters, 6 choice of main dishes, 4 fixed depending on the seasons + 2 main courses per week, choice of desserts). À la carte: Around €30. Wine by the glass. American Express. Groups welcome (business meal, baptism, wedding). Terrace. Paying public parking Commandant Lamy just opposite.

This restaurant from another time with a retro setting elaborates a traditional, simple and generous home cooking prepared with fresh products. The all-inclusive menu formula has not aged and still satisfies customers: the welcome cup of drinks, several successive starters, a slice of smoked salmon with its glass of vodka, homemade terrine, choice of main course, roasted squail, filet mignon with camembert sauce, Auge valley chicken breast or the daily special, assortment of desserts and a half bottle of wine, mineral water or soft drink. What could be better?

LA FARIGOULE
82, rue Meynadier ✆ +33 (0)4 93 38 94 95
emile0@hotmail.fr

Open all year. Daily for lunch and dinner. Children's menu: €10. Daily special: €10. Wine by the glass. Full menu at €17, for lunch and dinner. Pasta dishes €10. Meat dishes €17. Credit card not accepted. Terrace.

It is in the pretty Meynadier shopping street that this small bistro-restaurant is located. The atmosphere is friendly, paintings on the walls and tables with red and white Vichy squares, and an efficient and attentive service. The cuisine is simple and quality is always with go: fillet of roasted red mullet, dish of the fisherman, stuffed vegetables, clafoutis, lemon pie with meringue, apple pie, tarte tatin, chocolate fondant... a friendly stop in one of the most authentic neighborhoods of the beautiful French Riviera.

GRILL AND WINES
5, rue Notre-Dame
✆ +33 (0)4 93 38 37 10
www.grillandwines.com
contact@grillandwines.com

Open all year. Tuesday to Saturday from 12pm to 2.30pm and from 7pm to 10.30pm. Booking advised. À la carte: Around €45. Children's menu: €12. Lunch menu: €16 (small starter, main course or main course, dessert and bottle of water). Wine by the glass. American Express, Chèque Restaurant. Groups welcome. Terrace. Activities.

Grilled or roasted meats are honoured in this chic bistro and wine bar: lamb shoulder, chateaubriand, grilled black Angus ribs, simmental prime ribs and its marrow bone, famous parillada (whole meat pieces cut on the board). But you should not forget to discover the various homemade terrines and the sea bass in salt crust for 2 people. Note: the lunch formula at low prices and the nice wine list, all served in a friendly and warm atmosphere.

L'ARDOISE

5, rue Rouguière ✆ +33 (0)4 93 68 60 43

Open daily for lunch and dinner. Menu €17. À la carte: Around €15 (to €30). Children's menu: €9. Lunch menu: €12 (main course and dessert). Chèque Restaurant. Terrace.

This small bistro near Rue d'Antibes deserves a lunch break. It is in a traditional setting, between red and cream colour walls, on dark wooden tables that we enjoy dishes with regional names such as the homemade Provençal daube, the fisherman's dish in bouillabaisse way, the well garnished Provençal dish (marinated sweet peppers, eggplant or courgette fritters, squid with parsley and tapenade toasts). Everything is cooked with fresh products guaranteeing the menu's quality. As for the desserts, they are homemade: tarte tatin, caramel cream, chocolate fondant, lemon tart and tiramisu will delight the most gourmands. In summer, you can sit on the terrace to enjoy the dynamic life of the neighbourhood. Dinner time inspires a cosy atmosphere. To try at any time of the day!

LUX CAFÉ

144, rue d'Antibes ✆ +33 (0)4 93 45 07 65

Open all year. Monday to Saturday from 8am to 8pm. Booking advised. À la carte: Around €15. Fixed rate formula: €13.50 (daily special, drink, coffee). Wine by the glass. Take-away pastries €5 the share or €6.50 to taste on the premises. Terrace. Take-away.

Ideally located on the most trendy street of Cannes, this restaurant opens for breakfast time where you can enjoy freshly squeezed juices, until late in the afternoon for tea time with its excellent homemade pastries. At lunchtime, all is homemade and varied, elaborated in brasserie spirit with fresh ingredients for those in a hurry to eat on the go with choices of Asian dishes (bo bun, various woks) but also salmon tartare, various quiches, vegetables or Black Angus for lovers of good meat...

SEA SENS

Five Seas Hôtel Cannes

22, rue du Bivouac-Napoléon

✆ +33 (0)4 63 36 05 06

www.five-seas-hotel-cannes.com

Closed in January. Open Tuesday to Saturday from 7.30pm to 10pm. Brasserie open daily for lunch and dinner. Booking advised. Menu from €65 to €115. À la carte: Around €60 (starter around €30, main course from €35 to €78, dessert €20). Brasserie: à la carte around €35, menu from €19 to €39. Groups welcome. Terrace. Valet. Activities. Parking.

The restaurant is on the roof of the hotel in Cannes, on the fifth floor, two atmospheres and two types of cuisine are offered. The central bar, near the entrance on the left offers a separated space which extends the terrace creating an ideal lounge for an aperitif. It is completed by the colourful brasserie section with a festive atmosphere where simple and classic dishes make up the menu. The gourmet restaurant room has a view on Suquet. The Chef prepares a cuisine which he likes eating, inspired by his travels and based on products of excellence. Jérôme de Oliveira, the Chef pastry, continues your pleasure with delicious sweetened delicacies.

LE CIRQUE

30, rue Hoche

✆ +33 (0)4 93 30 02 38

Closed from January 22nd to March 1st, 2017. Open Monday to Saturday from 8am to midnight. À la carte in 2 parts: first part around €12 and second part around €17. American Express.

In this café bistro, you enter a universe where conviviality reigns as a Master surrounded by walls of stones and notched lamps. This restaurant, located in full heart of the city, offers a funny and creative Mediterranean and Rhone valley cuisine: pan bagnat of the circus, salad niçoise and tuna tataki, green asparagus bouquet and speck, candied shoulder of lam and gnocchis, rack of pork and potato waffle... A real treat to enjoy with a good bottle of wine, the Cirque also has a well provided wine cellar!

LE PARK 45

The Grand Hotel

45, la Croisette

✆ +33 (0)4 93 38 15 45

www.grand-hotel-cannes.com

info@grand-hotel-cannes.com

«Maître Restaurateur» label. Closed from December to January. Closed in July and August, and from December 9th to February 5th, 2017. Open Tuesday to Saturday from 12pm to 2.15pm and from 7.30pm to 10pm. Booking advised. Menu veggie €55. À la carte: Around €50 (starter around €30, main course around €40, dessert around €20). Wine by the glass. American Express, Diners Club. Accessible to the armchairs, WC adapted. Garden. Terrace. Valet. Parking. 1 Michelin star.

It is possible to have lunch or dinner on the Croisette without the town inconveniences (noise, pollutions...). Sit in the restaurant with its exposed wine cellar or on the terrace in front of a large and long green carpet under the shade of palm trees. To complete your bliss, taste a subtle cuisine that relies on producers, suppliers and impeccable craftsmen of taste: Jean-Paul Véziano in Antibes for his breads, the oil mill Sainte Anne in Grasse, Marie Luxe the fish wholesaler for her fresh seafood, Patrick Duler for his cured meats and Gascon pigs... Mediterranean flavours and local products perfectly prepared by the Chef Sébastien Broda, one Michelin star, and tasty desserts prepared by Pascal Picasse.

CRÊPERIE OF THE CROISETTE

82, boulevard de la Croisette
✆ +33 (0)4 93 94 43 47
www.creperiedelacroisette.com
tcl1@bbox.fr

High season: open every day from 8.30am to 10pm. From October 16th to April 14th, closed on Monday. Buckwheat pancake up to €16.50. Crepe with wheat from €3.50. Salads up to €16.50.

On the mythical Boulevard de la Croisette, the gourmands can enjoy authentic pancakes in a contemporary and warm setting. The choice is varied: Andalusian, Provençal, with smoked duck breast, andouillette or vegetarian... These pancakes can be eaten with all sauces with a bowl of cider or a glass of wine. On sunny days, you can enjoy the terrace facing the palm trees and the sea.

LA PALME D'OR

Grand Hyatt Cannes Hôtel Martinez
73, la Croisette
✆ +33 (0)4 92 98 74 14
www.cannesmartinez.grand.hyatt.com
lapalmedor.martinez@hyatt.com

♿

Closed from January to March. Open Wednesday to Saturday from 12.30pm to 1.30pm and from 8pm to 10pm. Booking advised. À la carte: Around €100. Fixed rate formula: €74 (the Croisette in mouvment). Wine by the glass. Menu collection: €185. Menu Inspiration of season: €205. Checks are not accepted. American Express, Diners Club. Terrace. Valet. Parking. 2 Michelin stars. Certification Green Globe.

This twice Michelin-star restaurant is managd by the Chef Christian Sinicropi who remains faithful to the concept that offers twice a year new ceramic crockery designed to receive his culinary compositions. This approach, which is certainly unique in the world, follows precise steps: seeking the form, design, identity and reflection of the artist then selecting the product – very important for him -, and preparing the recipe. We find originality, taste and precision especially with the spider crab cooked like a caramel sauce, iodized round and sharp subtleties, the triple A Greffeuille Allaiton lamb cooked for 72 h, citron and Granny Smith apple available in sorbet, tart, marmalade and crystal matrix. One of the most gustatory travels!

LA PLAGE MAJESTIC BARRIÈRE

La Croisette
✆ +33 (0)4 92 98 77 30
www.lucienbarriere.com

Annual closing 1 week in November and 3 weeks in December. Open every day from 12pm to 4pm. And from 12pm to 6pm in July and August. Booking advised. À la carte: Around €40. Wine by the glass. Fixed formulas starter and main course: €41 or main course and dessert: €32. American Express, Diners Club. Groups welcome. Terrace. Parking nearby.

This 2,600 m^2 area has the largest façade overlooking the bay of Cannes. This beach offers two special features: its eco-responsible design, in terms of material manufacturing and the products and waste management and its dismountable function. Indeed, it is the first beach of La Croisette to meet the standards of the coastline law and therefore became the greenest beach of the most famous Cannes's boulevard. This new bold construction with glass panels and sliding roof, very white, with boat canvas that gives a maritime mood, houses the restaurant with 500 m^2 brand new kitchens. Pictures of celebrities, in black and white version, who stayed in Hôtel Majestic Barrière, adorn the flat surfaces and accompany you during your meals which sublimate the Mediterranean specialties.

LE JARDIN

15, avenue Isola Bella
✆ +33 (0)4 93 38 17 85

Open all year. Daily for lunch from 12pm to 2pm and for dinner from 7.30pm. Closed for dinner. Except for groups: daily special, à la carte, fixed rate formulas and menu. From April to end of October, à la carte, wood fired pizza, salads, pasta, skewers and grilled meats and fish on the wood fire...

Le Jardin is mainly known by regulars . And it is for a good reason, the entrance is on the same level as the bar leading to a large garden and a winter lush garden beautifully lit up at night hidden in a side street behind the façade. The setting has rich colours, very relaxing which is one of the advantages and assets of this restaurant somewhat isolated from the central Cannes. As for the cuisine, the complete and attractive menu offers simple dishes made from fresh, seasonal ingredients. You will probably find your happiness in this haven of peace with a warm welcome that will seduce you.

LE JARDIN SECRET

2, rue des Frères
✆ +33 (0)4 93 38 72 63
lejardin.secretcannes@gmail.com

Closed from November to March. Low season: open Wednesday to Saturday from 7pm to midnight. High season: Monday to Saturday from 7pm to midnight. Tapas between €12 and €20.

This unusual restaurant located in the charming historic district of Le suquet in Cannes promises culinary discoveries for those in search of new flavours. An original decor, a bit vintage, composed of antique objects and greenery, sit in the lovely inner courtyard, safe from prying, to enjoy a regressive cuisine. The tapas dishes are generous and tasty. For the sweet touch, a plethora of pretty desserts are feast. Homemade with fresh ingredients. The reception and service is friendly and relaxed.

LUCI SERA

5, rue Batéguier
✆ +33 (0)4 89 89 14 48
www.lucisera.fr
contact@lucisera.com

Open every evening on reservation (except Sunday off season). À la carte: Around €30 (starters around €8. Dishes around €22. Dessert €10). Terrace. Valet.

Just behind the Croisette, this restaurant offers an authentic italian cuisine. The elegant and refined decor is an invitation to intimate gourmet breaks. Bruschetta, grilled peppers, linguine with clams, tagliatelle with vegetables, veal cutlet a la Milanese, stuffed sardines, roasted squids, and also the unmissable transalpine desserts like the tiramisù or panna cotta. Important note: the carte evolves according to the seasons, to cook only with fresh ingredients. The wine list has been carefully selected to go with the main courses. An address of charm!

LA MAISON CORSE
11, rue de la Miséricorde
✆ +33 (0)9 67 81 07 47
lamaisoncorse@outlook.com
Open all year. Tuesday to Sunday from 9.30am to 2pm and from 6.30pm to midnight; Sunday from 9.30am to 2.30pm. À la carte: Around €17 (dish).
In the heart of the old Cannes Le Suquet, sit at table, have a drink while enjoying a typically Corsican dish: stew of wild boar, figatelli, veal lasagnes, lentils with Corsican sausage, fiadone... Here, the products are authentic, of quality, and directly imported from Corsica. Enough to enchant your tastebuds for a delicious moment with flavours of the South. As for the delicatessen side, you'll find artisanal products which make the identity of the Corsican gastronomy: farm charcuterie, cheeses or prepared dishes without forgetting good bottles as well as other specialties to (Re) discover. Buon appetitu!

LA MOME
6, impasse Florian
✆ +33 (0)6 30 04 51 68
✆ +33 (0)4 93 38 60 95
www.lamomecannes.com
contact@lamomecannes.com
Open every day from 7.30pm to 0h30. À la carte: Around €60 (starter up to €36, main course up to €54, dessert up to €16).
In a chic and trendy decor with bright colours, you're comfortably seated on velvet armchairs to enjoy original Mediterranean dishes. From the burrata accompanied by market vegetables and truffle cream via braised octopus or the tagliata of beef fillet to the creamy waffle chantilly and Nutella and biscuit with lemon, you'll appreciate the flavours and the quality of products that are finely prepared. La Môme can also prepare all your events: cocktail, dinner buffet, full or partial privatization, local DJ... The service is excellent, always welcoming whatever the period. Congratulations!

LE 360°
Radisson Blu hotel and thalasso Cannes
2, boulevard Jean-Hibert
✆ +33 (0)4 92 99 73 10
www.restaurant-le-360.com
Open all year. Every day from 12.30pm to 2pm and from 7pm to 10pm. Booking advised. À la carte: Around €35. Wine by the glass. Daily menu for lunch: starter and main course or main course and dessert: €32 or starter + main course + dessert = €42. Daily menu for dinner: starter + main course + dessert: €50. Menu Discovery (for dinner): €79. American Express. Groups welcome. Terrace. Valet.
The restaurant nestled on the terrace of the hotel offers a double satisfaction, the pleasure of the eyes, and certainly the most beautiful circular view of Cannes, which goes from the Esterel to the tip of the Croisette, via the port, the Lérins islands and the old town and the delight of your tastebuds with Mediterranean cuisine of chef Reynald Thivet at the service of well-being: lobster gratinée with girolles and hazelnuts, scallop carpaccio, rolled sole saltimboca way, large roasted pork chop, or the vegetable wok with soy sauce. The Chef's dish is the bass in salt crust, a wonder! To end your meal deliciously, try the chocolate-orange fondant with vanilla ice cream.

BELLA STORIA
51, rue Félix-Faure
✆ +33 (0)4 93 39 03 95 / +33 (0)6 13 45 03 25
www.bellastoria-cannes.fr
«Maître Restaurateur» label. Open all year. Every day from 12pm to 2.30pm and from 7pm to 10.30pm. Booking advised. Menu from €18 to €30. Children's menu: €10. Daily special: €13 (daily special + drink + coffee, Monday to Friday). Wine by the glass. American Express, Chèque Restaurant. Groups welcome. Terrace. Take-away.
At Bella Storia, italian cuisine is sublimated. Nothing astonishing knowing that this restaurant is the property of the Foppiani family which also offers an Italian catering at 31 rue Meynadier for all your events. You'll find on the menu of the restaurant a large choice of fresh raviolis but also lasagnas, stuffed vegetables, risotto as well as a wide range of fish and meats. In summer, you can also have pizzas. As for the desserts, you can enjoy tiramisù, panna cotta, creme brulee or special chocolate fondant and its vanilla ball inside, the whole is homemade. Delizioso!

GASTON & GASTOUNETTE
6-7, quai Saint-Pierre
✆ +33 (0)4 93 39 49 44
gastongastounette@orange.fr
Open daily for lunch and dinner. Booking advised. Lunch menu: €27.50 (starter, main course, dessert. Starter, main course or main course, dessert at 22,50€). Evening menu: €40. Groups welcome (reception seminars). Terrace. Air conditioning.
Gaston & Gastounette is a real institution in Cannes with its unusual setting for lunch breaks. This restaurant particularly dedicated to seafood has built the reputation of this area in Cannes opposite the old port. You are seated in a large chic and colourful setting with a modern and baroque spirit – painted walls, chandeliers, round convivial tables with white tablecloths, benches and armchairs in iridescent violet. The menu presents regional specialities like the bourride, the bouillabaisse, fried food, fish in salt crust. crispy cod with tapenade chantilly or kidney flambés. These copious and tasty meals has made for a long time the reputation of the place open for business or family meals.

L'ASSIETTE PROVENCALE
9, quai Saint-Pierre
✆ +33 (0)4 93 38 52 14
www.assiette-provencale.fr
contact@assiette-provencale.fr
Open daily for lunch and dinner. Menu from €25 to €30. À la carte: Around €25 (starter around €17, main course around €25, dessert around €10). Wine by the glass. Terrace.
The tables on the terrace have a new pleasant setting created along the Old Port. The chalkboards on the bright walls of the dining room – with a honey flooring and dark or pearl grey chairs - show the dishes mainly turned towards the sea: homemade fish soup with its rouille and croutons, wolffish fillet à la plancha, roasted codfish and its squash pumpkin gratin, whole fish from the market with flavours from the Mediterranean shrub. A range of starters and meats will suit every taste in this restaurant where black and white portraits of great French actors give a nostalgic and artistic touch; these echo the neat culinary work and the respect of the products.

TABLE 22
22, rue Saint-Antoine
✆ +33 (0)4 93 39 13 10 / +33 (0)6 61 70 49 53
www.restaurantmantel.com
Castles & hotels collection. Culinary college of France. Open for dinner Tuesday to Sunday and for lunch Thursday to Sunday. Menu from €35 to €60. À la carte: Around €70 (main course around €40). Small salted and sweetened plates from €4 to €10. American Express. Charter Sea quality of Lérins 2015. Groups welcome.
Noël Mantel, old of mobility Fair, is a culinary reference resident of Cannes which it is useless to present to an initiated public. Recently, it transformed the name and the concept of its restaurant nested in the middle of this swarming street of world which goes up towards the heights of Suquet to propose there a Mediterranean "street food" (onion, donuts of zucchini flowers, or pie lemon-yellow) in a resolutely contemporary decor. More accessible prices which do not prevent the chef from continuing to decline a more elaborate à la carte with the Mediterranean colors which evolves with the season of the Forville market located

The boulevard de la Croisette, Cannes.

near: squid fricassée juice emulsified with the ink juice, risotto cooked with Italian with ceps and juice of veal, Saint-Pierre to the lemon grass, loin of lamb roasted with thyme and garlic confit, braised and frozen veal shank. The reception of Brenda Mantel is charming and the very professional service of the team in room.

Sleeping

BEST WESTERN CANNES RIVIERA & SPA

16, boulevard d'Alsace
✆ +33 (0)4 97 06 20 40
www.cannesriviera.com

Open all year. 61 rooms (and 5 suites). Single room from €94; double room from €102; suite from €153. Buffet breakfast: €17. Garage: €19 (private and closed). Accepted payments Visa, Union Pay, JCB. American Express, Diners Club. 3 accessible rooms for disabled people. Seminars. Receptions and weddings. Internet access. Free Wifi. Satellite TV. Spa.

The face of Marilyn Monroe is portrayed on the facade of this hotel, bystanders cannot miss it! Mythical, when you are at the entrance of the town of Cannes, it recalls us that we are in the city of the cinema where this hotel can accommodate visitors with warmth and elegance. The rooms are magnificently comfortable and the contemporary and refined decoration is an invitation to spend very pleasant stays. The hotel also has a lobby and a English library-style bar, as well as a large canopy for the breakfast room and a spa. On the roof, you can relax by the swimming pool while enjoying the magnificent panoramic view. Unquestionably, Best Western Cannes Riviera is the right address for couples, between friends or with family.

L'ANCIENNE LAITERIE

18, avenue Sainte-Marguerite
✆ +33 (0)6 71 00 54 84 / +33 (0)4 93 47 02 33
www.lanciennelaiterie-cannes.com
lanciennelaiterie@gmail.com

Open all year. Apartment 1 room from €90 to €170 per night. Superior apartment 1 room from €120 to €205. Loft suite from €135 to €230. Parking: €7/day. Animals free. Minimum stay 2 nights. Pets allowed. Free Wifi.

This is an unusual but very attractive place. The four duplex and two lofts are located in a former dairy farm of 1880 in La Bocca, 300 metres away from the sea. Everything is brand new and the charming owner Valérie has renovated this small complex with much taste and originality with a design combining original decoration and a high quality service (DVD player, Wi Fi, iPhone station). The loft is incredible as there is a subtle blend of recycled unusual objects and also "design". The place also has an outdoor terrace, an on-site private parking and a fully equipped kitchen. There is a bus and train station nearby. In brief we just love the place. Please note that you can hire the whole place.

LE CAVENDISH

11, boulevard Carnot
✆ +33 (0)4 97 06 26 00
www.cavendish-cannes.com

Closed from December to March. Reception 24/24 (spoken languages: French, English, Italian, Russian). 34 rooms (certain smokers). Double room from €105; suite from €195. Buffet breakfast: €20. Garage: €25. Checks are not accepted. American Express, Diners Club. Free Wifi. Cleaning service. Canal+. Bar offered for the guests of the hotel from 6pm to 9pm. Excursions on request.

This charming "boutique hotel" is located in a residence dating from the 19th century, down Carnot Boulevard the main boulevard of the Cinema Capital city. This innovative concept is based on discreet service and on a luxurious setting for a "human scale" stay. The 34 spacious white-washed rooms reveal a sweet and refined Provençal atmosphere with lilac, olive green, sky-blue and mimosa yellow tints. The four rooms nestled in the Belle Epoque rotunda display a very particular charm.

The noble furniture goes with the modern top-class equipment. The owners Christine and Guy Welter, receive each client as a privileged guest. Note that the bus which links to Nice airport, stops right in front of the hotel (Place Vauban stop) and a partnership with a private beach allows you to get a free mattress if you stay for at least 3 nights if you book on the website or directly at the hotel.

FIVE SEAS HOTEL CANNES
1, rue Notre-Dame
✆ +33 (0)4 63 36 05 05
✆ +33 (0)4 63 36 05 19
www.five-seas-hotel-cannes.com

Closed from December 12th to January 24th. Reception 24/24 (spoken languages: French, English, Italian, Russian, German). 45 rooms (100% non smoker, half being suites). Single room from €148; suite up to €1,110. Buffet breakfast: €35. Closed parking: €35 (per day). American Express. Pets allowed. Seminars. Receptions and weddings. Internet corner. Free Internet access. Free Wifi. Cleaning service. Restaurant Sea Sens 1 Michelin star. Delicacies corner Intuitions By J by Jerome de Oliveira, world champion of pastry. Product sales. Satellite TV. Hammam, whirlpool, sauna. Activities. Spa By Cinq Mondes and Carita. 1 yacht at disposal for your cruises and private parties.

The spirit of motionless voyage is present in this unusual hotel. Each object brought back from all corners of the world, each painting in the lobby or each furniture reminding of the great travel trunks is an invitation to an escapade which goes up to the Cinq Mondes and Carita spa or from the swimming pool on the roof terrace which offers a stunning view of the Suquet. Travel is still an omnipresent theme at the Sea Sens. The menu designed by Arnaud Tabarec, new Michelin star chef, honours faraway dishes. Finally, the gourmet lounge Intuitions By J where you will give into the sweet treats of Jérôme de Oliveira – world champion of pastries – is the last curiosity. It is definitely a unique experience.

© LAWRENCE BANAHAN – AUTHOR'S IMAGE

Beach along side La Croisette.

OKKO HOTEL
6, place de la Gare
✆ +33 (0)4 92 98 30 30
http://cannescentre.okkohotels.com

Open all year. Reception 24/24. Double room from €90 to €300. Buffet breakfast included. Free Wifi. Satellite TV. Sauna.

The Cannes Train Station has been transformed in a few months, it is now all in white. This revival comes with the arrival of a new brand: the OKKO Cannes hotel. It is elegantly integrated in the neighbourhood of the station. You'll enter it by a rather discrete entrance and a lift which leads you to the 6th floor to the luminous reception.

The concept of the OKKO group is resolutely modern and generous: an «all inclusive» offer. It integrates the room obviously, but also the buffet breakfast, the wi-fi, on-demand movie and even the small snacks to nibble during the day to finish by the Italian aperitif (with antipasti and wine bar). The idea is simple but it must had been found! After the check in at the reception, you enter a VIP space, a bit like an airport lounge in business class. This space located on the 6th floor is very vast (300 m^2) and has an attractive view on the roofs of Cannes and a pleasant terrace. It is a true place of life where to have breakfast, or work in the business corner or rest on a sofa... or even for the aperitif in the evening.... In short, you feel like home. The rooms resemble each other: 18 m^2, very functional and nicely designed. The rates are very competitive and especially without surprises because no extra charge. A great success which combines freedom and conviviality.

HOTEL FESTIVAL
3, rue Molière
✆ +33 (0)4 97 06 64 40
www.hotel-festival.com
infos@hotel-festival.com

Open all year. Reception 24/24 (spoken languages: French, English, Italian, Spanish). 14 rooms (100% non smoker). Single room from €69 to €159; double room from €89 to €189; triple room from €150 to €220. Breakfast: €9.80 (served in room). American Express. Pets allowed (on request and with supplement). Receptions and weddings. Internet corner. Free Internet access. Free Wifi. Cleaning service. Spa. Whirlpool, sauna. Public parking paying 50 m from the hotel.

The Festival hotel is cozy and charming although it is located in the middle of the town (reception upstairs of a building). It offers a quiet and intimate atmosphere to live a perfect «cocooning». The recently renovated rooms are spacious, decorated differently and well equipped so as you enjoy a nice stay (air-conditioning, wi-fi, flat screen TV, marble bathroom...) The other highlight of the hotel is the spa with hot tub and sauna at guest's disposal with no extra charge. Massages are offered on request and booking. You will undoubtedly be pampered here whatever the reason of your stay, business or leisure.

HÔTEL MOLIÈRE

5, rue Molière
✆ +33 (0)4 93 38 16 16
www.hotel-moliere.com
reception@hotel-moliere.com

Closed from December 15th to April 1st. Reception 24/24 (spoken languages: French, English, Italian, German). 24 rooms (100 % non smoker, balcony for smokers). Single room from €90 to €130; double room from €120 to €240. Breakfast: €11 (continental). Extra bed: €20. Pets allowed (5 to €10). Free Wifi. Cleaning service.

This fully renovated hotel offers a moment of serenity in a chic and green setting. Rooms are uncluttered and warm, most of them have a balcony and a view over the garden and have all the necessary comfort (air conditioning, WiFi, LCD TV...). Apart from its ideal location, right in the city centre, only 100 m away from the Croisette and the Palais des Festivals, the hotel has a pleasant garden, where you can relax and have your breakfast under the rays of Cannes sun. Combining serenity and elegance, this establishment corresponds to all types of stays: romantic, in family, with friends or business. Up to you to choose!

HOTEL SPLENDID

4-6, rue Félix-Faure
✆ +33 (0)4 97 06 22 22
www.splendid-hotel-cannes.com
contact@splendid-hotel-cannes.com

Open all year. Reception 24/24. 62 rooms. Double room from €88. Breakfast: €19 (buffet served in the breakfast room and on the terrace – €14 continental served in the room). Extra bed: €30. Rooms and facilities for disabled guests, ask for information by telephone. Pets allowed. Seminars. Receptions and weddings. Free Internet access. Free Wifi.

The Splendid displays its elegant early century architecture above the famous alleys of plane trees facing the old port of Cannes. The terraces and balconies of the 62 rooms of this small palace offers the prettiest and most authentic scenery of Cannes with the area of Suquet in the background. Its central position is ideal to enjoy the long summer evenings in the city centre, on the Croisette or by the sea. The absolute comfort, ancient refined furniture and sophisticated equipment complete the «familial house spirit» of this hotel renowned as one of the most beautifuls gems of Cannes hotels.

Leisure

TAHITIAN ADVENTURE

✆ +33 (0)6 60 08 02 72
www.tahitian-adventure.fr

Open from 9am to 7pm. Reservations on the site. Coastline discovery €40 per person. Checks are not accepted.

You are invited to experience a coastal discovery on a Polynesian pirogue with family or between friends. Accompanied by a guide, thanks to this original means of transport for the French Riviera with a slender hull linked to a side beam by two wooden arms, that you will explore, paddles in hands, the wealth of the region, creeks, islands... Five tours are offered: Cap d'Antibes, îles de Lérins, Pointe de l'Aiguille in Théoule-sur-Mer, the île des Vieilles near Anthéor and further on, towards the peninsula of Saint-Tropez, cap Taillat, located between the Lardier and Camarat caps. Breakfast or aperitive breaks are also planned.

Going Out

LE BAR À VIN

10, rue Marceau
✆ +33 (0)6 23 73 44 43

Open Monday to Saturday. Open from 6pm to 2am. Terrace. Catering facilities.

The amateurs and connoisseurs of good wines will be welcomed in this intimate place in a subdued and cool atmosphere to choose among a large variety of french and international wines . The Epicureans seated on high stools, in armchairs beneath the flat screen or at the tables on the mezzanine upstairs for a cosy pause accompany their drink with cheese or antipasti platters offered on the board.

BARISTA

6, rue Tesseire
✆ +33 (0)4 93 38 17 92

Annual closing 15 days in November. Open Monday to Saturday from 8am to 7.30pm. Choice of buckwheat pancake + a cider bowlful €10. Terrace.

The Barista is a restaurant and an "Espresso bar". It seduces by the dishes which it offers and by its cafe, a favourite of the connoisseurs. The restaurant offers in the morning a breakfast menu with orange juice, fancy pastries, toasts and hot drink. For lunch and up to 3.00 p.m., it's salads and pastas. Then, it's time for wafers and pancakes for the pleasure of the gourmets. Everything is made of fresh products. A very modern setting for this restaurant where it feels good to stop at whatever time of the day. They always welcome you warmly and the atmosphere is very pleasant.

MORRISON' S IRISH PUB

10, rue Teisseire
✆ +33 (0)4 92 98 16 17

Open Monday to Friday from 5pm to 2am; weekends from 12pm to 2am. Activities. Concerts.

Festive atmosphere, this pub in Cannes reminds us those you can find in Ireland. It has a typical decor of Anglo-Saxon pubs – predominant wood- and is the place to be for festive and cool evenings with friends. This place, impossible to circumvent for the nightlife in Cannes, is mainly attended by anglophones who come for live Irish or blues and rock concerts. Sports lovers never miss events broadcasted on giant screen (football, rugby, golf...).

MORRISON' S LOUNGE

8, rue Teisseire
✆ +33 (0)4 92 98 16 17

Open Monday to Friday from 5pm to 2am.

The most famous pub of Cannes declined into a lounge version, for relaxed trendy evenings. To the soft noise of clinking pints added to those of the cocktails on a lounge, electro, house music atmosphere, from Tuesday to Saturday. In a different atmosphere than the pub, you'll relax with the DJ, in a filtered and elegant decor. .

THE QUAY'S IRISH PUB

17, quai Saint-Pierre
✆ +33 (0)4 93 39 27 84

Open Monday to Friday from 4pm to 2am; weekends from 12pm to 2am. Terrace.

A very nice place with view of the Cannes old port, the pub displays a friendly atmosphere! The prices are affordable and beer flows non-stop on a *live music* background especially on Thursdays and Fridays for very friendly evenings. Guaranteed change of scenery for this unmissable rendezvous for Anglo-Saxons!

La Croisette

MA NOLAN'S IRISH PUB CANNES

6, rue Buttura ✆ +33 (0)4 93 68 10 82
www.ma-nolans.com
info@ma-nolans.com

Open every day from 11am to 2am. Terrace. Catering facilities. Animations. Concerts.

Near the Palais des Festivals et des Congrès, this is the third establishment on the French Riviera (after those of Nice cours Saleya and the port) dedicated to mom Nolan and created in the city of the international film festival in October 2012. A place to enjoy Irish beers or whiskeys and to eat throughout the day in a pub atmosphere of Dublin or Cork. It is also a place to watch sports events broadcasted on a large screen, attend live concerts and test your knowledge at the quiz, twice a week, to win lots of vouchers to order at the bar.

Shopping

One of the best cities for Shopping, Cannes offers the largest concentration of luxury shops per square meter in France! If the brands in la Croisette and the «Cannes Shopping Festival» fulfill the fashion addict, all tastes and all budgets will be satisfied in the fashion and accessories boutiques mainly concentrated in Antibes Street. Most picturesque and popular, Meynadier street regroups mostly foodcourts while the market of Forville exibits its stalls every morning from Tuesday to Saturday in a picturesque atmosphere.

Rue Meynadier: an air of gourmet village...

In the middle of Cannes, the pedestrian street Meynadier perpetuates a village-spirit amid brands that are mainly dedicated to food: caterers, fishmongers, cheese-seller, delicatessens, butchers, chocolate-maker are listed on a typical path to fulfill our market-basket and to prepare our meals. Morning walks during weekends have a gourmet aspect and a joyful and active atmosphere in this section of Cannes where the buds definitely outweigh the glitz atmosphere.

PASTRY CHOCOLATE SHOP PHILIPPE BRITO

79, avenue du Maréchal-Juin
✆ +33 (0)4 93 94 43 48
www.philippebrito.com

Open Tuesday to Saturday from 8am to 1pm and from 4pm to 7pm; Sunday from 8am to 1pm. Terrace.

It is in the basse Californie area that Philippe Brito, active member of the Union of the craftsmen pastry chefs, chocolate makers, confectioners, ice-cream makers of the Alpes-Maritimes holds his beautiful shop. Bright and modern, with his coulourful creations under beautiful windows. The most gourmet will have the choice: preciousnesses, macaroons, cakes, chocolates, pastries... Creations are original: «with simple materials the pastry can be rich not only in flavours but also in colors. Rediscover textures, play with flavors, be astonished by the forms, such is the creed of this family craft business». You can enjoy these softnesses on the lovely suuny terrace with a cup of tea, a hot chocolate, or a top of a range Alain Miliat fruit juice, or take them away.

LES ÉLEVEURS GASTRONOMES

14, place du marché Forville
✆ +33 (0)4 93 38 03 65
www.roger-junca.com
boutique.cannes@excelfoiegras.fr

♿

Open Monday to Saturday from 8am to 1pm and from 4pm to 7pm; Sunday from 8.30am to 1pm. Parkings nearby. American Express.

The gastronomes farmer Excel perpetuates the tradition of Roger Junca, creator of a delicatessen in Dax in 1949, by inviting you to share their unique culinary heritage, which sublimes flavours with duck foie gras from the Southwest. On site, delicatessen and snacks allow you to buy and enjoy a range of whole half-cooked «Label Rouge» IGP Landes foie gras, recipe with fleur de sel or canned as well as Southwest specialties and duck: aiguillettes, thighs, sleeves, chops, duck, duck tournedos, grilled duck, smoked duck breast, neck, terrines, mousse, pies, sausages, rillettes and another confit.

Guided tour of the Fort royal and the prison of the Iron Mask

State prison under the reign of Louis XIV, the jails of Fort Royal (completed by Vauban in 1637) have shelted one of the most famous prisoners in the history of France, "the man with the iron mask" whose identity has never been established despite the sixty assumptions and many legends. He stayed 12 years (1687-1698) under the supervision of Monsieur de Saint- Mars, then governor of the fort. An important prisoner, held in secret, he still raises a thousand interpretations. Many characters were mentioned: Fouquet (former Superintendent of Finance), Louis de Bourbon biological son of Louis XIV, an elder half-brother of Louis XIV, a twin brother kept away from the succession... From June to September, free guided tours of the fort are offered by young guides who welcome visitors on the island from the landing quay and distribute leaflets and all the practical information needed to discover the places. From the terrace of the fortress, do not miss the wide view that opens on the coastline.

■ **BARBARAC**
4, rue Félix-Faure ✆ +33 (0)4 97 06 55 51
High season: open every day from 9.30am and until 1am.
Change of name and of owner for this coloured window, a long time attached to a famous ice-cream shop in Saint Tropez. On the lively rue Félix Faure, Gelato Junkie will enjoy you with its homemade ice-creams, elaborated with fresh and natural ingredients, which are declined in multiple flavours, from the classical to the most original. Milkshakes, granites, in a pot or horn, for all the tastes. Special mention for the low-fat ice creams, ideal for pleasure without feeling guilty!

■ **LA MAISON CORSE**
11, rue de la Miséricorde
✆ +33 (0)9 67 81 07 47
lamaisoncorse@outlook.com
Open Tuesday to Sunday from 9.30am to 2pm and from 6.30pm to midnight; Sunday from 9.30am to 2.30pm.
The owner will welcome you with a smile in this charming delicatessen settled in the heart of the old Cannes Le Suquet. He will accommodate you and help you in the choice of your dishes, or will install you at a table for a drink, accompanied by a typically Corsican plate. All the products come directly from Corsica and will enchant your tastebuds. In the shop, you will find all the artisanal products which make the identity of the Corsican gastronomy, the farm charcuterie, cheeses, the simmered dishes, good bottles as well as other specialties to be discovered. Enjoy the mix of flavours, stew of wild boar, veal lasagne, lentils with Corsican sausage, fiadone. A dopu, é, buon appetitu!

In the surroundings

Lérins islands

Sainte-Maguerite

3 km long, 900 m wide, 180 ha of pine forests and eucalyptus. The island is crossed by broad avenues that intersect and join the walkway that goes around, following the rather rocky coastline, but which has many small discrete coves for swimming – it is also nice in the channel between the two islands. We cross a path lined with giant eucalyptus – where migratory birds can be found in season – and we follow a botanical trail marked with Mediterranean species, arranged by the National Office of Forests. Guided tours on request for this touristic and ecological path (the office is located near the landing-post). An oppidum (fortified city) was once there at the current location of the fort, was completed by Vauban in 1637. The prison housed famous prisoners and a legendary one «the Man with the Iron Mask.» An area full of history, Sainte Marguerite offers moments of pure relaxation. From the Pointe du Dragon, do not miss a breath-taking panorama of Cannes to Anthéor.

Stays within the community

The Community of Lérins opens its monastery section to men who wish to deepen their faith or confirm their vocation. These stays of 8 days minimum take place within the monastery sharing the daily life of the monks. Retreats that are open to all, without any particular ecclesiastical vocation, are also possible in the «hotel area» reserved for spiritual retreats; stays of one week maximum available to people who are looking for a place to relax and enjoy the silence. We can participate in the liturgical prayers and meals are taken in common.

Informations : www.abbayedelerins.com

MUSÉE DE LA MER ★★★

Île Sainte-Marguerite
✆ +33 (0)4 89 82 26 26
Laubeuf parking – Piers: Quai Laubeuf

Pier and parking: quai Laubeuf. Closed public holidays and every Monday. Open from October to March from 10.30am to 1.15pm and from 2.15pm to 4.45pm. Open from April to May from 10.30am to 1.15pm and from 2.15pm to 5.45pm. Open 7 days a week from June to September from 10am to 5.45pm. Free 1st Sunday of each month from November to March included, - 18 years, students - 26 years. Adult: €6. Reduced rate €3 (- 25 years, Resident of Cannes with written proof, groups starting from 10 people). Workshops for the 7 to 13 years all year, in school period, Wednesday and Saturday. Guided tour. Shop.

This museum occupies the oldest part of the Royal Fort of St. Margaret's on one of the two Lérins Islands. This Historical Monument site houses Roman cisterns in which underwater archaeology objects are exposed including a Roman and Saracen wreck found near the island. Ceramics, vases, jars and glasses are exposed on the first floor where you will discover fragments of Roman wall paintings from land excavations of Sainte-Marguerite as well as a reconstruction of the laconicum. In the State prison section, you will discover the cell of the Iron Mask. Finally, there is a section dedicated to temporary exhibitions of photographs. Do not miss the breathtaking view from the large terrace overlooking the prison that extends from Esterel to Cap d'Antibes.

Saint-Honorat

The small island of Saint Honorat belongs to the Cistercian monks of the Abbey of Lérins who exploit the natural resources since its founding in the 5th century by Saint Honorat. Many bishops came from this abbey and all have given their name to towns in Provence: Saint Cassien, St. Aigulf, Saint -Vallier. The actual church was rebuilt in 1880 on the site of the old abbey. The community cultivates vines and plants with which they make liquor «the Lérina.» They also produce excellent wines exported worldwide. Visits of this green jewel, ideal for meditation are highly regulated because of heritage. The fortified tower located at the southern tip, classified as historical monument, is the vestige of a defensive military structure of the 12th century to protect the island from invasion. From the top of the tower, the view is wonderful. The fortified monastery is one of the finest examples of feudal architecture in Provence. We can make a retreat for a few days and share the monastic life to find the slow pace of serenity. Information at the Abbey.

MONASTÈRE ET ABBAYE NOTRE-DAME-DE-LÉRINS ★★★

Ile Saint-Honorat
✆ +33 (0)4 92 99 54 24
www.abbayedelerins.com
info@abbayedelerins.com

Lérins abbey funded in the 410's on the Saint-Honorat island, is one of the oldest abbeys in the Occident. Inhabited now by a community of Cistercian monks of various nationalities, the areas where the community lives are not accessible to the public, except on local heritage days. However, the monastery-tower is open to the visit all year long: this impressive medieval keep, by the sea, which construction started in the late 11th century, and where lived monks from 1392 to 1788, is the first building in Alpes-Maritimes to be listed historical monument (in 1840). The abbatial church is open to the public as well. Taking part in liturgical prayers and attending the Mass with the monks are possible all year long, whereas individual or collective spiritual retreats at the abbaye hostelry are suggested in any season except in November. Monks grow 8 ha of vines and 150 olive trees on the island, and distil many liqueurs, especially the famous *Lerina*, which secret recipe is pass from generation to generation. You will find liqueurs, olive oil and red or white wines produced by the monks in the abbey shops or on line.

Ovens to redden fire balls...

A curiosity that can be seen on the Saint-Honorat Island: 4 ovens to redden fire balls dating from 1794 built at the instigation of Napoleon. The fire balls reddened by fire burned the wings and wooden decks of vessels. He would remain in France only a dozen ovens, including four on Saint-Honorat Island.

LE CANNET ★★★

Sightseeing

BONNARD MUSEUM ★

16, boulevard Sadi-Carnot
✆ +33 (0)4 93 94 06 06
www.museebonnard.fr
♿

Open Tuesday to Sunday. From 10am to 6pm from beginning of October to end of May (Thursday night until 9pm). From 10am to 8pm from beginning of June to end of September (Thursday night until 9pm). Closed on Monday and January 1st, May 1st, November 1st and December 25th. Full rate €5 (€7 during the temporary exhibitions). Reduced rate €3.50 (€5 during the temporary exhibitions). Guided tour (audioguide adult and young people €3). Shop. Activities. Terrace-garden. A unique museum in the world pays tribute to the painter Pierre Bonnard in a building labelled «Musée de France». The collections are spread on three exhibition levels on a surface area of 900 m^2 divided between a Belle Époque villa and a contemporary extension which also gathers vast spaces, a shop, a teaching room, a projection room and a terrace overlooking a beautiful garden. Each room is equipped with cards allowing visitors to better understand the works presented, from the Nabi movement to the construction of a personal and complex world. A multimedia audio guide is also available in several languages (paid), with a version suitable for young people.

Le Cannet and joy for life

Responding to its prime location, to its tranquillity and to the wide panorama that opens from the old core to the bay of Cannes and the Esterel mountains, the town of Cannet has decided to celebrate the pleasure of living and the colours magnified by the Riviera artist Tobiasse whose permanent exhibition can be discovered in the Saint-Sauveur chapel called "Life is a party" in the historic district of Old-Cannet (free entry). In the City Hall, former "Hotel des Anges", the hall which is the most visited is the wedding hall called «Bellini Hall» where you can see five works of the painter Emmanuel Bellini representing the joy of living in Le Cannet. Another symbol of the joy of life: the Wall of lovers of Peynet, honorary citizen of the town of Cannet who made this work in honour of all newlyweds. The fresco painted on the wall of an old house in Old-Cannet depicts newlyweds who fly above the Garden of Eden inspired by the town of Cannet.

Knife & Fork

TIVOLI

25, boulevard Sadi-Carnot
✆ +33 (0)4 93 45 42 73
brasserietivolicannet@gmail.com

Open all year. Tuesday to Friday from 8am to 10pm. Saturdays from 9am to 10pm. Monday from 8am to 4pm. Closed on Sunday. Iberian pork-butchery, black pig of Bigorre: tapas from €6.50. Daily special: €15.50 (to €17). Spanish sardines, Portuguese and Spanish tin-cans from €8.50. Cheese plate from €11: Mons cheese factory. Starter around €15. Meats around €24. Fresh fish around €24. Checks are not accepted. American Express, Chèque Restaurant. Terrace. Shop. Since June 2016, Christopher Vuillemin, sommelier, and Frédéric Roy, owner and former michelin-starred chef took over this unavoidable address of Cannet. Opposite the town hall and Musee Bonnard, the restaurant- bistro- wine bar Tivoli has refreshed by now offering a very wide range of wines carefully selected (author wines, worked in biodynamic, organic such as The domaine de la Réatière, Pierre Micheland, Chateau Revelette, Peter Fischer as Coteaux of Aix or Jean-François Ganevat for Côte du Jura...) that you can enjoy at any time on the sunny terrace or in the indoor room dedicated to the world of wine. To go with these 180 champagne and wine references, let yourself be tempted by some snails, Gillardeau oysters... a charcuterie plate before choosing fish or meat, and of course, finally, a dessert of the day. The menu also offers daily specials nicely prepared by the chef who creates a market cuisine according to the seasons.

VILLA ARCHANGE

Rue de l'Ouest ✆ +33 (0)4 92 18 18 28
www.bruno-oger.com
reservation@bruno-oger.com
♿

Relais & Chateaux. Open all year. Tuesday to Saturday from 7pm to 10pm; Friday and Saturday from 12pm to 2pm. Booking advised. Menu from €68 to €210 (menu at €68 only for lunch. From €98 to €210 with food and wine pairing). À la carte: Around €130 (main course up to €130). Wine by the glass. Chèque Restaurant. Groups welcome (up to 26 people). Garden. Terrace. Take-away. 2 Michelin stars. Catering on order. Private parking of 50 places with dock of reversal for the buses.
The Villa Archange of Bruno Oger is located in one of the buildings of the Villa Notre-Dame-des-Anges. This property of the town dating from the 18th century and designed like a private house, comprises two lounges and opens on a shady inner courtyard ideal for summer dinners. If you are among the 26 privileged people to be seated there, you can enjoy a frog carpaccio and clams with mild garlic and yellow wine, a lemon-lemongrass wild sea bass, gambas tartar with coriander, a veal shank cooked during 24 hours, mashed potatoes with truffles, Brittany lobster ravioli with Petrossian caviar and a dessert like the great traou mad with roasted Victoria pineapple.

You have understood that you are in one of the greatest restaurants of the French Riviera and everything is necessarily great. The Villa Archange can also accommodate 8 guests for an exceptional moment in the kitchen at the table d'hôte.

Sleeping

LE RANCH
Aubarède
275, chemin Saint-Joseph
✆ +33 (0)4 93 46 00 11
www.leranchcamping.fr
info@leranchcamping.fr

Since 1956. Open from April 16th to October 15th. Front desk open from 9am to 12pm and from 2pm to 8pm. Booking advised. Land of 2 ha. Rates room: April 16th – July 5th and August 30th – October 15: €50 for 2 people, €60 for 3 people, €72 for 4 people, July 5th – August 30th and during the Film Festival of Cannes: €60 for €2. €72 for 3. €82 for 4 people. Week in bungalow from €250 in low season and from €450 in high season; cheaper rates. Campsites from €16 in low season and from €18 in high season. Holiday voucher. Children's club. Games for children. Bathroom for babies. Pets allowed (supplement €1). Area for camper van. Catering facilities (snack). Activities. Navette du Ranch downtown. Indoor swimming pool. Playground for children. Covered terrace. Table football, billiards. Distributors of cold and hot drinks. New: petanque field.
Just a few minutes from the sandy beaches of Cannes, the Ranch Campsite is a 3 star establishment that has welcomed its guests for 60 years. The bungalows, chalets, apartments, and campsites are located in a wooded, green and relaxing park. The asset of the campsite is a regular city bus service that takes guests to the centre of Cannes, day and night. In low season, the pool is covered and heated; in high season, the campsite organises weekly entertainment for all. Le Ranch Camping faces the communal domaine de La Croix des Gardes, for nature lovers, jogging or hiking. The hotel is 2 km from the beaches of Cannes and less than 4 km from the city centre. It is ideally located and allows thanks to public transportation to visit the most beautiful places of the French Riviera, the coastline like Cannes, Nice or Monaco and the back country including Grasse. In the surroundings, tennis courts, gym, fitness trail, provencal market and shopping centers.

MANDELIEU-LA-NAPOULE ★★★

Located at the far west of the Alpes-Maritimes, Mandelieu La Napoule is on the outskirts of the Esterel massif, offering landscapes of sea and wild nature, real features of this site surrounded by red rocks that contrasts with the azure blue of the Mediterranean. Once land of predilections of Russian and British aristocrats at the end of the 19th century, the town chose mimosa for symbol, originally from Australia which took root in the massifs of Tanneron and Esterel. This tree with yellow flowers commonly called "the winters sunshine" on French Riviera, is celebrated every year in February in Mandelieu. Today, its exploitation contains ten local mimosists as well as a hundred around the city. The town, major nautical pole received the label "nautical station" in 1987, also offers a wide range of leisure and sports activities: sailing, scuba diving, golf, rowing, water-skiing, parks for walks, parasailing, motonautism... With six ports, including two maritime, dry port and three river offers the largest capacity of pleasure in the department.
For amateurs, there are also many sites of walks: the natural park of San-Peyre, the natural park of l'Aiguille, and a portion of the GR51, crossing the city. Departure is in front of the San-Estello leisure park and the arrival of the port of Théoule.
You will also have the opportunity to visit the Lérins islands in just 30 minutes by boat, departing from the Aiguille pier.

The festival of the Mimosa

The mimosa which is called «the winter sun» is the emblem of the town. Every year in February is held the Mimosa Festival, great popular demonstration which lasts 10 days. The festivities fill the streets and give rise to numerous events: Election of the Queen of the Mimosa, shows, carnival parades, floats, parades and day and night flower-parades, battles of flowers, or even hikes in the mountains of Tanneron to discover the splendour of the mimosa, gold of the hills.

TOURIST OFFICE OF MANDELIEU-LA-NAPOULE
806, avenue de Cannes
✆ +33 (0)4 93 93 64 64
✆ +33 (0)4 93 93 64 66
www.ot-mandelieu.fr
accueil@ot-mandelieu.fr

Open Monday to Saturday from 9.30am to 12.30pm and from 2pm to 6pm; Sunday and public holidays from 9.30am to 1pm. From November to end of January, closes at 6pm and Sunday 10-13. July and August: on weekdays 9.30am to 1pm and 2.30pm to 6pm. Sunday and holiday closes at 5pm. Free Wifi. Tourism label & Disability. Qualité Tourisme label and Famille plus. Classified 4.*
Due to the quality of its services to visitors, this Tourism Office is rated 4 * and received the Tourisme & Handicap,

The departmental forest park of San Peyre

This 18-hectare park located in the town of Mandelieu-La-Napoule is a nature reserve where the Mediterranean forest is protected and maintained. The walk is a little more than four kilometres and takes about two hours and can be done both in summer and in winter. After parking your vehicle near the Château de la Napoule, it is possible to start the walk by skirting it. From there, you can reach the botanical trail over three kilometres on gentle slope that goes through the park-forest. Walkers discover the typical flora of the Mediterranean type, arbutus, mastic, cork oaks, a collection of mimosas, exotic plantations and even a mini garden of succulents. Mount San Peyre is a volcanic cone consisting of a base on which the lava of a huge volcano of the primary era spilled. We can continue the path that winds to the top of San Peyre thus amounting to 131 m height; we find there an observation table and discover a huge panorama over the sea, the Esterel and the Alps.

Qualité Tourisme and Famille Plus labels. It offers all types of services: accommodation reservations, all-inclusive packages, selection of activities and entertainment to suit your interests and your budget. Free wi-fi.

Knife & Fork

LE BISTROT DE LA RAGUE

Port of Rague
✆ +33 (0)4 93 49 93 48
bistrotdelarague@outlook.fr

Open all year. In low season: open daily for lunch, Monday to Sunday and for dinner, Friday to Sunday. In high season: open daily for lunch and dinner. Live music Friday evening. À la carte: Around €40. Charter quality Mer de Lérins 2015. Groups welcome (up to 80 people). Public parking nearby. Free wi-fi. Spoken languages: Dutch, English and German. Terrace on the waterfront.

Esther and Didier welcome you in their warm and family establishment. Ideally located on the port of La Rague on the waterside, come and taste the dishes inspired by fresh and local products of the market as well as fish and seafood specialties such as fish soup and its rouille sauce, or fresh and smoked tartare duo, the salmon steak with its lobster and basil sauce, pan-fried scallops with sweet wine... The welcome is friendly and smiling, and the masters of the place will do everything to make you spend an exceptional moment in an idyllic setting.

BISTROT L'ÉTAGE DE L'OASIS

6, rue Jean-Honoré-Carle
✆ +33 (0)4 93 49 95 52
www.oasis-raimbault.com
contact@oasis-raimbault.com

Annual closing from mid-December to mid-January. Open Tuesday to Saturday from 12pm to 2pm and from 7.30pm to 10pm. Booking advised. À la carte: Around €45. Fixed formula: €32 (starter, main course, dessert, excluding drinks, for lunch and dinner Tuesday to Saturday). Wine by the glass. Diners Club, Holiday voucher, Chèque Restaurant. Groups welcome. Car valet. Shop. Parking.

This restaurant of the Raimbault brothers with two Michelin stars, is unique for its value for money and numerous assets: car valet service and order taken especially by a sommelier between others. The success of the original concept of «bistronomie» – gourmet dishes served in the bistro – relies on the quality of the dishes served, the low prices of its formula, the numerous suggestions on the blackboard and the 26 tables made up of wine cases. We love the simple dishes revisited by the Raimbault brothers working in the kitchen of l'Oasis: Stéphane, Antoine and François. Try the jarred snails with croutons, the calf's head with Ravigote sauce, the pluma de pata negra, the bouillabaisse de Saint-Pierre or the crepe souffle with Grand Marnier.

L'UCCELLO

Hauts de Lérins
217, rue Laurent-Gandolphe
✆ +33 (0)4 93 49 66 18

♿

Open all year. Open every day from 12pm to 2pm and from 7pm to 9pm (11pm in high season). Booking advised. Menu from €21 to €30. À la carte: Around €30 (to €35). Lunch menu: €16.50 (main course and dessert + coffee or starter and main course + coffee). Wine by the glass. Set menu: starter + main course + dessert €18.50. Holiday voucher, Chèque Restaurant. Groups welcome. Terrace. Catering and chef at home for a buffet, a meal, a wedding, a birthday, a cocktail on the premises, take-away, on site of reception.

The terrace bordered with hints of plants and the bright spacious dining room accommodate you every day for your lunch break. You will taste a traditional French cuisine and more precisely Mediterranean with multiple influences throughout the world: wide choice of pizzas and focaccias, fresh pasta, tagines, woks... You will also find on the menu more refined dishes such as the prawns risotto with gorgonzola and Espelette peppers, Nice royal aïoli of cod, Nice real stuffed vegetables, candied lamb shank with Maquis AOP honey, wok of scallop with coconut milk, ginger and lemon grass, raviolis stuffed with ceps and olive oil juice with truffle, Mediterranean stuffed squids... And to finish with a sweet and gourmet touch, let yourself be seduced by the originality of the fresh fruit gratin with limoncello. This contemporary address is right next to the living center of Mandelieu, the Tourist Office and exhibition congress Center.

LA MANDARINE

18, rue de la Poste ✆ +33 (0)4 93 49 98 83

Open all year. From October 15th to May 31st: open for lunch and dinner from 12pm to 2pm and from 6.30pm to 10pm except Saturday and Sunday for lunch. From June 1st to October 14th: open every evening from 6.30pm to 10.30pm-11pm. Menu from €20.50 to €26.50. Daily special: €9.50. American Express. Take-away. Wifi.

This small, friendly and pleasant hotel is located in the narrow streets which invite you to a stroll close to La Napoule castle. The setting recreates a travel spirit in a warm atmosphere. The owner, a Dutchman will perfectly answer you in four languages. The food, also crosses the borders. You will find on the menu a great range of fish, beef carpaccios, ribbs, fajitas or the famous Mandarine salad. We suggest you the homemade tiramisu to end your meal.

THE OASIS

Rue Jean-Honoré-Carle ✆ +33 (0)4 93 49 95 52
www.oasis-raimbault.com

Relais et Chateaux. Closed from mid-December to mid-January. 2 Michelin stars since 1992. Grandes Tables of the World. Open Tuesday to Saturday from 12pm to 2pm and from 7.30pm to 10pm. Booking advised. Menu from €69 to €282 (excluding drinks). À la carte: Around €140. Wine by the glass. Groups welcome. Garden. Terrace. Valet. Shop. Parking.

The history of this prestigious starred restaurant goes back to 1954, when Louis Outhier fell in love with this house. Then the Raimbault brothers took over in 1991 and lead it to the stars. In their flower-filled patio, Stéphane and Antoine continue to enchant their guests with a cuisine with Asian and Mediterranean influences: oyster sushi with yuzu, sea water granite with Japanese flavours, raw fish from the rising sun souvenir of Osaka, rice salad with shiso and Chinese cabbage, the famous truffle of L'Oasis and its jelly with yellow wine, brown crust of sea bass, delicious tarragon, steamed endives and butter of sea urchin with lime, fillet of beef wagyu... As for François, the pastry chef, he satisfies the lovers of sweet treats with the unmissable caravan of pastries and desserts.

QUAI 06

161, rue Yves-Brayer ✆ +33 (0)4 92 59 21 92
www.restaurant-quai06.fr

Open Tuesday to Saturday from 12pm to 3pm and from 6pm to 11.30pm and Sunday from 12pm to 3pm. In season open every day for lunch and dinner. Menu from €18.50 to €24.50. Children's menu: €8.50. Lunch menu: €12.50 (main course and dessert + coffee). Holiday voucher, Chèque Restaurant. Terrace. Large private parking. Seminars. Theme parties.

With an urban décor and a *steack house* carte, Quai 06 brings you to the States. North American flavours, meat lovers will be charmed: burger, bagel, grilled meats, ribs... Freshness is guaranteed and all is home made from the hamburgers bread to the steack, chopped on the spot. You'll also enjoy the desserts: cheese cake, muffin and donuts. Saturday evenings are animated when the restaurant organizes thematic evenings: the Eighties, gypsy, karaoké, disguised... For the sport fans, all games are broadcasted with a friendly formula which offers pizza and beer, or a glass of wine. We loved it!

LA VOILE BLEUE DU BISTROT DU PORT

4, avenue Henry-Clews
On the quay of the port of Mandelieu-la-Napoule (under the station Total)
✆ +33 (0)4 93 49 80 60 / +33 (0)6 18 46 73 73
bistrotduport@wanadoo.fr

Open all year. Thursday to Tuesday for lunch and dinner; Wednesday for lunch. Menu from €26 to €32. À la carte: Around €55. Fixed rate formula: €19 (starter and main course or main course and dessert). Groups welcome. Wifi. Interior and external terrace. Possibility of privatizing part of the room for any type of events. Pets allowed. Pedestrian area. Spoken languages: English, Italian.

This restaurant located in the port pays tribute to the sea thanks to the marine colours of its decoration and its menu dedicated to seafood. While being seated on the terrace, on the verandah in summer with a view of the moored yachts or comfortably seated in the dining room, you will discover a traditional cuisine, fish, shellfish and seafood, mussel puff pastry soup, sole fillet with Noilly Prat and homemade fettuccinis, roasted red mullets, fine basil stuffing, rougail sauce or the Saint Honorat bouillabaisse. Meat aficionados will also be pleased with the copious and tasty dishes like the veal cutlet and cream, the beef fillet with green pepper. Finally the gourmets will appreciate the homemade desserts specialities like the iced nougat on raspberry coulis or the iced truffles with vanilla custard. You will be warmly welcomed by an experienced team. A real pleasure!

LE VOILIER

4, avenue Henry-Clews
On the quay of the port of Mandelieu-la-Napoule (under the station Total)
✆ +33 (0)4 93 49 56 00

Open all year. Daily for lunch and dinner. À la carte: Around €30. Daily special: €12. Holiday voucher. Terrace.

This establishment (which belongs to the same owner as the next door restaurant La Voile bleue du Bistrot du Port which now has a panoramic terrace above the restaurant), has a soft, lounge and contemporary setting with a stunning view of the port, and a delightful varied menu, with a large selection of fresh products, various tasty salads, homemade pizzas, hearty burgers, provençal dishes, small stuffed vegetables, courgette flowers, aioli, without forgetting the suggestions of meat, fish and seafood.

Sleeping

ERMITAGE DU RIOU

26, avenue Henri-Clews
✆ +33 (0)4 93 49 95 56
hotel@ermitage-du-riou.fr

Annual closing from December to beginning of March. Reception 24/24. 33 rooms (non smoker). Low season: double room from €109. Buffet breakfast: €24 (per person). Extra bed: €70. Parking (external offered and closed at night). Spoken languages: French, English, German and Italian. American Express, Diners Club. Pets allowed (in the hotel rooms with €20 extra per animal and night; not authorized at the restaurant). Seminars. Receptions and weddings. Internet corner. Free Internet access. Free Wifi. Cleaning service. Product sales of Domaine de Barbossi (wines, honeies, nougats, olive oil...). Satellite TV. Free bicycles at disposal. Shuttle to the other activities of the estate (riding, golf, tennis).

Located opposite the marina of La Napoule and along the Riou river and the oldest golf course of the French Riviera, this charming house completely restored in the spirit of Mediterranean villas has undergone a full renovation by its new owners. All rooms and suites, extremely refined, bright and uncluttered, combine white and blue sea or warm chocolate tones, all in a bright atmosphere. All are decorated with works of Art. Some open on the Mediterranean, others on the Estérel massif and the golf. Don't miss the varied menu of cocktails offered by the lounge bar near the pool.

Leisure

RIVIERA GOLF OF BARBOSSI

802, avenue des Amazones
✆ +33 (0)4 92 97 49 49
www.ddeb.fr
rivieragolf@ddeb.fr

Open all year. Green Fee: 18 holes + golf car from €98 to €120. Green Fee: 18 holes + car + series + shoes from €130. American Express. Catering facilities. Shop. A practice of 15 stations, including 9 covered, 3 compact holes and a putting green.

Located in a beautiful natural environment made up of pine trees, mimosas and lakes, this 18 hole golf course designed on the foothills of the Esterel by the American architect Robert Trent Jones Sr offers a total of 5,444 m distance. The undulating course is quite technical, and requires great skill. It is decorated with some difficulties that will delight the experienced golfers. A restaurant with a wonderful terrace which opens onto the green, awaits you to revive you after your course.

SAINT-LAURENT-DU-VAR ★

Set in the middle of the Alpes Maritimes coast line, halfway between Cannes and Monaco, Saint-Laurent-du-Var has all the advantages of a modern city and an old village with the bonus of a whole range of nautical pleasures. Ancient natural border of Nice county until 1860, the city was the border between France and the Sardinian kingdom. The crossing of Var river was often made when water was low. The wooden bridge that made it possible to cross the river has often been worn by water or was demolished during the wars. It is only after 1860 that a stone bridge was built for the road and the railway side-by-side. The city, very much affected by the bombings of 1943 and 1944, was mainly rebuilt but many monuments of the old Saint-Laurent remain as the church place Castillon rebuilt in the 12th century and remodelled in the 16th century with a Provençal romanesque style that houses a reliquary containing a tibia of saint Benoit, founder of the Benedictines. Around the church remains a part of the old village with its old characteristic streets. The port of Saint-Laurent with its 18 acres of mooring, shops, restaurants and bars is the stronghold of daytime and night time entertainment of the town relayed by the large mall of Cap 3000.

Knife & Fork

BISTRO QUAI

Port of Saint-Laurent-du-Var
✆ +33 (0)4 93 26 48 83 – www.bistro-quai.com
bistro-quai@hotmail.fr

Open all year. Open Tuesday to Saturday from 12pm to 2.15pm and from 7pm to 10.30pm. Booking advised. Dishes around €18. Wine by the glass. Fixed rate formulas from €16. Covered and heated terrace.

Here, everyone is satisfied. Starting from the attentive and smiling welcome to the quality of the dishes available on the wall-mounted blackboards that celebrate a good looking traditional cuisine with creative tastes. The contemporary setting punctuated with brown-beige reflects the spirit of an elegant bistro and the lively atmosphere ensures the well-being of the regular customers spoiled by Jean-Christophe Tiberghien and his team. The refined dishes, basil zucchini flowers tempura, tomatoes coulis, swordfish steak, pan-fried vegetables with Espelette pepper, are accompanied with carefully chosen wines and desserts such as the Nutella fondant and the lemon meringue pie deliciously end the meals, you can enjoy all of that a few meters from the sea and the moored boats along the quays of the seafront.

BEACH CLUB

Beach, Restaurant, Lounge Bar
2,promenade des Flots-Bleus
✆ +33 (0)4 69 00 13 48

See page 49.

Promenade des Flots Bleus

You'll appreciate the seaside of Saint-Laurent-du-Var by walking along from the parking of the Cap 3000 shopping centre to the «promenade des flots bleus (walk of blue waves)» while going through the esplanade des Goélands facing the sea with benches and pergolas. Walkers enjoy a car-free area near the waves, animated by the terraces of restaurants, ice cream parlours and cafes. You can also walk to the marina in Saint-Laurent-du-Var and its captaincy.

«Petite Camargue», bird sanctuary

Nicknamed «La Petite Camargue», this bird sanctuary is situated between the shopping centre of Cap 3000 and the Nice Côte d'Azur airport at the estuary of the Var. Privileged transit place of migratory birds you can access by parking your car on the south parking of the mall. In this site classified as "nature reserve", there are more than 260 species of birds almost half of those surveyed in Europe. This delta, formed at Saint Laurent by the Var and the Mediterranean, is a wetland with small swamps where migratory and aquatic birds meet: herons, warblers, snipe, kingfishers, egrets, pink flamingos... Do not forget your binoculars when exploring the site, the opportunity to make a "green" walk, decorated with wooden panels containing the names and characteristics of the Birds that could be observed.

LA CABANE
167, promenade des Flots-Bleus
✆ +33 (0)4 93 07 07 70

Open all year. Tuesday to Sunday from 11am to 11pm. Booking advised. À la carte: Around €35. Fixed rate formula: €16.50 (main course and dessert). Daily special: €13.50. No menus but many daily specials. Terrace.

This restaurant on the Promenade des Flots Bleus has an exotic setting and a festive identity. Here, everything is bright and flowery, like the good humour of the team! The lively large terrace that looks like a «a bamboo hut», similar to a rum distillery in the islands, has a bar where you can enjoy colourful cocktails with various flavors. You'll also find flavoured rhums and old AOC rhums on the menu which displays suggestion of the day available on the blackboard according to the seasons. Here, everything is prepared with fresh products and quality meats – veal chop with sage, rack of lamb with herb coating, beef stew – as well as splendid wild fish. Regulars come for the famous roasted octopus and the pan-fried scallops. Fresh pastas and mixed salads (prawns/artichokes or lobster/pineapple) complete the menu for friendly meal breaks in a holiday atmosphere by the water. The most gourmands will end on a sweet note with an excellent cheese cake and the famous rum baba of the chef. We love the nicely presented plates of fresh fruits. Véronique, Christophe and their team will always welcome you with a smile.

EVASION
Cap 3000
✆ +33 (0)4 92 27 06 50
http://restaurant-evasion.com
contact@restaurant-evasion.com

Open Monday to Saturday from 10am to 10pm; Sunday until 3pm. À la carte: Around €30 (main course and dessert + drink). Lunch menu: €16 (pizza + a glass of wine + coffee). Several fixed rate formulas for lunch. American Express. Groups welcome. Terrace. Wine by the glass.

Facing the sea, this establishment with a modern decor serves traditional cuisine with south accents. The menu offers tasty starters, pastas in sauce (farfalle with meatballs and Perugian sausage with tomatoes, fusilli with fresh tuna in the Sicilian way), meat and fish freshly prepared and other homemade pizzas with fine and crunchy dough using fresh ingredients. As for desserts, the classics and other suggestions will allow you to finish your meal on a pleasant sweet touch. The service is friendly and the setting is most pleasant.

PANASIA
Cap 3000 – Avenue Eugène-Donadeï
Level 1
✆ +33 (0)4 93 26 05 38
www.panasia.fr
contact@panasia.fr

Open all year. Every day from 8.30am to 11pm and Sunday from 8.30am to 5pm. On the premises or take-away. Children's menu: €10.90. Bento only take-away from Monday to Friday €10.90. Restaurant Vue sur Mer access Parking 4.

A new concept of Asian cuisine has settled on the Côte d'Azur. Panasia offers a Far Eastern bistronomy, a fusion of great traditional dishes from various countries combining different flavours on one table. A journey to Vietnam, China, Japan or Thailand while peacefully seated in your chair: Vietnamese chicken salad, sushi, pad thai, bo bun, pot of fish Sichuan way, bento... As for the desserts, taste original specialties such as the dorayaki stuffed with red beans, Japanese cheesecake, mochis with matcha... a parade of dishes, a mixture of flavours. A gustative delight thanks to the freshness of the products and the nice recipes worked by a most professional team. To try immediately!

Going Out

THE TUBE
Port of Saint-Laurent-du-Var
✆ +33 (0)4 93 31 88 62
letube06@orange.fr

Open Thursday to Sunday evening from 11pm as well as public holidays. Snacking.

Their motto? Infinite begins here... at 11pm! The Tube is a trendy nightclub that opened its doors in June 2014 on the port of St Laurent du Var. If at first sight, the space is not very large, you will be quickly conquered by its festive and friendly atmosphere, a promise of beautiful evenings, all in a relaxed and unpretentious atmosphere because here, you are accepted for who you are. The decoration is trendy and minimalist: wide and comfortable white sofas, a large bar, design ceiling lights and mirrors, small black tables, transparent or plexis chairs... As for the menu, it displays cocktails at reasonable prices. So, ready to party?

Shopping

CAP 3000
Avenue Eugène-Donadeï
✆ +33 (0)4 93 31 10 35
www.cap3000.com
♿
Open Monday to Saturday from 10am to 9pm. Lafayette Gourmet 8.30am – 9pm. Games 4 to 12 years from 10am to 7pm every Wednesday, Saturday and public holidays; every day during school holidays. Restaurants sea view open Monday to Saturday from 8.30am to midnight and Sunday from 8.30am to 3pm. Exceptional openings some Sunday and public holidays. Relaxation areas. Concierge services. Taxis. Letter-box. ATM. Reception. Reception Lignes d'Azur every Wednesday from 10am to 1pm and from 2pm to 5pm (except public holidays). Information and subscriptions. Free: cloakroom, toilets. Parking reserved to the guests of Cap 3000: 3 hours free per day without purchase condition (overtime: €3) + 2hours extra offered with your loyalty card Cap3000 from €50 of purchases. American Express, Chèque Restaurant.
Cap 3000 is the first largest Shopping Center in the French Riviera, the only one open until 9 pm. All the major brands are represented. You can find there the Galeries Lafayette, a Lafayette Gourmet and more than 150 specialised shops and areas: fashion and trends (clothes for everyone, leather, shoes, accessories, jewellery, watches), health and wellness (beauty, health, hairdressers, hearing, optics, solar), leisures & travels, home (decoration, hi-tech), banks, dry cleaning, medical office, culinary delights (food, wine cellar, delicatessen and gourmet food) as well as many restaurants and tea rooms. You can download the free iPhone app «CAP 3000» to follow the news and many good plans. Also discover the loyalty card. Works for redevelopment and extension of the place are underway.

YELLOWKORNER
Cap 3000 shopping centre
Avenue Eugène-Donadei
✆ +33 (0)9 66 97 18 60
www.yellowcorner.com
contact@yellowkorner.com
Instead of offering 10 prints at €5,000, Yellow Corner chooses to publish 1,000 of them at €50.
Discovering the photographic art through the great names or the young talents of tomorrow and to get one of their works in limited edition at low prices, is possible with this concept created in 2006 by two passionate about photos. The most beautiful fashion, sport, urban, views, landscapes photos... obtained from laboratory, on silver photo paper of top quality then numbered with a certificate of authenticity.

THÉOULE-SUR-MER ★★★

OFFICE DE TOURISME DE THÉOULE-SUR-MER
2, boulevard Corniche-d'Or
✆ +33 (0)4 93 49 28 28
www.theoule-sur-mer.org
ot@theoule-sur-mer.org
From October 1st to April 30th, open Monday to Saturday 10am at 5.30pm. From May 1st to September 30th, open Monday to Saturday from 9am to 7pm. From June 19th to September 18th, open on Sunday from 10am to 1pm and from 3pm to 7pm and public holidays from 9am to 1pm.
Booklets in several free tongues on the manifestations of the city and common the surrounding (Le Trayas, Agay), you will find here all which you need to know about the news, trott them and the activities organized with Théoule on sea. The Tourist Office also offers to the visitors a free internet access, for those which have a computer or a smartphone. Relaxation area on the square of the office to settle and consult its e-mails or of documentation.

Knife & Fork

LES FRÈRES DE LA BAIE
Parking du Chateau
Promenade de la Darse
✆ +33 (0)4 92 97 80 20
See page 55.

JILALI B
Figueirette
16, avenue du Trayas
✆ +33 (0)4 93 75 19 03
www.jilalib.com
contact@jilalib.com
♿
Closed from mid-November to beginning of February. Open Tuesday to Sunday from 7.30pm to 9.30pm; Wednesday to Sunday from 12.15pm to 2.30pm. Booking advised. Menu from €39 to €59 (or €85 or €120 drinks included, for lunch and dinner). À la carte: around €55. Lunch menu: €29 (starter, main course, dessert, only on weekdays). Wine by the glass. American Express. Groups welcome. Garden. Terrace. Take-away. Parking. Wifi.
Through the bay windows of the room or on the panoramic terrace, a heavenly visual delight is offered, with majestic Esterel's red rocks that dip in the Mediterranean sea, as a background. Pleasure extends to the plate with the typical Mediterranean cuisine, prepared by Jilali, rockfish soup from the Bay of Theoule, coquilles Saint Jacques ceviche with Richerenches truffe and whipped celery, roast suckling lamb, pastoral salad and hen Retour du Marché, grilled or roasted Lobster and crayfish from our ponds, risotto accompanied by thyme flower and lemon,confit seasonal vegetable with Spéracèdes olives and spinach shoots, bouillabaisse tasting.

The regional park of Esterel

L'Esterel is a volcanic mountain range of 320 km ^{2} – hence its red rocks – of low altitude. Most of it is protected and has a forest that is managed by the NFB. Departmental park of about 370 acres, owned by the Conservatoire du Littoral, it covers the towns of Mandelieu-la-Napoule and Theoule-sur-Mer. This natural zone has many ecological treasures, both in terms of flora and fauna. It houses some thirty species of heritage interest: bobcats, bats, deer and birds including some raptors such as the peregrine falcon, great horned of Europe and the little Duke. Animations and outings are carried out by the Departmental Committee of cliff-of climbing Monges which can be accessed from the parking of the marina of Theoule. Further is the entrance of an underground path that go up towards Trayas hill, till the foot of the rock.

CHEZ PHILIPPE
Port of Théoule
Promenade de la Darse
✆ +33 (0)4 93 49 87 13
www.restaurantchezphilippe.com
mikoul8@hotmail.com

Closed from October 31st to February 1st. High season: open daily for lunch and dinner. Closed on Monday and Sunday for dinner in low season. Booking advised. Menu from €38 to €48. À la carte: Around €50. Wine by the glass. Seafood platters from €38 to €95. Bouillabaisse from €45 to €95 per person. Dessert €10. American Express. Charter qualité Mer of Lérins 2015. Groups welcome (organization of weddings, baptisms, birthdays, banquets.). Terrace. Take-away. Activities. Parking.

This family-run restaurant is located on a white sandy beach lined with palm trees on the waterfront. Sylvie will warmly welcome you in the dining room, while her son Sébastien offers daily suggestions on the board and prepares dishes essentially with seafood. Discover among others, every day a new suggestion based on meat or fish. Seafood lovers will also be charmed by the magnificent plates for two and by the delicious and generous bouillabaisse. Stephanie will sublimate your meal with the great chocolate fudge cake and its warm chocolate. Michael will, for his part, find the suitable wine for you from his nice wine cellar.

Sleeping

TIARA MIRAMAR BEACH HOTEL****
47, avenue de Miramar
✆ +33 (0)4 93 75 05 05
www.tiara-hotels.com

Open all year. Reception 24/24. Double room from €220; suite from €620. Buffet breakfast included. Garage (free – free covered parking). Spoken languages: French, English, Italian. Tiara Hotels & Resorts. American Express, Diners Club. Pets allowed. Seminars. Receptions and weddings. Internet corner. Free Wifi. Cleaning service. Catering facilities (bistro M open daily for lunch and every evening (in summer, closed for lunch)). Spa by Sothys. Satellite TV. Hammam, whirlpool, sauna. Excursions.

Set up with cliffside at the waterfront, this establishment on the spot has all that one wishes to pass a formidable stay. The rooms with refined and Eastern decoration offer almost a whole a view on the Mediterranean. The services of the hotel are also very numerous: heated indoor swimming pool in winter, private beach Red Rock the summer, relaxation area including sauna, hammam, whirlpool, fitness but also two restaurants, the Bistro M with its panoramic view on Estérel and the sea, and Moya, establishment of beach proposing a summer à la carte.

TIARA YAKTSA*****
6, boulevard de l'Esquillon
✆ +33 (0)4 92 28 60 30
www.tiara-hotels.com
reservations.yaktsa@tiara-hotels.com

Relay & Castles. Closed from January to April. Tiara hotels & resorts. Reception 24/24 (spoken languages: French, English, Arabic, Italian). 21 rooms (100% not smoker). Double room from €312; suite from €472. Buffet breakfast included. Beds free babies. Parking (external free). American Express, Diners Club. Room adapted for disabled people. Pets allowed. Seminars. Receptions and weddings. Free Wifi. Cleaning service. Restaurant Blue Gold. Menu €85 (tasting). Card. Spa. Satellite TV, Canal+. Whirlpool.

The natural elegance of the decor posed above floods, is a perfect ecrin for this hotel 5 stars, Relais & Châteaux member, including suites and rooms with the Eastern spirit, and thus opening on a garden with the Mediterranean petrols. The undeniable romanticism of the place continues in the privacy of a spa area and on beds with hangings placed in the middle of a green lawn prolonged by the pool. The travel Zen continues once sat at table within the restaurant Blue Gold where Mediterranean flavours explode, flowers of zucchini to Mediterranean and lemon-flavoured carpaccio of prawns, jumped squids with vintage, roasted lobster and spring vegetables of season, roast fillet of beef and gnocchi of potatoes to truffle, fishing punt with vervain, apricot roasted with rosemary... The restaurant's terrace embraces the sea, just like the suite «Penthouse» of 80 m ^{2} with its private whirlpools. Wealth and refinement of the southernmost culture here are resolutely celebrated between quiet, luxury and pleasure.

Leisure

JETSCOOL

Port of Figueirette – 7, avenue de Trayas
✆ +33 (0)6 11 14 30 06 / +33 (0)6 69 36 30 03
www.jetscool.com – info@jetscool.com

Open every day from 9am and from 6pm. Jet skiing from €80 the 30 min. Flyboard: initiation course €150, sensation course €80. Located in the middle of the port of Figueirette between Agay and Mandelieu at 10 minutes from the village of Théoule sur mer, Jets'Cool accommodates sea impassioned with strong sensqtions in a zouk and very relaxed atmosphere... cool! From 30 minutes to 5 hours hikes framed by qualified state instructors by the French federation of Motonautisme. Special mention for Sunset at sunset!

GOLFE-JUAN ★★★★

Knife & Fork

LE BISTRO DU PORT

53, avenue des Frères-Roustan
✆ +33 (0)4 93 63 70 64
www.bistrotduport.com

♿

«Maître Restaurateur» label. Annual closing from mid-November to mid-December. From October to May, restaurant closed Sunday for dinner and Monday. From June to September, restaurant closed Saturday for lunch and Monday. Booking advised. À la carte: Around €60. Daily special: €15.50. Wine by the glass. Set menu €20.50 (starter and main course or main course and dessert). Menu €25.50 (starter + main course + dessert). American Express. Groups welcome. Terrace. Charter Mer de Lérins 2015.

Fully renovated, Bistrot du Port remained faithful to its original spirit. Indeed, this family business is simple and friendly, like the owners, the brothers Mathieu and Thomas Allinéi. Here the cuisine is authentic, refined and tasty. The short carte offers only seasonal ingredients and fresh fish, coming from daily arrivals or local fish. Guaranteed wild, it is prepared with artichokes, a la provencale, with white wine, in salt crust... or just roasted in a wooden fire to preserve its taste. Traditional specialties: bouillabaisse and grilled fish. Crayfish or lobster is served on order. All the desserts are home made and you'll discover daring and inventive flavours (the macaroon in a hull of ink and creamy passion fruit, the religieuse with lemon and coulis of acidulated basil, the chocolate variation around Japan...).

BRUNO

Le Vieux Port – 27, avenue des Frères-Roustan
✆ +33 (0)4 93 63 72 12

♿

Closed of December 20th to the beginning of March. Closed weekly Tuesday and Sunday for dinner off-season. Open daily for lunch and dinner. Booking advised. Children's menu: €10 (syrup, 4 choices of main dishes, ice-cream ball). Lunch menu: €20 (starter, main course, dessert). Daily special at €14. Main course around €16. Holiday voucher, Chèque Restaurant. Reception of groups. Organization of private or professional events. Large terrace and big room.

By taking over the establishment created by her grand-parents in 1950, the granddaughter of BRUNO and her husband maintained tradition and quality. The products are fresh and varied: steak with its marrowbone and salt flower, wok with prawns and Saint-Jacques, grilled fish like sea bass or bream of approximately 750 grams but also several specialties like the special fondue of the sea or the Brasero, small artisanal barbecue where one cooks fish, prawns, cuttlefish, scallop, or beef with cheese. Apart from the specialties, you'll find pizzas, salads, burgers and fresh chopped steak. The whole in a friendly and cordial decor, which recalls the family past of the restaurant. Old photos fixed on the walls, a large floral terrace, decorated trees and a charming small fish pool overhung by a splendid mill, you'll find the print of the first owners. A charm decor, within walking distance of the old port of Golf-Juan, a tasty cuisine and traditional served by a friendly and cordial couple.

LE CAFÉ BLEU

Port Camille-Rayon
✆ +33 (0)4 93 63 48 02
www.restaurant-lecafebleu.fr
contact@restaurant-lecafebleu.fr

Open on Wednesday, Thursday, Saturday and Sunday from 9am to 6pm; Friday from 11am to midnight. Set menu at €24.50 (starter, main course, dessert). À la carte: Around €35. Pasta (spaghetti, ravioles or raviolis niçois) from €10 to €15. Terrace. Activities.

On the Camille-Ray port, this brasserie, tea room, and ice-cream shop, welcomes you throughout the day. The cuisine is traditional and prepared with fresh ingredients such as fish soup, rouille and croutons, tartare, thinly sliced chicken with cream, salmon steak virgin sauce, floating island, crème brûlée... In the afternoon, after your stroll on the docks, a gourmet stop is a must, beautiful sweet pancakes, waffles, or a choice of ice-creams. Jazz evenings on Fridays.

NOUNOU

Boulevard des Frères-Roustan
✆ +33 (0)4 93 63 71 73
www.nounou.fr
info@nounou.fr

From end of December to mid-November the restaurant is open daily for lunch and dinner. House specialties from €58 to €104. Fish around €45. Meats around €30.

This fish restaurant with an ancient charm is a must for its bouillabaisse. In a blue and white decor opening directly on the beach, Nounou serves a very refined seafood cuisine: lobster salad, salmon tartare, shrimp cocktail, oysters, fisherman's bouillabaisse, crayfish or lobster, grilled fish, in parchment t or in salt crust... As they are all authentic and tasty, you'll enjoy these Mediterranean dishes while admiring the sea. A choice address for all seafood lovers!

RIO' S BANANA CAFÉ

Port Camille-Rayon
✆ +33 (0)4 93 63 79 79
http://rios-banana-cafe.com
info@rios-banana-cafe.com

Open every day from 11am to 2am in the morning non-stop. Free WiFi. Billiards. Sports Channel. Find the news on the Facebook page! À la carte: Around €30. Daily special €12.90. Burgers from €13.90 to €26.90. Tapas from €1.40 to €6. Groups welcome. Terrace. Activities.

The evenings are festive and animated by live concerts every weekend and also for themed evenings: rock, salsa, Halloween... The decor is acidic which gives life to this bistro pub offering a pleasant view of the port. The cuisine is simple in a «brasserie» spirit. The menu offers various salads, omelettes, tapas, salmon with tarragon, tuna steak, rump steak, whole duck breast, chicken wrap and an important choice of burgers including the Delux burger with foie gras!

LA SIRÈNE

49, avenue des Frères-Roustan
✆ +33 (0)4 93 63 59 19

Annual closing in December. Open Thursday to Tuesday from 8.30am to 11pm. À la carte: Around €35 (starter around €12, dish around €20). Roasted fish of the day: €25. Accepted luncheon vouchers. Checks are not accepted. Holiday voucher. Terrace. Spoken English. Located 600 m from the SNCF train station. Kitchen open on the room.

This emblematic restaurant of Golfe-Juan opened since 1985 has been delighting his customers for generations. Kindness, politeness, smile and conviviality are the watchwords of this family-run and warm restaurant. A perfect service without neglecting the cuisine. We find on the menu simple dishes prepared with fresh products: squid doughnuts, roasted scampi, fries and mussels, pizza, aioli... And the homemade desserts are also simply delicious!

Sleeping

HÔTEL DE LA MER

226, avenue de la Liberté
✆ +33 (0)4 93 63 80 83
www.hotelmer.com
contact@hotelmer.com

Annual closing from December 10th, 2016 to January 8th, 2017. Reception until 9pm (contact the establishment for a late arrival until 11pm). 34 rooms. Single room from €57 to €97; double room from €65 to €119; triple room from €109 to €133; suite from €139 to €299. Buffet breakfast: €12 (€8 for the child up to 8 years). Cot €15. Closed parking: €10. Parking under video surveillance. Holiday voucher. Games for children. Seminars. Receptions and weddings. Free Wifi. Cleaning service. Activities.

The rooms have been recently renovated by the new owners and yet have kept the beautiful Provençal frescoes dating back to the 1970s. This is a family hotel. By the way, families, as well as groups of friends can stay here at low costs, a few steps away from the beaches and nautical activities. All the rooms overlook the sea or the swimming pool; they are calm and air-conditioned, they have a small personal refrigerator and TNT. Profit from the solarium, the bar and the swimming pool in the evening. A tourist information desk can help you organize your holiday outings with the support of your hosts.

VALLAURIS ★★★

«Vallis Aurea», Vallauris, means the golden valley owes its name to the Roman people. During the middle Ages, the production of olive oil was the main activity of the municipality. Its territory was subsequently ceded to the monastic brotherhood of the Lérins islands in 1036 by the Bishop of Antibes, to the great despair of its inhabitants. Vallauris is finally released in 1787 by Louis XVI's decision, shortly before the Revolution. Pottery perpetuates a tradition for over 2,000 years. Already in Gallo-Roman times, bricks and pots were made. Ravaged by the plague during the 16th century, 70 families, including many potters, from surrounding Genoa, settled in Vallauris. The village is in possession in its basement, a clay ground of high quality easier to work with but also to cook. Despite the difficulties of communication, the production of pottery develops. Workshops become real factories in the late 19th century, companies appear, giving rise to small industry. The arrival of materials best suited to modern life such as cast iron, stainless steel or aluminium also allows pottery to move towards artistic ceramics. Picasso lived in the village from 1948 to 1955. He will engage in 1946 in ceramics, after meeting with manufacturers and visited the annual exhibition of potters. He will create plates and dishes based on his favourite themes- the bullfight, the owl, goat or woman – shaped in the nymph and fauna clay. He realised in nearly 20 years 4000 original works, some of which were copies. Jean Marais is one of the other artists who influenced the city in which he moved in 1980. This painter, sculptor and actor experiments pottery and ends up liking it. He opened in

1975 his own workshop and Vallauris the statue of "La Robellissière" in 1991. Died in November 8, 1998, the artist lies in the old city graveyard.

■ TOURIST OFFICE OF VALLAURIS GOLFE-JUAN TANAGRA

67, avenue Georges Clemenceau
✆ +33 (0)4 93 63 82 58
www.vallauris-golfe-juan.fr
contact.tourisme@vallauris.fr

♿

Open Monday to Saturday from 9am to 12pm and from 1pm to 5pm.

The team offers a personalised and multilingual welcome in the offices of Vallauris or of Golfe-Juan. Besides the printed guides, you will also find informmation, events and audio guides available online to be downloaded free on smartphones. Shows tickets sales.

Knife & Fork

■ LE CLOS COSETTE

1, avenue du Tapis-Vert
✆ +33 (0)4 93 64 30 64
www.lecloscosette.com

High season: open Tuesday to Sunday from 12pm to 2pm and from 7.30pm to 10.30pm. Closed Sunday for dinner in low season. Booking advised. À la carte: Around €35 (dish around €20). Lunch menu: €12.50 (€17.50 starter, main course, dessert). Wine by the glass. Menu from €29.50. Chèque Restaurant. Groups welcome (organization of receptions and private parties or professional). Terrace. Activities.

Located in a former pottery of the 1960s, Clos Cosette welcomes you in a setting with carefully decorated stone walls and wooden beams. The different spaces offered by the restaurant ensure privacy and comfort: first of all, the flowery terrace, hidden from the street by a hedge of shrubs. Relaxation and freshness are guaranted with the continuous sound of the fountain. Then, the entrance, formerly a smoking lounge, decorated by many artists or craftsmen work, pleasant for an aperitive or waiting for the meal. Finally, the lovely refined room with a permanent exposition of paintings. The owner of the place, Philippe Demier runs the kitchen to satisfy your appetites and tastebuds. In addition to the traditional specialties, homemade duck foie gras, snail soup with garlic cream, homemade terrine of young rabbit, braised veal sweetbread with morel sauce, he always prepares a selection of fresh fish and grilled meats. The customers are loyal and find with pleasure the good plans of an address that become unmissable over the years.

■ LA VIOLE FLEURY

50, avenue Georges-Clemenceau
✆ +33 (0)4 92 90 34 83 / +33 (0)6 70 39 44 47

♿

Closed from December 19th to December 31st. Open on Tuesday and Wednesday from 7.30am to 7pm; Thursday to Saturday from 7.30am to 10pm; Sunday from 8am to 7pm. Booking advised. À la carte: Around €25 (starter around €6, main course around €15, dessert around €5). Wine by the glass. Groups welcome. Terrace. Take-away.

The former cabaret and shop of the famous ceramist Roger Capron has found a new lease of life with the establishment of a winstub with a cosy and family atmosphere. If you wish to taste Alsatian specialities traditionally elaborated in a warm atmosphere and with an excellent value for money, you are at the right address. On the menu: flammekueche, alsatian quiche, Alsatian sauerkraut, sea sauerkraut, chicken vol-au-vents, Alsatian tart with seasonal fruits...

VILLENEUVE LOUBET ★

■ OFFICE DE TOURISME DE VILLENEUVE-LOUBET

16, avenue de la Mer
Rue de l'Hôtel-de-Ville ✆ +33 (0)4 92 02 66 16
www.villeneuve-tourisme.com
info@villeneuve-tourisme.com

From September to June, open Monday to Friday from 9am to 12.30pm and from 2pm to 5.30pm. Saturdays open from 9am to 1pm. In July and August Monday to Saturday from 9am to 1pm and from 2pm to 6pm. Sunday open from 9am to 1pm. Free guided tours. Free Wifi. Qualité Tourisme label.

The offices of the Tourist Office are labelled Tourism & Handicap with sensitized staff. They offer visitors free Wireless internet via IKD network. On request from the members in stay, get access codes valid 30 min. multilingual free Brochures. Charming welcome. Access to disabilities driving, visual, auditory and mental.

FRENCH RIVIERA: THE COASTLINE

The architectural Marina Baie des Anges

Witness of the architectural boldness of the sixties, the Ministry of Culture recognized «Marina Baie des Anges» as a whole architectural characteristic of the building heritage of the twentieth century. Initiated in 1960, the construction took place over nearly 25 years, today's 16 hectares shelter a marina and 4 giant pyramids evoking huge white waves peaking at 70 m above sea level. With nearly 1,500 homes, «Marina Baie des Anges» is a monument erected to the glory of the civilization of leisure in the late twentieth century. The genesis of the project and the vagaries of the construction is the starting point for guided tours offered by the Tourist Office. We discover the unusual story and visit the extensive gardens along the Mediterranean. Dates and times for visit are available on request.

Sightseeing

MUSÉE ESCOFFIER DE L'ART CULINAIRE

3, rue Escoffier © +33 (0)4 93 20 80 51
www.fondation-escoffier.org

Free the first Sunday of the month, and as from July 2016 audio guides (€4) in French, English and Italian are offered. Free for under 11-year-olds. Adult: €6. €3 students, without employment and disabled people. From February 1st to May 30st, and October. Thee Museum is open daily from 10:00 am to 1:00 pm and from 2:00 pm to 6:00 pm. Closing Months: November - December From June 1st to September 30th, The Museum is open daily from 10:00 am to 1:00 pm and from 2:00 to 7:00 pm. Free the 1st Sunday of each month. In our temporary exhibitions, events - tastings are open only to visitors who have paid their access.

This museum has been established in the house where Auguste Escoffier (1846-1935) was born thanks to the patronage of his disciple Joseph Donon who bought the building and funded the works. It goes back over the career of this great master-chef who was the chef of the Carlton in London. You will discover during the visit some personal items of the «King of cooks and cook of the kings», documents related to the art of cooking through history and also menus of famous meals among which the one of 1870's Christmas Eve during the Franco-Prussian war where the animals of the Vincennes zoo served as games! Auguste Escoffier, the predecessor of our actual great chefs, is the creator of the peach melba which was imagined to pay tribute to the singer Nelly Melba. This museum-foundation presents its collections in a space of more than 300 m² in a charming setting in Provençal colours. Guided games for children, temporary exhibitions and professional traineeships are also offered in this historical place.

Knife & Fork

L'AUBERGE FLEURIE

11, rue des Mesures -Village
© +33 (0)4 93 73 90 92 / +33 (0)6 64 82 10 54

Winter, open for lunch Wednesday to Sunday and for dinner Tuesday to Saturday. Summer, open for lunch Thursday to Sunday and for dinner Thursday to Tuesday. Open from 12pm to 3pm and from 7.15pm to 10.30pm. Booking advised. Menu from €29 to €72. À la carte: Around €45 (starter around €20, main course around €33, dessert €9). Lunch menu: €15.90. Menu on the board for lunch €25 (starter, main course, dessert). Groups welcome. Terrace. Qualité Tourisme label.

This address of great charm run by Philippe Guichoux offers a cuisine inspired by fresh market products: roast veal cutlet and its poêlée of season, casserole of calf's kidneys, steak with marrow, foie gras escalopes, raviolis verde, prawn risotto... For the desserts, the classics reveal a creative touch with much refinement: soufflé with limoncello, millefeuille of the moment, gourmet coffee... Off-season, you'll enjoy the comfortable and coloured dining room with a chimney, and at the return of nice days, you'll love the authentic terrace in a green and floral setting in the heart of the peaceful village of Villeneuve-Loubet, just beside the Escoffier museum of culinary art.

LA FLIBUSTE MARTIN'S RESTAURANT

Marina Baie des Anges port
The Commodore © +33 (0)4 93 20 59 02
www.restaurantlaflibuste.com

«Maître Restaurateur» label. Open all year. Closed Sunday for dinner and Monday in low season. High season: every day from 12pm to 2.30pm and from 7pm to 10.30pm. Three forks and a plate in the Michelin Guide. Booking advised. À la carte: Around €65 (starter around €20, main course between €30 and €40, dessert €10). Lunch menu: €17.50 (€28 and €33). Groups welcome. Terrace. Valet. Parking nearby.

As soon as you are seated, Roger Martins presents you the catch of the day, that can be line-caught fish or wild sea bass, saint-pierre, sea bream, capon, gilthead sea bream and sargo...

They are simply grilled then rapidly cooked in the oven, to fully appreciate the taste of their flesh and served with white butter sauce or a virgin sauce. The highlight of the menu is sea food and acclaimed dishes like fresh squid fritters, local salad, tartar sauce and 5-year-old Léonardi balsam vinegar. The meat lovers are not left behind with the roast rack of lamb covered with herbs and rosemary juice. Note the arrival of the young chef Stéphane Garcia, Toque d'Or 2016, which will form a duo of choice with the Chef Jean Claude Plais. Innovation promised for 2017!

RISTORANTE VILLA MARINA
Marina Baie des Anges port
✆ +33 (0)4 93 22 61 77
villa.marina@orange.fr
Open daily for lunch and dinner. À la carte: Around €30. Fixed rate formula: €15 (main course and dessert + drink). Daily special: €10.
Villa Marina has an ideal location facing Villeneuve-Loubet harbor. A large terrace shaded by beautiful palm trees and bathed by sun rays or a comfortable spacios interior dining room. This restaurant offers a sunny cuisine, Italian and Provencal inspired by sea products: grilled fish, choice of pasta with prawns, vongole, fish, risotto, gnocchis and pizzas but also beautiful fresh salads and meats with sauce: fillet with ceps, lamb coasts with pistachios. The desserts are made home-made: tiramisù, tarts, panna cotta... The reception is pleasant and relaxed. You'll spend a good moment there, in all conviviality.

Sleeping

PERLA RIVIERA
369, avenue de La Colle ✆ +33 (0)4 93 20 97 58
www.perlariviera.fr
contact@perlariviera.fr
Logis (2 cheminées). Open all year. Reception until 10pm (spoken languages: French, English, Portuguese). 27 rooms (100% non smoker and including 15 giving on the swimming pool). Single room from €66; double room from €85; triple room from €105. Buffet breakfast: €9. Extra bed: €15. Garage: €9 (closed box and free outdoor parking 44 places). Holiday voucher. Seminars. Receptions and weddings. Free Wifi. Cleaning service. Catering facilities (Logis 2 cocottes). Restaurant The Ô . . . Closed Sunday and Monday lunchtime in low season. Open every day in high season. Fixed rate formula starter and main course or main course and dessert: €22.50 only at lunchtime. Card around €17.90. Wines by the glass. Children's menu €11.50).
If you want to escape the fuss of the seafront, this unstarred hotel, worthy of a 3 stars is for you: 15 rooms overlook the pool and the hills, a wine bar awaits you before going to table where the Chef prepares a regional cuisine with foie gras, smoked salmon, marrow-bone, candied duck legs. Note a beautiful terrace of 150 m^2 with a panoramic view on the hills and castle of Villeneuve-loubet.

RESIDENCE SEA SIDE PARK
2686, RD 6007 ✆ +33 (0)4 93 22 08 08
www.seasidepark.fr
contact@seasidepark.fr
Open all year. Inter-hotel. Reception 24/24 (in summer – more restricted schedule in winter). 72 rooms (100% non smoker). Low season: studio/apartment from €174 per week. High season: studio/apartment from €620 per week. Breakfast: €11. Extra bed: €10. Garage: €8 (free outdoor parking). Spoken languages: French, English, Italian and Spanish. Checks are not accepted. American Express, Holiday voucher. Staff attentive to the reception of disabled people. Before any reservation, you are invited to directly contact them in order to evaluate together the conditions of reception and accommodation. Pets allowed (extra charge). Receptions and weddings. Free Internet access. Free Wifi. Cleaning service. Billiards. Fitness room.
Slightly off the road linking Villeneuve-loubet to Antibes, this address with a modern architecture offers spacious rooms, between 25 m^2 and 48 m^2 with a capacity of 2 to 6 people. The rooms are impeccable, nicely decorated and very well equipped: microwave, dishwasher, hob, wi-fi... The rooftop swimming pool offers a beautiful view of the sea, the horizon and mountains as background. The Vaugrenier park is at nearby proximity, and the beach just a few steps away.

Leisure

The label "Family Station" suits well Villeneuve-Loubet who favours funny, educational and touristic activities specifically dedicated to families. The town has a rich natural heritage accessible to local people and visitors. The two natural departmental parks are areas where one can breathe freely, can walk and relax but there are also playgrounds, leisure and outdoor sports (biking, jogging, fitness ...). On the sea side: there are nautical activities and leisure activities on the beach especially suitable for families and children. On land, the discovery of the fauna and flora of villeneuvois natural areas is done due to the different interpretation-paths.

Going Out

THE PITCHER
Marina Baie des Anges port
Avenue de la batterie
✆ +33 (0)6 81 44 95 25
oliver.mba@hotmail.fr
Open all year. Monday to Saturday from 5pm until 0h30. Checks are not accepted. Terrace.
In the heart of the port of Marina Baies des Anges Pitcher is the ideal place to relax after a harassing day at work (or at the beach) and enjoy the view of the moored boats. For a dinner on the go, a afterwork with colleagues, a game of billiard or simple reunion with friends in a relaxed atmosphere and warm and friendly place. And if you get hungry, the pub offers flammekueche and pizzas cooked in a delicious wooden fire!

LE VILLAGE DES FOUS ★★★
2559, route de Grasse
✆ +33 (0)4 92 02 06 06
www.levillagedesfous.com
contact@alpesazuraventures.fr
Open from April 1st to November 12th, 2017. From 12 years and adults: €15. From 4 years to 11 years included: €13. 65 years and more (on presentation of an ID): €8. Discount starting from 5 people. Holiday voucher. Picnic areas, snack area and free parking at disposal.
Flying bathtub, nuts area, kupardessutête hut, 13 m high tower... In this amusement park/ village impossible to get bored: the games are varied, enough to spend a recreation afternoon with family. A great moment!

Grasse.

FRENCH RIVIERA:
THE MOUTAINSIDE

GRASSE ★★★★

Grasse was separated from the Var County in 1860 to form with the Nice county, the Alpes-Maritimes which is the sub-prefecture. It is on the limestone hill of Puy that was built the medieval village which remains the historical heart. Grasse specialised in tanning leather in the Middle Ages: the tanned skins were then exported to Italy. A craftsman had the idea of creating the first perfumed leather gloves: it enables the development of «Glovers' perfumers» which acquired a deserved reputation among the nobility. The Place aux Aires, crossed by a canal, was long the stronghold of tanners. When the leather industry declined, the perfume one took its place with the passion for creams, soaps and scented waters with rare scents requested by all the courts of Europe: lavender, myrtle, jasmine, rose, carnation, mimosa, tuberose, violet... In the late 18th century, Grasse experienced an extraordinary development of perfumery which is still blooming today: the Provençal town perched on a hill is considered the world capital of perfume.

TOURIST OFFICE
Place de la Buanderie
✆ +33 (0)4 93 36 66 66
www.grasse.fr
info@grasse.fr
Low season: open Monday to Friday from 9am to 1pm and from 2pm to 5pm; Saturday from 10am to 1pm and from 2pm to 5pm. High season: Monday to Saturday from 9am to 7pm; Sunday from 10am to 7pm.
On site: wi-fi area, rest area, shop, electrical and mechanical bike rental, sales centre. The Place de la Buanderie hosts also the bus station.

The festival of jasmine

Cultural event based on perfumery, it is the event in summer to pay tribute to this rare flower historically associated to the economy of the city. This provencal tradition celebrated every first weekend of August, was created in August 1946. In 1948, the jasmine festival is introduced in its current form: parades of floats lavishly decorated and floral parades decorated with the rhythm of fifes and tambourines, flower-battles, fireworks... A unique opportunity for the public to be sprayed by jasmine water by fire-fighters!

Sightseeing

MOLINARD ★★
60, boulevard Victor-Hugo
✆ +33 (0)4 93 36 01 62
www.molinard.com
cdemets@molinard.fr
Open all year. Every day from 9.30am to 6.30pm. Open until 7pm in July and August. Free tour of the museum and the soap factory.
Founded in 1849, the Maison Molinard has been a family business for five generations. In 1860, Molinard created perfumes which were sold in elegant Baccarat crystal bottles. In 1891, Queen Victoria bought her perfumes there. In 1900, Gustave Eiffel designed the structure of a distiller and foreigners (already) come to admire the magnificent collection of furniture from the 17th and 18th century in the Provence lounge. In 1921, Molinard launches the inimitable Habanita who had a complete success! In the early 1930s, Lalique and Baccarat signed the beautiful bottles. Go and have a look on the spot. Everything is there, nothing has changed: the architecture of the house is wonderful, the collection of old bottles is unique as well as the furniture on which the collections are displayed. The family proudly carries the label *«made in France»*. Indeed, Molinard is the only perfumer in Grasse to hold the label *Entreprise du patrimoine vivant* (EPV) (meaning Living Heritage Company). You should follow do a training in the creative workshop, where a smell helps you combine the notes. You can take your creation of perfume, in a 50 ml spray and his numbered certificate. It is magical! Upon presentation of guide: 10% discount on perfumes.

INTERNATIONAL MUSEUM OF PERFUMERY MIP - ★★★
2, boulevard du Jeu-de-Ballon
✆ +33 (0)4 97 05 58 00
✆ +33 (0)4 97 05 58 01
www.museesdegrasse.com
Closed on December 25th, January 1st and May 1st. Annual closing 3 weeks in November (starting from November 11th). Low season: open every day from 10am to 5.30pm. High season: every day from 10am to 7pm. Free for under 18-year-olds. Adult: €4 (€6 during the temporary exhibitions). Rental audio-guided: €1. Tourisme & Handicap label. Audio-guided, supports in Braille, specific course for young people (as of 7 years). Guided tour. Shop. Activities. Library.
Created in 1989 and fully renovated in 2008, this unique museum is dedicated to the preservation and the promotion of the international heritage of smells,

flavours and fragrances. It showcases the history and the originality of the industrial jobs and the famous perfume house. The MIP (International Museum of Perfumery) tackle the history of the fragrances in all aspects: raw materials, manufacturing, industry, innovation, trade, design, uses through various forms – art works, decorative arts, textiles, archaeological evidence, unique pieces and industrial platforms. Bold architectural project of Frédéric Jung, leant with authentic 14th-century ramparts, the museum (3 500 m^2) was extended by annexing adjoining buildings (the Pontevès hotel, the current museum and the Pélissier building) around a large transparent nave with landscaped gardens and terraces. New rooms were created: a temporary exhibition room, an auditorium, educational rooms for school's entertainment, entertainment rooms for children and adults and a children welcome at the entrance of the museum. The International Museum of Perfumery also offers temporary exhibitions, thematic tours and experiences (olfactory and culinary workshops). Do not miss to visit the MIP Gardens in Mouans-Sartoux to discover the perfume plants from Grasse.

Knife & Fork

LOU CANTOUN

4, avenue Louis-Pasteur
✆ +33 (0)4 93 42 22 57
restoloucantoun@gmail.com

Open Monday to Friday for lunch; Friday for dinner. Set menu at €16.50 (starter + main course + dessert). Children's menu: €7.50. Lunch menu: €13.50 (starter and main course or main course and dessert). Daily special at €11.

Located at the Plan, the establishment has a room with colors of the South and a small terrace. Warm welcome and hearty dishes made the reputation of Lou Cantoun. Many regulars get together for lunch. The dishes are different each day, you always have two choices. You can enjoy pasta, meat but also of fish. An elaborate and varied home made cooking which will charm your tastebuds for a very reasonable price without forgetting that the cuisine is carried out only with fresh ingredients. The desserts are also home made and vary like the main courses. The place is not so big, so think of booking.

ASPEN COUNTRY CLUB
In the tennis-club of Grasse
190, route de Cannes ✆ +33 (0)9 52 77 34 90
www.tcgrasse.com – contact@tcgrasse.com

Open all year. Open daily for lunch, dinner on reservation only for groups. Monday to Saturday from 9am to 7pm. Facebook page for the daily menus: www.facebook.com/aspencountryclub. Booking advised. Set menu at €14.90 (daily special, dessert and drink). Lunch menu: €9.90. Wine by the glass. Possibility of delivery or take-away. Groups welcome. Garden. Terrace. Games area for the young children. Free parking on the premises.

Aspen is a haven of peace, almost hidden inside the tennis club of Grasse. Not easy to find if you are not from Grasse but once there, what a delight! The large indoor room which has been completely renovated opens onto a terrace overlooking the tennis courts and a large garden. Unique for the region and indeed we are still in an urban area. Florent and his team love simplicity and real things. This restaurant offers a generous cuisine that uses fresh products. Pasta, woks, burgers and bagels are all original. In summer, meat and fish are served as carpaccio and Tartar. Have your meal with a glass of wine, while comfortably seated in the sun... The greediest will conclude with a sweet note as all desserts are homemade: the chef is indeed a pastry cook. Pastry courses for children are organized on Wednesdays and during school holidays. A nice place having an excellent quality/price ratio and a very nice welcome from Florent, the owner, who shares his good humour every day.

AUBERGE DE PROVENCE
2, place Saint-Donat
Plascassier ✆ +33 (0)4 93 42 40 83
www.aubergedeprovence.fr

Cuisine Niçoise and Provençale. From April to October: open every day for lunch and dinner except Wednesday. From November to March Thursday to Tuesday for lunch; Friday and Saturday for dinner. Children's menu: €10 (up to 10 years). Lunch menu: €15 (daily special + gourmet coffee). Wine by the glass. Menu Auberge €27: starter + main course + dessert. Terrace.

Plascassier is one of the hamlets attached to Grasse. Edith Piaf died there in October 1963. It is worth the visit because it has at least two pearls. One is the pretty small Saint-Pancrace church, built in 1646, the other is the Auberge de Provence which has just been taken over by Eric and Carine Graziotti. Both have already an establishment in Valbonne, the Bistro du Sommelier, that they created in 2013. Impassioned by wines, Eric also wishes to share the niçoise cuisine of his childhood. In the room, Carine welcomes you with a smile. And the terrace makes it possible to also enjoy the sun. An address to be rediscovered.

LA FLEUR DE LYS
2, avenue Chiris ✆ +33 (0)4 93 36 33 19
restaurantlafleurdelys@sfr.fr

Open Tuesday to Saturday for lunch and dinner. Booking advised. Menu from €27 to €37. Children's menu: €8.50. Daily special: €16.50 (except weekend). Daily specials at €18. Smart parking: Hôtel de Ville.

The hotel has recently been taken over but has kept the same spirit: traditional and refined cuisine. It is now the Chef Frédéric Bogé who works in the kitchen. After working with grand chefs such as Serge Gouloumes (Le mas Candille) or Alain Llorca, he is now in the capital of perfumes where he offers tasty cuisine made with fresh local products. Squid, veal cannelloni, roast quail as well as fish, according to the catch of the day. Regarding the desserts, let yourself be tempted by a whole lemon or gourmet coffee. Remember to book.

VAROUJ
115, route de Cannes ✆ +33 (0)4 93 09 08 01
www.auberge-lesaromes.com
auberge-les-aromes@wanadoo.fr

Open all year. Monday to Saturday for lunch and dinner. Menus €15, €29 and €35. Children's menu: €15 (up to 12 years). Lunch menu: €15 (starter and main course, or main course and dessert). Holiday voucher, Chèque Restaurant. Garden. Terrace.

The Andoniand family has been owner of the address for more than ten years and Sir, who is in the kitchen, gave his name to the restaurant. Its cuisine is an invitation to travel, a gourmet getaway on a tour of Armenian and Greek specialties. Diners as if you were there, mezzes various and delicious, moussaka, stuffed eggplant, grilled keuftes, sparse keufte to give kebab and lasagne to feta... We end with pastries of Greece or Armenia, Lebanon desserts like the baklava (made with almonds) or mouhalabieh (custard flavoured with honey and orange blossom). If does not tell any guests, the restaurant offers more traditional French dishes, fried meat or fish cooked in tinfoil... In the evening, you can choose one of the three menus or à la carte. Provençal setting is warm and friendly atmosphere and family. On sunny days, you can enjoy a large and very pleasant covered terrace, which opens onto a lovely garden. It is not known any longer if flavours on the plate or air... The property is located on the ground floor of The auberge Les Aromes (see section hotel).

Napoleon road

Napoleon left Elba Island on the brig the Inconstant with about 900 men and landed at Golfe-Juan in the late afternoon on 1st March 1815. They broke the bivouac at 2am to head to Grasse following impassable parades due to snow. In Grasse, Napoleon abandoned a car and two guns before resuming his forced walk to Paris to reclaim his throne. "The victory had to be in my haste," he said. The Emperor and his guard crossed the Provence and the Alps to reach Grenoble in 6 days, or 324 km via Grasse, Digne and Gap! Thus a prodigious epic due to the ways and terrible time. This route took the name of the Emperor to become the first tourist route having a historical character. If it does not exactly follow the paths of that time – many of which have also disappeared – Route Napoleon (RN85) gives a good idea about the journey made in 1815.

Old town of Grasse

Sleeping

AUBERGE LES ARÔMES

115, route de Cannes
✆ +33 (0)4 93 09 08 01
www.auberge-lesaromes.com
aubergelesaromes@gmail.com

Open all year. 5 rooms. Double room from €78 to €93; triple room from €100 to €115. Breakfast: €8. Open parking. Four-people room from €122 to €137. Holiday voucher. Wifi. Catering facilities (from €15 to €35).

The Andoniand family has been running this charming inn for a little more than ten years now. An ideal location halfway between Grasse and Cannes with a beautiful view over the hills of Grasse. The bedrooms are beautifully decorated with rich colours and shades of Provence. They are particularly large and all have a bathroom, a flat screen LCD television, telephone, air conditioning and wi-fi. There, the restaurant Varouj offers Eastern, Armenian and Greek specialties and traditional French dishes. The wonderful welcome from this family will make you feel almost like at home, and you will spend a relaxing stay in this nice setting. It is advisable to book as the rooms are limited.

LA BASTIDE SAINT ANTOINE

48, avenue Henri-Dunant
✆ +33 (0)4 93 70 94 94
www.jacques-chibois.com
info@jacques-chibois.com

Relais & Chateaux. Open all year. Reception 24/24. 16 rooms. Double room from €400 to €480; suite from €760 to €1,000. Breakfast: €29. Extra bed: €56. Parking (free). American Express, Diners Club. Pets allowed (small onds without supplement). Seminars. Receptions and weddings. Free Internet access. Free Wifi. Cleaning service. Catering facilities. Sale. Satellite TV. Whirlpool. Animations. Excursions (by reservation).

This is the wellness address where the Provencal art of life is fully expressed. Located in the middle of an 5 hectares olive grove in the countryside of Grasse, the Bastide of Saint Antoine dates back to the 18th century. This large house offers a stunning view from the restaurant and rooms facing the Esterel and the bay of Theoule. It is surrounded by a park where it is good to walk among the ancient trees and all the essences of Provence. Opio, Peymeinade, Saint-Vallier... These names evoking small villages nearby are also those of the 9 rooms and 7 suites. Each of them has a warm, elegant and refined style, spacious bathrooms with tubs and massage showers. The rooms have a more contemporary style as they have an extension where some have a private hot tub on the terrace. La Bastide offers packages for 2 people depending on the season and the cultural activity in the region. It also organizes themed holidays such as the discovery of wine or an introduction to the creation of perfumes.

BEST WESTERN ÉLIXIR GRASSE

Rue Martine-Carol
✆ +33 (0)4 93 70 70 70
www.bestwestern-elixir-grasse.com
resa@bestwestern-elixir.com

Open all year. Reception 24/24. 63 rooms. Double room from €107 to €218. Buffet breakfast: €15. Closed parking included. Continental breakfast at €8. American Express, Diners Club. Pets allowed. Seminars. Receptions and weddings. Free Wifi. Catering facilities (restaurant open in the evening Monday to Saturday. (7pm to 10pm) Menus from €32.50 to €38). Satellite TV, Canal+. Spa and wellness space.

Grasse and perfume

Grasse is famous since the Middle Ages for its green leather. The leathers are imported unprocessed and tanners prepare them with a new technique, favoured by the abundant presence of masti in the scrub which is used as tan to give the leather its colour. From the mid-thirteenth century, the drapers and tanners corporations are organized. Tanners who need water are on the Place aux Aires. In the sixteenth century, some begin to perfume the luxury gloves as it was thus done in Spain and Italy. It is Catherine de Medici who introduced it in France and Louis XIII in 1614 created the title of Maître Parfumeur (Master Glover) at the Court of France. In the seventeenth century, perfumed leather became increasingly popular: belts, vests, shoes... Then the tendency changes, changes occur (in 1724, the perfumers-glovers split from the tanners' corporation) and Grasse then specializes in perfumery. The discovery of the process of cold enfleurage to extract the fragrant of the most delicate flowers will transform the perfumery which then becomes industrial. The workshops in the centre, too narrow, are transferred to larger premises; many settled in ancient monasteries that were confiscated from the clergy during the Revolution; perfumers buy huge country sides to cultivate. The outdoor cultivation is made possible by irrigating the land. They get fragrant essences of exceptional quality, due to the climate: rose, jasmine, daffodil, carnation, tuberose, orange blossom, violet... The 1850s mark the conquest of markets and the development of aromatic crops in region. Leon Chiris from Grasse acquired in 1894 the first patent for volatile solvents. The perfume industry is running, it then becomes international and Grasse occupies a very important place, if not the first.

A full renovation in 2014, a change of name and brand: Élixir hotel has been redesigned and peacefully approaches the future. The 63 fully-equipped rooms (satellite TV, wi-fi, bathroom with bath-tub or shower) are worth the 4 star categories. The exterior classical architecture does not reflect the contemporary and slightly hushed atmosphere inside. There is also a garden, a swimming pool which is very nice in summer and a large terrace. Open 7 days a week, the Élixir restaurant, managed by the chef Frédéric Bogé, offers trendy «bistronomic» cuisine. A creative and modern culinary approach with real traditional recipes that have been completely revisited. The hotel is suitable for families or business customers (reception and conference halls).

Guesthouses

MOULIN SAINTE ANNE

9, chemin des Prés
✆ +33 (0)4 83 05 58 05
✆ +33 (0)7 81 79 41 01
www.moulinsainteanne.com
contact@moulinsainteanne.com

Open all year. 3 rooms (2 apartments (weekly rental)). Double room from €119 to €170. Breakfast included. Wifi. Satellite TV.

Le Moulin Sainte-Anne is a splendid building of the 18th century which was been renovated and transformed into guest rooms. Nestled in a green and rural setting of the Grasse countryside, Le Moulin Sainte Anne has 3 rooms and two apartments. Lovers of old stones will love the atmosphere from this magical place full of history. The renovation is exceptional because it has succeeded in conserving the old print of this former oil mill while giving it a comfort worthy of a 4-star hotel. The rooms are very spacious, from 34m^2 for the smallest to 53 m^2 for the suite with balneotherapy bathroom. Two independant apartments complete the offer. They can be rented for a week and are well equipped and nicely furnished and decorated. Once you are there, you enjoy the huge garden which stretches over 6,000 m^2, a charming small pool and the river that runs below the property. Breakfast is served on the south-facing terrace in summer. We love this very exceptional place!

In the surroundings

Opio ★★

L'OREE D'OPIO

30, route de Nice
✆ +33 (0)4 93 09 45 91
www.loreedopio.com
oreedopio@orange.fr

Open all year. Tuesday to Saturday for lunch and dinner. July and August open on Monday and Sunday. Menu from €23.90 to €38. Children's menu: €10.50. Lunch menu: €16.90 (main course, 1/4 of wine and coffee). Everything is cooked over a wood fire, giving a special flavour to the dishes. Chef Erik Bernard likes preparing products from the South-West and truffles depending on the seasons. The star products of the restaurant are obviously duck and foie gras prepared in several ways: half-baked, fried, and pickled or as salad. There are also: pizza tartuffo (truffles), the Landes salad, veal with artichokes and as desserts, enjoy the zabaglione with figs, peach cocktail with green tea and raspberry, chocolate fudge... Every day fresh fish coming from the market are served, so good when cooked in a salt crust. Véronique Hurson ensures an attentive reception. The restaurant has a large veranda which is covered in a semicircle, very bright and nicely decorated with plants. These two beautiful terraces are a great asset to spend a good time outside as soon as the weather is fine.

CLUB MED GOLF

Chemin de Tour
Domaine de la Tour
✆ +33 (0)4 93 09 71 00
www.golf-passion.org

Open all year. 9 holes. By 30. 1380 Mr. Architecte: Cabell Robinson. Rates included in the Club Med package. Secured cloakroom. Shop. Catering facilities from 12.30pm to 3pm. Hotel.

On the heights of Cannes, in the heart of the Club Med in Opio, this golf has thirty-seven bunkers and large and shallow greens, making it an excellent introduction and improvment course.

MILL OF OPIO

2, route de Châteauneuf
✆ +33 (0)4 93 77 23 03
www.moulin-dopio.com
accueil@moulinopio.com

Low season: open Monday to Friday from 9.30am to 12pm and from 2.30pm to 5pm. High season: Monday to Friday from 10am to 12pm and from 2.30pm to 6pm. Opening of the shop: in summer Monday to Saturday, from 9.30am to 1pm and from 2.30pm to 7pm, in winter Monday to Saturday, from 9am to 12.30pm and from 2pm to 6.30pm (except Monday morning).

This former mill dates back to the 15th century. Taken over in 1848 by M. Authion, the wheel at the time was powered by the waters of la Brague. When Roger Michel inherited, he changed the traditions and set up a more productive mill. More than seven generations later, the site is still run by his descendants who modernised it while staying attached to an approach of quality. Small producers and individuals can have their olives pressed there. The oil produced at the mill is of exceptional quality: they received several medals at the General Agricultural Competition in Paris. The shop is located in the old mill: you can admire the former olive dressed-stone press, the old millstones with wooden gears intact for two centuries years... They sell oil (AOP Nice, sweet, fruity and flavoured), table olives as well as a selection of regional products and condiments prepared without additive or dye: tapenade, anchoïade, mustard, saussoun, aubergine caviar, artichokes, peppers and dried tomatoes without forgetting honey, jams and syrups.

Peymeinade

■ **LE JARDIN DE CAMILLE ET QUENTIN**
32, avenue de Boutiny ✆ +33 (0)4 93 60 02 08
www.lejardindecamilleetquentin.fr
Closed during All Saints holidays. Closed on Wednesday and Sunday for dinner, except in summer (July and August) from 12pm to 2pm and from 7pm to 10pm. Booking advised. Children's menu: €9.90 (up to 12 years). Menus: €24.90 and €30.90. Accepted luncheon vouchers. Holiday voucher. Groups welcome (up to 80 people). Terrace with brumisator. Air conditioning. Changing table for baby.
Le Jardin de Camille et Quentin has flourished in Peymeinade since September 2010. The menus offer a beautiful selection of starters and various meals with an excellent value for money. The menu is between traditional cuisine – roasted duck breast, beef tenderloin sauce with porcini or foie gras – and Mediterranean cuisine – lamb with herbs, toast with tapenade, bream on basilica-courgette spaghetti. It also offers revisited classic bistro style such as beef tartare with a knife, cheeseburger or hamburger with foie gras and fig chutney. Those who love lobster will be delighted to find fresh ones in the pond. The restaurant also prepares a selection of pizzas and gourmet desserts as well as an amazing wine list that combines great wines and regional crops. The plates are copious and nicely presented; the service is attentive and efficient. The room sometimes seems a bit noisy because it is always full. But on sunny days, you can enjoy the quietness of the large terrace. A nice and friendly place to share.

■ **AU PAYS D'AUDREY**
Domaine du Mas de l'Olivine
16, chemin des Lazes ✆ +33 (0)6 61 77 26 54
www.aupaysdaudrey.fr
Open all year. Guided tours all year, on reservation, €5 per person.
The domaine de Mas de l'Olivine is a farm property of two hectares which dates from the 18th century. A family estate that brings together more than 300 olive trees. Exceptional scented plants, emblematic of Grasse, are grown there in the traditional way. Centifolia rose, Tuberose, Jasmine, Iris or orange blossom... A real immersion in the heart of these flowers. Guided tours are made all year round. A shop sells products made with the transformed flowers on site. The property can be privatized for weddings, baptisms or other festivals, with a quotation on request.

SAINT-VALLIER-DE-THIEY

Sightseeing

■ **SOUTERROSCOPE DE BAUME OBSCURE**
2600, chemin Sainte-Anne
✆ +33 (0)4 93 42 61 63 / +33 (0)6 80 90 70 59
www.baumeobscure.com
From February to mid-November Tuesday to Sunday. Closed on Monday (except if public holiday or school holidays). Annual closing from mid-November to beginning of February (possibility of visiting only for groups during this period). From February to March every day from 10am to 4pm (hour of the last departure of visit). From April to June from 10am to 5pm. From July to end of August from 10am to 6pm. From September to mid-November from 10am to 5pm. Group rate (as of 10 people): €7. Free for under 4-year-olds. Adult: €9. Child (from 4 to 12 years old): €5. Option treasure hunts: visit 2hours in the cave + 1hour outside €14 adult, €10 child. Recommended by the Park. Catering facilities. Picnic tables. No pets allowed in the cave. Parking.
The Baume Obscure cave is hidden in an unspoilt, natural space in the middle of a vast, forested limestone plateau on the route Napoléon, 20 minutes from Grasse. You get there by car on a renovated communal road that has retained the touristic character of a forest path. By means of a marked, 700 m track 60 m underground, guided by music and light, one discovers a fascinating and mysterious world. The Souterroscope is an automated museographic spectacle. The audiovisual «sound and light» show magnifies the natural marvels of the site and makes it possible to observe the crystalline concretions, small lakes and fossils at one's own pace. The music has, moreover, just been changed: more zen, now, it immerses visitors into a more peaceful atmosphere. If you reserve in advance, a speleologist can accompany you and explain what you are seeing: history of the cave, geology, hydrology, mineralogy and cave fauna. More entertaining visits also are organised so that the place can be explored with a treasure hunt. The novelty this year is that the hunt takes place outside in the forest as well: it lasts 3h (2h in the cave + 1h outside). In July and August, nocturnal, educational and entertaining events are organised several times a week for all publics: guided visits of the cave by torchlight and outside spectacles (musical, theatrical, film projections, specialised lectures on nature, astronomy...). An on-the-spot snack-bar provides light refreshment, hot and cold, every noon and in the evening when there are cultural events. Bring closed shoes to visit the cave and a sweater, even in summer.

Knife & Fork

■ **LA LANTERNE**
3-5, rue Adrien-Guébhard
✆ +33 (0)4 93 42 67 46
www.restaurant-la-lanterne.com
♿
Open all year. Daily for lunch and dinner. Booking advised. À la carte: Around €16. Children's menu: €8.90. Wine by the glass. American Express, Holiday voucher, Chèque Restaurant. Groups welcome. Take-away. Activities. Parking nearby and free.
An address where the reception is warm, the staff is

friendly and the cuisine is traditional (stuffed mussels, steak of the chef and its vegetables or chips); pizzas (Neapolitan, sicilian, queen, chorizo, oriental, calzone); couscous on Thursday; aioli Friday and Indian specialties with a thousand spices, samossa with meat or vegetables, Madras chicken, lamb Biryani, all accompanied by naan, the dishes prepared by the chef Sathish Nathesan, to enjoy with Indian background music.

■ **LE RELAIS IMPÉRIAL**
Route Napoléon (N.85)
2/4, place Cavalier ✆ +33 (0)4 92 60 36 36
www.relaisimperial.com
Logis. Open daily for lunch and dinner. Booking advised. Menu from €22 to €49. Children's menus from €7.50 to €11.50. Menu at €20 with the grill pizzeria of the relay. Terrace. Take-away.
Relais Imperial (former horses stable where Napoléon stopped) is an institution in the region which enjoys its guests. The dining room is splendid with exposed beams and hunting lodge style decoration of the great century. The glassed conservatory extends it and allows you to eat under the sun in all seasons. A simple and neat decoration that can host private parties. The hotel offers two types of catering services. On one side, a traditional cuisine made with fresh ingredients and with four set menus. On the other side, a grill pizzeria with a wide choice of pizzas but also salads, pasta or grilled meat. A warm welcome and a gourmet cuisine are the key words of this restaurant.

SAINT-CÉZAIRE-SUR-SIAGNE

Fortified village built on the steep cliffs overlooking Siagne, once harvests were stored there during the Roman conquest before conveying them to the port of Forum Julii (Frejus), which resulted the nickname «granary of César». In the 14th century, at the request of the count of Provence, it was closed by three fortified gates to protect the population from the bandits, pillaging and epidemics: the romanesque door of Saint-Ferréol, the door of Mons and Tour. The castle is part of the medieval fortifications: property of the famous family Cresp, it became communal in 1818 and now houses the town hall. Along the steep streets, you will discover the remains of the ramparts, the passages under vaults and doors with lintels. You can see two more chapels which became private homes and a hospital run by the knights of Saint-Blaise. The stone washhouse dates back to 1868 and the fountain aux Mulets: they were built to mark the arrival of water in the village thanks to a machine on the canal de Siagne.

Knife & Fork

■ **LOU SAN FERIOU**
12, place du Général-de-Gaulle
✆ +33 (0)4 93 70 73 52
www.restaurant-lou-san-feriou.fr
michel@raybaud.com
Open Tuesday to Saturday from 12pm to 2pm and from 7pm to 9pm; Sunday from 12pm to 2pm. Closed on Monday. Booking advised. Children's menu: €9.50. Lunch menu: €13.50 (daily special, dessert, coffee). Daily special €10. Chèque Restaurant. Groups welcome (up to 40 people). Baby chairs. Terrace. Free parking nearby.
Sandrine livens up this place with her husband Michel. The rustic dining room with exposed stones and the nicely decorated tables create a cosy atmosphere. It has a large covered terrace on the square in the pedestrian area. There is also a new summer terrace which is shaded and intimate.
Sandrine cooks Provencal style traditional meals in the kitchen. She strictly selects local products: fresh food or olive oil (used to enhance her famous aioli that all the regular customers enjoy); and artisanal pasta (ravioli, gnocchi made in the neighbouring village). She loves preparing tripe, pieds paquets, calf's head... and game during the season.
On her carte, in addition to the Provençal specialties, there are large salads and barbecue in summer with homemade fries. As for the dessert: crème brûlée with lavender, floating island, fruit tiramisu... Wines from producers are sold in jug or by the glass. And if you want to be sure of finding a table to enjoy all these tasty dishes, consider booking.

In the surroundings

Cabris ★★

LE FLAMBEAU
27, rue Frédéric-Mistral
✆ +33 (0)4 93 77 51 42
leflambeau@yahoo.fr
Open daily for lunch and dinner. À la carte: Around €15. Terrace. Activities.
Le Flambeau has several assets. You will find a traditional cuisine with meats and fish but also pizzas. The establishment also offers takeouts or deliveries: burgers, pasta, pizzas. Also *live* saturdays: such a success that booking is strongly recommended! A space for second-hand goods and déco was created: objects of quality are exposed there and put to sale for the happiness of bargain hunters. Activity which reinforces the cordial and friendly spirit which reigns in this place to discover urgently.

LE PETIT PRINCE
15, rue Frédéric-Mistral
✆ +33 (0)4 93 60 63 14
«Maître Restaurateur» label. Open Friday to Wednesday for lunch; Friday to Tuesday for dinner. Booking advised. Children's menu: €12. Daily specials: €13.50 (starter and main course or main course and dessert with 1/4 wine or coffee). Menus €26, €32, €40.
Countess Marie de Saint-Exupéry lived in Cabris from 1934 to 1971: she was the one who agreed that the restaurant is named after the hero of her son, the writer Antoine de Saint-Exupéry. The rustic dining room, with exposed beams and stonework, is decorated with reproductions of water-colours from the eponymous book. It is extended with a veranda, and a terrace surrounded by trees and plants open to the small meadow of the village. Christelle Joubert took over the premises in 2010 and now occupies the kitchen with her assistant Giovanni. From the room, we can see them at work. They serve a Mediterranean cuisine based on fresh products that have been purchased locally. The food is tasty; the plates are well-filled and beautifully displayed delight the eyes before the palate. Her lamb shank confit with spices, melting in the mouth, is already a classic of high quality. The 3 proposed menus enables to vary the pleasures and come back, especially since the menu is renewed each season. The welcome is friendly. During a meal, we'll go back to a princely childhood in this serene setting.

HÔTEL L'HORIZON
100, promenade Saint-Jean
✆ +33 (0)4 93 60 51 69
hotel-horizon.cabris@wanadoo.fr
Logis (2 cheminées). Closed from October 15th to April 30th. 22 rooms. From €91 to €159. Breakfast: €13. Internet access. Free Wifi. Satellite TV. Private parking.
A charming hotel located in the heart of the village of Cabris. The comfortable rooms enjoy stunning views of the bay of Cannes to the Saint-Cassien Lake, via the Esterel hills. You can also enjoy this panoramic view from the pool where you can peacefully breathe the fresh air, at about twenty minutes from the coast. A stop that will be an opportunity to discover the village and enjoy hiking and lots of other activities in Cabris.

Spéracèdes ★★

LA SOLEILLADE
3, rue des Orangers
✆ +33 (0)4 93 60 58 46 / +33 (0)6 64 29 45 03
www.la-soleillade.com
Gluten-free friendly. Open all year. Reception until 7pm. 5 rooms (100% non smoker). Double room from €57 to €75. Breakfast: €7.80. Extra bed: €15. Spoken languages: French, German, English. Pets allowed. Seminars. Free Internet access. Free Wifi. Cleaning service. Restaurant open daily for lunch and dinner, closed on Sunday evening and Monday. Daily special: €10. Menu from €16.50. Product sales.
It is a solar address due to its name and atmosphere in this old building from the late 19th century. Nicole Breuer runs the place with her German husband Horst and the Franco-Vietnamese chef Agnes Dans. Former teachers, it is without regret that they all left their job for this adventure. This trio gives spirit and good humour which delight the customers. The rooms are cosy, nicely furnished and have a bathroom. There is a terrace for relaxation and another is dedicated to the restoration. The food is traditional, regional and family: aioli, calf's head, spring rolls, small fish fry, fettuccine with braised zucchini for vegetarian and some gluten-free dishes. Nice wine list focused on AOP of Provence and other wines, exclusively French. Vietnamese meals on request. A smart family hotel in this peaceful village.

BIOT ★★★

Charming medieval village known for its glassware, Biot is identified with the history of the handicraft creation of potters: you will find on the territory of the town all the materials for this craft including clay, sand, manganese and feed stone. Already called «century of the Jar» in the 18th century, the village included forty factories and then the famous Jarre de Biot was exported to various Mediterranean ports and sometimes even as far as India and the Americas. The period of postwar will reveal the artistic identity of this town: it was at this time Raymond Peynet decided to bring life to "his amoureux" or that Fernand Léger sized his first relief. In 1997, the town received the label city and crafts for the glass works that exports the name of the village in the world. You can visit the village through the themed itineraries , the old way, the geological way, the glass or the handicraft (brochures available at the Tourist Office).

Sightseeing

Biot has the privilege to have been able to preserve its old authentic village. You must get lost in the maze of streets to admire its architectural beauty. It is classified by the Historic Monuments. Former Celtic-Ligurian habitat, Biot was occupied by the Romans for five centuries.

The seat of a Commandery of Templar Knights from 1209 to 1312, he subsequently became a garrison of the Knights of Malta. In Roman times, Biot was already known for pottery. In late 19th century, the clay pots used for transporting foodstuffs are gradually abandoned. It was around the mid-12th century that the city develops the work of decorative pottery and especially of glass, crafts for which it has been awarded the City and Crafts. Discover Biot means to enter a world in which you can admire the skills, the workshops of master glassmakers that are open to the public. Artists also have fell in love with the city.

Raymond Peynet (1908-1999). Set in the tower of the walkway from 1946 to 1976, he loved meeting his friends for the hallowed game of bowls, like as if they were having aperitif. Active member of the village, he took part in fiestas and created posters repeatedly. Made Honorary Citizen in 1952, an exhibition room is devoted to him at the Tourist Office.

Fernand Léger (1881-1955). The painter lived in Biot from 1951 to 1955. Museum dedicated to him was built in 1957. Inaugurated for the first time in 1960, it became a national museum and was opened again in 1969 by André Malraux, then Minister of Cultural Affairs.

Knife & Fork

LES TERRAILLERS
11, chemin Neuf
✆ +33 (0)4 93 65 01 59
www.lesterraillers.fr
contact@lesterraillers.com

Open Friday to Tuesday from 12pm to 2pm and from 7pm to 11pm. Booking advised. Menu from €74 to €120 (menu truffle in season €130). À la carte: Around €110. Children's menu: €25. Lunch menu: €43 (every day on weekdays starter, main course, dessert, 59€ with glass of champagne, 2 glasses of wine and coffee). American Express. Groups welcome (small group). Garden. Terrace. Parking. Valet in season. 1 Michelin star.

This high class restaurant built in an authentic pottery of the 16th century has preserved its charm of yesteryear with vaults, old beams, exposed old stones, antique furniture, all complemented by a lovely outdoor terrace which is flowered and shaded. In the room, Chantal and Pierre Fulci are professional and ensure a good welcome. In the kitchen, their son Michaël Fulci who took over the kitchens brings passion, youth and modernity. Only the lunch menu changes every Saturday, prepared by the chef when he comes back from the market. Every week, he creates new recipes where respect for seasonal products with the pleasure of the eye and taste. The other meals change according to the seasons and when the change of the menu. Extensive wine list with over 300 references and very nice plate of farmhouse cheeses selected by Master Perrin from La Ferme Fromagere. A cuisine of passionate people, subtle, creative, contemporary and which is consistent and modern.

THE CLUB
95, avenue de Roumanille
✆ +33 (0)4 93 65 00 00
www.leprovencal.com
info@leprovencalgolf.com

Low season: open every day from 7.30am to 5.30pm. High season: every day from 7.30am to 8pm. Daily special: €13. Fixed rate formula main course and dessert + mineral water: €18.50.

In the heart of Provençal Golf, Le Club is a chic brasserie in which you can eat during the opening hours of the golf. A sober and refined decoration, an attentive service: everything is made for you so that you can have a good time. Three terraces allow you to enjoy all the sunny days on the coast. As for the catering, it is the Chef Christophe Seine who will delight your tastebuds with dishes prepared according to the morning market. Breakfasts are served from the first hours. It is even possible to organize dinners, cocktails or festive meal. Last but not least, a catering service run by the Chef Jean-Laurent Depoil as well as a pastry service with David Orhant come to perfect an already complete offer.

In the workshop of the glass Masters Antoine and Robert Pierini.

Abbey of Château du Canadel

The oldest heritage of the town, the Abbey was originally a monastery built in the fifth century attached to the brotherhood of monks of Lérins in the year 1055. It was then a relay on the road to Saint- Honorat. The monks began the construction of the chapel and then in the twelfth and thirteenth centuries, they built the Abbey which adjoins. It initially served as a guest house to Pere Abbé when going to meetings of the Bishops of Vence and as winter residence. Requisitioned during the Revolution in 1789, it was sold to a rich Neapolitan who later sold it to a chef of the Negresco in Nice. The latter created a hotel-restaurant "L'Abbaye chez Joseph" in 1938. During the after-war period, the Abbey was a cultural mecca that received many artists, movie stars or singers. The atmosphere changed with the death of Joseph. After years of closure, it was reopened in 1997. With a 3-star hotel and a gourmet restaurant "541", the Abbey is still a gourmet address having great charm and character whose cloister and the chapel are both included in the inventory of historical monuments since 1927. Of the castle, only the tower with battlements and the porch Canadel which was the old gate, are still there.

LA COLLE-SUR-LOUP ★

ALAIN LLORCA

350, route de Saint-Paul
✆ +33 (0)4 93 32 02 93
www.alainllorca.com
reservations@alainllorca.com

♿

«Maître Restaurateur» label. Open all year. Closed on December 24th in the evening. Every day from 12.30pm to 1.45pm and from 7.30pm to 9.45pm. Booking advised. Menu from €65 to €150. À la carte: Around €50. Children's menu: €25. Lunch menu: €42 (valid all the week, excluding drinks). Wine by the glass. American Express. Groups welcome. Garden. Terrace. Valet. Take-away. Shop. Parking. 1 Michelin star.

Today, the cuisine of Alain Llorca goes to the essential. Refined, looking for the best, he does not disperse himself into table setting which often masks tasteless food. His culinary influences always sail in the county of Nice to Spain, where he comes from. Italy is also available with the arrival of Italian craftsman who produces exclusively for the hotels Llorca, ravioli, gnocchi and other specialties, including the famous agnolettis. The grill space, which faces the entrance of the restaurant, is also a big asset of this address with cooking "live" of Chalosse pigeon and foie gras by grilled cooking, Alpine lamb of the Haute Provence cooked on the grill, beef, from Bavaria or the Charolais, cooked on the roaster. The epilogue of the meal is signed by Jean-Michel Llorca, one of the best pastry chefs of the French Riviera, that makes the desserts, traditional and modern, creative, with lightness mark.

GOURDON ★

Gourdon is a medieval fortified village whose history dates back to the 9th century when the counts of Provence held their border to be isolated from the county of Ventimiglia. Built on a rocky outcrop at 760m of altitude, only one entrance orders it. You leave the car parking (required) below and on the path climbs the main street, we pass in front of the Saint-Pons romanesque chapel surrounded by a small garden. The Saint-Vincent church of provençal romanesque-style was built between the 10th century and 12th century: it just has a beautiful romanesque font with an angels head and the reliquary busts of sainte Luce, saint Just and saint Vincent. From the Victoria square, one enjoys a unique panorama stretching along 80 km, from Nice to Théoule and which features the mouth of the Var, Cap d'Antibes, the Lérins islands, the mountainous massifs of the Maures and the Estérel mountains and closer, the hamlet of the Pont du Loup which marks the entrance to the gorges du loup. The square owes its name to the Queen of England who visited Gourdon on March 28th, 1891 accompanied by the princess of Battenberg and the duchess of Argyll, a fact recounted in a newspaper at the time. The village is the starting point for beautiful walks on marked trails offering exceptional views including chemin du Paradis, Haut-Montet, the tour of the plateau Cavillore or Balconies of the French Riviera...

LA TAVERNE PROVENCALE

Place de l'Eglise
✆ +33 (0)4 93 09 68 22 / +33 (0)6 07 01 71 09
www.lataverneprovencale.com
contact@lataverneprovencale.com

♿

Closed at the beginning of December and from the end of Christmas holidays until the end of January. Low season: open every day from 9am to 7pm. Open for lunch and dinner 7 days a week in July and August. Booking advised. Set menu at €24. Children's menu: €14. Checks are not accepted. Groups welcome. Terrace. Parking.

This beautiful restaurant is the oldest in the village. It was created in 1933 by E. Reymond in an ancient building. Since then, it has been managed by the same family, and now by Marie-Christine Bousckri. Beautiful stone walls façade adorned with blue shutters, a kitchen open to the large dining room, large terrace offering a superb view of the sea... Many generations of customers, friends and personalities have come here to savour a traditional cuisine. Everything here is typical of Provence: Provencal medley (stuffed vegetables, tapenade, tart, eggplant caviar), homemade terrine, meat stew... Trout (almonds, meuniere or blue) and crayfish (nage or Bordeaux) from the fishpond to be served in your plate! A daily special is proposed at lunchtime according to the market. Do not miss the honey almond tart, a creation of the house. Tea shop and a shop of traditional products to be visited at place Sainte-Catherine.

■ **AUBERGE DE GOURDON**
Route de Caussols
✆ +33 (0)4 93 09 69 69 / +33 (0)6 13 22 46 77
www.aubergedegourdon06.fr
aubergedegourdon@sfr.fr
Open every day and public holidays from 8am to 7pm. Closed on Friday from mid-November to mid-April. Menu at €22.50 (starter + main course + dessert). Children's menu: €9.80. Daily special: €12. Set menu: €15 (starter + dessert), €18.50 (starter and main course or main course and dessert). Holiday voucher. Groups welcome (birthdays, seminars, receptions, etc). Terrace. Parking.
Located at the foot of the village, the inn of Roland Chiroleu is a nice friendly place, because this accomplished athlete hosts the paragliding club. The setting and the atmosphere is as warm as the owner's welcome. Here, we enjoy provençal regional cuisine, rich in flavours and fresh ingredients. According to the seasons and market, Roland gives suggestions on the blackboard, a choice of pasta but also the grilled meats. The dishes are hearty. The Provencal dish is a speciality consisting of homemade terrine, crisps of chard, barbajuans, goat cheese toasts, panisses, stuffed vegetables, sometimes sanguin mushrooms with oil. The desserts, favourite of the Chef, are unmissable: gratin of fresh fruit, apple tarts caramel sauce, crumble with seasonal fruit, tiramisu, homemade iced parfait with honey. In the afternoon, beverages, waffles, ice cream, sandwiches... are served in the dining room or on the garden terrace. This Epicurean is also an amateur beekeeper and in his secret garden, he harvests honey twice a year in June (spring taste of thyme and lime of Gourdon) and mid-September (Caussols lavender scent). He can also sell it – if there are any left.

MOUANS-SARTOUX ★

Knife & Fork

■ **LE PETIT BOUCHON**
4, rue de la République
✆ +33 (0)4 93 75 65 43
www.petitbouchonmouans.com
contact@petitbouchonmouans.com
Open all year. Every day all year, closing Monday only. Menus Bouchon €24. Menu Tablier €34. À la carte: Around €35. Chef's suggestions on the slate. Chèque Restaurant. Terrace.
By creating a «bouchon» in the old village, the audacious bet of the associates Ludovic Lercier and Laurent Boismare was to bring here the culinary heritage of Lyon. They have succeeded in creating this identity. The room is full of objects from Lyon in a rustic atmosphere of yesteryear. During fine weather, the terrace extends in both pedestrian streets around the restaurant, which is ideally located in a corner. The authentic cuisine offers a variety of specialties: frog legs, pork cheek confit, duck pie with mushrooms, sausage, chicken liver cake, pudding, sausages, kidneys, veal stew... Here, everything is for our pleasure. The plates are generous and the dishes are well presented. The wines naturally come from Burgundy, Beaujolais, Crozes-Hermitage, Côtes du Rhône, etc. The menu follows the seasons in order to ensure freshness and quality. Ludovic, the chef displays his suggestions on the blackboard. Efficient service and outstanding hospitality from a friendly and attentive staff. Have a break there to enjoy a happy moment full of taste... Lyon at lunch time!

■ **L'ARDOISE DU PRIMEUR**
22, rue Durand-de-Sartoux
✆ +33 (0)6 05 06 85 63
patrick.girard613@hotmail.fr
Open all year. Every day from 10am to 11pm. Children's menu: €5 (less than 5 years). Daily specials: €12.80. Wine by the glass. All the main courses are at €9.95, the desserts at €5.50. Groups welcome (up to 15 people). Terrace. Take-away. Parkings at the village.
In the centre of the village, in the room with a bistro-spirit of this small restaurant or on the heated terrace, enjoy the simple, traditional and family cuisine of Patrick Girard, who concocts homemade meals (on blackboard) with fresh products: warm goat cheese, small stuffed vegetables, ravioli roquefort sauce, tartare with fresh fries, supreme chicken with curry sauce, burgers, pies... As a bonus, a friendly welcome and unbeatable prices. What else?

Sleeping

DOMAINE DE L'ALBATROS

1000, chemin des Plaines
✆ +33 (0)4 92 28 40 00
www.domaine-albatros.com
contact@domaine-albatros.com

Open all year. 58 rooms. Low season: from €75 to €120. High season: from €95 to €130. Breakfast: €10. Parking. American Express. Pets allowed (€7 per day). Free Wifi. Satellite TV.

A charming property located in the countryside of Grasse in a green oasis, on the edge of the golf course Saint-Donat. The rooms are modern, comfortable and large. They are equipped with all the modern comfort: air conditioning, a flat-screen television, separate toilets... The suites have a private terrace and a sofa bed. And then there are the Cottage villas. Designed in duplex, they can accommodate from 2 to 6 people (ideal for 4). Each has a private garden overlooking the golf course and pool. On the ground floor a sitting room, a kitchen and two rooms upstairs. Another asset of the hotel: a nice central swimming pool facing the park. As for sports and relaxation: the golf course that borders the complex (inquire for packages), ten tennis courts, an equestrian centre nearby and a spa on site to decompress.

Shopping

LES DÉLICES D'AURILE

6, rue de la République
✆ +33 (0)4 92 92 81 10
✆ +33 (0)6 25 47 63 72
www.lesdelicesdaurile.fr
contact@lesdelicesdaurile.fr

Except school holidays from 1pm to 7.30pm, closed on Monday. Small school holidays from 1pm to 7.30pm every day and public holidays except December 25th and January 1st. July and August every day from 1pm to 11pm. June and September every day except Monday from 1pm to 7.30pm and from 1pm to 10.30pm Friday and Saturday. A ball: €2.50, 2 balls: €4. Take-away. Table service. Terrace.

The greediest have found their address! With your tongues ready for pleasure, the ice-cream lovers roam the streets of the charming village of Mouans-Sartoux until nightfall because they have nomadic greediness. The ice-cream is made from whole milk, eggs, sugar and natural flavourings or fruits. They are invariably served in a pot or in cone of different sizes with a choice of different flavours that vary according to the seasons. You just have to dip the spoon into the pot to realize the beautiful creamy texture. The setting is cozy and the atmosphere is friendly and family in the small room or on the terrace. Note that for the holidays, the Délices d'Aurile also creates logs and frozen desserts. Foodies will also enjoy the pancakes and waffles from October to late April. A nice address, discrete, full of heart and flavours.

In the surroundings

Auribeau-sur-Siagne ★

LA TABLE DU VILLAGE

66, route du Village ✆ +33 (0)4 93 60 06 45
www.la-table-du-village.blogspot.fr

Closed for the New year holidays. Open Thursday to Monday for dinner; Thursday to Tuesday for lunch. Booking advised. Set menu at €35 (gourmet menu). À la carte: Around €35. Children's menu: €12. Wine by the glass. Checks are not accepted. Terrace. Parking. When Daniel Stoecklin cooks, he chooses local products from small producers, as his ravioli with porcini mushrooms, cream sauce and gravy (fresh ravioli made by a local craftsman) or a Valcluse trout (fish farming in Auribeau-sur-Siagne) with thyme and lemon. You may also like the charcuterie plate of the back country, the semi-cooked homemade foie gras, gingerbread of the Chef with gégéride jam and finally flambéed Suzette pancake. Every Friday, there is an aioli and an Alsatian menu is offered once a month. In the room, his wife Marie-Jo will advise you wisely for the choice of your wines. In summer, enjoy the shadowed terrace, where you can enjoy lunch or dinner while admiring the view of the valley.

Pégomas ★

LE GRILL DE LA MOURACHONNE

3, place du Logis ✆ +33 (0)4 93 77 96 60
www.legrilldelamourachonne.com

Open all year. Daily for lunch and dinner. À la carte: Around €25. Children's menu: €9.90. Daily special: €10.90. Groups welcome (the restaurant proposes menus adapted to groups). Baby chairs. Terrace. A large car park is at disposal in front of the establishment.

Located in the city center on the banks of the Mourachonne river, the Grill of the same name offers a varied and quality cuisine to his guests. A family-run restaurant held by Catherine and Pierre Petit as well as their son Maxime since July 2012. In addition to a large room decorated with care, the restaurant has also a terrace to enjoy the surroundings. Part of it was covered last year, offering a large protected surface. The dishes are copious and varied. Fish or meat, each piece is a product of quality. Everyday, a series of suggestions on a blackboard in addition to the carte. A wide choice for all tastes. For dessert, the tiramisu with caramel deserves a special mention. During the whole service, the establishment is always full. So a tip: book before coming.

HÔTEL LES JASMINS

531, avenue Frédéric-Mistral
✆ +33 (0)4 93 42 22 94 / +33 (0)6 32 67 77 27
www.hotel-lesjasmins.com

Logis (1 cheminée). Single room €45; double room €74. Half-board: €69 (per person). Breakfast: €8. Parking included. Wifi. Catering facilities (logis 1 cocotte).

Located in the heart of Pégomas, this hotel has the advantage of enjoying a central location yet very quiet surrounded by greenery.
The place is ideal to stop and enjoy a walk around to explore the Siagne valley. Also at 15-minute drive from the seaside. Alone or with family, all configurations are possible in the 14 spacious and comfortable rooms. The restaurant is open on week days and also on the weekend.
A warm and friendly welcome awaits you every day of the week. In winter, you can admire the hills covered with mimosas surrounding the whole village.

MOUGINS ★★★

Above the modern town of Mougins, you will find the Mougins Village at 260 metres altitude. You will first discover the extramural part built after the 18th century, and then get inside the ramparts of the medieval core built in the middle Ages with a stunning snail shape. The Mougins fame began in the late 19th century. Its climate attracts many tourists, and artists succombed to the charm of the village: in 1924 Francis Picabia, surrealist avant-garde painter settled there. Equally conquered by its attraction, Picasso spent the last 12 years of his life there, between 1961 and 1973. It is in the «Mas Notre Dame de Vie» that he created his last works. Other personalities also marked the place: Jean Cocteau, Paul Eluard, Man Ray, Fernand Léger, Robert Desnos, René Clair, Isadora Duncan, Christian Dior ... The charm of the village still inspires many artists who carry out their work in galleries or work in their workshops there. The image of Mougins is also associated with gastronomy. In 1992, the town was dedicated the most starred city in France while each year, it returns to the art of the table by organising the Festival International de la Gastronomie in September.

TOURIST OFFICE OF MOUGINS
39, place des Patriotes ✆ +33 (0)4 92 92 14 00
www.mougins-tourisme.fr
tourisme@villedemougins.com
From Cannes, take the N85 towards Grasse. Mougins is located 7 km from Cannes.
Qualité Tourisme label. Low season: open every day from 10am to 5pm. High season: every day from 10am to 7pm. June and September: Monday to Saturday, from 10am to 6pm.
The tourist office of Mougins offers several themed tours allowing you to really enjoy your stay in this beautiful town with the charm of yesteryear. There are several themes: the old village, the chapel Notre-Dame-des-Vies, Picasso and Mougins, the chapel of St. Barthélemy or even the ride along the water that relates the history of fountains and pond in the village. For those who prefer to organize themselves freely, download all of these courses on the website of the Office.

Sightseeing

The authentic streets of the old centre of the village of Mougins curl on themselves and have many architectural treasures. On Sainte-Anne Square is a bust of Commander Lamy who became famous in Chad at the time of colonial conquests, whose capital (now Djamenah) long bore the name of Fort-Lamy.
The Saracen door on the Church Square is the last vestige of fortifications built in the 14th century. A bronze Ceres overcomes one of the oldest fountains of the village while the city bears the ancient arms. Note that at No. 26 Vaniers Street, paintings dating from 1510 representing two monks were discovered, one of which holds a book and the other a pike.

© LAWRENCE BANAHAN – AUTHOR'S IMAGE

Mougins.

Knife & Fork

LE MOULIN DE MOUGINS
Avenue Notre-Dame-de-Vie
✆ +33 (0)4 93 75 78 24
www.moulindemougins.com
reservation@moulindemougins.com

Open Monday to Saturday for lunch and dinner; Sunday from 11.30am to 5pm. Corner tapas/lounge open Tuesday to Saturday, from 6pm to midnight. À la carte: Around €55. Wine by the glass. American Express, Diners Club.

Facelift for the Moulin de Mougins. After having undergone major works after the bad weather of October 2015, the hotel made a few changes. The cuisine is now open, the terraces are more spacious and the parking is more accessible. Without forgetting the wheel of the mill that now turns. The hotel where Roger Vergé worked for many years honours fresh ingredients. Guests can enjoy a fillet of black Angus, lobster from the Atlantic or tataki of bluefin tuna from corsica. On sundays, a brunch is served between 11: 30 am and 5pm. Finally, a tapas corner, near the bamboo plantation, allows you to enjoy the place while having a drink with cheese, meats or even oysters.

LE CANDILLE
Le Mas Candille
Boulevard Clément-Rebuffel
✆ +33 (0)4 92 28 43 43
www.lemascandille.com
info@lemascandille.com

Relay & Castles. Open all year. Low season: Wednesday to Sunday for lunch and dinner. High season: every day for dinner; Wednesday to Sunday for lunch. Booking advised. Menu from €95 to €135. À la carte: Around €115. Lunch menu: €62 ("Menu of the market" 1 Candille aperitif, 2 glasses of wine, mineral water and coffee). Wine by the glass. American Express, Diners Club. Groups welcome. Garden. Terrace. Valet. Parking.

Michelin-starred Chef Serge Gouloumès, present since the opening gave up his headquarters a few years ago in David Chauvac, his right arm. A nouvelle cuisine to be discovered in the dining room with light grey walls built by the raspberry touches the Bohemian crystal chandeliers and plum armchairs in the large, bright dining room and its ceiling of Jean Honoré Fragonard, the native, who gives the pleasant impression lunch open-air, or on the pleasant terrace with views of the grasse hinterland. The restaurant at La Pergola summer is open from May to mid-September and allows you to eat summer large plates or snacks, by the infinity pool.

Sleeping

LE MAS CANDILLE
Boulevard Clément Rebuffel
✆ +33 (0)4 92 28 43 43
www.lemascandille.com
info@lemascandille.com

Relais & Chateaux. Reception 24/24. 45 rooms (including 7 suites. Non smoker). Double room from €515 to €815. Buffet breakfast: €29. Parking (external free). American Express, Diners Club. Pets allowed (except in La Pergola). Seminars. Receptions and weddings. Free Internet access. Free Wifi. Gourmet restaurant « Le Candille « open daily for lunch and dinner. Summer Restaurant « La Pergola « open from May to mid-September by the swimming pool. Satellite TV, Canal+. Hammam, whirlpool, sauna. 3 outdoor pools including one heated all year. SPA Shiseido, treatments, massages.

Mas Candille has different unique atmospheres in a vast landscaped park offering exceptional comfort, a setting of absolute tranquillity and elegance. The Mas, with the restaurant and 20 rooms, dates back to the 18th century. It was originally a farm where vine and olive were cultivated. The name «candille» is a Provencal word and means candle, referring to the cypress trees, centenarian guardians. The «Bastide» is an extension built in 2000 is an oasis dedicated to well-being: it has 19 rooms, 1 suite, and the Shiseido Spa, the first in France, which offers Qi-Shiseido massages combined with a range of treatments to meet your wellness. Finally, in 2009 the «Villa» was created. It is a set of 6 luxurious suites from 55 to 70 m^2 with modern facilities built below the terrace in two buildings that are integrated to the environment with their hanging Provencal gardens. Large infinity pool, fitness centre, etc... The gastronomic restaurant «Le Candille» has one Michelin star, is open daily for lunch and dinner. Eat in the dining room or on the terrace with panoramic views over the valley and surrounding hills. The restaurant "La Pergola" is open from May to mid-September near the swimming pool for lunch; bar service and snacks throughout the day. The Mas is in itself a sanctuary of peace, a haven of serenity.

General view of Mougins.

LES ETOILES DE MOUGINS

INTERNATIONAL FESTIVAL OF GASTRONOMY

23 | 24 | 25 JUNE

Free entrance

#LesEtoiles2017

LESETOILESDEMOUGINS.COM

A typical house of Mougins.

■ **LE MAS DU GOLF**
348, avenue de la Valmasque
✆ +33 (0)4 92 28 88 20
www.lemasdugolf.com
contact@lemasdugolf.com

Reception 24/24 (spoken languages: French, English, Italian, Spanish, Arabic). 24 rooms (100% non smoker). Double room from €89 to €149. Buffet breakfast: €12. Parking included. Checks are not accepted. American Express, Holiday voucher. Seminars. Internet corner. Free Internet access. Free Wifi. Cleaning service. Airport shuttle on request, paying service. Satellite TV, Canal+. Excursions (possible on request).
Near the Golf Country Club of Cannes Mougins and the Royal Mougins golf club located at 6 km only, this establishment created in 2011 consists of three independent buildings in the middle of a park of 3,000 square meters. Mostly on the ground floor and open onto the garden, the rooms are bright, air-conditioned, soundproofed and are fully equipped. Double, twin or triple rooms, all reveal a contemporary setting, high comfort bedding with duvets and bathrooms with a large shower area. Breakfasts are served in a room which opens on the garden and swimming pool. The Mas can also host meetings or conferences in a pleasant green and wooded setting.

■ **LA LUNE DE MOUGINS HOTEL & SPA**
1082, avenue du Général-de-Gaulle
✆ +33 (0)4 93 75 77 33
www.hotel-lunedemougins.com
contact@hotellunedemougins.com

47 rooms. Single room from €95 to €170; double room from €115 to €190. Breakfast: €16 (€10 for under 12-year-olds). 2 rooms adapted to the disabled guests. Call to book depending on your specific needs.
Charming hotel on the heights of Cannes, la Lune De Mougins is surrounded by greenery, in the regional park of Mougins. A comfortable hotel where you can relax and resource yourself. Its restaurant, le Citrus, serves mediterranean cuisine with fresh ingredients. A bar is also open 24 h/24. And for even more relaxation, an outdoor pool with a shady terrace awaits you.

SAINT-PAUL

■ **TOURIST OFFICE OF SAINT-PAUL-DE-VENCE**
2, rue Grande ✆ +33 (0)4 93 32 86 95
www.saint-pauldevence.com
tourisme@saint-pauldevence.com
From June 1st to September 30th, open from 10am to 7pm. From October 1st to May 31st, from 10am to 6pm. Closed from 1pm to 2pm weekends and public holidays.
This office organizes many commented guided tours on different themes such as built heritage, artists, religious heritage, in the footsteps of Marc Chagall, the street in the Middle Ages, the cemetery or the White Penitents chapel decorated by Folon. These services are offered to individual customers but also for groups (minimum 10 people). Count between one or one and a half hour for the visit. The Tourist Office has recently been awarded grade 3 for the quality of its services.

Sightseeing

■ **FOUNDATION MAEGHT** ★★★★
623, chemin des Gardettes
✆ +33 (0)4 93 32 81 63
www.fondation-maeght.com
Info@fondation-maeght.com
Open all year. Low season: every day and public holidays from 10am to 6pm. High season: every day and public holidays from 10am to 7pm. The ticket office closes 30 min before closing. Closed at 4pm the 24th and December 31st. Free for under 10-year-olds. Adult: €15. Group (10 people): €10 (+ students and -18 years). Reduced rate: €10. Possibility to take photos and film: €5. Between two temporary exhibitions, certain rooms can be closed to the public: rate is consequently reduced. Guided tour with the Tourist Office: €7 + €15 admission fee. Catering facilities. Shop. Activities. Library.
The Aimé and Marguerite Maeght Foundation is a unique example of a private foundation in Europe. This temple of modern and contemporary art was opened on July 28, 1964 by André Malraux, then minister of Cultural Affairs. The site, which celeberated its 50th anniversary was entirely designed and funded by the couple who asked the Catalan architect Josep Lluís Sert to manage its appearance, in cooperation with the artists (painters and sculptors) who created the foundational works, often monumental, integrated to buildings and gardens such as the labyrinth of Miró, Giacometti court, mosaics of Chagall and Tal-Coat, the fountain of Bury, pelvis and the Braque stained glass windows. It is an exceptional place, hidden in a landscape of great beauty, a meeting place, research, education... The foundation is completely autonomous. Each year, it organises numerous monographic and thematic exhibitions. With 200,000 visitors a year, it is the second most visited museum of modern art in France.

Knife & Fork

THE CARUSO

1, Montée de la Castre
Place de l'Eglise ✆ +33 (0)4 93 24 36 47
www.lecarusodesaintpaul.fr
le-tandem@orange.fr

Open Thursday to Tuesday for lunch; the weekend for dinner. Menu from €28 to €35. À la carte: Around €50. Lunch menu: €25 (starter and main course or main course and dessert). Lunch menu at €31 with starter, main course and dessert.

In the heart of the village, blackboards with gourmet suggestions frame the entrance of Caruso, taken over summer 2012 by Celine at the reception and Barthelemy in cuisine. The two small rooms are connected by some steps and offer a comfortable setting; paintings hung on the white walls facing the stone walls. Smart atmosphere, all beige and white. One comes here to taste a gastronomy of the south where tradition mixes with creativity. All is minute-prepared and worked out with fresh ingredients from market. Lobster raviolis with emulsion of bisque, marinated salmons, Black Angus fillet of beef... The evening, some pizzas are added to the carte. Pleasant welcome and elegant service.

LA FONTAINE RESTAURANT

10, montée de la Castre
✆ +33 (0)4 93 32 58 01
www.restaurant-lafontaine.fr
contact@restaurant-lafontaine.fr

Open every day from 10am to 10pm. Children's menu: €16. Main courses between €19 and €40. Terrace.

In the heart of the medieval village, it is in a cosy and warm setting that the team of La Fontaine restaurant welcomes you every day. A sleek and stylish decor, a sophisticated cuisine and dishes made with fresh ingredients made the reputation of the establishment. Le Chef Jérôme Garello works in the kitchen. Parillada and its giant prawns are one of the specialties of the establishment. Two menus are available: one for lunch with bistro-style dishes and a second with more elaborated choices in the evening. This year, La Fontaine tents to take down the Maître Restaurateur label. Tasty and very popular table. It is better to book before coming.

LE TILLEUL

Place du Tilleul ✆ +33 (0)4 93 32 80 36
www.restaurant-letilleul.com

Open all year. Exceptional closings are communicated on the site. Daily for lunch (last sitting at 2.45pm) and for dinner (last sitting at 10pm). Booking advised. À la carte: Around €50. Children's menu on request. Lunch menu: €25 (starter, main course or main course, dessert). Lunch menu starter, main course, dessert €29. Wine by the glass. American Express. Groups welcome (on request by e-mail). Terrace. Take-away at the snack « Les Gourmandises du Tilleul «.

Well located after the gate of the old city walls that gives access to the heart of the village, this charming address is like a family home in which you can peacefully rest. On the terrace which is in the shade of a centenary lime tree, or in interior rooms with open views over St. Paul, the atmosphere is different at different hours of the day, from breakfast at 8h30 until dinner at 7.30pm... The Chef Bastien Hodé works with seasonal products with which he likes to add exotic flavours. He offers two menus: a faster one for lunch; and another which is more ambitious for diner. The meals are regularly renewed. In the afternoon lemonade, tea and snacks are available.

LA VAGUE DE SAINT-PAUL

45, chemin des Salettes
✆ +33 (0)4 92 11 20 00
www.vaguesaintpaul.fr
reservation@vaguesaintpaul.com

♿

Low season: open Wednesday to Saturday from 7.30pm to 9.30pm; Wednesday to Sunday from 12.30pm to 2.30pm. High season: every day from 12.30pm to 2.30pm and

Saint-Paul-de-Vence.

© VALÉRY TRILLAUD

Saint-Paul-de-Vence.

from 7.30pm to 9.30pm. Booking advised. Lunch menu: €25 (2 dishes, water and coffee included). Wine by the glass. Lunch menu 3 main course at €29 (water and coffee included). Menu dinner 3 main course at €39 (excluding drinks). Menu Carte blanche at €69 (excluding drinks). American Express. Groups welcome (organization of receptions, evenings, seminars, cocktails). Garden. Terrace. Shop. Parking.

This year, the restaurant changes name and Chef. You will therefore now enjoy the creative mediterranean cuisine of chef Akhara Chay at the Jardin de la Vague. After being trained at Ghislaine Arabian and Alain Ducasse, he worked in renowned establishments including the Royal Barriere of Deauville and Le mas Candille in Mougins. Several set menus are offered for lunch and dinner, as well as a large choice on the carte. Mediterranean flavours are honoured and will pleasure your taste buds. As for the setting, it is modern and uncluttered, like the rest of the hotel.

Sleeping

■ LA VAGUE DE SAINT-PAUL
45, chemin des Salettes
✆ +33 (0)4 92 11 20 00
www.vaguesaintpaul.fr
reservation@vaguesaintpaul.com

The hotel closes in November and January. Reception 24/24 (spoken languages: French, English, Spanish, Italian). 50 rooms (including 4 suites and 2 equipped rooms for disabled guests). Low season: double room from €100 to €215. High season: double room from €130 to €250. Half-board: €39 (per person, excluding drinks, only in the evening). Buffet breakfast: €18. Closed parking (external, free). American Express. Pets allowed. Seminars. Receptions and weddings. Internet corner. Free Internet access. Free Wifi. Cleaning service. Restaurant Au jardin de la Vague. Open Wednesday to Sunday midday in low season and every day in high season. Lunch menus 2 main course at €25 and 3 main course at €29 (water and coffee included). Spa. Satellite TV. Hammam, whirlpool, sauna. Excursions.

The history of this building with the shape of a wave, located in a green oasis is not trivial. Built in the late 1970's by an architect capable of giving unusual cures to concrete, it has long been the global showcase of a high-tech company, but was then abandoned. Rehabilitated, it reopened under the leadership of Swiss investors. Vague has become a contemporary and minimalist hotel, open to a demanding clientele: furniture is designed by a great designer, eco-friendly approach in the choice of materials, optimized spaces. The 50 rooms and suites having a minimalist design are luxuriously equipped (minibar, safe, LED screen TV, air conditioning, iPod station...). The terraces overlook the gardens and the pool in the middle of the park. Luxurious services that can be accessed freely: gym, spa, business centre. There are private rooms for receptions and seminars. On the occasion of the fiftieth anniversary of the Maeght Foundation, located nearby, the hotel managed by Thierry Naidu and the Phoenix hotel management offers a package dedicated to the discovery of this exceptional art museum. We urge you to dive into this wave and enjoy it.

LE HAMEAU

528, route de La Colle ✆ +33 (0)4 93 32 80 24
www.le-hameau.com

Closed from November 15th to February 14th. It is recommended to consult the site of the hotel to profit from best rates codes promotion GO. 17 rooms (including suites). Double room from €98 to €255; suite from €150 to €335. Buffet breakfast: €15. Closed parking. American Express. Pets allowed (€15/day). Free Wifi. Sale. Satellite TV. Sauna. Solarium. Bowling green. Infinity pool. Fitness.

This former Provencal farmhouse of the 18th century has remarkably been restored and now welcomes very selective tourists. A jewel in a green case, a successful combination of the past, of authenticity and modernity, for the choice of colours, fabrics and flowers, it has welcomed prestigious guests, including Chagall... Its 17 rooms and independent suites are bright and all different. With traditional Provencal furniture, old tiles on the floor, with or without terrace. They are all very comfortable: air conditioning, telephone, TV, internet, mini- bar, room service. This haven of peace is charming; from the infinity pool we have a wide view over the village of Saint Paul. There is a relaxation section with a hot tub (near the pool), sauna and hammam. Possibility of massages upon appointment. A roof terrace has been converted into a solarium and offers a superb view of the sea... 5000 m^2 of terraced gardens, multitude of flowers and orange trees provide a total escape from everyday stress. Caring welcome and excellent service. Escape guaranteed.

Leisure

BOULES GAME

At the entrance of the village

Free access 24/24.

This boules game dates back to the beginning of the century, but here, the petanque (or set of balls) is forever associated to Yves Montand and Lino Ventura. Experts will watch out this ground located at the entrance of the village in front of the remparts wondering exactly where the accomplices used to play... No surprise thus if the Tourist Office of the town offers a guided tour on this theme in which you'll learn all about it: doublette, triplette, how to point, draw, square and... kiss Fanny! Impossible to circumvent.

Going Out

THE ARTIST

Intramural – 3, montée de l'Eglise
✆ +33 (0)4 93 24 37 48
quenardfrederic@gmail.com

Open all year. Low season: Thursday to Tuesday from 8am to 6pm. High season: every day from 8am to 9pm. Daily special between €10 and €13.50. Gourmet coffee at €8. Tea from €3.50. Terrace.

An old cartery transformed into a charming tea room and bakery at the same time. A déco which refers to the cinema world, in homage certainly to all the actors who remained in Saint Paul. The establishment has just been taken over by two new managers who preserved the formula of the place. In the morning, you stop to buy your bread, have a café. Midday, you can enjoy a beautiful salad, a savory pie or a pancake. In the afternoon a place for tea time with a tea carte of «Dammann Frères». (30 varieties for tasting and sale). In short, whatever the timing of the day, a small gourmet break always extremely pleasant.

Shopping

CUTLER OF SAINT PAUL

7, place de la Mairie
✆ +33 (0)4 93 58 21 69
ateliercouteaux@free.fr

Open from beginning of March to mid-November, every day from 10.30am to 6.30pm.

The origin of these knives comes from Tulle in Corrèze where a passionate opened his factory of handmade knives in 2004. He then creates his first pocket knife, the Corrézien; it immediately attracts the most demanding in terms of cutlery, with attention to detail and perfection without any possible comparison. The regional collections are inspired by local and cultural heritage of each region: Provence, Brittany, Alsace, Languedoc, Corrèze... Located in front of the Town Hall of Saint-Paul-de-Vence (church square, this shop offers a wide selection of models of regional knives, including the famous Saint Paul (knife with the shape of a siren, homage to the painter Chagall which was often inspired by sirens, and loved Saint-Paul-de-Vence). Pocket knives, table knives, penknife and unique pieces can be discovered in this exclusive shop or on their website.

TOURRETTES-SUR-LOUP ★★

Knife & Fork

AUBERGE DES GORGES DU LOUP

4, route de Grasse – Le Pont du Loup
✆ +33 (0)4 93 59 38 01
www.auberge-gorgesduloup.com

Closed from mid-November to mid-December and from mid-January to mid-February. Open Tuesday to Saturday for lunch and dinner and Sunday for lunch. Booking advised. Menu from €16 to €32. À la carte: Around €30. Children's menu: €12. Wine by the glass. American Express, Holiday voucher, Chèque Restaurant. Groups welcome. Garden. Terrace. Parking at disposal.

The Blavette husbands are the owners of the Auberge des Gorges du Loup. A place rich in traditions as well in cuisine as in the room. The carte is inspired by flavours of Provence: snails cassoulet with mushrooms, fish soup and its rust, poultry with olives... You'll also find some «Tahitian» dishes: fish marinated in a Tahitian way, fillet of sea-bream with vanilla, creme brulee with Tahitian vanilla. Each summer, an evening Tahitian is organized in July. Reception in music, chains of flowers and dance shows are on the program. The charm of the inn continues in its ten rooms (see hotel section).

Sleeping

■ **AUBERGE DES GORGES DU LOUP**
4, route de Grasse
Le Pont du Loup
✆ **+33 (0)4 93 59 38 01**
www.auberge-gorgesduloup.com
info@auberge-gorgesduloup.com

Closed from mid-January to mid-February and from mid-November to mid-December. Tables et auberges de France. Reception from 9am to 11pm. Spoken languages: French, English, German, Spanish. 10 rooms (100% non smoker). Double room from €65 to €80. Breakfast: €10 (continental and €15 American). Extra bed: €15. Closed parking (free). American Express, Holiday voucher. Pets allowed. Seminars. Receptions and weddings. Free Wifi. Cleaning service. Catering facilities (menu from €16 to €32 - carte around €30 - children's menu €12). Satellite TV.

The Auberge des Gorges du Loup is located at the entrance of the Gorges du Loup, it is a beautiful place for people wishing to explore a very rich and varied natural territory. The owners warmly welcome you with ten comfortable rooms, bathroom or shower, TV and free wi-fi. The rooms are like the authentic Provençal surroundings. You can have lunch on the shaded and very flowery terrace. It is a true country haven, ideal for relaxation. The restaurant room has a distinctly rustic and cosy decoration: huge fireplace, straw chairs, copper pots and a chandelier made from a cartwheel... Here, meals highlight local flavours and the stays have a southern atmosphere in a pleasant rural conviviality.

VALBONNE - SOPHIA-ANTIPOLIS ★★

«Here the future has found its roots». This is the motto of the city, rich in its complementarity between heritage and sciences of the future. Valbonne Sophia Antipolis gathers the historic village of Valbonne and the technopole Sophia Antipolis who is more than 55% of its territory. The small village of yesteryear had a deep transformation with the creation of the park. From 1,600 inhabitants in 1970 to 12,900 inhabitants in 2012, it had to adapt to new challenges, build, innovative, change its urban landscape to accommodate a cosmopolitan population of about 80 different nationalities while maintaining the 2/3 of its territory in green area. The new district of Garbejaïre Haut-Sartoux, located in the heart of Sophia Antipolis, is a living area, culture and leisure founded by a unique architecture that respects nature and forms part of a perfectly preserved landscape. Valbonne received the label flowered City. It is also the first department to have signed with the charter UNICEF friendly City of children. Beyond these distinctions, Valbonne Sophia Antipolis since December 2010 is the first French city signatory of the world pact of the UNO. This pact officializes commitment of the city that adopted the ten universal principles dictated by international organization of human rights, the standard and the working conditions, the environment and the fight against corruption.

The Arches in the heart of the historic village.

TOURIST OFFICE OF VALBONNE

1, place de l' Hôtel-de-Ville
✆ +33 (0)4 93 12 34 50
www.tourisme-valbonne.com
office@tourisme-valbonne.com

Open from June 15th to September 15th, Monday to Saturday from 9am to 12.30pm and from 1.30pm to 5.30pm. Open from September 15th to June 15th, Monday to Friday from 9am to 12.30pm and from 1.30pm to 5.30pm, Saturday morning from 9am to 12.30pm.

Located at l'Hôtel de Ville square, in the village of Valbonne Sophia Antipolis, you will find here complete information about the city and its heritage as well as the local transport network and the many festivals and events organized by the Town. The welcome of the public is in French and English by a dynamic and friendly team.

Sightseeing

VALBONNE VILLAGE ★★

Place de l'Hôtel-de-Ville
✆ +33 (0)4 93 12 31 00
www.ville-valbonne.fr

At the end of the Middle Ages, the Black Death, the great drought and the barbarian invasions had led to the desertification of the region, which had been ruined and abandoned. In 1519 on the initiative of the prior Don Antonio Taxil and the goodwill of Augustin de Grimaldi, Bishop of Grasse and commendatory of Lérins, the village of Valbonne is built around the abbey due to an act of habitation that conceded men to honour the heritage of the parish church. *Vallis Bona*, the «good valley» along the coastal river of La Brague is then repopulated by communities from neighbouring villages and the back country. The old village unlike most Provençal villages is built on a rectangular grid plan called orthogonal based on the model of Roman cities that merge the main street, the perpendicular street and the central square. Real defensive walls, the tall and narrow houses did not have doors on the outside. Beautifully preserved, the village has preserved its authenticity over the centuries by expanding outside the old centre.

© VILLE DE VALBONNE SOPHIA ANTIPOLIS – ROBERT PALOMBA

The globe «World» of Jean-Claude Meynard, stands on Vallis Bona.

Knife & Fork

À LA MAISON

2030, route de Cannes
✆ +33 (0)4 92 98 97 13
alamaisonresto@gmail.com

Open Tuesday to Saturday for lunch and dinner all year except in August open Monday to Saturday only for dinner. Daily special: €11.90. Fixed rate formulas starter and main course or main course and dessert: €16.90. Starter + main course + dessert: €20. Terrace.

This address offers an original and new concept in the area. A retro atmosphere with a vintage decor that all generations love. Formica furniture and antique objects composes the large dining room of about sixty people. There is even a bed or a corner with foosball! A large terrace is open as soon as the fine weather is back. Inside, Odile Isoul, the hostess, welcomes you with Emma at her sides for the service. In the kitchen, Charles offers fusion cuisine that varies with the seasons: wok, tartare of meat or fish, many kinds of burger, revisited sausage or bone marrow. Many formulas are available for lunch, dinner is chosen on the carte. A trio that works well and which seems to have found a perfect balance. And for more originality, an orange 2CV is planted in front of the hotel. You can't miss it!

LE BISTROT DU SOMMELIER

21, rue Eugène-Giraud
✆ +33 (0)4 93 12 17 95
www.lebistrotdusommelier.fr
bistrotdusommelier@gmail.com

Open all year. Closed on Wednesday all day and Saturday for lunch. Set menu at €35 (menu bistro: starter and main course + cheese + dessert). Daily special: €12. Wine by the glass. Lunch menu at €16.50 (daily special + gourmet coffee). Terrace.

It is in this little bistro located in the heart of the streets of Valbonne village that Eric and his wife Carine have settled after having worked in beautiful Côte d'Azur houses. They have completely renovated the place and the red, white and black colours give this place a certain charm. A small outdoor terrace completes the room. In the kitchen, the products bought at the market are offered on the blackboard every day. Angus skirt steak, larded Provencal monkfish or sautéed veal with parsley. For the desserts, the chocolate fondue will delight the gourmets, like the tiramisu with red fruits or the coconut-banana crumble. A true delight. Without forgetting that Eric was primarily a sommelier, the wine list is amazing and well-stocked! You can thus enjoy nearly 25 wines by the glass at very reasonable price. Connoisseurs will also be delighted with great bottles.

FRENCH RIVIERA

VALBONNE SOPHIA ANTIPOLIS

Historic village

Provencal market

Nature preserved

Exhibitions Street festival

VSA

VILLE DE VALBONNE SOPHIA ANTIPOLIS

04 93 12 34 50 - www.valbonne.fr

LE CISTE ET LA BÉGUDE

Château de la Bégude
Route de Roquefort-les-Pins
✆ +33 (0)4 93 12 37 00
www.chateau-begude.com
restaurant@chateau-begude.com
♿

Open all year. Le Ciste open every evening Tuesday to Saturday from 7.30pm to 9.30pm. Menu at €45, €65 and €95. La Bégude open every day from 12pm to 2.30pm (open for dinner, except Sunday, when Le Ciste is closed) Menus at € 26 and €32. Booking advised. Wine by the glass. American Express, Diners Club, Holiday voucher, Chèque Restaurant. Groups welcome. Garden. Terrace. Free parking. Take-away: foie gras on reservation and macaroons.

The Chef Gabriel Degenne created two atmospheres and different services at Château de la Bégude. For lunch, the brasserie La Bégude offers a carte with Mediterranean flavors served on the terrace overlooking the golf course from the first rays of sun. For diner, the restaurant Le Ciste offers a gourmet menu with elaborate dishes: poeléed duck foie gras, creamy corn of the moment, blue crystal shrimp served in two ways as starters, colourful veal with fennel seeds in butter, wild bar grilled with flavours of Provence, artichokes in barigoule, foam of stock fish in dishes, ravioli with kalamansi, sour orange emulsion for dessert. You have a choice of 3 menus: Château, Prestige and Dégustation. Finally, on the roof of the restaurant, you can drink cocktails and enjoy some tapas at the lounge bar La Terrasse.
A beautiful culinary stop in a peaceful and green setting.

LE COIN DE LA RUE

8, rue des Arcades
✆ +33 (0)9 80 57 02 50 / +33 (0)6 59 25 40 72
www.lecoindelarue.fr
geraldinerogue@gmail.com

Open every day for dinner. À la carte: Around €50. Daily specials: €18.

Located in a quiet narrow street, near the main square of the medieval village, the establishment is beautifully located with a terrace surrounded by greenery. Inside, everything has been completely renovated, even the kitchen. The style is nearly the same in shades of beige and taupe. All the dishes are seasonal and displayed on the slate. The lobster ravioli, homemade foie gras terrine or fish tempura are tasty and make the reputation of the restaurant. As for the desserts, you have many choices: fresh fruit salad, gourmet coffee or Irish coffee served with mini-pastry. A cuisine made with local products and organic vegetables. Whether for a romantic dinner, a birthday with friends or a business meal, Le Coin de la Rue is the place for you. The welcome is always friendly and adapted to each guest. English is spoken fluently. You can also speak in Swedish or Norwegian. A gourmet and pleasant stopover.

EL BRAZERO

1016, route de Cannes ✆ +33 (0)4 92 28 03 73
www.elbrasero.fr
elbrasero@orange.fr

Open Tuesday to Friday and Sunday for lunch; Tuesday to Saturday for dinner. Menu from €28 to €35 (paella at €14.50). Children's menu: €7.90. Lunch menu: €15.10 (daily special + dessert). Tapas: €3.50 the unit. Board at €10.50.

Live a Spanish evening thanks to El Brasero. This restaurant specialized in spanish cuisine takes you to the country of flamenco and bullfighting. On the menu: a delicious paella with fresh ingredients, meat of Argentina or seafoods. The establishment serves till 2pm for lunch and 10pm for diner. Add to that a warm welcome and here are all the ingredients for a successful time. Thursdays as of 6pm until 7.30pm, the place offers a *after work with* tapas at the unit or in formulas (tortilla, pan con tomato, patatras braves...) while some Fridays, flamenco evenings are organized to start the weekend on a good foot. A parking of about fifty places allows you to park with no worry.

Sleeping

LA BASTIDE DE VALBONNE

107, chemin Font-de-Cuberte
✆ +33 (0)4 93 12 33 40
www.bastidevalbonne.com

Open all year. 34 rooms. Low season: double room from €95 to €200. High season: double room from €125 to €250. Buffet breakfast: €15 (served in room: €18). Extra bed: €25. The breakfast is free for children under 4 years old. Wifi.

A charming place which has been renovated with taste and harmony in Provencal tones. 34 rooms and large suites with bright refined colours, fully equipped, satellite TV, air conditioning, telephone, wi-fi, safe. Some rooms have a balcony or terrace overlooking the pool and the flowered garden with palm trees and herbs that smell the south. The breakfast is served as a buffet, in the dining room or outdoor on sunny days (extra charge for room service). A perfect haven to relax whatever the purpose of the travel: romantic getaway, family vacation or business trip. Snacks are available in high season. Parking under surveillance. Excellent welcome from Catherine and Fabrizio Ferro, attentive owners who are eager to welcome you at their best.

BEACHCOMBER FRENCH RIVIERA

3350, route des Dolines
Sophia Antipolis ✆ +33 (0)4 92 96 68 78
www.hotel-resort-frenchriviera.com

Open all year. 155 rooms (from €105). American Express, Diners Club. Seminars. Free Wifi. Catering facilities (fixed rate formula daily special, dessert, water and coffee at €21. Open daily for lunch and dinner). Satellite TV. Hammam, sauna. Golf academy – Tennis academy.

Beachcomber is the luxury hotel-resort of Sophia Country Club located in a 12 hectare park in the protected forest of Valmasque. The 155 rooms (Club, Prestige, and 2 suites) are soundproofed, air-conditioned, all highly equipped. The restaurant offers a seasonal cuisine prepared by the Chef Franckie Quenette. You have lunch in the air conditioned dining room or on the sunny terrace by the superb pool. The elegant lounge bar, open every day from 10am to midnight, favours relaxation and discretion. For more relaxation a unique area of 700 m^2 dedicated to well-being and fitness, with exclusive treatments. Here the concept of «sport, tennis, art of living» is developed with formations from the Tennis Academy and the Golf Complex.

CHÂTEAU DE LA BÉGUDE

Route de Roquefort-les-Pins
✆ +33 (0)4 93 12 37 00
www.chateau-begude.com

44 rooms. Single room from €90 to €230; double room from €110 to €290; suite from €170 to €500. 2 equipped rooms for disabled guests. Two restaurants: Le Ciste and La Bégude. A golf 18 holes.

Located in the heart of a protected estate, Château de la Bégude is a haven of peace where tranquility and well-being are the keywords. This 4 -star hotel composed of 44 rooms and suites with extra comfort revolves around a bastide and a sheepfold dating from the 17th century. A 18 -hole golf course, a swimming pool open in summer and tennis courts are as many amenities you can enjoy during your stay. A gourmet restaurant, Le Ciste and a brasserie, La Bégude, will allow you to enjoy a tasty mediterranean cuisine. Le Château de la Bégude can also be privatized for events such as weddings, baptisms or birthdays.

© VILLE DE VALBONNE SOPHIA ANTIPOLIS – ROBERT PALOMBA

Each Friday morning, Valbonne village is one of the largest markets of Provence in the region.

VENCE ★★★★

Vence is a pure gem that is lucky not to have lost its soul. A kind of magic, a timeless grace lives in this charming and privileged town.

Chagall, Dubuffet, Dufy, Matisse, Soutine… The greatest artists experienced a real fascination and inspiration for this city with multiple facets.

On the foothills of the Alps, a balcony on the Mediterranean and the Riviera, prestigious hotels and traditional accommodation blends to make Vence a renowned and popular tourist site, one of the last secret gardens of the French Riviera.

The medieval town, one of rare of the Middle Ages having preserved its ramparts, shelters historical treasures including Fontaine du Peyra and Cathédrale Notre Dame de la Nativité both listed as Historical Monuments.

TOURIST OFFICE OF VENCE

8, place du Grand-Jardin
✆ +33 (0)4 93 58 06 38
www.vence-tourisme.fr
officedetourisme@vence.fr
Access from the A8, exit N ° 48, interchange Cagnes

January, February, November and December: open Monday to Saturday, from 9am to 5pm. From March to June, September and October: open Monday to Saturday, from 9am to 6pm. July and August: open Monday to Saturday, from 9am to 7pm and Sunday from 10am to 6pm. Tourism label & Disability.

The multilingual team of the tourist office of Vence welcomes visitors throughout the year in their office situated on place du Grand-Jardin. You will be informed freely about the local touristic offers with brochures and useful maps. Ideas for tours and discoveries around heritage sites (chapels and fountains) are offered. Guided tours of the historic city and the Côte d'Azur des Peintres (upon reservation) are regularly ensured by a counsellor in English, French, German and Italian.

Sightseeing

LES NUITS DU SUD

Place du Grand-Jardin ✆ +33 (0)4 93 58 40 17
www.nuitsdusud.com
nuitsdusud-com@ville-vence.fr

From July 6th to July 29th, 2017. Free for under 10-year-olds. Presale at €15. Full rate at €25. Weekend pass at €60 (3 entrances).

Each summer, les Nuits du Sud, ephemeral concert hall, plays musics of yesterday and today. You will dance and swing under the night sky of Vence. The festival Les Nuits du Sud likes being always closer to music and all kinds of music. You will see renowned artists as well as emerging ones. The festival likes discovering and helping artists of the region. Two places are taken over by the festival: the place du Grand Jardin and the salle des Meules. For tis 20th birthday, the festival has decided to mark it with two more events. Les Nuits du Sud took place in April, called Printemps des Nuits du Sud: it took place in the room La Carpa, a transitory concert hall, on Place du Grand Jardin. Nuits intimes have also been created. It is a monthly rendez-vous, in the room des Meules, dedicated to emergence. A rich and dense year to celebrate their 20 years of existence!

Villa le Rêvé.

UFO turism at the col de Vence

If all the regions in France have their fairies, witches or ghosts tales, the Riviera with the plateau of the hill of Vence also has one! Secluded but easily accessible by car, it is located 963 m above sea level. At the top the magnificent panorama opens from Italy to Cannes. The fauna and flora of the plateau are very rich and some stones having unusual shapes give the site a special atmosphere. The soil is full of rocks that seem to spring from the ground, why before it was called "Plateau of Idols" or "Plateau of the Moon". It is a place full of history and mystery. It was occupied by the Romans, then by the Templars. More recently many testimonies relate strange phenomena at night: the appearance of lights or huge clouds of dust, heady sounds, rock fall, spherical shapes invisible to the naked eye appear in pictures...So many events that make some people believe that they are on a site that is visited by other forms of life... We can find on the floor, unexplained circular mark that was discovered in 1993. But now, the sharpness of the borderlines is fading but grass still does not grow there. Today, the plateau of the valley of Vence is one of the sites that are famous by those who are «enthusiast about strange things» and mysteries.

Knife & Fork

L'AMBROISIE
37, avenue Alphonse-Toreille
✆ +33 (0)4 93 58 78 58 / +33 (0)6 14 70 83 24
www.ambroisie-vence.com
bruno.seillery@cegetel.net
Open Thursday to Monday for lunch; Thursday to Tuesday for dinner. Menu from €29 to €36. Cookery classes.
The property is located in a former 17th century convent which has retained its character, with vaulted stones and walls. As for the cuisine, it is a soft blend between flavours of Southwest France and Provence. Warm escalope of foie gras with cherries, beef sirloin of Haut-Béarn vineyard sauce, john dory fillet cooked on the skin, sautéed vegetables, vinaigrette with basil, dish of fruit sorbets, chocolate tear and its orange ice cream. A generous wine list at rather tight prices. An excellent address where you come back with pleasure.

LES BACCHANALES
247, avenue de Provence
✆ +33 (0)4 93 24 19 19
www.lesbacchanales.com
info@lesbacchanales.com
Open Thursday to Monday for lunch and dinner. Tuesday or Wednesday opening for groups starting from 30 people on reservation. Menu from €65 to €105. Lunch menu: €32 (2 choice of main dishes, except Sunday and public holidays). For lunch from €32 to €65; evening from €65 to €95; Sunday and public holidays €55 and €75. American Express. Garden. Terrace. Activities. Parking. 1 Michelin star.
In a beautiful villa end 19th century with a contemporary decor, Christophe Dufau, starred Chef is always in search of new ideas and combinations of new flavours. Here, all is different, all is pretext to discovery. Christophe Dufau doesn't know about routine. Each week he invents a new menu and creates main courses at the image of his original and colourfull art collection present in the house and garden. He always elaborates with regional products in a radius of 250 kilometers. You can discover his cuisine at a very attractive price.

MICHEL ANGE
1, place Godeau ✆ +33 (0)4 93 58 32 56
lemichelange06@gmail.com
Open all year. Tuesday to Sunday for lunch; Friday and Saturday for dinner. Menu from €23 to €28 (starter + main course + dessert or starter/main course or main course/dessert). Lunch menu: €17 (starter and main course or main course and dessert). Daily special at €14. Terrace.
A nice restaurant located in the old town. This year, you may notice the change of the manager of the restaurant and a beautiful upscale, whether it in the dishes or the decor.
Finished with pizzas for a sunny cuisine of Nice inspiration. You eat on the spot in summer, in winter you can settle in the small nice room recently renovated. The terrace is now heated in winter. Michel in cuisine offers all the specialties of the azur capital: ravioli, stew, stuffed vegetables, stockfish... Every Friday, you can enjoy the famous «aïoli». Some grandmother recipes revisited by the chef make the delight of the connoisseurs such as calf's head, tripe of the day, stuffed sardines. We also like fresh fish like sea bream. As for sweetness, let yourself be tempted to the chocolate tart and red fruits, the tart with walnut and caramel or tiramisu. Everything is «homemade». Here no fuss with a generous and cheap cuisine.

CRÊPERIE BRETONNE
6, place Surian ✆ +33 (0)4 93 24 08 20
Open all year. Open daily for lunch and dinner. À la carte: Around €25. Terrace. In the historical centre of Vence, in an authentic decor and a typically Breton atmosphere, you will enjoy the buckwheat cakes and pancakes made of wheat whose prices are reasonable. On sunny days, this little creperie extends its pleasant terrace at the foot of the nearby fountain on the Surian Square. We love the original recipes such as cake with scallops and leek fondue which reminds of the musts in Bretagne. Sweet side, the pancake with baked apples is simply delicious. Compositions that make the whole originality of Crêperie Bretonne, without forgetting the traditional cider. A good time in perspective in a very pleasant setting. To be sure to have a table, don't come too late because the room is quickly filled.

Aerial view of Vence.

LA RÉGENCE CAFÉ

10, place du Grand-Jardin
✆ +33 (0)4 93 24 02 10
www.laregencecafe.com
la-regence-cafe@wanadoo.fr

Open all year. Every day from 11am to 11pm. Evenings Live Music Friday and Saturday evenings. Set menu at €29 (starter, main course, dessert). À la carte: Around €25. Children's menu: €7. Daily special: €11. Wine by the glass. Free Wifi access. Brasserie. Restaurant. Pizzeria. Bar. Tea room. Ice-cream shop. Groups welcome. Terrace.
The «new» Regence has come back for nearly three years now. You can sit on the large sunny terrace, one of the most beautiful of Place du Grand Jardin, or in one of the three interior rooms (air-conditioned), each with their little cozy corners. The terrace is also the ideal place to enjoy concerts of Nuits du Sud. The menu changes according to the seasons with woks, tartars, burgers, or salads. Suggestions are daily offered. We like the chicken wok and its chinese noodles with exotic perfume or the mixed grill of the sea and its aïoli (tuna, salmon, prawns, and fresh scallops). A «snacking» break (omelette, toasted sandwiches, quiches) is also possible throughout the day. We appreciate the hospitality of the place, we like the aperitif with its «bistro» plates served as snacks and their loyalty card with discounts of 10% on your bill. You can find all the news for musical events on their Facebook page. In short, a must in Vence that should be (re)discovered without hesitation.

CÔTÉ JARDIN

10, rue Isnard
✆ +33 (0)4 93 24 78 13
www.cotejardinvence.com
cotejardinvence@yahoo.fr

Open all year. Low season: Tuesday to Saturday for lunch; Friday and Saturday for dinner. High season: Monday, Friday and Saturday for dinner; Tuesday to Saturday for lunch. Booking advised. Daily special: €13. Menu 2 main courses €18 or 3 main courses €22 for lunch and €32 for dinner or à la carte: Around €30. Garden. Parking: Marie Antoinette free from 6pm to midnight.
Côté Jardin is a little oasis in Vence, in the ruelle du cinema opened four years ago, run by the charming Fanny. On sunny days, you can enjoy the private garden and its beautiful terrace overlooking the Baous and the

Matisse chapel. The cuisine is fresh, tasty and simple with an excellent price/quality ratio: cod aioli, prawn wok with crunchy vegetables, barigoule artichokes, grilled Iberian pork... Don't miss the delicious lemon meringue pie. The cuisine is homemade and you can feel it.

■ LES PETITS TABLIERS

7, avenue Marcellin-Maurel
✆ +33 (0)9 81 45 97 95
lespetitstabliersvence@gmail.com

Open Tuesday to Saturday from 8.30am to 5pm. Lunch menu: €16.50 (daily special and dessert of the day). Breakfasts between €6 and €8.50. Two menus for the 0-2 years at €2 and €5 and two menus for the 3-10 years at €5 and €7.50. Baby chairs. Activities.

A paradise for children and adults! While parents eat, children have a dedicated space and also special dishes for their baby mouths. An original and welcoming café-stroller created in May 2014 which serves fresh and sometimes organic products. Varied daily specials, burgers, sandwiches and salads are on the restaurant's carte menu, the prices are very reasonable. But there is more: Les Petits Tabliers also organizes workshops on Tuesday, Wednesday and Saturday. On the programme: discussion between moms, gardening or hobbies... You can even organise a birthday party, wedding or baby shower. They certainly don't lack ideas. And that's the reason why this place is warm and friendly for a stopover. Note however that the restaurant is not only for parents.

■ LA TABLE DU CANTEMERLE

258, chemin Cantemerle
✆ +33 (0)4 93 58 08 18
www.table-cantemerle.fr
info@hotelcantemerle.com
♿

«Maître Restaurateur» label. Closed from mid-March to mid-October. Schedule of the restaurant depending on the season. Closed Sunday for dinner and Monday. « Well-bing bubble» day with lunch drinks included, access to the spa area (swimming pool, hammam and fitness space) and 1hour of treatment at the choice (face or body) from €119/pers. Booking is essential. Menu from €37 to €56. À la carte: Around €55. Children's menu: €16. Lunch menu: €25 2 main courses – and €31 3 main courses, menu freshness Tuesday to Friday for lunch. Wine by the glass. Buffet of the sea at will €59 or or €76 per person with a half-bottle of white wine all Friday for dinner on reservation. American Express, Holiday voucher. Groups welcome. Garden. Terrace. Private parking. Organization of meals and party evenings. Personalized menu on request.

Since 2008 Jerome Héraud is the manager of the hotel and kitchen. He cultivates his own organic herb garden as he likes to have fresh products. Most of the products he uses are directly from producers and are of controlled origin. He likes combining flavours, the abundance of local products from Provence with other tastes from elsewhere. For lunch, he proposes fresh food which include grilled food, crispy wok vegetables, salads, gazpacho... and a selection of low-calorie meals. In the evening, he reveals a gourmet cuisine that revives the taste buds. A «wellness bubble» day allows you to combine lunch at Table du Cantemerle and a relaxing time at the hotel's spa. The wine list is a mixture of fine wines and also what the producers specially like, and as always there is a great respect for vintage and local ones. You will be served in the renovated room or on the shaded terrace overlooking the pool and the green park. A peaceful setting, with generous and sincere food that make this table a delight.

Sleeping

■ HÔTEL MIRAMAR

167, avenue Bougearel
Saint Michel plateau
✆ +33 (0)4 93 58 01 32
www.hotel-miramar-vence.com
contact@hotel-miramar-vence.com

Open all year. 18 rooms. Season: from €78 to €178 (superior rooms with balcony and panoramic view) triple rooms possible, quadruple and suite of 2 rooms for 4/5 people. Extra bed €20 (€23 in high season). Low season: double rooms from €58 to 98. Breakfast: €10. Pets allowed (€10). Internet access. Free Wifi. Satellite TV.

The Miramar hotel is nestled in the heart of a former mansion, and located at 5 minutes from the historic centre of Vence. Transformed into a charming hotel, this property which is close to the city centre of Vence has an elegant and classic design as well as quality services. The 18 rooms are named after flowers of Provence: *bleuet* – blueberry -, *capucine* – nasturtium – ... They are equipped with all the comfort needed and are decorated with Provence-inspired colours. The panoramic terrace offers a stunning view over the sea and the *Baous*. Breakfasts are served here. You can also have a drink at the bar. The swimming pool in the middle of a tree-filled garden is charming and you will appreciate the quietness of the place.

■ HÔTEL, SPA & RESTAURANT CANTEMERLE

258, chemin Cantemerle
✆ +33 (0)4 93 58 08 18 / +33 (0)6 66 91 74 81
www.cantemerle-hotel-vence.com
info@hotelcantemerle.com

Open from mid-March to mid-October. 27 rooms and suites from €140 to €587. Reception 24/24 (spoken languages: French, English, German, Spanish, Italian, Russian). Half-board: €65. Breakfast: €22. Extra bed: €50. Parking (private free). Child free up to 5 years with parents. Up to 12 years, reduced rate. American Express, Holiday voucher. Pets allowed. Seminars. Receptions and weddings. Internet access. Wifi. Cleaning service. La Table de Cantemerle restaurant. «Maître Restaurateur» label. Satellite TV. Hammam. Spa. Massages wellness. Solarium. Heated indoor pool. Outdoor pool.

The address celebrated its 30 years last year. This charming hotel located on a wooded hill in a charming and bucolic setting has two swimming pools. Its two buildings lie in the middle of a lush private park of 1 hectare. The rooms are very spacious and have private terraces that open on the garden and unveil an elegantly Provencal decor with pretty contemporary touches. Comfortably equipped with minibar, safe, air conditioning, satellite TV and free wi-fi connection. Room prices freely gives access to all services offered by the hotel: heated outdoor pool with sun loungers and parasols, also heated indoor pool and hydro-massage jets, steam room, fitness room and solarium. During your stay, you can relax in the spa of the hotel which offers beauty cares, massages and an access to the fitness room (treadmill, rowing machine, bike). Cuisine side, «La Table du Cantemerle», distinguished as Maître Restaurateur handled by Jérôme Héraud who is also the manager of the hotel, offers an exquisite cuisine with southern flavours. A petanque field is at the disposal of guests for friendly moments!

Guesthouses

■ LA BASTIDE DE FREINET

114, chemin du Pioulier
✆ +33 (0)4 93 58 82 88 / +33 (0)6 16 92 59 15
www.labastidefreinet.fr
info@labastidefreinet.fr

Gîte de France (3 épis). Open all year. 2 rooms. Double room from €70 to €120. Breakfast included. Parking. Free Wifi.

A charming Provencal house nestled on the hills of Vence. Southwest exposure with a beautiful view and a large garden with swimming pool. Beatrice Gomont, the owner, offers 2 spacious and bright rooms. Private terrace opening onto the garden with bay window. The decor is neat, of contemporary style. Guests have at their disposal a dedicated space which is located in the garden level with summer terrace and a cosy lounge with fireplace. In summer, you can sunbath on the lounger, near the swimming pool. In short, it is a real haven of peace which is a few minutes drive from the village of Vence. Ideal for a quiet break with your lover or family. The common areas are spacious; we feel a bit like at home, away from the bustle of a regular hotel. You should book in advance as there are only 2 rooms and the value for money is excellent.

Going Out

■ K'FE MALTE

16, rue du Marché ✆ +33 (0)4 93 32 52 36 / +33 (0)6 95 42 82 82 – www.kfemalte.fr

Low season: open Tuesday to Saturday from 5pm to midnight. High season: Monday to Saturday from 5pm to 1am. Beer from €4. Credit card not accepted. Terrace. Activities. Concerts. Possible privatization of space for private parties up to 20 people. Find the news of K'fé Malté on Facebook.

This little beer bar ideally located in the heart of the historic centre of Vence, offers over fifty varieties of French craft beers. White, blond, amber, red, dark or black, they can be enjoyed on the terrace or in the room where it is hot. The beer list is also regularly changed in order to make you discover continuously new products. A selection of wines from Var and Ventoux, fruit juice, original smoothies and hot wines complete the list of drink which can be served with tapas, gourmet sandwiches, plates of charcuterie and cheeses, salads or cold soups. The meal is prepared as far as possible with products from fair trade, from organic and local market. They serve a unique menu during *live* concerts or theme evenings organized in the vaulted cellar. Dates and programming of the festivities are displayed on the doorstep but also on the Facebook address. A festive and convivial spot, this funny café is run by the friendly duo Joelle and Patrick. It can be privatized to organize your own private party.

Shopping

■ RIVA DOLCE

10, place du Grand-Jardin
✆ +33 (0)4 93 59 16 43 – www.rivadolce.fr
contact@rivadolce.fr

Low season: open Tuesday to Sunday from 9am to 7pm. High season: Tuesday to Sunday from 9am to 11pm. Cup of ice cream from €7, scoop of ice-cream from €2.

Sweet lovers, stop here for a delicious greedy break! This shop in Vence has a lovely terrace and depending on the time of the day, becomes an ice cream maker, tea lounge, creperie and chocolate-maker. About fifty ice-cream flavours made with the best selected products and entirely incorporated into the recipe (fruits represent 60 to 70 % of the composition of ice-creams). Your taste buds will enjoy incredible flavours, difficult to find elsewhere like the ice-cream with candied pieces of ginger, the one with speculoos biscuits of Bruges or the salted caramel, orange blossom, violet or even more uncommon like Malabar, Kinder Bueno, or the famous «Gargamelle» a completely blue ice-cream! Pancakes (sweet and salted), hot and cold drinks. In winter, you will also enjoy a nice selection of chocolates to crunch (Voisin chocolates, brand from Lyon). Add to this the friendly welcome of Fred and you will surely be enchanted!

In the surroundings

Gréolières ★★

■ **LE RELAIS**
1, rue du Ribas
✆ +33 (0)6 11 05 08 03 / +33 (0)4 93 32 03 86
p.murati@wanadoo.fr
Open Tuesday to Sunday. Service from 7.30am to 5pm. À la carte: Around €15. Limoncello or coffee offered. WiFi free.
For breakfast, lunch or just for a drink, Le Relais welcomes you in the heart of Gréolières. The terrace with a view on the mountains is an invitation to relaxation. Inside, the room is decorated in tons of red creating a warm atmosphere. As for the cuisine, you will discover a regional cuisine with provencal flavours. We loved the gourmet coffee which is very hearty. The Corsican draft beer with chestnuts is also very appreciated. An address where you enjoy coming back. Booking recommended on week ends.

La Gaude ★★

■ **LA GAUDRIOLE**
4, rue Centrale ✆ +33 (0)4 93 24 88 88
jeanmarc.ducousso@sfr.fr
Open Tuesday to Saturday for lunch and dinner; Sunday for lunch. Daily special: €9 (suggestions between €7 and €14). Average price à la carte between €22 and €30. Label Nissarde Kitchen. Terrace.
This restaurant in the center of the village celebrates regional cuisine, tasty and generous at the same time. It has just been labeled Niçoise Cuisine. The carte is long because there is pizzas, fresh home-made pasta (with ceps, red marrow or garlic with Parma ham and fresh tomatos), and the dishes of cuisine niçoise, of course. You'll find donuts of fillets of red mullet with mixed green salad, small octopuses a la niçoise, wild boar stew, merda di can (translation: gnocchis with spinaches) which accompanies the stew and in season the stockfish or stuffed vegetables. In winter one settles in the warmth of the rustic vaulted dining room and in summer, one benefits from the little square at the bottom of the church. Friendly atmosphere, excellent value for money, come to join the regulars of this well-known restaurant of the inhabitants of Gaude.

■ **NÉRÉIDES CROISIERE**
Le Plan du Bois
46, avenue des Oliviers
✆ +33 (0)6 10 34 76 61
www.croisieres-nereides.com
contact@croisieres-nereides.com
Mediterranean cruises 6 days low season: €650, high season: €690. Down payment 50 % of the amount of the course to validate your reservation. For the reservations 15 days before the departure, the totality of the amount of the course will have to be paid.
Courses and cruises are on the program of this cruise school. You will here learn all about manoeuvring, sailing, navigating, security, maritime regulation, reading maps and the marine weather. Embark on board a sail ship in a friendly and cordial atmosphere, navigate on the Mediterranean sea for several days and discover stunning landscapes thanks to the outings framed by a qualified State instructor.

SAINT-JEANNET ★★

Knife & Fork

■ **LA TABLE DES BAOUS**
42, rue Nationale ✆ +33 (0)4 93 24 90 63
www.latabledesbaous.fr
contact@latabledesbaous.fr
Open all year. Annual closing during Christmas holidays (open for December 31st). Monday to Wednesday for dinner; Thursday to Sunday for lunch and dinner. Menu from €24.90 to €29.50. À la carte: Around €30. Children's menu: €10. Daily specials on the slate, from €16. Terrace.
This beautiful restaurant was created by the chef Sebastien Liprandi after he spent some times with others who encouraged him to settle. In the old village, he renovated a former restaurant into a trendy place with «bistro chic» style. The cutleries are beautifully displayed in the room with soft colours or on the small

The vineyards of Saint Jeannet

The history of Saint-Jeannet is linked to the wine culture until the early 1960s. The «Saint-Jeannet tardif» after war was even feeding luxury groceries in Paris during the end of year celebrations. The development of the horticultural industry, although the expansion of land had took over the wine culture, there are still some irreducible, a dozen farmers are still doing their wine. Only the Rasse family, wine-maker from father to son, carries on a business of much importance on 4 ha in the the Sausses district. Their red and white wines are on the tables of many restaurants of the region. If you are on the way to Sausses at the valley of Mouré, stop the estate of the last great vineyards of the town and take time for a tasting of the rosé «tuilé» or the Cuvée Pressoir Romain, or Georges Rasse...
Vineyard des Hautes Collines of the French Riviera 800 chemin des Sausses ✆+33 (0) 4 93 24 96 01

The cliff of Saint-Jeannet

This cliff of 807 m dominates the Riviera. To discover this panorama from the wash house of the village, we go up to the Verger square and we follow the streets of Baou. At 1500 m from the village, we leave the main road to turn left and reach the top in about 1h15. Recognized climbing site, this cliff has 457 climbing paths of 6-200 m in height and approximately 18,000 m of climbing enable all the techniques to be practiced.

Approach routes for the climbing-routes:

- **The site of the Source:** from the Notre-Dame chapel, take the path down to the valley of Cagne then the path towards Castellet which leads to the foot paths.
- **The site of Ressauts** (southeast side): from the Sainte-Barbe Square, go up the street of Baou to the reservoir and follow a path with indications.
- **The site of Grande Face** (southwest side): same access as for the site of the Source (for experienced climbers).

terrace in the shade of the vine on sunny days (the road is sometimes closed during summer, which gives a truly village atmosphere to the place). The welcome is friendly from this generous man who only works with fresh seasonal products and who buys products from nearby producers: Gattières vegetable, oils and wines from the estates of Saint Jeannet (wines from the Rasse vineyards)... You will taste the difference in your plate while enjoying the delicious flavours. The Chef declines several propositions on the blackboard-menu based on what is available in the market and every day prepares 4 starters and 4 main courses which you can choose: fish or shellfish, offal, poultry or white meat, red meat (beef flank steak), risotto with fresh vegetables (broad beans, artichokes). The homemade desserts are fabulous: puffed lemon or casserole with caramelized apples with dried fruit... The wine list is mainly organic, with excellent references. A culinary discovery that should not to be missed in order to share the pleasures of the senses with the demanding customers who regularly come back.

THE AZUREAN HILLSIDES

Ideally perched between sea and mountains, the villages of Le Broc, Carros, Gilette and Gattières overlook the right bank of the Var Valley at about 15 km north of Nice. This privileged location offers visitors a range of extremely varied Mediterranean landscape, a kind of transitional space between the back country and the coast. These villages have exceptional touristic attractions – heritage of great value, preserved natural environment... – but are still quite unknown to the main classical tourist tours of the region. Yet they are as charming as the villages which enjoy international fame, and all have preserved an authentic look.

Carros ★

Sightseeing

This old village is entirely listed and has fortunately preserved its medieval appearance and authenticity. The feudal castle, built in the 12th century, constantly overhauled, and not always happily, has now two towers connected by a curtain wall, a donjon and the Puy tower. The former chapel of the castle has become the parish church. Place du Puy: a windmill; a very detailed orientation table enables you to admire the magnificent panorama.

- **In the village**: the bell tower, remains of Notre-Dame-de-Colas; the church; Villa Barbary; the castle and the International Center of Contemporary Art; the old windmill; the craft-market.
- **In the vicinity**: the monastery of Carmel; the oratories: there are four on the territory of Carros. Strategically located at the crossroads, they must have been there to anticipate the rest of the travelers. Also worth a visit: the laundry, the chapel of Selves, the engraved stones with Roman inscriptions (in the village), the Forest Park in Carros City.

Knife & Fork

LA FORGE
Avenue Fernand-Barbary
✆ +33 (0)4 93 29 31 50
www.restolaforge.com
restaurant.laforge.carros@gmail.com

«Maître Restaurateur» label. Assiette Michelin guide. Open Thursday to Tuesday for lunch; Thursday to Sunday for dinner. Booking advised. Menu from €33 to €65. À la carte: Around €40. Children's menu: €10. Lunch menu: €18 (starter, main course or main course, dessert and €23 starter, main course, dessert – on weekdays only). Wine by the glass. No lunch menu in summer and during school holidays. Menu ode to truffle at €65. American Express. Groups welcome (up to 40 people). Terrace. Parking.

This nice village address gets better as years go by. The brand proudly displays since 2013 the label Maître Restaurateur, the result of a well deserved work. Claude (in the dining room) and Karine Scutéri (the Chef) revived this former communal inn. A decidedly modern decor in old stones: two beautiful vaulted rooms and a TV broadcasting the images of the work carried out in the open kitchen on the first room in shades of red and orange. In the cuisine, Karine likes to elaborate a cuisine in female touches as she nicely says. Her dishes, exclusively homemade, pay tribute to white truffle and the revisited traditional products: cuttlefish à la plancha, marshed potatoes, olive oil sauce, bellota Iberian pork pluma, Brie cheese fondant... The wine list features appelations of the region and the selection of desserts, chocolate brownies, Karine's delicacies revive the great classics in sweet version. On sunny days, you'll enjoy the serenity of this village by sitting on the pleasant terrace, adding wellness to the pleasures of the table.

Gattières ★★

ESCALE D'AZUR
455, chemin des Prés
✆ +33 (0)6 13 01 33 36 / +33 (0)6 76 10 98 41
www.escale-azur-gattieres.com

Gîte de France (2 épis). Open all year. 4 rooms (and an apartment). Double room from €87 to €100. High season: studio/apartment €950 per week. Breakfast included (for the rooms). Free outdoor parking. Wifi. Air conditioning in all the rooms.

This Stopover leads to a superb villa nestled in the heights of Gattières. The landscape is simply grandiose with a panoramic view on the old village and its neighbouring hills. Joelle and Jean-Jacques renovated this beautiful building with great refinement and offer to their guests four high-standard rooms bearing flower names: Mimosa, Tangerine, Cornflower and Poppy. Each one enjoys an individual access to the pool. High quality services: individual terrace, flat-screen TV, bathroom with bathtub or shower, separate toilets, hairdryer. Every small detail is well thought, there is even a bathrobe for guests... The house has a tree-lined garden on three levels in various fragrance, magnolia, cedar and palm trees. You can even practise your shooting on the petanque field. The swimming pool is on the center and offers a dream view. A pool house with barbecue, bread oven, fridge, electric hotplate, tableware (etc.) is at the disposal of guests. Such accessible comfort with an excellent quality/price ratio will make you fell like a privileged person.

LE BEAU SITE
60, voie Venciane ✆ +33 (0)4 92 08 21 00
www.lebeausite-gattieres.com
contact@lebeausite-gattieres.com

Open all year. 5 rooms. Low season: double room from €92 to €97. High season: double room from €97 to €104. Breakfast included. Parking. Meal with starter, main course and dessert at €24. Wifi. Catering facilities. Satellite TV.

A small jewel recently renovated which deserves to be known. Le Beau Site was taken over in 2013 by Joelle and her husband Pierre and they completely refitted it. What a beautiful surprise when you arrive! A panoramic view on the Var valley, the sea and the mountains of Mercantour. Still a hotel last year, the Beau site is from now on chambres d'hôte. The huge open space lounge opens on large bay windows is divided into several spaces: the lounge corner with sofa and fireplace, the dining room. A pleasant family atmosphere. The owners travelled much and have settled here and their furniture comes from the four corners of the world. Decoration is harmonious and combines acidulated colours with antique furniture. The 5 rooms are small but elegant and have a panoramic view. Two of them have a private terrace. The breakfast, on fine days, is taken in the nice southern garden. Possibility to dine on the spot on reservation. And it is Joelle, who works in the kitchens. A stop we highly advise.

Gillette ★★

LOU COUNTEA
7, place Docteur-Morani ✆ +33 (0)4 93 73 97 50
www.restaurant-loucountea.com
joel.laugier@restaurant-loucountea.com

Open all year. Tuesday to Saturday for lunch and dinner; Sunday for lunch. From June to end of September open Sunday for dinner. À la carte: Around €30. Children's menu: €9.50. Lunch menu: €14 (starter/main course or main course/dessert and glass of wine, served Tuesday to Friday for lunch). Wine by the glass. Menus of specialties Sunday at €28 and €38. Holiday voucher, Chèque Restaurant. Groups welcome. Terrace.

Homecoming for Joël Laugier who established Lou Countea in June 2012 in his hometown Gillette. He began as a butcher with his father in the family business that he has kept until today. He just extended the walls and redefined the space; the room of the restaurant has a bay window overlooking the kitchen. He inherited from his mother the taste of authentic cuisine, rooted in local traditions of the valley. He prepares sausage, tripe, chipolata sausages with garlic, head cheese that he serves himself. Olive oil, pressed at the mill of the village, comes from the tercentenary olive trees. You must taste the specialties of Estéron such as the potato gnocchi, spinach chard, sweet tart of chard (the recipe that differs from that made in Nice) for which he won the first prize of Capelina just for his pissaladière. Stockfish Emilie as a tribute to his mother, goat's cheese of the Haute Vallée of Estéron (Amirat), tome of Tinée's cow... As you can imagine, they perpetuate here the expertise of a culinary heritage of yesteryear and that's worth a detour: it is delicious.

THE VALLEY OF THE ROYA

The valley of the Roya links Côte d'Azur to Piedmont. It includes a variety of beautiful hilltop villages full of history and traditions: Sospel is a medieval city, Saorge is a former feudal platform, Tende is a gateway in the preserved universe of Valley des Merveilles... Away from the tourism hustle in summer, it is a paradise for hiking, white-water sports and cultural activities. The road follows the river through beautiful landscapes. Discover a timeless route tracing back the authenticity of the past with its baroque churches, fortifications and religious heritage.

BREIL-SUR-ROYA ★★

Built along a loop of the Roya river, Breil stretches to the foot of the Arpette mountain (1,610 m), a natural defense rampart. The former city was disenclosed in the late 19th century by to the road linking it to Ventimiglia in Italy then with the arrival of the train. Breil has long been a stopover on the Route Du Sel, this mule path between Piémont and the Mediterranean. Enlarged for motor vehicles after the creation of the port of Nice, it became the «Voie Royale» linking Nice to Turin allowing the transit of goods. Breil has kept from medieval time the narrow streets and the covered passageways (*courreou*) and the ligurian architecture, the arcade squares, the houses with colourful façades, the decors painted in trompe-l'oeil and the glazed tiles of the bell towers. Capital of the canton, Breil was given to France in 1860. The hamlets attached to it became French only in 1947: Libre, famous for olive-tree cultivation, and Piène-Haute, at the top of a rocky outcrop.

Breil-sur-Roya.

■ **TOURIST OFFICE OF BREIL-SUR-ROYA**
17, place Biancheri ✆ +33 (0)4 93 04 99 76
www.breil-sur-roya.fr
tourismebreilsurroya@wanadoo.fr
Low season: open Sunday to Friday from 9am to 12pm and from 1.30pm to 5.30pm; Saturday from 9am to 12pm. High season: Monday to Saturday from 9am to 12.30pm and from 2pm to 6pm; Sunday from 9am to 12.30pm.

Knife & Fork

■ **LE FLAVIE**
17, boulevard Jean-Jaurès
✆ +33 (0)4 93 54 65 74
www.leflavie.eresto.net
leflavie@gmx.fr
Annual closing from beginning of November to mid-December. Open daily for lunch and dinner except Thursday all day and Friday for lunch. À la carte: Around €30. Wine by the glass. Terrace. Parking. Wifi. Musical evenings in summer.
This address still has a brewery spirit, nicely decorated and comfortably furnished, and it deserves its reputation in the Roya Valley, both for its good quality products and for the traditional and family cuisine. Meats are labelled (Montbéliard, Charolais, etc...) and the meals are prepared according to the seasons. You will find veal liver in old-fashioned way, veal kidneys, sausage from Lyon, cabbage stew in cast iron casserole, Creole chicken (the boss who cooks comes from Réunion Island) but also in summer, there are beautiful Provencal salads. The desserts are homemade: tiramisu, chocolate mousse and creme caramel. The portions are generous. Note that there is also the small bar in the lobby and the large flowered terrace which is sunny in spring and shaded in summer. Nice welcome and attentive service of the owner. Excellent value for money.

Sleeping

■ **CAMPING AZUR ET MERVEILLES**
650, promenade Georges-Clemenceau
✆ +33 (0)4 93 04 99 76
✆ +33 (0)4 93 62 47 04
www.camping-azur-merveilles.com
Qualité Tourisme label. Open from April 1st to October 31st. Booking advised. Supervised daytime (July and August). Land of 1 ha. 40 campsites (+ 10 chalets and 1 mobile home for 4 people). Exposure: mid--shaded/sunny. All inclusive pitch package 1 person €15, 2 people €22. Night €77 in mobile home (4 people) and €99 in HLL (for €6.107 July and August). Week: mobile home (4 people) from €412 to €577 and in HLL (6 people) from €494 to €618. Holiday voucher. Games for children. Pets allowed (with vaccination certificate up-to-date. €2.50 per animal). Area for camper van. Wifi.
This beautiful municipal complex has a swimming pool and camping site "Azur et Merveilles **" which is certified

Breil-sur-Roya.

«Quality Tourism». Located in a green park entirely closed near the river, it offers 40 pitches for caravans, tents and motorhomes, equipped with modern sanitation, and 10 light leisure houses (HLL) for 6 persons, comfortable and well equipped with: 3 bedrooms, bathroom with shower and sink, separate toilet, kitchenette, terrace. There is also a mobile home with 2 bedrooms for 4 persons. Welcoming office during peak season. BBQ area available. There are several varied activities and water sports in the river, for children and adults. You may prefer hiking or climbing tours in the nearby Valley des Merveilles. The municipal swimming pool is next to the camping site and the access is free for guests residing there. Initially outdoors, it is now covered with a roof which can be opened and is also heated. The pool is monitored and younger ones have their paddling pool. In July-August: there are swimming lessons, water aerobics and fitness classes or aquatic zumba

Leisure

ROYA EVASION

11, boulevard Rouvier
✆ +33 (0)4 93 04 91 46 / +33 (0)9 61 61 68 38
www.royaevasion.com

Open all year. Voucher gift. Holiday voucher.

The whole team of Roya Évasion trains mountain lovers and white-water sports lovers in these magical places where sensation and adventure are everywhere. They offer hiking, trekking or snowshoes hiking all year round. Via Ferrata, mountain biking and enduro in the Marcantour, or even canyoning to explore sublime canyons like the wild Carleva, Le Guiou with clear waters, the tropical Barbera or the top Maglia. Without forgetting the kayak-raft (for one person), the canoe-raft, rafting and tubbing. There is something for all tastes and all pleasures, enough to dazzle the eyes and lungs.

SAORGE ★★

In the middle of the Roya valley, Saorge is at the bend of a turn. This medieval city, perched on the mountain above the gorges is a «monumental village»: it is one of most beautiful in France! It has cobbled streets and stairs, houses of the 15th century decorated with remarkable doors and lintels whilst the roofs are covered with red or green schist slate of Roya.The lively history of this town on the Route Du Sel was closely associated with that of Nice's county. It has changed Sovereignty several times: Sardinian, it was conquered by Massena in 1794 who had its ramparts demolished. From 1814 to 1860, it was again Sardinian until its final affiliation to France. The Saint-Sauveur church, now Baroque jewel, was probably built in the 15th century on a Romanesque church and transformed in the Baroque style in the 18th century. Its facade has visible traces of columns painted in trompe-l'oeil. The high altar (1732) built by a craftsman of San Remo is a marvel of marble marquetry. Organ of Italian Lingiardi (1847) fully restored in 1979 and played since then during concerts and religious events. Its carillon of the 19th century is regularly played by the hands and feet of the master bell-ringer of Saorge.

LA BRIGUE ★

The village La Brigue is a little away from the D6204 to Tende. It is located at 770 m high, along the Levenza river, an affluent of Roya, close to the Italian border. Formerly a hunting area of king Vittorio Emanuele, this part of the territory was annexed to France in 1947. Populated by rich merchants and shepherds, whose history mingles with the powerful lords of Lascaris,. It has an architectural heritage composed of 7 buildings classified as Historical Monuments. The medieval heart of the village contains the most identified fine collection of emblazoned or historiated lintels, in the middle of the 15th century till now, made in a black schist once used in the region, or with the green stone of Tende.

TOURIST OFFICE

Place Saint-Martin ✆ +33 (0)4 93 79 09 34
www.labrigue.fr – Info-labrigue@orange.fr

Low season: open Monday to Saturday from 9am to 12.30pm and from 1.30pm to 5pm. High season: every day from 9am to 12.30pm and from 1.30pm to 5pm. The village of La Brigue is located in the heart of the Roya valley, a short distance from the Italian border, in this part of the territory handed over to France in 1947, once hunting area of king Vittorio Emanuele, a little away from the RN204 that goes to Tende.

VIA FERRATA ★★★

Tourist Office – Place Saint Martin
✆ +33 (0)4 93 79 09 34
www.labrigue.fr
info-labrigue@orange.fr

Elevation: 250 meters. Open every day and public holidays from 9am to 12.30pm and from 2pm to 5.30pm. From November to May, the tourism office closes at 12pm and 5pm. Via ferrata is accessible all year, following weather conditions. Recommended between April and October. Access adult: €5, child and group starting from 6 people: €3.50. Prohibited under 12-year-olds.

Overlooking the medieval village and its vertical 80 meters cliffs, the itinerary is athletic. It is a succession of equipments suspended on 600 m long and 250 m high, for steep sensations. The highlights of this beautiful tour are the seven rope bridges and a zip line of 120 meters. Buy the tickets at the Tourist Office. The bureau des guides of Tende, located rue Sébastien-Grandis 6bis offers half days to discover the course safely with supervision and equipment in order to progress without danger.

Reservation: ✆ +33 (0)4 93 04 67 88 or www.mercantour-roya.com.

SAINT-DALMAS-DE-TENDE ★★

Located on D6204, 4 km before Tende towards the Italian border, this small village was once the frontier post of Nice – Cunéo railway, which explains the impressive size of its station, built in 1928 and marked by the Mussolini era. At the time of its full activity, it was an important depot and workshop maintenance of steam engines and railway ears of fifteen paths.

In the chapter of curiosities, or exploits – railway – it is interesting to note, if you go from Nice to Tende by train, that the railway wins altitude, without having to make loops in the valley. This trick is the equivalent of a lock for waterways! In La Brigue, a spiral tunnel of 300 m ray dug in the depth of the mountain leads the way to rotate, by winning altitude and to stand 50 feet higher. Indeed, the railway must go up to 700 in 35 km of course, when you need only 25 of them for the road to get to the same result below valley.

The helical tunnel allows you to pass the important level cahnges. Saint-Dalmas-de-Tende is the starting point for excursions to the mont Bégo and the valley des Merveilles.

LE PRIEURÉ
Rue Jean-Médecin
✆ +33 (0)4 93 04 75 70
www.leprieure.org
contact@leprieure.org

Open all year. Daily for lunch and dinner. Booking advised. Menu starter + main course + dessert at €18. À la carte: Around €30. Children's menu: €9. Lunch menu: €13 (starter and main course or main course and dessert). Holiday voucher. Groups welcome (reservation required). Garden. Terrace. Organization of private events or professional seminars. Catering at home (Vallée de la Roya exclusively). This unusual address is located in the beautiful setting of a former converted monastery. The renovation was tastefully done. In winter, you will be welcomed in a vast vaulted and bright room overlooking the river. On sunny days, you will surely choose to go on the large terrace facing the garden. The hotel can accommodate private or business events in the former chapel of the Priory which was transformed into a banquet hall that can welcome up to 150 people. The food is traditional with regional accents, the evolutionary menu changes regularly. Among the meals, there is a choice of starters, grilled meats or with sauce, two fishes, and for the sweet, a variety of greedy desserts. The restaurant has a remarkable private island nestled between the two arms of the Roya River. It can be booked for organizing outdoor brunch or group lunch from 20 people. The Chef will then prepare a custom barbecue menu. A wonderful idea to act as Robinson peacefully... A Priory with multiple attractions, to be discovered for an excellent value for money.

TENDE ★★

The village of Tende is nestled at 850 m altitude at the foot of the eponymous col is the largest town of the Alpes-Maritimes consisting of Tende, Saint-Dalmas-de-Tende and the hamlets of Castérino, Viévola, Granile and Canaresse. It is on its territory that the remarkable Vallée des Merveilles in the Mercantour national park is located. The col of Tende at 1,871 m is the less high and the most direct passage of the Alps between Provence and Eastern Piémont. The military fortresses that overlook it offer stunning views of Monte Rosa Massif located at 4,364 m. Like all the villages of this valley, Tendes' domination changed several times: in 1581, the county of Tende was acquired by Maison de Savoie, the territories of Tende and La Brigue were definitively given to France with the peace treaty of Paris on 10th February 1947.

Festival of Saint Eloi

Since the Middle Ages, the road of salt started from Nice to join Piedmont. In the Savoyard domination, this mule track became a fundamental exchange zone and Tende was on the way. Salt came from the salt marsh of Camargue on ships docking at the port of Nice and Villefranche. The bags were loaded on mules to Tende, city stage where the mean of transport changed as tendasques mules were known for their durability and strength. The Dukes of Savoy and the kings of Sardinia, used the tendasques mule for transporting military equipment and supplies to their troops often warred on either side of the col of Tende. They quickly grouped to form a corporation and created the Brotherhood of Muletiers of Tende, under the patronage of Saint Eloi, which still exists today. The members perpetuate the celebration of St. Eloi every second Sunday of July, during which the horses and mules were blessed. These animals, heirs of an ancient tradition, are adorned with festive attire and led by the Prior of the year, are the stars of a ride through the village.

Contact: Brotherhood of Saint Eloi, district Colombera 06430 Tende (http://fetesainteloi.fr)

TOURIST OFFICE OF TENDE
103, avenue du 16-Septembre-1947
✆ +33 (0)4 93 04 73 71
www.tendemerveilles.com

Low season: open Monday to Saturday from 9am to 12pm and from 2pm to 5pm; Sunday from 9am to 12pm. From May to end of September every day from 9am to 12pm and 2pm at 6pm.

The friendly team gives all information on routes and conditions for hiking and provides documentation of the park, the road of the forts of Tenda and the trails of the perched villages.

Knife & Fork

LA MARGUERIA
19, avenue du16-Septembre-1947
✆ +33 (0)4 93 04 60 53

Open all year for lunch and dinner except Tuesday. July and August, open 7 days a week. À la carte: Around €18. Daily specials: starter €9 to €13. Pizzas from €9. Tickets Restaurant accepted. American Express, Holiday voucher, Chèque Restaurant. Groups welcome (up to 60 people – on reservation only). Terrace.

Located in the main street that crosses Tende, this family-run restaurant offers Mediterranean cuisine with Italian accents, as well as cheese specialties such as tartiflette, Raclette, Savoyard fondue or the reblochonnade. You will also find on the menu a large choice of pizzas baked in a wood fire and, in summer, gourmet dishes prepared with fresh ingredients. Without forgetting the excellent wine list of craftsmen, mostly natural, from the region – Abbaye de Lérins, Clos Saint-Joseph -, from the four corners of France – H. Milan, Clos Saint-Vincent, M. Bouchet, H. Villemade – and Italy – G. Rinaldi, for instance. Tables is set for lunch and dinner in the dining room, decorated with raw wood and stone, and on the terrace to enjoy the fine days from a magnificent view of the mountains above the roofs of the city. A nice address that combines warm hospitality and good value.

LE MIRAMONTI
5, rue Antoine-Vassalo ✆ +33 (0)4 93 04 61 82
www.lemiramonti-restaurant.fr
sarl.noa0036@orange.fr

Closed from mid-November to mid-January and 15 days in April. Low season: open Tuesday to Sunday from 12pm to 2.30pm; Tuesday and Thursday to Saturday from 7pm to 9pm. High season: Monday to Saturday from 7pm to 9pm; every day from 12pm to 2.30pm. Menu from €17 to €24. À la carte: Around €27. Children's menu: €8. Daily special: €10 (to €11.50). Wine by the glass. 6 rooms from €41 to €48. Half-board €86 for 2 people and €67 single person. Chèque Restaurant. Accessible to wheel chairs only at the restaurant. Groups welcome (100 people in winter and 150 in summer). Garden. Terrace. Take-away. Parking. Wifi access. Organization of excursions in 4x4 in the valley des Merveilles.

Miramonti is located in the heart of the city, a few steps away from the station and the Musée des Merveilles. A rustic dining room, a large sunny outdoor terrace and a small summer garden, that's for the decor. The

traditional and family cuisine offers tendasques and Italian specialities, fresh pasta, meats and cheeses of the region. Enjoy country trout en papillote, cooked with lemon and white wine, Arrabiata spaghetti – tomatoes and pepper – or the tagliatelle with mushrooms. The wine list includes names from Italy, Corsica and French terroir, at reasonable prices. As for the accommodation, Miramonti features 6 comfortable rooms located above the restaurant, equipped for 3 or 4 people. Three of them have showers and toilets, the others share a bathroom. The management organises daily trips to the Vallée des Merveilles from the hotel. Ask for information on site for rates and schedules.

In the surroundings

Castérino

Little mountainous spot at 1500 m height in the middle of a vast valley, Castérino is found at the gateway to the National Park of Mercantour and the Valley des Merveilles. Hamlet of the town of Tende, it has a beautiful Nordic activities centre, a serene atmosphere of far north under the sun of the south: cross country skiing, dog sledding, snowshoeing, snow ski touring. The resort is for the whole family, easily accessible, with twenty kilometres of slopes. In summer it is the ideal place to watch the marmots and birds of prey, for hikings on horseback or mountain biking, hiking or hiking in 4x4 vehicle to discover the wonders of the park with a licensed tour-guide.

INDEX

D

E

F

G

H